The psychological treatment of depression

Over the past decade, Cognitive Behaviour Therapy (CBT) has become established as an effective treatment for clinical depression. Research studies throughout the world have found that CBT is as effective as the best anti-depressant drugs in the short term, and that it has longer-lasting effects than medication.

The Psychological Treatment of Depression describes the wide range of cognitive behavioural techniques in great detail, enabling therapists to put them to practical use. The author draws together assessment and treatment techniques of proven efficacy, describing them in *usable* detail, and setting them in the context of current psychological theories of depression. Some of these techniques are suitable for out-patient or primary care work, others for in-patients who may have been severely depressed for a long time. Some techniques lend themselves to long-term strategies, others to brief therapy interventions. In all cases, the techniques are explored in sufficient detail that practitioners new to CBT can feel confident about using them and that those already using them can update their skills. The final chapters discuss recent advances in research on vulnerability to depression and recent theories about what processes underlie successful therapy.

Basic and clear, with explicit case studies, sample dialogues, checklists, and other helpful aids, the book is a splendid working manual, a field guide for all mental health practitioners in any discipline who want to apply or incorporate the successful methods of CBT into their work with depressed patients.

The psychological treatment of depression

A guide to the theory and practice of cognitive behaviour therapy

Second edition

J. Mark G. Williams

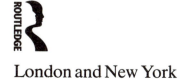

London and New York

First published by Croom Helm in 1984

This second edition first published in 1992 by
Routledge
11 New Fetter Lane, London EC4P 4EE

Simultaneously published in the USA and Canada by
Routledge
29 West 35th Street, New York, NY 10001

Reprinted 1995

© 1984, 1992 J. Mark G. Williams

Printed and bound in Great Britain by
Mackays of Chatham PLC, Chatham, Kent
Typeset by LaserScript, Mitcham, Surrey

British Library Cataloguing in Publication Data
A catalogue record for this book is available from the British Library.

Library of Congress Cataloging in Publication Data
A catalog record for this book is available from the Library of Congress.

ISBN 0–415–12873–0 (hbk)
ISBN 0–415–12874–9 (pbk)

Contents

Tables and figures

TABLES

FIGURES

Preface to the first edition

It was not until the late 1960s and early 1970s that behavioural and cognitive approaches began to be applied in the treatment of clinical depression. Like the earlier applications of behavioural techniques for anxiety-based disorders, researchers have since used a variety of strategies to investigate efficacy and elucidate the factors affecting successful treatment outcome. Single case studies in the early writings have given way to treatment analogue studies and subsequently to larger scale outcome studies with clinical groups. There now exist several careful reviews of these studies. Although each of these points to areas in the outcome literature where there are problems in interpretation, the reviewers converge on the same conclusion: 'Generally, behavioural and cognitive strategies can have a significant effect on depression' (Rehm and Kornblith, 1979); 'From these studies, there appears adequate evidence that depressives can respond to psychological intervention' (Whitehead, 1979); 'Several of the specific behavioural and cognitive-behavioural interventions appear to have survived initial tests of efficacy' (Hollon, 1981).

These reviewers also agree that combinations of cognitive and behavioural techniques seem to be more effective in ameliorating depression than either alone and their conclusions suggest that clinicians may be optimistic in using such techniques or combinations of techniques in their therapeutic practice; but how to proceed? The problem is that, although some techniques have rationales and procedures which have been clearly documented by their proponents (e.g. the excellent *Cognitive Therapy Manual* by Beck *et al.*, 1979), this is by no means true for all the techniques which the reviewers of outcome studies cite as being effective therapeutic strategies. Some techniques which hold out clear promise as effective practices are to be found only in partial descriptions, scattered throughout the behavioural literature. When such studies are reviewed, the reviewer rarely has sufficient space to give more than one or two sentences to describe the technique under consideration. We end up knowing something of what might be most therapeutic for our clients, but little or nothing about how to go about it. It is to help fill this gap that this book has been written.

The techniques I have chosen to describe represent a range of those currently practised by cognitive-behavioural therapists. Some are suitable for inpatient management, others more suitable for outpatient or primary care work. Some are suitable long-term strategies, others more suitable for brief therapy interventions. The therapy chapters form the central portion of the book. Their aim is to describe the techniques in sufficient detail to be useful for clinicians who want to apply such methods in their work with depressed patients, and as such, they are not written as a justification of these methods over and above alternative treatment approaches. Had space permitted it might have been possible to give details of more broad-based psycho-therapeutic approaches, or of the new and challenging field of clinical ecology. (Readers interested in introductions to these fields might refer to Malan (1979) and Rippere and Adams (1982) respectively.) Unlike the arguments surrounding the growth of behaviour therapy for anxiety-based disorders, there is now a more constructive debate between proponents of different therapeutic schools. Each is more prepared to believe that patients differ in the extent to which they benefit from the techniques of the different therapeutic schools. The responsibility of practitioners of each orientation is to make plain what methods are used in their particular therapy so that individual clinicians may choose rationally which approach is appropriate for which patient. Such a description of cognitive-behavioural techniques is what is attempted as the central aspect of this book.

Preceding the core therapy chapters is a chapter on assessment which gives a representative range of techniques (e.g. Beck, Hamilton) in full. The therapy chapters are followed by a section on training exercises which aims to give clinicians ideas to use in development of their own skills.

The book begins and ends on a theoretical note: the first two chapters set the context for psychological approaches to depression; the last two raise some basic theoretical and research issues. I hope these more theoretical sections will be of interest to students of psychology, clinical psychology and psychiatry in their 'abnormal psychology' or 'experimental psycho-pathology' courses. However, the book will have fulfilled its purpose if it provides for the clinician an introduction to and encouragement to try out techniques, the utility of which can only ultimately be judged in the clinical situation itself.

Acknowledgements for the first edition

This book grew out of a series of teaching seminars and workshops I gave while at the Department of Psychiatry, University of Newcastle-upon-Tyne between 1979 and 1982. I am grateful to many people for their support, encouragement and ideas during this period, but especially to some colleagues with whom a great deal of this work was discussed: Will Barker, Anne Goodwin, Veronica Gore, Charles Lund, Angus McGregor, Ian McKeith, Jan Scott, Lindsay Shrubsole, Debbie Spaull, Stephen Tyrer and Ian Wilkinson. Since moving to Cambridge, I have been grateful for discussions with Fraser Watts, and throughout the period I have been helped by talks I have had with Chris Brewin.

Secretarial assistance has been a great asset in the drafting and re-drafting of the text, and thanks are due to Sue Lowe and Gerry Mulholland in Newcastle, and to Sharon Basham in Cambridge.

For permission to use their scales and questionnaires, I am grateful to Professor A.T. Beck, Professor Max Hamilton, Dr Ivy Blackburn and Ian Wilkinson.

Less direct, but no less important support came at the inception of the project at work and home: at work, from Peter Britton and Donald Eccleston, colleagues whose encouragement was highly valued; at home, from my wife Phyllis, and from Robert, Jennifer, and Anne-Marie whose love and support has been a source of strength throughout.

Finally, there are two people who deserve special mention; two clinical psychologists who died within a few weeks of each other at about the time this book was started; May Davidson and Roger Garside. One started me in my career as a clinical psychologist; the other was a source of valued support as a colleague when I joined the Department of Psychiatry in Newcastle. To the memory of May Davidson and Roger Garside, I should like to dedicate this book.

Mark Williams

Preface to the second edition

At the time of writing the first edition, cognitive behaviour therapy was still in its infancy. Over the last eight years, however, it has become established as an effective method of psychotherapy. In particular, it has led the way in promoting the use of structured psychotherapy for depressed patients as an alternative or addition to antidepressant medication. The aim of this second edition, therefore, remains that of encouraging clinicians to try cognitive and behavioural approaches with their clients. For this, therapists need not only an up-to-date review of the outcome literature, but also a clear introduction to the rationale and aim of each technique used in these studies, together with detailed description of how to proceed with each technique. The central chapters provide this information, and I have added more details on how to initiate therapy, and on how, later, to deal with underlying fears and assumptions with which patients can find great difficulty in coping. I am grateful to Arlene Weissman and to Michael Rosenbaum for permission to reproduce the Dysfunctional Attitude Scale and the Self-Control Schedule which should help assess these aspects of patients' problems.

Since the publication of the first edition, there has been extensive research on the outcome of cognitive therapy. This new edition provides an update on these developments, the most significant of which has been the finding that cognitive therapy reduces relapse. A second body of research has accumulated showing that cognitive therapy techniques, sometimes suitably modified, can be effective in helping people with chronic unremitting depression. I have included a new chapter reflecting these developments, and giving details of techniques to use in an inpatient setting.

A further development has been the use of experimental cognitive psychology to help understand the process of change in psychotherapy in general, and cognitive therapy in particular. The final chapter, which is new, reviews several different attempts to understand the critical processes underlying therapeutic change, and integrates them using new findings from research on autobiographical memory and problem-solving.

Finally, I have become aware that the first edition assumed a great deal of basic knowledge about the phenomenon of depression itself. The readership of this edition turned out to be much wider than I had predicted. I greatly welcome this interest, and have written a new introductory chapter for those who may be unfamiliar with issues relating to prevalence, incidence and diagnosis of depression.

Much of the new agenda for the second edition came out of workshops and training groups in Cambridge and elsewhere. I am indebted to Nacho Quemada, Gillian Rose, Simon Barnett, Peter Bentham, Keron Fletcher, Kevin Green, Paula MacKay, Steve Feast, Andy Thornton, Jane Shapleski, Katherine Foreman, Steve Jones and Ann Palmer for the helpful discussions we have shared on the practical aspects and difficulties of applying cognitive behaviour therapy. Special thanks are due to Jan Scott, Andrew MacLeod, Tracey Shea, Irene Elkin and Melanie Taylor for reading and being prepared to comment on portions of the text. Thanks, too, to Sharon Gamble for wordprocessing it all.

This edition of the book was written in the last few months of my eight-and-a-half years at the Medical Research Council's Applied Psychology Unit at Cambridge. I should like to thank my colleagues there, particularly Alan Baddeley, Andrew MacLeod, John Teasdale and Fraser Watts for their support and encouragement, and for many helpful discussions on the theory and practice of cognitive approaches to emotion. It is also a fitting time to thank those who have supported me during my time in Cambridge, especially, more recently, in my role as worker-priest: Andrew McKearney, Rob and Wendy MacIntosh, Peter and Rachel Nancarrow and John and Margaret Robson. Finally, to Phyllis, my wife, and to Robert, Jennie and Annie, thanks for everything.

Mark Williams
Bangor
1992

Chapter 1

Introduction

A man was walking in the hills when he fell down a disused mineshaft. He fell fifteen feet, then became wedged. He dare not move lest he fall further. He cried out for help. Eventually another walker heard his cries. This walker was something of an expert at rock-climbing, pot-holing and generally getting out of fixes. Instructions were shouted down the mineshaft – where to put feet, hands and body to get into the correct position for climbing out. But the man wouldn't move. The walker muttered something about getting more help, and moved off. After some time a second walker heard the cries and came to help. This walker instantly recognized the man's distress and confusion. He realized that the man did not have the courage to move while feeling so hopeless about his situation. So he gave him reassurance, put him at his ease, made him feel better. The man did feel better, but he was still in the mineshaft. He did not move. So the second rescuer went away to fetch more help.

Eventually a third walker arrived on the scene. Like the first, he had rock-climbing experience. Like the second, he realized that the man would not make any move whilst he was so upset. Furthermore he knew two things: that the man in the mineshaft was unlikely to take the rescuer's word for it that moving in a certain way would not make matters even worse; second, that from the top of the mineshaft it was impossible to know precisely what the man's position was, what the risks were of moving. He would first have to ask the man to make small movements (which from experience needed to be of minimal risk) and then to ask for a report on their effects. As victim and rescuer gathered more information, the victim's courage returned. Slowly he moved, took more risks. In time he was free. End of parable.

Depression is a little like the disused mine shaft. Everyone becomes a little depressed from time to time. But sometimes, the depth of depression outweighs a person's abilities to cope. Mood spirals downwards, the person experiences hopelessness and despair, and almost total emptiness, feels unmotivated to do many of the things they used to find enjoyable, or feels that they would rather not meet other people. It is no accident that the metaphors we used to describe increasing severity of depression speak of 'depth' or 'spiralling downwards'. Whereas anxiety 'rises', depression 'deepens'. Hence the parable. The severely depressed person finds themselves trapped, in darkness, not daring to make any move for fear of making things worse, helpless about their prospect of escape.

The story captures what is important about structured psychotherapies. They are not mere techniques telling a person how to get out of a bad situation, able to be taught mechanically. Neither are they merely offering a safe relationship. They aim to provide a careful combination of the two. The 'skilled rescuer' is the one who is able both to teach the specific things which it will be necessary for the trapped person to do in order to climb out, and to forge a relationship with the person which will give them the courage to try after so much has failed. Of course, a therapist's personality may occasionally be sufficient so long as the person already has the necessary skills to cope with difficulty. Indeed, this may be why some placebo therapies sometimes work quite well, by encouraging those who normally use active problem-solving strategies to mobilize their skills. But for some people, dealing with their difficulties has exceeded their capacity. In this case sheer force of personality of a therapist will not be sufficient.

The value of individual structured psychotherapies for depression, of which the best known are social skills training (Hersen *et al.*, 1984; Sanchez *et al.*, 1980), interpersonal psychotherapy (Klerman *et al.*, 1984) and cognitive-behaviour therapy (Beck *et al.*, 1979) is that they provide information and specific exercises for depressed patients who find they have fallen into the depths. This book describes a range of techniques. The techniques are focused around one of these psychotherapies, cognitive-behaviour therapy, but many (e.g. task assignment) are common to all structured psychotherapies.

Although much of the book is concerned with 'techniques', the parable reminds us that these need to be embedded in a supportive relationship. Techniques are not mere mechanical devices in which certain wheels can be turned and certain responses produced. A.T. Beck and his colleagues, who have brought together many of the techniques to be described in this book under the heading of cognitive therapy, have also emphasized the qualities of empathy, warmth, genuineness and unconditional positive regard in the therapist. Appropriate and delicate use of humour, challenge, sympathy and encouragement are fundamental. Yet the research evidence suggests that the quality of the relationship is not sufficient for therapeutic progress. Studies of unstructured psychotherapy for major depression have been disappointing (see Whitehead, 1979; DeRubeis and Hollon, 1981). Furthermore if one systematically varies the subcomponents of treatment *within* a single session (for example, by simply exploring a negative thought, versus collaborating to challenge its validity), differences in depressed mood can be detected, despite the factor of the relationship with therapist remaining constant (Teasdale and Fennell, 1982).

No book can help much in developing the personal qualities of accurate empathy into which therapists will need to embed their techniques. However, knowledge of strategies for assessing and coping with depression can help the therapist by giving him or her a clarity of perception which may better withstand the tendency to become so drawn in to the hopelessness of the patient that the therapist ends up feeling only despair and pessimism for the patient. For this reason, the techniques of assessment and of behavioural and cognitive intervention form the central aspect of this book. Exercises to use in further training, including a checklist to help evaluate one's own developing competency as a therapist will be found in Chapter Nine.

Knowledge of the techniques themselves is not sufficient. For unless a therapist has an overall framework from which the techniques are derived, they will not know in which direction to go if one approach is not proving helpful. For example, if task assignment is being used by the patient, it is important to know in what framework it is being used. Is it being used to increase the number of pleasant activities; or to increase their enjoyability (a reinforcement theory of depression); or as a homework assignment to learn social skills (a social skills framework)? Or is it being used to discover what undermining images and thoughts occur to the person when they try to engage in activities (a cognitive framework)? At different times in therapy, this same technique may serve any or all of these purposes. Without having the framework clear, the therapist is unlikely to communicate successfully to the patient what is the purpose of the assignment. Worse, the therapist will be unclear how to review the homework at the next session. If the homework has not been performed (as often happens) it makes a great difference which framework was guiding the assignment. Only on this basis can the therapist decide what the next move in therapy may be. For this reason, the next two chapters will focus on the psychological models or frameworks which underlie behavioural and cognitive approaches to depression, and the final chapters will pursue the cognitive model in greater depth. The first requirement of anyone who seeks to treat depressed patients is to know a lot about depression. It will be very important early on in therapy to allow the patient to ask questions and to be able to give answers about what depression is. I will therefore start by summarizing some of the major facts and figures about depression.

SO WHAT IS DEPRESSION?

People become depressed for many reasons, for varying lengths of time to varying degrees. When depressed, different people have various ways of coping. At any one time, 4–5 per cent of a population meet the criteria (detailed below) for clinical depression (Paykel, 1989). In any one year approximately one in ten of the population will have an episode of depression (Amenson and Lewinsohn, 1981). Yet most people cope without seeking treatment. Twenty–five per cent of episodes of depression last less than a month; a further 50 per cent recover in less than three months. For some, the depression may simply pass without their having to do anything. Others will have used a range of different self-help strategies (Parker and Brown, 1979; Rippere, 1977).

We have already noted that 4–5 per cent of the population is depressed at any one time, but in order to give such a figure, we need to have defined clearly what we mean by 'depressed'. The term 'depression' is used very often in our day-by-day conversation to describe a normal downswing of mood. Such downswings in mood may be adaptive. In rather the same way that normal anxiety and fear can warn of danger and prevent more serious harm, so depression may remind of losses and spur a person to find ways of re-engaging with activities or friends. But just as anxiety can become abnormally generalized and severe, so depression can present for the person more problems than it solves. Although the distinction is probably one of degree rather than of kind, what happens when the depression deepens is that more symptoms are 'drawn in'. The result is clinical depression, a 'syndrome', that is a cluster of symptoms that tend to occur together. But these symptoms are themselves very diverse. They include emotional changes (feelings of sadness often referred to as 'dysphoria', the opposite of euphoria); cognitive changes (low self-esteem, guilt, rumination, memory and concentration difficulties); behavioural changes (agitation or retardation, reduced engagement in social or recreational activities) and bodily changes (sleep, eating and sexual problems, aches and pains, loss of energy). Some of these have been seen as central to a diagnosis of depression and are shown in Table 1.1. Other symptoms are excluded because, although they very commonly occur in depression, they also occur when a person has other psychological problems. For example, 'avoidance' occurs in phobias, and 'ruminations' occur in obsessions, 'passivity' occurs in schizophrenia and 'irritability' occurs in mania. Most methods of diagnosis have a number of other categories so that the many people with a wider spread of less intense (though often very persistent) symptoms may be diagnosed. Table 1.2 shows these more peripheral symptoms given by one diagnostic system. The criteria which need to be met for this mild form of depression are much more relaxed. If it were only these milder symptoms which were suffered by 5 per cent of the population at any one time, this would not be surprising. But studies of the prevalence of depression in the community have used the more stringent criteria given in Table 1.1 to assess how many people in the population are depressed. The regularity with which such studies find a figure around 4–5 per cent suggests this proportion is reliable.

Table 1.1 List of symptoms used to diagnose major depressive disorder (Spitzer *et al.*, 1978)

      A.   Persistent low mood (for at least two weeks)*

plus B.   At least five** of the following symptoms

        1. Poor appetite or weight loss, or increased appetite or weight gain (change of 1lb a week over several weeks or 10lbs a year when not dieting)

        2. Sleep difficulty or sleeping too much

        3. Loss of energy, fatigability or tiredness

        4. Psychomotor agitation or retardation (but not mere subjective feeling of restlessness or being slowed down)

        5. Loss of interest or pleasure in usual activities, including social contact or sex not attributable to delusions or hallucinations

        6. Feelings of self-reproach or excessive inappropriate guilt (either may be delusional)

        7. Complaints or evidence of diminished ability to think or concentrate such as slowed thinking or indecisiveness not attributable to obvious formal thought disorder

        8. Recurrent thoughts of death or suicide, or any suicidal behaviour

plus C.   Sought or was referred for help, took medication or has impaired functioning

plus D.   Has no symptoms suggesting schizophrenia

---

* If one–two weeks, 'probable' rather than 'definite' diagnosis is made.
** If only *four* symptoms present, 'probable' major depressive disorder is diagnosed.

Table 1.2 List of symptoms contributing to diagnosis of 'minor depressive disorder'*

---

1. Crying
2. Pessimistic thought
3. Brooding about past unpleasantness
4. Preoccupation with feelings of inadequacy
5. Feeling resentful, irritable, angry
6. Needing reassurance/help from somebody (feeling of clinging dependency)
7. Feeling sorry for yourself
8. Physical complaints which do not seem to be caused by any physical illness

---

* This can be diagnosed if depression has persisted for two weeks accompanied by two or more of the symptoms listed in Tables 1.1 and 1.2 (see Spitzer *et al.* for details).

SEX DIFFERENCES

The prevalence figures given above are not the only figures which emerge sufficiently often to be thought reliable. No less often, researchers find that the proportion of women who are depressed by these definitions exceed the proportion of men (Paykel, 1989). Women are between two and three times as likely to be depressed as are men (Weissman and Klerman, 1977). The reasons for this remain uncertain. Young women with young children are particularly vulnerable and this has led some to suggest that women's disadvantaged role with regard to opportunities for paid employment and their increased responsibility for unpaid child care is the major cause. The correlation between onset of depression, increase in life stress and the absence of social support (Brown, 1989) is wholly consistent with this conclusion.

What is less clear is whether women are more vulnerable than men if they have never been depressed before. Note that studies finding sex differences are *prevalence* studies – that is, they are assessing the proportion of men and women who are depressed, randomly sampled from a population at a single point in time. But this does not tell us whether the depression being reported by a person is the *first* episode a person has ever had, or the third or the twenty-third. The excess proportion for women may arise because they are more likely to experience repeated episodes once they have been depressed, not because they were more vulnerable in the first place. There is now evidence to support this idea.

Amenson and Lewinsohn (1981) carried out a longitudinal, prospective study of 1,000 people in the community. They found, as others have before and since, that the prevalence of depression was higher in women than men. But because the study was prospective, they could count what proportion of men and women became depressed for the first time during the period of the study. They found this figure (the incidence of new cases) to be 7.1 per cent for men and 6.9 per cent for women. Furthermore, they found that the episodes of depression did not last any longer in women than men, nor were women more likely to have their first episode at a younger age than men.

This implies that the difference in prevalence rates arises because women who have had one episode of depression are more likely to relapse than are men who have had a similar episode. Amenson and Lewinsohn were able to confirm this. One-fifth (21.8 per cent) of women who had had a previous episode became depressed again. Although men who had been depressed before were at greater risk of future depression than those men who had never been depressed, the risk was substantially smaller than that of women. Only 12.9 per cent became depressed again. Since Amenson and Lewinsohn were careful to exclude from the analysis a large number of psychological and social factors which might have explained these sex differences, the result appears reliable. We are left with needing to explain not the increased vulnerability of women, but their increased vulnerability to repeated episodes following a first episode. We have already mentioned the stresses and potential loneliness of a child care role. This is clearly important. Another possibility is that the hormonal changes of a woman's menstrual cycle, though not generally sufficient by themselves to bring about clinical depression, may nevertheless tend to re-activate memories and attitudes from a previous period of major depression once this has occurred for other reasons. I shall return to how such re-activation may occur in Chapter Ten, when I shall distinguish between vulnerability for a first episode, vulnerability for relapse or recurrence, and vulnerability for the episode of depression to persist.

DISTINCTIONS BETWEEN DIFFERENT SORTS OF DEPRESSION

Depression is a syndrome, with clusters of symptoms which tend to occur together. In this book I shall deal only with unipolar depression – that is, with people whose depression, at times when less severe, approximates to normal mood, rather than being punctuated by periods of euphoria. In these latter cases of 'manic depressive disorder' or cyclothymia (the term if the mood swings are less severe), mood swings up as well as down. This is a far less common disorder, occurring in 0.5 per cent of the population. That is, about one in ten of all depressions are of this type. Although the first episode of mania can be precipitated by a life event (Ambelas, 1979) there has not yet been any systematic attempt to study the cognitive processes involved in manic depression or its implications for psychological treatment (though see Healy and Williams, 1989 for one possible account of how the biological processes underlying circadian rhythms may interact with dysfunctional attitudes and attributions to produce mania).

Within the far more common unipolar depression, many attempts have been made to identify subclusters of symptoms within the syndrome. The distinction which has aroused most controversy, yet become most firmly embedded within psychiatric thinking, is that between *endogenous* and *reactive* depressions. The distinction was originally intended to capture the difference between those whose depression arose 'from the inside' (from biochemical disturbance in the brain) and separate them from those who were depressed in reaction to external stresses (sometimes called 'exogenous' to parallel the term endogenous). Yet from the earliest days of research in this area, many more differences than simply 'presence or ab-sence of a life event' were taken into account when deciding whether the depression was 'endogenous' or 'reactive'.

One of the ways of assessing endogeneity which has lasted longest was derived from a list of symptoms and their weightings derived in a study which examined response to electro-convulsive therapy by Carney *et al.* (1965) (see Table 1.3). This 'Newcastle Scale' is still widely used in diagnosis today. But is it a reliable and valid distinction that is being made?

Other statistical analyses suggest that, if there are subclassifications to be made, they are more complex than endogenous–reactive. One such analysis identified four categories: anxious depression, hostile depression, retarded depression and agitated depression (Overall and Hollister, 1966). Another

Table 1.3 Newcastle diagnostic scale for endogenous
depression (Carney *et al.*, 1965)

	Score
Adequate personality	+1
No adequate psychogenesis	+2
Distinct quality of mood	+1
Weight loss	+2
Previous episode	+1
Depressive psychomotor activity	+2
Anxiety	−1
Nihilistic delusions	+2
Blames others	−1
Guilt	+1

such analysis is that by Young *et al.* (1986) who also found four groups distinguished by two dichotomous features: the presence or absence of anhedonia (lack of ability to experience pleasure) and the presence or absence of 'vegetative' features (e.g. changes in sleep and appetite). It is certainly the case that endogenous depression is preceded by stressful life events as often as other depressions are (Paykel, 1989). Studies which appear to show that non-endogenous patients have experienced more life events have relied on self-report rather than independently checked events. Such self-reports can be unreliable (Robins *et al.*, 1990). This has encouraged some to suggest that the term 'endogenous' should only be taken to describe a certain cluster of symptoms, and not be taken to refer to how the depression was caused. The result of this is that when the word endogenous is used nowadays, it most commonly refers to cases where certain features are found (see Table 1.4). Other cases are simply called 'non-endogenous' so as not to imply that all other cases are reactive.

One might have expected that clarifying the term in this way would have helped research into the biological factors which may be causal in depression. In particular much research effort has gone into the search for biological markers (bodily signs indicating the level or integrity of a biological system). Although discussion of this research is beyond the scope of this book, progress in this area appears to have been disappointing. For example, early hopes for the Dexamethasone Suppression Test (DST) have foundered. In this test, dexamethasone is given to patients to see if the mechanism which controls natural cortisol output in the body is shut down or suppressed (as it should) by the presence of dexamethasone. Although non-suppression occurs more often in endogenous patients than in non-endogenous (showing that the hypothalamic-pituitary-adrenal system is faulty) it is not unique to endogenously depressed patients. Non-

Table 1.4 List of symptoms used by Spitzer *et al.* (1978) to distinguish endogenous-type depression

From group A and B a total of at least four symptoms for probable, six for definite, including at least one symptom from group A.

A. 1. Distinct quality to depressed mood, i.e. depressed mood is perceived as distinctly different from the kind of feeling (s)he would have or has had following the death of a loved one
   2. Lack of reactivity to environmental changes (once depressed doesn't feel better, even temporarily, when something good happens)
   3. Mood is regularly worse in the morning
   4. Pervasive loss of interest or pleasure

B. 1. Feelings of self-reproach or excessive or inappropriate guilt
   2. Early morning wakening or middle insomnia
   3. Psychomotor retardation or agitation (more than mere subjective feeling of being slowed down or restless)
   4. Poor appetite
   5. Weight loss (two lbs a week over several weeks or 20 lbs in a year when not dieting)
   6. Loss of interest or pleasure (may or may not be pervasive) in usual activities or decreased sexual drive

suppression has also been found in mania, in schizophrenia, in dysthymic patients and in patients with anorexia nervosa. Indeed, some have suggested that the fault in the hypothalamic pituitary system could be secondary to other factors such as weight loss (see Free and Oei, 1989 for more extended discussion of this issue). This has made a recent report conclude: 'The initial DST status does not powerfully or consistently supplement clinical methods of diagnosis of major depression for predicting short-term responses to adequate doses of tricyclic antidepressants or ECT' (APA Task Force on Laboratory Tests in Psychiatry, 1987: 1257).

But does the endogenous/non-endogenous subtype difference relate differently to psychological variables? The small number of studies which have been done give a slightly mixed picture, the evidence weighted against the distinction being important. DST non-suppressors are equivalent to DST suppressors in questionnaire measures of dysfunctional attitudes (Rush, 1983; Norman *et al.*, 1987). In one recent study Robins *et al.* (1990) found that dysfunctional attitudes measured by the Dysfunctional Attitude Scale (DAS) (Weissman and Beck, 1978) was significantly lower in endogenous patients than non-endogenous (distinguished on the Research Diagnostic Criteria). However, in another recent study of our own, we found that endogeneity assessed by the Newcastle Scale did not correlate with dysfunctional attitudes (Williams *et al.*, 1990).

Studies of response to cognitive behavioural treatment have found a similar picture: that endogeneity does not predict response. Blackburn *et al.* (1981), Kovacs (1981) and Beck *et al.* (1985) looked to see if the presence of endogenous symptoms made patients any less likely to respond to cognitive therapy. They did not. Note, however, that these studies (as with most other outcome studies of cognitive therapy that have been done) excluded psychotically depressed patients (i.e. those who had delusions and/or hallucinations); and have used outpatients, thereby excluding the most severely depressed hospitalized patients. The definition of endogenous can be either lax or relatively restrictive (for example, both the DSM IIIR definition of major depression, melancholic subtype and the older Newcastle Scale are more restrictive than the endogenous category of Spitzer *et al.*'s (1978) Research Diagnostic Criteria), and no study of more severe inpatient depressives has been large enough to see if using a more restrictive definition would predict treatment response.

As psychological treatments move further towards treating more severe patients, it would be well to keep an open mind on whether diagnostic distinctions will be helpful. Although subtype differences may well turn out to represent markers of severity (Kendall, 1976), it remains true that several studies have found that patients with 'endogenous' symptom clusters differ in several respects from patients without such symptoms. They differ in their style of rumination (Nelson and Mazure, 1985), in the content of their thoughts (Matussek and Luks, 1981), in the ease with which distraction can reduce their negative thinking and mood (Fennell *et al.*, 1987) and the ease with which imagery techniques can help compensate for poor concentration and memory (Watts *et al.*, 1988). Though these differences may not be reflected in *overall* response to psychological treatment, they may be determining which techniques within a therapy package are most helpful for different kinds of patient. Such information is evidently of value in discovering which procedures will best meet the needs of which patient.

Discussion of the nature of depression has brought us full circle to treatment issues. That is not surprising. The most important aspect of any clinical syndrome (no less true of other aspects of our environment such as tables and chairs) is not so much what it is 'in itself' – its essence – but how it responds when you do something to it. This book is not about 'doing something to', but it is about doing something for and with depressed people. We start, in the next two chapters, by describing the psychological frameworks that underlie the cognitive-behavioural therapy approach.

Chapter 2

Psychological models of depression I
The behavioural background

In the 1960s and early 1970s, clinical psychologists concerned themselves mostly with the behavioural treatment of anxiety-based disorders: phobias, obsessions and general anxiety. Where other problems were tackled, it was because they were assumed to have an anxiety component, e.g. tics, stammering, sexual problems. Careful analysis of the situations in which the anxiety arose, followed by relaxation, desensitization, exposure, response prevention, massed practice, etc. – these were the staple diet of the behavioural practitioner. Somehow, depression was not thought the appropriate target for such interventions.

Firstly, depression appeared more 'biological', and if so the behavioural aspects would be mere symptoms. The development of antidepressant drugs had appeared to confirm the theory that depression was the result of deficiencies in some combination of biogenic amines in the brain. Secondly, although some depression was thought 'reactive', where the trauma was great, the depressive response seemed understandable and not requiring any special theory. Where the trauma was little, and the depressive response apparently out of proportion, there were psychodynamic explanations available. Thirdly, the symptoms of depression are many and various. The earliest behavioural speculations about depression had spoken of depression as 'extinction' (behavioural repertoire being weakened due to insufficient reinforcement relative to the effort expended – the response cost). Yet such notions did not seem to do justice to the variety of symptoms in depression. Indeed, as we saw in the last chapter, a person may be diagnosed depressed on the grounds of low mood, suicidal ideas, appetite disturbance, sleep disturbance, feelings of self-reproach and concentration or memory problems, without reduced behavioural output or 'extinction' being a major feature. Yet it is with such behavioural formulations that this review of the background to cognitive-behaviour therapy must start. Whatever their deficiencies as complete explanations of the phenomena of depression, they were arguably the most significant development in clinical psychological theorizing since the interpretations of phobic reactions as conditioned emotional responses earlier in the century. They broke the mould of predominant explanations for depression: the biogenic amine theory on the one hand and the psychodynamic theory on the other.

I shall start by reviewing some early behavioural formulations, and then trace their more recent development. Finally we shall see how the theory of learned helplessness builds a bridge from behavioural towards cognitive approaches.

EARLY BEHAVIOURAL FORMULATIONS

Reduced frequency of social reinforcement

Early behavioural formulations of depression attributed the symptoms to 'inadequate or insufficient reinforcement' (Lazarus, 1968). However it was not clear whether 'inadequate' implied reduced frequency or quality of reinforcement. By contrast, theories which spoke of reduced frequency of social reinforcement were more specific. 'Frequency' is a particular concept and 'social' limits the otherwise wide term 'reinforcement'. It is a theory most often associated with Lewinsohn (e.g. Lewinsohn *et al.*, 1970). According to Lewinsohn, low rate of response contingent positive reinforcement has consequences in terms of the respondent behaviour of the individual (elicits crying, dysphoric mood, etc.) and is itself sufficient explanation for reduced behavioural output in depression. In the early stages of depressive breakdown, symptoms may be maintained by reinforcement from others (the 'secondary gain' phenomenon), but later on close family and friends are more likely to stop rewarding the person's behaviour. They may try to avoid the depressed person altogether, thus further reducing frequency of rewards available in the environment.

However the concepts are not so circumscribed as may be supposed. The concept which is important but missing is that of the S^D, the 'discriminative stimulus' (Ferster, 1966). This is the stimulus in the environment which signals the availability of reinforcers in rather the same way in which a laboratory animal may learn that food will only be available when a small light is on, and then only when it presses a bar. If a person were to become less sensitive to stimuli in the environment which normally 'announce' the availability of rewards, then the effect on behaviour would presumably be the same as reducing frequency of actual reinforcement. These are very different models, but are almost indistinguishable solely on the basis of their behavioural effects. Furthermore, 'reduced reinforcement' paradigms are too narrow. A truly comprehensive theory would include a greater number of parameters of reinforcement – frequency, duration, magnitude and the amount of behaviour required to obtain the reinforcer (the response cost).

Loss of reinforcible behaviour

This theory is ascribed to Ferster (1966, 1973) and refers to the reduction of reinforcible behaviour in the repertoire (for any reason). Simply put, if the behaviour is not there to be rewarded, it will not be rewarded. Such reduction in behaviour characteristically follows large and/or sudden environmental changes, which change the stimulus conditions which normally control behaviour. It may also result from reinforcible behaviour being squeezed out of the repertoire by the need to escape or avoid stress, or by increase in hostility which reduces other people's willingness to give 'social reinforcement'. Clearly this formulation is very similar to those of 'inadequate or insufficient reinforcement' mentioned above.

Aversive control

This theory attributes reduced behavioural output to the fear that anything a person does will be punished. Although several authors have pointed out that depression may result from unusually intense and prolonged anxiety (Lazarus, 1968; Wolpe, 1972) this is different from explaining actual performance deficits in depression in terms of expectations of unpleasant consequences. This is despite the fact that (although anxiety and depression are distinguishable as clinical syndromes), anxiety is very often a component in the depressive state, especially in mild depressions. The significance of 'punishment' or 'stimuli signalling punishment' becomes more clear if Gray's analysis of their equivalence with 'frustrative non-reward' and 'stimuli signalling frustrative non-reward' (respectively) is borne in mind (Gray, 1987, 1990). In the circumstances of bereavement, for example, the individual is besieged by stimuli which have normally signalled the presence of their loved one: 'the alarm clock which he always turned off', 'the television programme she always used to watch' and so on. Yet the person is not there when they look around – paradigmatic of 'frustrative non-reward'. Many of the stimuli in the environment must thereby become signals for such non-reward, and reduction in behaviour ensues as certainly as if the behaviour was being systematically punished. This formulation seems inadequate to explain the generalization of behavioural deficits in depression, yet if one extends the theory to include 'conditioned inhibition' – the reduction in behavioural output owing to the presence of stimuli signalling that no reward is available – it may yet explain a wide range of phenomena.

Loss of reinforcer effectiveness

According to this theory (Costello, 1972a) sufficient reinforcers may be available in the environment and the individual might still be capable of procuring them, but for some reason they have lost their *potency* as reinforcers. This is in contrast with those theories which would predict that only techniques which increase total amount of rewarding events or those which teach the necessary skills (e.g. assertion training) to procure such rewards will ultimately be effective in alleviating depression. The formulation seems particularly useful in accounting for depressions which do not seem to follow any loss event (and although many do, a substantial minority do not). It also seems to account for the finding by people who are depressed that their discomfort and dysphoria may be increased when they attempt to do things which they formerly found pleasurable – an aspect of the syndrome which has been ignored by many theorists. If individuals expect from past experience to get pleasure from an activity then they find it is not rewarding, a frustrative non-reward effect will follow, increasing discomfort accordingly.

How does loss of reinforcer effectiveness come about? According to Costello, it may result from endogenous changes in the biochemical mechanisms known to underlie consummatory motivation, or it may result from the disruption of a behavioural chain by the loss of a single reinforcer in that chain. It is this latter behavioural formulation which is potentially of interest to the psychological therapist. It sounds rather as if a single loss may have general consequences by its chain disrupting effects, in rather the same way as a house-buying chain of several agreements may be upset by the disruption of one purchase in the chain. The difference here is that all the 'contracts' are being made within the behavioural repertoire of a single individual. Put differently, the stimuli, responses and reinforcers in a person's behaviour are mutually interdependent (Costello, 1972b), and it may be that some people's greater proneness to depression reflects the fact that the mutual interdependence of their behaviour is particularly strong and needs to be weakened. It resembles most closely the clinical observation of an individual 'putting all their eggs in one basket'. A patient who says 'If I can't have my lover back, there is nothing for me' is defining all rewards in terms of a dependence on one particular state of affairs – a state of affairs over which they may have little control in any case. A person who has a 'network' of rewards which is dependent on one or two central components (be it love, job, status, children), is vulnerable to disruption in the chain and as a consequence to generalized loss of reinforcer effectiveness. Eastman gives a helpful analogy:

> Consider a tightly stretched net, made of some elastic filament. The knots in this net represent behaviours, stimuli and reinforcers, while the filaments between them represent the interdependencies. If a single knot is excised, a large hole appears: the net effectively collapses. This represents the disruption of the relationships between behaviours, stimuli and reinforcers that Costello calls a 'loss of reinforcer effectiveness'. If the net is only loosely stretched in the first place and if there are inbuilt holes (some behaviours, etc. are not interrelated with others), then the removal of one knot will have only a small effect on the total.
>
> (Eastman, 1976: 282)

EVALUATION OF EARLY BEHAVIOURAL FORMULATIONS

Table 2.1 shows a summary of the four behavioural formulations, set out according to the factors which render a person vulnerable to, which precipitate or which maintain the depression. What is the evidence that these models are valid? Up until the early to mid-1970s there was very little evidence. The problem was that these models were not expressed sufficiently precisely to generate testable experimental or clinical predictions. Even the more precise formulations, which generated the greatest amount of evidence, suffered from the problem of correlational evidence. Take, for example, the 'reduced frequency of social reinforcement' model of Lewinsohn and his co-workers in Oregon. Their theory is broadly as laid out in Table 2.1, and has vulnerability (lack of interpersonal skills), precipitating (loss event), and maintaining (inadequate or insufficient response contingent positive reinforcement) components. Many writers have pointed out the insufficiency of correlational data in establishing this model. The fact that fewer activities are associated with low mood does not imply that the behaviour changed prior to the mood. Indeed, Lewinsohn's own practice in obtaining these correlations would easily allow the opposite to be the case. This is because, in asking subjects in his experiments to rate the number of activities which occurred on any particular day, they are always instructed in a daily frequency check to count an activity as having occurred only if it was 'at least a little pleasant'. For example, if watching television is on a subject's activity schedule, then if TV-watching was not experienced as enjoyable (a common occurrence) the subject does not check that particular activity on that day (Lewinsohn, 1975). Small wonder then that Lewinsohn and his colleagues obtain significant correlations between subjects' daily ratings of frequency of activities and daily mood ratings. On a 'good day' (assuming affective state to be prior) a subject will enjoy more activities, so his 'frequency' rating will rise. It is not valid to conclude from correlations thus obtained that rate of behavioural output is prior to affective change. (Sanchez and Lewinsohn (1980) have, as I shall report later, attempted to address the issue of causal primacy between mood and assertive behaviour, but there are problems in interpreting even these data.)

In the following section, I shall review research on those models which have become precise enough to gather evidence for and against them. Although each has been concerned with the central aspect of 'adequate reinforcement' for the maintenance of behaviour, each has focused on different aspects. *Social skills theory*, the most direct successor to the earlier formulations, continued to emphasize the reduced frequency of social reinforcement. The second, *self-control theory* emphasized the depressed person's inability to reinforce their own behaviour. The third, *learned helplessness*, focused not on the reduction of reinforcement, but rather on the independence between behaviour and reinforcement.

Table 2.1 Summary of four behavioural formulations

Vulnerability factors	Precipitating factors	Maintaining factors
1. *Reduced frequency of social reinforcement*		Insufficient response contingent positive reinforcement
Lack of social skill (Lack of ability to recognize and use reinforcers)	Loss of reinforcer	Secondary gain (reinforcement of depressive behaviour)
2. *Loss of reinforcible behaviour*		
	Environmental change or situation that can be altered only by emitting very large amount of behaviour	Reduced frequency of behaviour which others or environment can reinforce.
3. *Aversive control*		
Excessive sensitivity to stimuli signalling impending punishment or non-reward	Loss of expected reinforcement (or actual punishment) following behaviour	Same as 1.
4. *Loss of reinforcer effectiveness*		
Large mutual interdependence of stimuli, reinforcers and behaviour	Loss of one or more reinforcers in the network	Generalized loss of potency of reinforcement

SOCIAL SKILLS DEFICITS IN DEPRESSION

Early descriptions in the literature certainly seemed to support the view that depressed people have social skills deficits. The observations of Lewinsohn and co-workers (Lewinsohn *et al.*, 1970; Libet and Lewinsohn, 1973) seemed to indicate that depressed individuals differed from non-depressed individuals in at least five areas: the total amount of verbal behaviour; the number of times the individual initiated behaviour (i.e. not a reaction to another); the degree to which the individual distributed their behaviour equally towards a group of others; the latency to respond to behaviour of another; and the rate of positive/reinforcing behaviour.

The problem with these conclusions was that they were largely derived from uncontrolled observations of depressed individuals in their homes (where the entire interpersonal structure may be biased as much by the 'non-depressed' family members as by the behaviour of the 'depressed' individual). Other data were derived from observations of groups of depressed individuals without extensive comparisons with non-depressed subjects.

Whether one judges these initial descriptions to be right or wrong depends on how one defines social skills. Social skills have been assessed in many different ways from 'molecular' to 'molar' aspects: observer ratings of the minutiae of behaviour (e.g. eye contact, head nods, etc.); observer ratings of number of positive and negative actions and reactions; self-monitoring of such positive and negative actions/reactions; structured interviews of interpersonal adjustment; and self-ratings of difficulty with interpersonal situations. Different definitions and different methods of assessment produce different results. For example, Coyne (1976) found that depressed individuals had a marked alienating effect on people to whom they were talking in a twenty-minute telephone conversation, but apart from the length of time the depressed person spent talking about themselves, the precise measures of social behaviour (total amount of speech, number of approval responses such as 'yeah', 'hm-hmm' and 'yes', number of hope statements, and degree of 'genuineness') did not distinguish depressed from non-depressed patients or control subjects.

A similar conclusion emerged from a very careful analysis of social interaction in depression by Youngren and Lewinsohn (1980). They examined the behaviour of seventy-five neurotically depressed outpatients in comparison with sixty-nine non-depressed psychiatric controls and with eighty normal controls. On five subscales of the Interpersonal Events Schedule (social activity, assertion, cognition, give positive and receive positive) the depressed patients rated themselves as less skilled than did normals and non-depressed psychiatric controls, consistent with ratings made by peers and by independent coders. However, the independent observers found no difference between depressed and non-depressed patients in the minutiae of social behaviour: activity level, initiation level, actions elicited, positive reactions elicited, negative reactions elicited, speech rate, speech volume, eye contact, smiling, facial expression and gestures (illustrators vs adaptors). Similarly, Lewinsohn and Amenson (1978) assessed a number of specific categories of overt behaviour but found that only the more global ratings tended to differentiate depressed patients, and to be associated with therapy improvement. A further study by Kornblith et al. (1983) also found that improvements in general ratings of depression over twelve weeks of self-control therapy were not paralleled by any changes in specific social behaviour.

Only one study appears to have shown differences between depressed patients and non-depressed controls in social skills at the 'molecular' level (Bellack et al., 1983). From a careful analysis of videotaped role-plays of eight positive and eight negative scenarios, they found differences on speech duration, voice tone, gaze, posture, request/compliance content and overall assertiveness. Note however that of these, only speech duration was objectively measured, the remainder were subjective ratings on five-point bidirectional Likert-type scales. There were in fact two other measures made objectively (response latency and number of smiles) and neither of these differed between the depressed and non-depressed group. Added to the fact that these behaviours were assessed in role-play situations, whereas Coyne (1976), Youngren and Lewinsohn (1980) and Kornblith *et al.* (1983), who found no molecular differences, took observations from genuine interactions, it can at least be said that the level of specific skills elements has not so far yielded as sensitive a measure of interpersonal difficulty as do more global ratings of behaviour. But if the patients and observers agree that there is something wrong with the interpersonal behaviour of depressives, and if these errors cannot be detected at the molecular level, where do they originate?

I have already referred to Coyne (1976), who studied twenty-minute telephone conversations in forty-five subject pairs. One member of each pair was an undergraduate subject, the other member of the pair (the target) was either a depressed patient (N = 15) or a non-depressed patient (N = 15) or a non-depressed control subject matched for age and social class with the patients (N = 15). All subjects in the experiment were women. Results showed that the non-depressed subjects felt more depressed, anxious and hostile following interaction with depressed patients than after interaction with non-depressed patients or controls. They also wished to have significantly less future contact with these individuals. Furthermore, there were significant associations between mood disturbance following the conversation and extent of rejection of opportunities for further contact. It was found that the depressed subjects spent more time talking about themselves (talking freely of deaths, marital infidelities, hysterectomies, family strife and 'a variety of other intensely personal matters'). In the absence of measurable differences in the elements of the interaction Coyne concluded that it is this *content* – the inappropriate self-disclosure – which determined the other's reaction, and accounts for the global ratings of interpersonal inadequacy.

Two further studies while finding broadly similar results, add some important information. Hammen and Peters (1978) pointed out that Coyne had only used female subjects and targets. They used both males and females in the role either of interviewer or interviewee, with the interviewee taking the role of a depressed or non-depressed person in five-minute telephone conversations. They replicated Coyne's finding of mood disturbance in interviewers after talking to a 'depressed' person, and of more rejection of 'depressed' people by the interviewers. But the predominant finding was that opposite-sex 'depressed' individuals were rejected far more than were same-sex 'depressed' people. Furthermore, by having interviewees play roles, the *content* of the interview could be controlled in this experiment. Specifically, there was no more personal information divulged by 'depressed' than by 'non-depressed' role-players, so that Coyne's speculation that overexposure of one's own life problems might be responsible for alienating the other person seemed not to explain these results. The 'depressed' interviewees mentioned the same range of problems, but, unlike 'non-depressed' interviewees, blamed themselves and expressed hopelessness about the eventual resolution of the problems. Wortman *et al.* (1976) have in fact found that such disclosure of a personal problem with blame attributed to the self elicits more negative reactions than if external circumstances are blamed.

Howes and Hokanson (1979) asked thirty male and thirty female undergraduates to interact with a 'depressed', 'non-depressed', or 'physically ill' confederate for seven minutes while waiting for an experiment to begin. Although subsequently the subjects rated the 'ill' confederate as 'functionally impaired' to the same extent as the 'depressed' confederate, they significantly more often rejected the 'depressed' individual. This rejection was not, however, correlated with mood disturbance, levels of which did not vary with the type of confederate with whom subjects were interacting.

These three experiments taken together provide strong evidence that depressed individuals alienate those with whom they interact; that this alienation is stronger for opposite sex interactions; that part of the effect may be mediated by the affect induced in the non-depressed partner, and that it seems to be the mentioning of personal problems with self-blameful and hopeless statements attached which causes both the mood disturbance and the alienation in the non-depressed recipient. Interestingly, the fact that two out of the three studies used telephone interactions demonstrates that deficiencies in observable non-verbal communication, such as eye contact and posture, are not necessary for such alienation to occur.

ASSERTIVENESS AND MOOD: WHICH COMES FIRST?

In evaluating the earlier behavioural formulations, I remarked that correlations between depression and the behavioural variable of interest (e.g. pleasant activities) was not sufficient to say which came first. Sanchez and Lewinsohn (1980) have attempted to address the issue of causal primacy between depressed mood and assertive behaviour. Each variable was rated on a daily basis by twelve patients over a five-week period. In addition to computing the same day correlation between the two variables (which turned out to be –0.5) they could also compute the cross-lagged correlations for each subject. That is, they computed the correlations between any day's assertion rating and the day before's and day after's mood rating. They found that the averaged correlation for their twelve subjects, between any day's depressed mood and next day's amount of assertive behaviour, was –0.017 and not significant. The correlation between any day's assertive behaviour and the next day's mood was 0.5, and significant. They conclude that their results 'suggest that rate of emitted assertive behaviour may indeed be better able to predict subsequent level of depression than level of depression can predict subsequent rate of emitted assertive behaviour' (p.120). This conclusion is somewhat premature. Firstly, the choice of computing correlations with a lag of one day is quite arbitrary. It is very likely that interactions between mood and behaviour are quite complex – certainly complex enough to justify experimenting with lag 2 or lag 3 to assess this complexity. Secondly, they make no mention of how the autocorrelations were derived for each subject. It seems that they did not make allowances for the statistical dependence of scores for one day on scores of the same variable for previous days. Thirdly, none of the statistical assumptions underlying the use of cross-lagged correlation analysis appears to have been met (Kenny, 1975; Cook and Campbell, 1979). Finally, and most damaging to their conclusions, they draw conclusions about the difference between two correlations on the basis that one is statistically significant and the other is not. That is invalid. They should have tested the specific hypothesis that there was no difference between the correlations. In fact, when the difference between these correlations is computed, the t-test value is 0.81 which is not significant. These data do not therefore allow the conclusion that one variable predicts the other in one direction better than the reverse. However, the results remain very suggestive, and provide better evidence than most theories have done for the relevance of assertive behaviour in maintaining depression.

Taken together with the evidence that depressed people alienate others, the evidence cited above suggests that downswings in mood may often follow attempts at engaging in interpersonal relationships. These attempts may have gone wrong not because of lack of social skills, but because of what the depressed person has wanted to talk about. Inappropriate disclosure may make the social situation genuinely more difficult for them. Once the other person has been alienated, it may take better social skills than *most* people have to rescue the situation. Thus, it may not be that depressed people have poor social skills. It may be rather that they find themselves (because of what they talk about) more often in social situations which would exceed most people's capacities. It is hardly surprising that they withdraw altogether from such situations. If this is the case, the important thing for therapy to tackle is not social skills, but the person's negative and self-blameful way of talking to others. I turn now to a model of depression which focuses more on attitude to the self. In it, self-blame (or lack of self-reward) is seen as one of three problems in attitudes to the self (the other two being self-monitoring and self-evaluation).

SELF-CONTROL THEORY OF DEPRESSION

This model emphasizes problems that depressed people have in giving themselves sufficient reward. Rehm (1977) developed Kanfer's (1970) self-regulation model which divided the control that an individual has over their own behaviour into three stages: self-monitoring, self-evaluation and self-reinforcement. These processes may be illustrated by way of the paradigmatic 'self-control' experiment. In it, an individual performs a task (e.g. attempting to recognize which of three nonsense syllables in an array has occurred in a prior list). Following their choice, subjects can be asked to *monitor* their success or failure rate, to *evaluate* their level of success relative to subjective standards of accuracy, and then to give themselves a *reward* in proportion to how deserving they think they are. Using such techniques, it has been found (Bellack and Schwartz, 1976) that self-evaluation and reinforcement do not necessarily correlate with actual accuracy. In two such experiments subjects were given verbal recognition tests consisting of thirty nonsense syllables, presented on slides, one at a time (one second each). Following a brief rest period, subjects saw thirty slides with three nonsense syllables on each. Their task was to identify the syllable they had seen before. Each set of three was presented for five seconds. College students usually have a 50–60 per cent recognition accuracy on this sort of task. Subjects evaluated each response (on a 0–10 scale in one experiment) and administered reward to themselves by pressing a button which lit up an orange lamp. No feedback about a subject's accuracy was provided. The results were clear. There was no correlation either between actual performance and subject's evaluation of their performance, or between their actual performance and the amount of reward that they gave to themselves. The maximum number of self-rewards was thirty. Subjects varied between zero and twenty, but those who gave themselves low ratings and low numbers of self-reward had done no worse on the task than those who gave themselves a large amount of self-rewards and evaluated their performance highly. Clearly large individual differences in self-evaluation and self-reward styles exist for this task. How much more variance would there be outside the tight control of the experimental laboratory?

Such experiments have made it clear that self-monitoring involves more than the passive registration of stimuli in the environment (Rehm, 1977). Rather it is an active scanning which selectively perceives and encodes into memory. Whereas non-depressed individuals perform this function appropriately, depressed individuals are hypothesized to attend selectively to negative aspects of themselves and their world. Self-evaluation is performed on the basis of criteria that are set too high to achieve, so that overt and covert rewards are rarely awarded. Thus the basis for normal rates of behaviour (self-regulation) in the relative absence of external control is diminished, and the depressed individual's behavioural repertoire is disrupted. In further statements of the self-regulation model, Kanfer and Hagerman (1981) amplify the distinction between the monitoring of one's own behaviour and evaluation of it according to current criteria. These criteria may be short- or long-term. Short-term criteria usually centre around performance or behaviour which is relevant only to the immediate situation of specific limited goals (e.g. stumbling when running to catch a bus may mean nothing more than a grazed knee and a ten-minute delay in getting to the office that morning). Long-term criteria, however, often relate to maintenance of enduring personal goals (e.g. stumbling when running in the athletic trials to determine who represents your country in the Olympics). In these examples, the situation clearly predefines the criteria which can be used to judge the significance of the same event (stumbling), but most situations are not so clear-cut. Failing to see quickly what you require in a supermarket is a common event, which, if thought about at all, may cause a non-depressed person to conclude that they are not 'on form' that day. A depressed person may conclude that they are dementing, because they will see it in the context of other similar events over a long time period. So it may be extremely important whether long-term or short-term standards are accessed in response to ambiguous situations. Accessing the wrong criteria for self-evaluation leads to poor or absent self-reinforcement and increased self-punishment.

Evidence consistent with Rehm's 1977 formulation has taken the form of results showing that depressed and non-depressed subjects do indeed differentially reward and punish themselves as predicted by the theory (Rozensky et al., 1977; Lobitz and Post, 1979). The theory has also led to several successful treatment studies (e.g. Fuchs and Rehm, 1977; Rehm et al., 1979), which although not reviewed in Chapter Four because they used a group rather than individualized approach, have found that an approach which combines self-reinforcement, thought monitoring and evaluation and activity monitoring can be very helpful.

LEARNED HELPLESSNESS AND DEPRESSION

Social skills and self-control theories emphasize the adequacy or inadequacy of rewards provided by other people or by oneself. By contrast, in learned helplessness theory, Seligman and his colleagues came to emphasize not the adequacy of reinforcement, but the contingency between actions and reinforcement.

In 1967, Overmier and Seligman, in the course of investigating the effects of Pavlovian fear conditioning had found that dogs given inescapable and unavoidable stressors in one situation (the Pavlovian Hammock) later failed to learn to escape or avoid a similar stressor in another situation (the shuttlebox). Further research found similar phenomena in cats, fish, rats, mice, birds, primates as well as man.

Maier and Seligman (1976) outlined three outcomes of exposure to uncontrollable aversive events:

1. *Motivational deficits*: Animals that had been exposed to inescapable stress did not subsequently initiate escape responses in the presence of such stress.
2. *Cognitive deficits*: Animals that had been exposed to inescapable stress

were slower to learn that their responses could control future stresses; i.e. if the animal made a response that produced relief, it had trouble 'catching on' to the response–relief contingency (Seligman, 1974). In humans, this effect of uncontrollability had been shown by assessing the number of trials taken for a subject to 'catch on' to the pattern underlying a series of anagrams. Subjects given prior exposure either to inescapable noise or insoluble discrimination problems took longer to perceive the pattern (Hiroto and Seligman, 1975; Miller and Seligman, 1975).

3. *Emotional changes*: Maier and Seligman presented data from a number of sources to support the claim that inescapable trauma had emotional effects: there was evidence that following only one such trauma in dogs, subsequent helplessness deficits dissipated over forty-eight hours, which they suggested hinted at a transient emotional (hormonal) effect; human subjects who performed tasks while being shocked but were not allowed to take time-outs when they wished, had been found to show consistently higher blood pressure than subjects who were allowed to specify when they wished to take time-outs (Hockanson *et al.*, 1971).

The hypothesis proposed by Seligman and co-workers to account for these phenomena was 'learned helplessness' (Seligman, 1974, 1975). It assumed that organisms could learn not only about the contingencies between instrumental responses and the outcomes of those responses but also could weigh up the probability of their behaviour resulting in a specific outcome. When the probability of reinforcement, given a specific response, does not differ from the probability of reinforcement in the absence of that response, responding and reinforcement are independent, i.e. the organism has no control over outcomes. The learned helplessness hypothesis argued that motivational and cognitive deficits and emotional changes follow when an organism has learned that responding and outcome are independent. The motivational deficits follow inescapable stress because part of the incentive for making such responses is the expectation that they will bring relief. The cognitive deficits follow inescapable stress because, having acquired a cognitive set in which responses are irrelevant to outcomes, it will be harder to learn that responses control outcomes when they actually do. The presence of emotional changes did not follow directly from the helplessness hypothesis, but Seligman cited evidence that exposure to uncontrollable trauma produced more conditional fear, ulcers, weight loss and defecation in animals, than controllable stress.

However, it was the suggestion that this learned helplessness phenomenon could be a model of reactive depression in humans which gave the greatest impetus to research, particularly in the attempts to find human analogues of the animal work. Just as animals exposed to inescapable stress showed later motivational, cognitive and emotional changes which undermined effective instrumental responding, so reactive depression may have resulted from stress perceived as uncontrollable which would lead to the expectation that future reinforcements would be out of the person's control. This expectation was hypothesized to lead to the passivity of depression (motivational), the negative expectations of depression (cognitive) and the affective disturbance in depression (emotional).

A great deal happened in the few years after publication of Seligman's book on helplessness (1975). For example, it soon became clear that many of the human laboratory helplessness demonstrations did not require a 'learned helplessness' model to explain them (Coyne *et al.*, 1980; Williams and Teasdale, 1982). Coyne *et al.* referred to the similarity between helplessness phenomena and the large number of studies using similar procedures (to similar effect) in the test anxiety and achievement motivation literature. They surmised that if laboratory helplessness phenomena were anxiety-based, they ought to be alleviated with 'pleasant relaxing imagery' inserted between pretreatment and test phases. They indeed found that instructing subjects to imagine a pleasant mountain scene 'in order to relax you' prevented deficits on twenty patterned anagrams following uncontrollable noise pretreatment. Williams and Teasdale (1982) found evidence that behavioural deficits on laboratory tasks used in helplessness research could be reproduced in subjects who had a low expectancy of success on a task thought to be of low importance, and in subjects who had a low expectancy for an important task who then met initial difficulty performing that task. Explanations of these results were proposed in terms of four variables: expectancy of success, motivation to succeed, amount of effort required and the cost of effort. No explanation in terms of perceived or expected non-contingency between action and outcome was necessary.

Alternative explanations for helplessness deficits have continued to appear. In one such recent study Mikulincer (1989) proposed that learned helplessness deficits were due to 'off-task cognitions'. Subject's proneness to cognitive interference was assessed prior to being given failure or no failure feedback in the first phase of an experiment. The subsequent test task used to assess helplessness varied in its memory load. Consistent with the hypothesis, only subjects defined as vulnerable to cognitive interference showed helplessness, and then only on the high memory load test task. Furthermore, accuracy on the test task was associated with the frequency of reported off-task cognitions. Once again, no explanation in terms of non-contingency between action and outcome was necessary.

However, the most significant development in learned helplessness theory has come, not from outside the helplessness camp but from within it. At about the same time as Seligman's landmark book, *Helplessness*, was published and certainly by the time the large review paper on 'Learned helplessness' by Maier and Seligman (1976) appeared in print the theory was being substantially modified. A draft paper was even then circulating between London, Pennsylvania and Oxford. A number of doubts about the robustness of the model had occurred simultaneously to Seligman himself (on sabbatical in London in the mid-1970s), to Lyn Abramson in Pennsylvania, and John Teasdale in Oxford. Their important paper in 1978 (Abramson, Seligman and Teasdale) represented a 'reformulation' of learned helplessness as applied to humans, in attributional theory terms. I shall start the next chapter, which will focus on cognitive accounts of depression, by examining this attributional reformulation.

Chapter 3

Psychological models of depression II
The cognitive foreground

When psychologists refer to cognitive models of depression, they are usually referring to one of two theories – that of Aaron Beck, who has been writing about the influence of thoughts, images, attitudes, and schemas on mood since at least the early 1960s (see Beck, 1964); and that of Martin Seligman, whose theory of learned helplessness I reviewed in the previous chapter. Seligman's theory differed from that of Beck in that it grew out of laboratory research with animals. It was nevertheless a 'cognitive theory' in the sense that the animal or human was presumed to be computing and comparing two probabilities (or expectations) of outcomes given a response versus the absence of a response. By contrast, Beck's model grew out of observation of the thoughts, images and dreams of depressed patients. It made use of concepts from the rapidly expanding field of information processing (most notably the concept of the schema) and quickly became the framework within which a structured psychotherapy developed. Originally, the links between these two cognitive theories were very tenuous, because of their different origins (see Seligman, 1981 for his description of similarities and differences). When the original learned helplessness account ran into difficulties, it was reformulated in terms which took into account a variable (attribution) which was very similar to the notion of dysfunctional attitude developed by Beck (1976). But it was a much more tightly formulated notion than dysfunctional attitudes, since it was able to benefit from several years of careful research into attributional processes (see Weiner, 1986). As such, the attributional formulation led to a large number of studies examining correlational and longitudinal relationships between attribution and depression. Because the attributional theory grew out of the helplessness framework reviewed in the previous chapter, I shall review it before reviewing that of Beck.

THE ATTRIBUTIONAL REFORMULATION OF DEPRESSION

A summary of the main proposals of the attributional reformulation was given by Seligman in a 1981 paper. The new model had four premises, the co-occurrence of which was hypothesized to be sufficient for depression to occur:

1. The individual expects that a highly aversive state of affairs is likely (or a highly desired state of affairs is unlikely).
2. The individual expects that he will be able to do nothing about the likelihood of these states of affairs.
3. The individual possesses a maladaptive attributional style so that negative events tend to be attributed to internal, stable and global causes, and positive events to external, unstable and specific causes.
4. The greater the certainty of the expected aversive state of affairs and the expected uncontrollability, the greater the strength of motivational and cognitive deficits. The greater the importance to the individual of the uncontrollable event, the greater will be the affective and self-esteem disruption.

For a reason which is not entirely clear, most subsequent interest has focused on the third premise, that maladaptive attributional style predisposes the individual to react in a depressive way to the presence of aversive events or non-occurrence of positive events. This component of the model states that attribution for an uncontrollable event determines the individual's response to that event. For example, if an exam was failed you might say to yourself either that you failed because you didn't have the necessary ability or because you didn't try hard enough (both internal attributions). Note however that ability is a rather more unchanging or 'stable' cause for your failure than effort. Effort may be increased the next time the exam comes around whereas ability is seen as rather less changeable. Or you may say that you failed because the exams set by that examination board are always very difficult (another 'stable', but this time 'external' attribution) or that it was just bad luck and next time may be OK ('unstable' and 'external'). Table 3.1 shows these four possible attributions and their categories.

These attributions may also be either global or specific. You may say you hadn't the ability either specifically, because it was, for example, a statistics exam which for you correlates with no other exam performance, or globally, because you are just no good at taking formal exams and don't understand anything on any of your college courses anyway. Clearly one would expect differences in attributions such as these to make a large difference in the

Table 3.1 Possible attributions for failing an exam

	Stable	*Unstable*
Internal	Low ability	Low effort
External	Task difficulty	Bad luck
Also: *Global/Specific* (see text)		

behavioural and affective impact of the original event. The theory proposes that negative events attributed to internal (personal), stable (unchanging) and global (wide-ranging) attributions will be more devastating emotionally. In particular, internal attributions for failure (and external ones for success) tend to lower self-esteem; stable attributions for failure (and unstable ones for success) tend to produce long-lasting deficits; and global attributions for failure (and specific ones for success) produce depressive deficits which generalize to many situations.

Note that this attributional component of the model is only one of four premises. Early research neglected the other premises, for example the first and second premises that an event perceived as uncontrollable is deemed a necessary co-occurrence of the other premises for depression to occur. That is not to say that depression cannot occur by other means (biological, prolonged anxiety or heavy workload, etc.), but that on this theory, all four premises are necessary. A detailed discussion of these aspects of the model will be found in Chapter Ten.

The researchers who have looked at the attributional component of depression have found ambiguous results. Some of these are detailed in Chapter Ten, but it is appropriate here to mention some studies which have examined these variables in some depth. Hargreaves (1985) examined fifty depressed patients (divided equally between the sexes) who had been referred to psychiatrists or psychologists for management of depression. The sample included inpatients, outpatients, daypatients and general practitioner patients. All were between the ages of sixteen and sixty-five years, with no psychoticism, mental deficiency or organicity, and no history of alcohol problems or drug addiction. All had a Beck Depression Inventory (BDI) score of at least 15.

Control subjects, matched for age and sex (twenty-five males and twenty-five females) were recruited from a subject panel. Depressed and control subjects completed the Beck Depression Inventory; the Attributional Style Questionnaire (which gives a score of an individual's tendency to see positive and negative events as caused by internal, stable or global factors, as well as a rating of the importance of the outcome) (Seligman *et al.*, 1979); the Locus of Control Scale (Rotter, 1966); a Self-Esteem Questionnaire (Rosenberg, 1965); and the Eysenck Personality Questionnaire (Eysenck and Eysenck, 1975). Thus it was possible not only to see if depressed patients were characterized by any particular attributional style, but also to examine the personality correlates of attributional style.

In answer to the first question, no differences in attributional style were found between the depressed and control groups. Furthermore, when the correlates of attributional style on Seligman's questionnaire were observed, they were disappointing. For example, there was no significant correlation in the depressed group between Seligman's internality scale and the Rotter Locus of Control internal–external score ($r = -0.252$ and -0.003 for internal attribution to success and failure respectively). For non-depressed subjects these correlations were $r = -0.414$ (p<0.01) and 0.128 respectively. This is hardly very good convergent validity evidence for the model. The corresponding correlation between internality and self-esteem is slightly more encouraging: internal attribution for failure vs. self-esteem $r = 0.435$ (p<0.01), but the corresponding correlation for success attributions which should be significant in the opposite direction is only $r = -0.190$. (The finding that attributions for failure produce results more consistent with the model than attributions for success has occurred elsewhere, e.g. Metalsky *et al.*, 1982; Jack and Williams, 1991.)

Hargreaves also examined differences between her depressed and control groups in extraversion and neuroticism. She found large and highly significant differences, the depressed group being less extravert and more neurotic. There was no relationship between these personality variables and attributional style.

This study provides virtually no support for the attributional reformulation. Is there an explanation for this? There are two possible explanations of the results which preserve the integrity of the attributional model to some extent. The first is that the definition of depression in this study was a cut-off score on the BDI, rather than a diagnosis of primary depression. Referral to a helping agency for treatment of depression does not guarantee the diagnosis in patients who may have been a mixed group. On the other hand, previous results which have been taken to support the attributional model have used cut-off scores with college students which are a rather more distant group from clinically depressed patients. The lack of diagnostic clarity can therefore hardly be taken as a major criticism relative to these other studies (e.g. Metalsky *et al.*, 1982). The second possible explanation is that many of the patients had perhaps become depressed by an alternative route. Seligman and colleagues do not maintain that their model provides the only way by which individuals become depressed – their premises are sufficient but not necessary for depression to occur. On the other hand, one might have expected some differences to emerge, even if only a proportion of the patients had a maladaptive attributional style. Further, we do not know which patients had suffered a life event prior to their depression. It is these patients for whom the attributional theory makes the most powerful prediction, and failure to find any relationship in this group would be damaging indeed to the model.

It would be misleading to give the impression that no investigation has found the hypothesized relationship between attributional style and depression. Raps *et al.* (1982) found that clinical depressives, but not hospitalized schizophrenics, had a maladaptive attributional style. The authors took this to illustrate that psychopathology by itself was insufficient to account for any differences between depressed and non-depressed individuals in attributional style. Most other findings have used college students (e.g. Seligman *et al.*, 1979; Golin *et al.*, 1981). There are now sufficient studies using other samples (e.g. women having their first babies; recently unemployed men) to obtain a clearer picture of the pattern of associations between attributions and depression. It is now clear that, even when the hypothesized results do occur, it is the attribution for negative, rather than for positive events which is associated with depression (Brewin, 1985). This has led to the revision of the original Attributional Style questionnaire, omitting those items asking about explanations for positive events, and adding more negative events to the questionnaire (Peterson and Vilanova, 1988). More significantly, it has led to a modification of the reformulated theory into what has been called the 'hopelessness theory' of depression (Alloy *et al.*, 1988). This 'reformulation of the reformulation' specifically emphasizes (a) that it is misattribution about aversive events (or non-occurrence of positive events) which is critical; (b) that such events must occur if the diathesis stress model is to be adequately tested; and (c) that tendencies to misattribute negative events may best be assessed when the individual is under stress, (c.f. Williams, 1984a) and which I discuss further in Chapter Ten.

Two other questions have persistently been raised with respect to the attributional reformulation of 1978. First, how necessary are the particular dimensions: are any of them redundant? Second, how complete is the model – are other attributional dimensions necessary? In answer to the first question, most doubt has been raised about the 'internality' dimension. Perhaps because internal attributions are complex, including both attributions for responsibility to the self ('I was part of the causal sequence') and self-blame ('My behaviour fell short of some internal or external standard') they have been inconsistent in their relationship to depression (Brewin, 1985).

In answer to the second question, Weiner (1986) has persistently argued that controllability is important. A recent study of children's attributions is consistent with the suggestion that controllability is indeed a moderator variable. Brown and Siegal (1988) suggested that only when a negative event is perceived as uncontrollable would internal, stable and global attributions lead to depression. They conducted a prospective study of 364 girls aged thirteen to seventeen years, assessing them twice, eight months apart. They measured depression levels, particularly focusing on the 176 who reported at least one negative event during the eight-month period. They were able to confirm their hypothesis. Only for negative events perceived as uncontrollable was there an association between a poor attributional style and increased depression. Furthermore, if the negative event was seen as controllable, the internal and stable global attribution style predicted a *less* depressed response.

To be fair to the reformulated helplessness model, this study might be seen to support its second premise (that for depression to occur an individual must not expect to be able to affect the outcome) rather than challenge the sufficiency of its third premise. The question of whether controllability is properly seen as an attribution or as a precondition off which explanatory style may feed, may seem academic. In any event, there are sufficient indications that an individual's beliefs about controllability contribute importantly to their future behaviour.

This reference to the second and third premises of the reformulated theory brings us back to the question of which of the four premises of the reformulated theory have received most interest. I shall return to the question of whether a negative event perceived as uncontrollable is necessary (the diathesis stress-model) in Chapter Ten. The emphasis of recent research has been the connection between maladaptive attribution style and ill-health. For example, Peterson et al. (1988) returned to material written by members of a Harvard class between 1939 and 1945. The mean age of the subjects had been twenty-five at this time. For this type of research, Seligman and his colleagues have developed CAVE (Content Analysis of Verbatim Explanations). Trained judges, who do not know any other information about the subjects, rate statements made in diaries, letters or interviews by experimental subjects many years before. Hence these researchers are able to carry out prospective studies of attributional concepts which were not themselves developed until years after the prospective study began! The study of the Harvard class showed that the attributional style of the students aged twenty-five predicted their state of health at age forty-five and sixty-five, even after partialling out their health at age twenty-five. This is only one of a number of such studies that have found that attributional style predicts later morbidity (see Seligman et al., 1988 for review).

Why does attributional style predict health over such a long interval? Could it be that it is not early attributional style which predicts later health, but mainly that attributional style predicts current health. In this case, the long time interval between attributional style at Time 1 and health at Time 2 arises because attributional style is a stable attribute. That is, attributional style at Time 1 correlates with attributional style at Time 2, and it is the concurrent correlation which is important. Burns and Seligman (1989) found evidence to support this suggestion. Independent judges rated diaries and letters from the distant past of their subjects (a mean of fifty-two years before) and also rated (blind) contemporary written responses to questions about their current life. Thirty people took part. The correlation between explanatory style for negative events then and now was 0.54.

These results, though they are not concerned with depression, are nevertheless relevant to psychological well-being. This is not only because of the close association between ill-health and depression, but because, if attributional style is as stable as this research suggests, long-term vulnerability to clinical depression will be a likely consequence.

Whatever the exact relationship between attributional style and depression turns out to be, the fact that maladaptive attributions do occur in *some* patients (Brewin, 1985) indicates that their possible role in all depressed patients must be looked for. Re-attribution training as a technique used by itself may be only minimally helpful for the largest proportion of patients, but that is not to say that it will not prove very helpful for some.

THE COGNITIVE THEORY OF DEPRESSION

Unlike the learned helplessness theory, Beck's cognitive theory of depression arose out of clinical observations rather than the animal or human laboratory. It is therefore to be expected that the observations which form the basis of the theory would have a great deal of validity in themselves. The key work from which our review of this theory may start is *Cognitive Therapy and the Emotional Disorders* (Beck, 1976).

In that book three main components of a theory of emotional disorders were outlined. The first component was the presence of *negative automatic thoughts* – 'automatic' by virtue of their coming 'out of the blue', often seemingly unprompted by events and not necessarily the results of 'directed' thinking. They seem 'immediate' and often 'valid' in the sense that they are often accepted unchallenged by the recipient. Their effect is to disrupt mood, and to cause further thoughts to emerge in a downward thought-affect spiral. Depressive thoughts can be characterized in terms of *cognitive triad* – a negative view of the self (e.g. 'I'm a failure'), the world (e.g. 'This neighbourhood is a terrible place') and the future (e.g. 'Everything will turn out badly').

The second component is the presence of *systematic logical errors* in the thinking of depressed individuals. Several categories (not mutually exclusive) have been distinguished: arbitrary inference (e.g. someone concludes that a friend has fallen out with them because they did not smile at him or her), overgeneralization (e.g. 'Failure on this exam means I'll never pass the other exams'), selective abstraction (e.g. a person only notices the few bad things in a report about himself); magnification and minimization (e.g. when a person exaggerates the effect of a negative event (catastrophizes) or minimizes the impact of a positive event); personalization (when a person attributes bad things to himself despite evidence to the contrary, e.g. 'If I'd thought to warn Mr Jones about the effects of overeating, he'd never have had a heart attack'); dichotomous thinking (all or nothing: black/white thinking, e.g. 'Only a miracle can make me well again', or 'If he leaves me, I may as well be dead').

The third component of the cognitive model is the presence of *depressogenic schemas*. These general, long-lasting attitudes or assumptions about the world represent the way in which the individual organizes their past and current experience, and is suggested to be the system by which incoming information about the world is classified. This is one of the earliest concepts in Beck's theoretical writings. In 1964 he defined the schema as a structure for screening, coding and evaluating impinging stimuli. In terms of the individual's adaptation to external reality, it is regarded as the mode by which the environment is broken down and organised into its many psychologically relevant facets; on the basis of the matrix of schemas, the individual is able to orient himself in relation to time and space and to categorise and interpret his experiences in a meaningful way.

According to the theory, depressive schemas develop over many years and, although they may not be evident, remain ready to be activated by a

Table 3.2 Factors in childhood history leading to depressive schemas

1. *Tangible loss*
   Loss of mother/father
   Loss of other relative, friend, person close to you (loss includes death, divorce, separation, desertion, prolonged ill-health)
   Prolonged ill-health as a child

2. *Expectation of loss (reality)*
   Loss of mother/father/other close person expected for long time before loss actually realized
   Disappointment by people relied upon
   Expectation of big reward for something done, which never materialized

3. *Expectation of loss (fantasy)*
   Loss (as in 2.) expected for long time, but did not actually occur

4. *Self-esteem lowering events*
   Difficulty in mixing with other children
   Being bullied over extended period
   Feeling of being different from peer group
   Feeling of being unwanted by parents
   Feeling of being unwanted by everyone ('no one cared')
   Feeling of being hated by everyone

5. *Reversal in valuation of object*
   Sudden change from loving someone very much to hating them
   Sudden change from self-respect to self-hate – feeling badly about self because of an event

6. *Background*
   Depression in close family members
   Severe punishment by either parent
   Overprotection by either parent, and/or
   Isolation from other children
   Strict rules by either parent
   History of parents pointing out faults but not good points

Table 3.3 Schemas which occur in personality disordered patients

- Dependency (e.g. feeling incapable of coping by oneself)
- Subjugation (e.g. letting others have their own way, being anxious to please)
- Vulnerability to harm or illness (e.g. worry about physical health or possibility of violent attack)
- Fear of losing self-control (e.g. worry about going crazy, losing control of emotions and impulses)
- Emotional deprivation (e.g. constant feeling of insufficient love and attention to meet needs, wanting deeper relationships)
- Abandonment/loss (e.g. feeling that one will be alone for ever, that it is inevitable that those now close to you will leave, constantly on the look out for signs of abandonment)
- Mistrust (e.g. feeling that others are going to attack or undermine you, even if they are appearing to be kind)
- Social isolation/alienation (e.g. the feeling of not 'fitting in', of being different and alienated)
- Defectiveness/unlovability (e.g. feeling of inherent defectiveness and that if only people could see me as I am, they would see how worthless I am)
- Social undesirability (e.g. feeling of being sexually, physically and socially unattractive; that no one would want to associate with someone as dull and boring as oneself)
- Incompetence/failure (e.g. most people are better or more competent than I am)
- Guilt/punishment (e.g. a basic feeling of deserving to be punished and 'no excuse will do')
- Shame/embarrassment (e.g. a feeling of being humiliated by one's own inadequacy, fear of others 'finding out')
- Unrelenting standards (e.g. need to push oneself to the limits, feeling that one could always do better)
- Entitlement/insufficient limits (e.g. feeling of irritation if frustrated or wronged); difficulty in setting limits (e.g. smoking, drinking); inability to settle to do routine jobs (e.g. dislike of constraints)

combination of stressful circumstances. Table 3.2 gives the sort of factors in child development which are supposed to cause the depressive schemas to be constructed over time.

Recently, Young (1989) has developed a comprehensive questionnaire to assess schemas. His work with personality disordered and difficult patients has suggested to him that there are fifteen major schematic categories, separate domains or themes within which the person is hypervigilant for signals. If these signals occur the patient concludes that they are vulnerable or failing or inadequate in a way defined by the schema. These domains are shown in Table 3.3. Whereas one would not expect all of these to be represented in depressed patients, several are likely to be. It will be important to investigate this in future research. Since there is often 'co-morbidity' between depression and long-standing personality difficulties, such new questionnaires as Young's become an increasingly important aid in therapy.

EVIDENCE FOR THE COGNITIVE MODEL

The evidence for the cognitive model is both correlational and experimental. Correlational studies show that individuals have more automatic negative thoughts when feeling depressed (using thought checklists or less structured diaries on which to record thoughts – see Chapter Seven). It is also possible to classify these thoughts according to the logical error being made at the time. There is little doubt also that depressives are selective in their recall of rewards and punishments, which favour the schema theory (Gotlib, 1981). There is also a great deal of experimental evidence (from laboratory mood induction research) that presentation of negative self-statements similar to those which occur naturally to depressed individuals can actually precipitate a downswing in the mood of formerly non-depressed subjects (see Chapter Ten). In fact, mood induction studies provide some of the best evidence that depressive cognitions may act in a causal capacity to affect mood (Goodwin and Williams, 1982). This research on induction of moods, and its opposite (the alleviation of depressed mood by experimental reduction in frequency of negative thoughts) is reviewed in Chapter Ten. This type of research contributes to that aspect of cognitive theory which suggests that cognitions affect mood (I call it the 'precipitation theory'). Different research strategies are required to test the notion that cognition renders some people more vulnerable than others to depressive onset and maintenance. I call this the 'vulnerability theory'. Since cognitive theory is explored in greater depth in this later chapter, I shall not discuss it further here. But it is worth noting at this point that the role of cognitions in the *aetiology* of depression, even if questioned, need not affect their status in the *maintenance* of depression. No matter how precipitated, a depressive reaction characterized by negative view of the self, the world and the future will tend to be more severe and more prolonged. Even those investigators who find little evidence for the antecedence of cognitions in the aetiology of depressive onset (e.g. Lewinsohn *et al.*, 1981) find that once depressed, the more negative the cognitive style, the longer it takes for the depression to remit. Thus the assessment of, and techniques designed to cope with the cognitive component of depression are likely to be very important. A review of the key treatment outcome studies (Chapter Four) justifies this conclusion.

CLINICAL COGNITIVE THEORY AND EXPERIMENTAL COGNITIVE PSYCHOLOGY

One of the major reasons why Beck's theory aroused so much interest among psychologists was that it paralleled closely research in experimental psychology. Interestingly, these two lines of research have existed in parallel for some years, and only recently have explicit links been made between them (see Williams *et al.*, 1988 for a review of this work). This experimental cognitive clinical research is still in its infancy, and yet to review it all would take us far beyond our present scope. Nevertheless, it is worth briefly examining the ideas from cognitive psychology which were influential initially in encouraging clinical and experimental cognitive psychologists to collaborate in building bridges between their hitherto separate interests.

The area of experimental cognitive psychology which seemed most relevant to biases in thinking seen in depression was the research into the errors made by non-clinical subjects when asked to make judgements about the world. Such judgements, about future probabilities, about the past, about explanations for events, are rarely error-free in the normal individual, since the information on which to base them is incomplete. This means that the normal subject must make inferences when remembering the past, perceiving the present, or generating expectancies about the future; inferences which may often be more due to factors internal or external to the individual of which the individual is not aware and which misrepresent 'reality'. Three areas of study will be mentioned: (a) heuristics used in making judgements under uncertainty; (b) hindsight judgements; and (c) biases in eyewitness testimony.

Normal 'biases' and their possible clinical counterparts

Errors in judgements under uncertainty

Tversky and Kahneman (1974) outlined several heuristics (rules of thumb) which people use when making judgements under uncertainty. One of these, the *availability heuristic* leads to a type of bias when people attempt to assess the likelihood of an event. It refers to the rule by which the frequency of an event or probability of an event is assessed by the ease with which relevant instances may be recalled. It is a useful rule in many instances, and may lead to correct conclusions: if you want to judge how likely it is that the traffic will be bad on a particular day at a particular time, it will be helpful to recall previous instances – and since instances of a large class of events are normally recalled better and faster than less frequent instances, assessing the probability of traffic hold-ups by judging the ease with which relevant instances are recalled may be accurate. But biases occur when there is differential retrievability for reasons other than increased frequency of instances. For example, if a friend has a heart attack, the fact that one single instance of heart attack is important to you (a 'salient feature') would make it easy to retrieve and lead you to overestimate the probability that you yourself are vulnerable. In this respect such biases, though leading to incorrect conclusions, may also be useful. People take greater precautions against being vulnerable to heart disease if a friend has had a recent attack. We take more safeguards against fire if there is fire down our *own* street (more salient) than if we read about a more remote fire in a newspaper. Nor is this excess caution merely a 'rational' process. A few years ago, I found myself carefully unplugging a tape recorder in my office (a caution I don't usually exercise) after I had been listening to a tape of a thunder storm in preparation to see a thunder-phobic client.

Despite the potential usefulness of such a heuristic, there can be little doubt that differential memorability may be a burden on the depressed patient, for the salient aspects of the depressed patient's past are often those times they have failed in the interpersonal, academic or occupational sphere. Lloyd and Lishman (1975) found that the more depressed the patient is, the latency to retrieve unpleasant memories becomes shorter relative to the latency to retrieve positive memories. Thus in making judgements on the future probability of successful outcomes, the 'availability heuristic' will, in implying that the incidents which are easier to retrieve from the past are the more probable in the future, dictate a pessimistic view.

Tversky and Kahneman also outlined an *anchoring heuristic* – this rule reflects the finding that different starting points yield different estimates which are biased towards (or 'anchored by') the initial values. The most striking demonstration of this bias is that if a roulette wheel is spun and the number observed just before a person is asked to estimate something (e.g. number of countries in the United Nations), the estimate varies considerably depending on the value of the roulette number observed beforehand. Tversky and Kahneman reported mean estimates of twenty-five countries and forty-five countries for wheel of fortune outcome of ten and sixty-four respectively.

What is so striking about this bias is the fact that the distracting values are so obviously irrelevant to the number being estimated. It is therefore not difficult to see how much more a subject may be biased by a relevant estimate of the same or similar value. For example, in research of biased recall in depressives, investigators have given depressed or non-depressed subjects a series of tasks at which they have either succeeded or failed (e.g. Nelson and Craighead, 1977). After completion of the series, subjects are asked how many they recall having succeeded at. The typical finding that depressed subjects give a lower success estimate has often been taken as evidence of a failure to *recall* success experiences. However, no independent evidence has been produced to support the hypothesis that these subjects actually cannot remember those tasks on which they succeeded. An equally likely explanation is that depressed subjects would have given a lower estimate of success rate before starting the series, and in giving their 'recall' values, are merely reflecting this general estimate. The ease with which normal subjects' estimates of neutral variables such as numbers of UN countries may be affected by irrelevant distracting numerical values makes unsurprising the extent to which depressed subjects bias their own estimates of self-referent variables.

Hindsight judgements

In the case of the 'anchoring heuristic' people were affected by a suggestion (the initial value) without being aware that they were so affected. The fact that the initial value could be determined at random showed how hard normal individuals find it to discard even uninformative information. The inability for normal individuals to ignore information is seen again in hindsight judgements. When confronted with an unfortunate accident, people tend to overestimate the probability that it would have occurred given only the prior information. People cannot, it seems, ignore the additional information that the event occurred, finding it difficult to reconstruct the uncertainties which would have faced people prior to the event (Fischhoff, 1977). Fischhoff points out how this bias makes people exaggerate the predictability of the past, and as a result systematically underestimate what can be learned from it. This bias has two implications for work with depressed patients. First, a constant source of frustration for the therapist working with depressed patients is how one bad event during the course of recovery may wipe out the positive progress by the patient in previous weeks. This occurs even if one has tried to prepare the patient for such bad experiences, e.g. by talking about them as an opportunity to use cognitive therapy techniques. Fischhoff's research suggests that following such a bad event, the previous positive events may not simply be being ignored by the patient, but may be being re-interpreted in the light of the subsequent event. A patient of mine had a good experience going swimming with friends and a few days later had a bad experience meeting other acquaintances at a party. It was not that being upset about the second event made her ignore the swimming event, rather she 'remembered' that it had been a struggle to get to the pool in fear of making herself look ridiculous, that it had been embarrassing to see herself in a swimming suit because of her weight problem, etc. and that on the basis of the swimming experience (thus re-coded) bad experiences in the future should have been entirely predict-table. Second, the hindsight bias implies that attributional theory accounts of depressed patients' dismissal of success as 'too easy' may be oversimple. This suggests that depressed patients may claim that their successes were 'predictable' rather than 'easy' (because of hindsight re-interpretations) and thereby they do not learn from these success experiences, i.e. success has little effect on future prediction.

Biases in testimony

Eye-witness testimony has been an extensively researched area because of the evident importance of determining sources of error in people's eye-witness statements. The particular type of error that concerns us is that found by Loftus and Palmer (1974) because it shows how the very language used in asking a question can bias the response. Loftus and Palmer found that following a road traffic accident, eye witnesses gave a higher estimate of the speed of the car when asked 'How fast was the car going when it *smashed* the other car?' as against 'How fast was the car going when it *hit* the other car?' This has been explained as the influence of the questioner on the respondent, i.e. the questioner's belief that the car was going fast influencing the witness. Note how such influence affects actual objective speed estimates – to all intents and purposes the database of the observer is being changed. To what extent then does the same bias apply to self-talk? Depressive's self-talk is often characterized by catastrophization (or magnification). It is often assumed that such catastro- phization is the outcome (product) of the biased selection of data on which to base interpretations. Loftus and Palmer's experiment raises the possibility that catastrophization itself affects a subject's estimates of the data to be interpreted. For example, telling oneself one is 'shattered' at the end of the day may lead to overestimates of the number of hours worked and underestimates of the number of rest pauses taken.

Heuristics and biases in thinking and judgements was only one of several seminal areas for collaboration between experimental and clinical re-searchers. Williams *et al.* (1988) review research on anxious and depressed patients which has studied concentration and memory deficits, attentional bias, memory bias, judgemental bias, schemas, thoughts and images, as well as examining the evidence for non-conscious processing. In that book we proposed an integrative framework which is able to guide further research in this area. Such cross-fertilization is already proving useful in under-standing potential blocks in problem-solving and depression which I will discuss in detail in the final chapter. It is a particularly helpful feature of Beck's model that it lends itself to such collaboration between the clinical and experimental domains.

ARE DEPRESSED PEOPLE GENUINELY BIASED, OR ARE THEY JUST REALISTIC?

A central aspect of cognitive and self-control theory is that depressives selectively attend to negative information and thus receive a distorted view of the world. An alternative view is that non-depressed individuals are unduly optimistic and that the apparent pessimism of the depressive is just how the world really is. There seems to be an increasing amount of evidence for this view.

For example, Alloy and Abramson (1979) confronted depressed and non-depressed students with a series of problems varying in actual con-tingency between performance response and outcome. Non-depressed sub-jects overestimated the degree of contingency for frequent and/or desired outcomes, but underestimated contingency between response and outcomes for negative outcomes. Depressed subjects were, by contrast, more accurate in their judgements. Nelson and Craighead (1977) found a similar result in a study of recall of positive or negative feedback on trials of an experimental task. Depressed or non-depressed students were given an ambiguous task on which they were either rewarded or punished on 30 per cent or 70 per cent of the trials. Depressed subjects recalled receiving less positive feedback than non-depressed (a distortion) but were more accurate in recalling the negative feedback when delivered at low frequency. Non-depressed subjects underestimated the amount of negative feedback (a distortion in the positive direction).

The conclusion that depressed patients may be more accurate in their assessment of themselves, the world and the future than overoptimistic non-depressed individuals is challenging indeed. These results would therefore be of great significance if they could be replicated in a clinical population. Gotlib (1981) examined rates of self-reinforcement and self-punishment on a memory task in sixteen depressed and twelve non-depressed psychiatric patients. A patient was classified as depressed if they (a) obtained a diagnosis of a 'definite' depressive syndrome according to the criteria of Feighner et al. (1972); and (b) had a score of more than 11 on the Beck Depression Inventory and a minimum of 14 on the Hamilton Rating Scale. Nineteen depressed hospital employees acted as a non-psychiatric control group. Results showed that whereas both psychiatric groups showed less self-reinforcement and greater self-punishment for their trial-by-trial performance than the non-psychiatric control group, only the depressed group showed biases in recall of the frequency with which they had rewarded or punished themselves. They recalled giving themselves fewer reinforcements and a greater number of self-punishments. The two non-depressed groups were not biased in their recall in this way. Thus it seems the analogue research was not replicated in this clinical study. There is one way in which the discrepant results could be reconciled, however. Whereas Nelson and Craighead's subjects received rewards and punishments which were administered by the experimenter, Gotlib's patients administered their own reward. Could it be that depressives are more accurate about externally delivered reinforcement, but biased in their judgements about internally generated responses? Only further studies addressed specifically to this issue in a clinical population will answer the question, though Garber and Hollon (1980) did find that depressed college students were more likely to vary the trial-by-trial expectancy of success on a task (as if the test was a matter of luck rather than skill) if it was themselves doing the task, but not if others were doing it. This study is not directly comparable to those of Nelson and Craighead or Gotlib, but it points to the importance of looking at whether the depressed patient is being required to make judgements about the external environment or reflecting his or her 'internal' state of optimism/pessimism.

Another paper which claimed to address the same issue is that by Lewinsohn *et al.* (1980) entitled 'Social competence and depression: the role of illusory self-perceptions'. They compared observer ratings of depressed and non-depressed patients' interpersonal behaviour, with self-ratings of their behaviour made by the participants. The sample consisted of seventy-one unipolar neurotically depressed patients, who were compared with fifty-nine psychiatric controls who were not depressed and seventy-three non-psychiatric (non-depressed) controls. These individuals participated in four forty-five-minute sessions during which they were rated for their interpersonal efficiency by independent coders, and after which the self-ratings were made. The important finding was that the discrepancy scores between observer and self-ratings of the depressed group were significantly smaller than those for the control groups at time 1. Over time there was no change in the non-depressed observer and self-ratings, but the depressed group changed their self-perception for the better, thus increasing the discrepancy between observer and self-ratings – in short, they became more benign and seemingly less accurate in their self-perceptions. The authors conclude that, since during the study depressed subjects' self-perceptions had become more unrealistic, 'perhaps the key to avoiding depression is to see oneself less stringently and more favourably than others see us'.

In interpreting these results, however, it is important to bear in mind their relativistic nature. What is being suggested is that certain individuals are more 'accurate' by virtue of the fact that they agree with another individual's assessment. But these 'other individuals' (coders) are presumably subject to the same influences as the non-depressed subjects in the experiment who were found to have a positive self-serving bias. (Note that a result that non-depressed subjects are overoptimistic is logically independent from the argument about whether depressed individuals are or are not accurate in *their* assessment of the world.) Just because the 'coders' were designated as 'independent' and not called upon to interact or make judgements about themselves, this does not mean that they themselves are free from bias. So where is 'reality' located in this? Consider this analogy: Mr Brown meets a person, Mr Smith. Mr Brown believes himself to have a high IQ, and judges Mr Smith to be rather a dullard. Suppose Mr Smith is depressed, and says to Mr Brown 'I'm dumb and stupid'. Mr Brown may concur. Who is being accurate here? Are we going to say that Mr Smith really is stupid on the grounds that they agree in their conclusions? By no means. Neither can we assert that depressed patients are being accurate in their self-judgements on the grounds that non-depressed individuals (subject, as we know, to their own misperceptions) say so. Of course, we would trust the independent coders more if, on a reliable coding system, they were able to produce behavioural evidence of the depressed person's interpersonal inefficiency. The same research team in fact examined a sample from the same population of individuals (Youngren and Lewinsohn, 1980) and found no actual behavioural evidence for the depressed persons' interpersonal deficits. Taken together with Gotlib's inability to replicate the analogue studies on the 'accuracy' of depressives, and keeping in mind the extensive clinical evidence of the depressed person's excessive pessimism and hopelessness, the validity of the conclusion that depressed persons are in fact seeing the 'real world' must remain in doubt. It must also be noticed that Beck's theory does not claim that patients are just pessimistic, but that they think in idiosyncratic ways. According to Beck they make logical errors in the way they think, for example arbitrarily inferring from the fact that a boyfriend does not answer the phone that he must be out with another woman. These errors of logic are not at all assessed or tested in the studies that have looked at whether people are being realistic or not.

BEHAVIOURAL AND COGNITIVE MODELS OF DEPRESSION – SOME FINAL REMARKS

When Blaney came to review the 'contemporary theories of depression' in 1977 he concentrated, rather as I have done, on Lewinsohn's theory implicating low rates of response-contingent reinforcement, on Seligman's helplessness model, and on Beck's cognitive model. He concluded that all of the elements suggested by any one of the three theories (rate of reinforcement, control and perception) are equally implicated in the other two. The inability to distinguish between the three models need not alarm, since, to some extent, the models use different universes of discourse to describe the same phenomena. Thus, Lewinsohn's behaviourally defined insufficiency of reinforcement may lead individuals to believe they are helpless, and be defined by Beck in terms of a cognitive distortion. One's theoretical perspective depends on how you choose to look at the evidence rather than on the basic evidence itself. In reviewing the outcome studies in the next chapter it will rarely be possible to distinguish the theoretical perspective on which the study is based.

Distinguishing the models has a major heuristic function however. Separately they can generate and test hypotheses which are more specific than would be possible if all were combined together. In a condition such as depression which is so complex a syndrome, this is no mean feat.

Notice how predominant the theme of *loss* is in every formulation of depression. The loss may be actual or perceived, but seems an almost universal phenomenon. This is consistent also with psychodynamic formulations of depression. There is a general finding of a large discrepancy between the real and ideal self, both because of raising the level of aspiration and lowering the estimate of actual achievement. Since many of these ideas predated the recent flourishing of experimental work in this area, is the experimental approach worth the energy spent on it? I believe the experimental approach indeed can produce novel insights, some of which may seem obvious once pointed out, but nevertheless advance our ideas about the clinical syndrome. Let me give just one example. Golin *et al.* (1980) examined the generality of pessimism in mildly depressed (BDI greater than 10) versus non-depressed (BDI less than 6) subjects. All subjects were given ten anagrams, the first six of which were standard, but the last four of which were either difficult, guaranteeing failure, or easy, guaranteeing success. Subjects were randomly allocated not only to the failure or success condition, but also to whether they were to receive a free cinema ticket on the basis of their performance on *this* task or whether they were to get a second chance. The dependent variable was how upset subjects became in reaction to the task (Multiple Affective Adjective Check List (MAACL), assessed just after the last anagram). Results showed an expected main effect for whether subjects succeeded or failed, but also an interaction between depression level and whether they were to get only one, or two chances. The depressed subjects were more upset than non-depressed if they failed when they thought they were to get only the one chance, but their mood was equivalent to the low level of the non-depressed subjects if they thought a second chance was available. The authors suggested that these mildly depressed subjects were not characterized by a 'general' pessimism. Rather (and this is the point which might not have been intuited prior to the results) the depressed subjects 'were prone to believe that the important goals they pursue must be attained by means of a single effort and that absence of reward associated with a single failure may be permanent and irreversible'. Of course only a mild manipulation in this analogue experiment – giving a second chance – was required to modify this expectation, but the authors note how much of the self-talk in clinical depressives is characterized by such phrases as 'The game is over', 'I don't have a second chance', 'Life has passed me by', 'It's too late to do anything about it' (Beck, 1976: 118). This dichotomous 'now or never' thinking fits with Beck's cognitive formulations very well. The Golin *et al.* study is a good example of how clinical and analogue research may converge onto a single phenomenon by different routes, each complementing the analysis of the other, but neither would have been helpful if research had remained at the purely descriptive level. The next chapter will overview some of the research which has applied these concepts in actual clinical treatment.

Chapter 4

Psychological treatment of depression
Outcome studies

Although theories about the aetiology, precipitation and maintenance of depression differ from each other, the treatment techniques predicted to be effective by the various models tend to converge. That is not to say that there are only a few methods used. On the contrary, I shall list over twenty techniques which have been applied, usually grouped in some multifaceted procedure, to clinically depressed patients. But each of these techniques could be argued to be affecting a subsystem of several of the psychological models outlined in Chapters Two and Three. In this chapter I should like to overview these procedures and the evidence for their effectiveness. In addition, I wish to discuss three other issues. First, the supposed commonality in procedures and in the factors mediating recovery. Second, the evidence for whether there exist any indications and contra-indications for the use of cognitive-behaviour therapy with depressed patients, or any evidence on which technique to use with which patient. Finally, the relationship of cognitive-behaviour therapy to pharmacotherapy will be discussed. In an early paper Whitehead (1979) outlined four general, though distinct, rationales from which cognitive and behavioural strategies were derived:

1. That the depressive behaviour *per se* constitutes the disorder and can be modified by suitable manipulation of reinforcers.
2. That depressive behaviour is a result of (or is maintained by) a reduced rate of positive reinforcement and that this reinforcement should be reinstated by a suitable manipulation.
3. That depressed individuals fail to respond because they believe themselves to lack any control over their environment. Treatment should be directed towards demonstrating their capability for such control.
4. That depression results from people's negative view of themselves and their circumstances and treatment is directed towards correcting this misconception.

Table 4.1 lists some clinical techniques used by cognitive-behavioural therapists, and corresponding rationales. Of course, there may be a difference between the supposed rationale and the actual therapeutic component of these techniques, but that is an issue which can be left until after the outcome research has been reviewed.

Table 4.1 Treatment components in cognitive-behavioural therapies*

1. Teaching self-monitoring of activities (2,3,4)
2. Teaching self-monitoring of mood (2,3,4)
3. Teaching self-monitoring of thoughts (3,4)
4. (Graded) task assignment (2,3,4) – teaching how to set appropriate goals
5. Teaching self-evaluation of behavioural achievement; mastery and pleasure techniques (2,3,4)
6. Teaching self-reinforcement for behavioural achievement (2,3,4)
7. Instructions in geographical control for negative thinking (2,3,4)
8. Instructions in temporal control for negative thinking (2,3, 4)
9. Teaching thought-catching and how to identify themes and dysfunctional assumptions in thought content (4)
10. Teaching 'distancing' of thoughts and assumptions by labelling as'hypotheses' (4)
11. Teaching how to evaluate evidence for 'hypotheses' (reality testing) (4)
12. Teaching how to deal with implications of thought evaluation (3,4)
13. Teaching how to find alternative rational responses to negative thoughts and assumptions (4)
14. Listing positive self-descriptions (3,4)
15. Using Premack principle to increase low frequency thoughts/activities (coverant conditioning) (1,4)
16. Contingency management (1)
17. Social skills/assertion training exercises (modelling, rehearsal, etc.) (1,2,3,4)
18. Re-attribution training (3,4)
19. Anticipation training (3,4)
20. Systemic resensitization (1,2)
21. Relaxation and desensitization (for anxiety component and initial insomnia) (2)
22. 'Alternative therapy' (3,4) 'decision analysis'
23. Role-playing (2,3,4)
24. Cognitive rehearsal (3,4)
25. Stress inoculation (2,3,4)
26. Teaching how to set up reciprocal contracts within relationships (1,2,3)
27. Thought stopping and/or distraction (4)
28. Instructions in increase of formerly or potentially pleasant activities (2,3,4)

* The numbers in brackets refer to the supposed rationales outlined in the text

RESEARCH ON THE EFFICACY OF COGNITIVE-BEHAVIOURAL TECHNIQUES

There have been several reviews of the outcome literature. Some of these are very good overviews of the early work (Rehm and Kornblith, 1979; Weissman, 1979; Whitehead, 1979; Blaney, 1981; Hollon, 1981). Other more recent overviews include the later studies (Dobson, 1989; Robinson *et al.*, 1990). These vary in their scope, particularly in the extent to which they include one-off uncontrolled case studies, analogue studies using student volunteers, or controlled single case or group design studies. In the review which follows, I shall consider only controlled studies which have used either clinically depressed patients or individuals who have come forward in response to advertisements offering treatment for depression. That is, I shall not consider those studies which use college students recruited for experimental purposes for course credit, etc. Second, because this book is concerned with individual therapy rather than group approaches, I shall consider only those studies using individualized treatment strategies. Third, because the reviews mentioned above are easily available for those who wish to follow up the more diverse methods, I shall confine my review to those studies mentioned by a majority of reviewers, together with studies which have been completed since these reviews were compiled. The aim in applying these constraints is to confine attention to the 'core studies' – those which most clearly represent the accepted body of opinion amongst cognitive and behaviour therapists on the efficacy of their treatment techniques. (Studies on inpatients are reviewed in Chapter Eight.) The number of techniques used in these studies varies. The overall picture emerges of therapeutic strategies which are enormously complex which makes it rather difficult to find out exactly what a therapist has done with any patient! Nevertheless, we shall proceed on the assumption that we are evaluating 'families' of techniques which do hold together to make a coherent strategy. I shall examine the studies in chronological order, since they overlap so much in terms of the particular combinations of behavioural and cognitive strategies used.

Hersen, Eisler, Alford and Agras (1973)

This study is a convenient place to start a review because it represents one extreme of theory about the nature of depression. This theory is that depression *is* the observable 'depressed' behaviour of the individual – increased frequency of crying, etc., and decreased frequency of constructive behaviours. Ayllon and Azrin (1968) had previously suggested that such behaviour could be modified by selective reinforcement of 'positive' behaviours incompatible with symptomatic manifestation. Hersen *et al.* used an ABA design in which blue tokens (index cards) were issued non-contingently (A), contingent upon occurrence of 'positive' behaviours (B), and again non-contingently (A). During the B phase, the target behaviours reinforced related to four areas: work, occupational therapy, responsibility and personal hygiene. Patients were expected to plan each day every morning during 'banking hours' during all phases of the study. Tokens could be exchanged for privileges according to a predetermined points system.

Three neurotically depressed inpatients were included in Hersen's study. Assessment during the study consisted of the Williams *et al.* (1972) rating scale which assesses amount of talking, smiling and activity on a time sampling basis. Results showed a marked diminution of observable depression during the contingency management phase. The impressions of the staff confirmed this result. They reported that the patients were less depressed in the B phase and more irritable in the A phases.

The significance of these results is weakened by the fact that the assessments were done by staff who, though blind to the experimental hypothesis, were not blind to the procedures used in the study, and therefore presumably knew what the investigators' intentions were. To some extent this problem is mitigated by the fact that the behaviour which was assessed was not that which was being reinforced in the study and was chosen to be as objectively assessable as possible. A more damaging criticism however is that all three were on psychotropic medication during the study. The fact that this remained unchanged for all three phases implies that the specific improvements noted could not be attributed to the drugs, however it is not known to what extent the drugs may have made the patients more amenable to the behavioural intervention. I shall discuss this question in the section below on the interaction of cognitive-behavioural therapies with pharmacological procedures.

Why does this investigation qualify as a 'core study'? Perhaps because it was one of the earliest controlled demonstrations of the potency of behavioural methods in this clinical population. One must bear in mind that until the late 1960s the predominant formulations of depression were either psychodynamic or biological. Neither of these theories would have predicted that contingency management would be effective. The fact that experimenter/therapist control was demonstrated was therefore an important result.

McLean, Ogston and Grauer (1973)

Three theoretical approaches provided the source-material for the rationale of this study of conjoint therapy. First, Ferster's analysis of depression as a response to 'diminished reinforcement field' (Ferster, 1966); second, Costello's analysis of depression as a loss of reinforcer effectiveness (Costello, 1972a); and third, Stuart's analysis of depression as an adaptation to maladaptive interpersonal encounters (Stuart, 1967). McLean *et al.* built upon these models, as well as work on social skill deficits in depression (e.g. Lewinsohn and Shaw, 1969) and derived a model of dysfunctional marital communication, in which 'the relationship between the patient and the spouse is characterized by a coercive communication pattern which precludes effective problem solving'. Their therapy was therefore aimed at modifying the couple's verbal interaction styles. Three categories of therapeutic strategy were used: (a) training in social learning principles; (b) immediate feedback as to the perception of verbal interactions between patient and spouse using cue boxes; and (c) training in the construction and use of reciprocal behavioural contracts. The 'cue box' was a box on which pressing one of two buttons operated red and green lights. Each box also had an electric counter for each light to record frequency of use of that button.

Couples were instructed to conduct short (twenty-minute) conversations at home on a topic which normally caused some friction (finance, child-rearing, etc.), and to push the red or green button as follows. They were to operate the red light if they perceived the other's comments to be negative (e.g. sarcastic, indifferent). They were to operate the green light if they perceived the other's comments to be in any way positive (e.g. complimentary, constructive). The aim was to 'provide immediate feedback as to how their verbal interactions were being perceived'. The idea was that, no matter how a comment is *meant*, it is how it is *received* which would determine the other's reaction. For example, one individual genuinely felt he was being constructive when he said 'you'd feel better if you didn't weep so much'. His partner (perhaps not surprisingly) perceived it as critical. Couples were told to hold these twenty-minute conversations five days a week for the first four weeks of treatment. Couples apparently found the cue boxes 'contrived but educational'. Details of reciprocal contracting methods are given in Chapter Eight.

Twenty couples (one member of each having been referred for treatment of a neurotic depression) were randomly allocated to this three-component treatment or to a control condition (in which case they were referred back to the referring agent and treated by routine methods which varied from antidepressant medication alone or in combination with social case work to irregular physician consultations). Experimental treatment took place in eight weekly sessions, one hour per week. Detailed assessment was made of verbal interaction style before and after treatment by careful analysis of tape recordings made by the couple of conversations between them. Outcome was additionally assessed by self-rating on the Depressive Adjective Check List (DACL) and by self- and spouse-rating of certain problem behaviours (social withdrawal, sleep disturbance, domestic or job incompetence, impaired concentration, poor motivation, inability to make decisions, suicidal preoccupation, decreased interest in hobbies, sports, etc. and decreased sexual satisfaction).

Results showed the experimental treatment to be superior to the control treatment on all outcome measures. These improvements were maintained at follow-up three months later. McLean *et al.* conclude that the result justifies the assumption that depressive states are associated with a failure to control one's interpersonal environment. They suggest that the efficacy of the experimental treatment

> appears to reside in its pragmatism and the ease with which patients and their spouse can be involved in monitoring and altering daily behaviours – patients . . . responded positively to the application of feedback techniques and to the specificity involved in reciprocal behavioural contracts.

The main problem with the study is its lack of adequate control procedures. Not only was there an unequal amount of time spent with the experimental and control groups, the control group's treatment was unsystematic and uncontrolled. Some may even have been inappropriate. Nevertheless, the investigation is justifiably included in this list of core studies since it further demonstrated the usefulness of some quite specific behavioural procedures.

As such, it was the main precursor of a major study six years later, based on the same principles, by McLean and Hakstian (reviewed below).

Padfield (1976)

This early study examined the comparative effects of behavioural and non-directive counselling on intensity of depression in 'rural women of low socioeconomic status'. Subjects for the study were recruited through physician referral and newspaper advertisement. Twelve weekly individual sessions were held in both treatments (thus controlling for therapy contact). The behavioural treatment was derived from Lewinsohn's writings, and consisted of teaching patients first to monitor then to increase the frequency of formerly or potentially pleasant activities (see Chapter Four for further details of this approach). Outcome was assessed using the Zung Self-Rating Scale, Lubin DACL, MacPhillamy and Lewinsohn's Pleasant Events Schedule, and the Grinker Feelings and Concerns Checklist. Results showed superiority of the behavioural treatment on this latter measure, but not the other three.

The fact that the behavioural group was marginally superior on one measure must be set against the lack of significant difference on the Pleasant Events Schedule – the measure which purported to assess the factors which were supposed to mediate the therapy's anti-depressive effectiveness. It seems that, ironically, what little effect this specific behavioural therapy had was not mediated by an increase in frequency of pleasant activities.

Taylor and Marshall (1977)

This study is important despite the fact it used solicited patients rather than true outpatient depressives. Forty-five subjects with BDI scores greater than 13 and whose self-reported depressed mood had lasted at least two weeks were recruited through advertisement. Although the mean BDI was 21.2 ('moderately severely depressed'), the possible difficulties in generalizing to clinically diagnosed cases must be borne in mind. Nevertheless, the study gains its importance from its careful control, and tight specification of the treatment packages used. Subjects were randomly assigned to one of four groups: cognitive only, behavioural only, cognitive and behavioural combined, and waiting list control. The rationale for the cognitive therapy given was that 'depressed mood is rooted in self-evaluation'. Subjects were taught how to become aware of thoughts which occurred between an event and consequent affective disturbance, and instructed to use alternative self-statements to cope with such situations when they occurred. With therapist's help, a list of positive self-statements was constructed, and subjects were instructed to read through the list before engaging in a high probability behaviour ('coverant control' using the Premack principle of making a high probability behaviour contingent upon a low probability behaviour). The rationale for the behavioural treatment was that 'depression results from insufficient positive reinforcement'. Subjects were given help in identifying situations which produced depressed mood, and in learning new alternative patterns of behaviour. Role-play, modelling and homework assignments to rehearse new techniques were used, often with the aim of promoting more assertive, socially skilled behaviour. The combined treatment would have made it impossible to spend more than half the time (on average) on each component. Despite this, the results of the six forty-minute sessions over four weeks showed a clear superiority for the combined treatment over each one alone, which in turn were superior to no treatment (assessed by BDI, MMPI (D) and visual analogue mood scales). The trend of these results was still clearly visible on follow-up assessment five weeks later.

This study is important because it was the first to address directly the issue of which elements in a cognitive-behavioural package are responsible for therapeutic progress. Padfield's earlier study had suggested that behavioural treatment by itself was not very powerful, and that even the gains that were noted were not due to changes in the supposed mediating variable (pleasant activities). The finding that integrating behavioural into a cognitive context (and *vice versa*) works better than spending the full time engaging in one or the other model has direct therapeutic implications if work with depressed patients bears it out. Surprisingly, there has been little work of this kind done using a clinical sample. The nearest is that of Wilson *et al.* (1983) and Rotzer-Zimmer *et al.* (1985) which will be reviewed below. Without going into detail, it is relevant at this stage to point out that these authors' findings are consistent with Taylor and Marshall's conclusion.

Rush, Beck, Kovacs and Hollon (1977)

During the 1970s the interest in cognitive-behaviour therapy grew very fast. Yet there was no satisfactory comprehensive outcome study to confirm what seemed to have been evident from single case work for some time. As late as 1976, McLean, in reviewing the evidence for the cognitive theory of depression wrote 'Currently there are several factors which limit the clinical utility of this model' of which the first was 'controlled clinical research is necessary to establish clinical efficacy. At the moment only several case studies are available'. The study by Rush *et al.* was a breakthrough then, not only for the practice, but also the theory of depression on which it was based. Despite criticisms that have been made of it, which I will mention later, it was possibly one of the most important contributions to clinical practice of that decade. The study itself was quite simple. Forty-one out-patients with a clear and unmixed diagnosis of depression, and scores of 17+ on the BDI and 14+ on the Hamilton Rating Scale, were randomly allocated to twelve weeks of either cognitive-behavioural therapy (up to twenty sessions – the mean number of sessions was fifteen, over an average of eleven weeks) or imipramine pharmacotherapy (up to 250 mg per day) and weekly supportive visits of twenty minutes each. Assessment was made by BDI, MMPI, Hamilton and the Raskin Rating Scale.

The results showed that both groups improved, but cognitive-behaviour therapy produced greater improvement than drugs. At the end of the twelve-weeks' therapy, the mean of the CBT group was within 1 s.d. of the mean for a non-depressed normative group and within 2 s.d. of the equivalent value for the MMPI (D scale). The mean of the drug group remained several s.d.'s above the non-depressed mean level on both assessments. Perhaps more significant clinically was the differential dropout rates for the two groups – 32 per cent for pharmacotherapy and only 5 per cent for the CBT. Most of these dropouts occurred in weeks 1–4 of the respective therapies. Retrospective analysis showed that those who dropped out were not distinguishable on demographic characteristics, history of illness factors, or pretreatment severity on clinical or self-rating scales.

Three main problems with the study have been raised. First, the drug group did not have equivalent therapist contact, so perhaps the effects were attributable to the additional support available in the CBT group. This complaint is reminiscent of that against McLean *et al.*'s (1973) control group, however they are not comparable. McLean's control group received a range of non-specific treatments unsystematically, but by contrast, Rush *et al.*'s control involved regular contact, systematic treatment with a plausible rationale. Second, the drug dosage was not as high as some pharmaco-therapists might have set it, thus favouring the CBT group treatment. Further-more, the design of the study necessitated drug withdrawal beginning at week 10 so that patients were drug-free at final assessment. It has been argued that a psychiatrist would normally keep patients on a maintenance dose of tricyclics. On the grounds, then, of dosage level and method of drug examination, the suggestion has been made that Rush *et al.*'s drug therapy was suboptimal. The response to these criticisms is as simple as it is obvious. There is no reason to suppose that the cognitive-behaviour therapy was not also suboptimal both in its method of delivery, and its termination at twelve weeks. Many behavioural psychotherapists would argue that 'maintenance' or 'tailing off sessions' are necessary in any psychological therapy to prevent quick relapse. (Actually, only one of the dropouts in the drug group occurred between weeks 10 and 12 of the trial, suggesting that it was not as upsetting as might be supposed.) In any event, the suboptimality argument fails because it applies equally to both treatments. Furthermore, no patient was admitted to the trial if they had a history of non-response to pharma-cotherapy, with no such constraint applied to patients with a history of psychotherapy 'failure'. Thus any bias in the sample would have favoured the drug regime's effectiveness. In the light of these considerations, Rush *et al.*'s results are all the more surprising, and important.

McLean and Hakstian (1979)

This studied the effectiveness of three active treatments: behaviour therapy (which actually included some cognitive components); short-term psycho-therapy and pharmacological therapy (amitriptyline, 150 mg/day). A plausible control treatment – relaxation training – was also used. Patients who were married or living as married encouraged their partners to attend to 'work together on the programme'. All treatments involved ten weekly outpatient visits (minimum of eight and maximum of twelve visits). Therapists had pretraining to maximize agreement about treatment procedures, as well as regular peer-monitoring sessions throughout the investigation. In addition, all sessions were audiotaped and sampled to monitor the use of techniques. The therapists in the *psychotherapy treatment* were using their preferred methods of therapeutic practice, and focused on the restoration of pre-episode level of functioning through the 'development of insight into the psychodynamic forces that initiated the current depression, and through the recognition of personality problems'. The *cognitive-behavioural therapy* was based on the rationale that 'depression is the result of ineffective coping techniques used to remedy situational life problems'. Patients were discouraged from ruminating upon negative ex-periences and encouraged to interact more with their environment. Therapy components included hierarchies of treatment goals, activity monitoring, and contingency plans for coping with stress. The *drug therapy* group were on medication throughout the trial and attended four weekly visits for a 'physio-logical review' of fifteen minutes each. Blood samples were drawn on two occasions (randomly specified) within the eleven-week period. Blood serum levels were checked to monitor compliance with self-medication as prescribed. Patients in *relaxation therapy* were given a rationale of depression as tension-induced. Patients received ten one-hour sessions of training together with homework assignments for relaxation practice and logsheets to monitor relaxation effectiveness.

The study used 178 outpatient depressives between the ages of twenty and sixty years. Their depression had to be of at least two months' duration prior to the study. Patients also had to be of sufficient severity to be functionally impaired (unable to work, socially withdrawn, suicidally preoccupied), and to be diagnosable as 'primary depressives' on Feighner *et al.*'s (1972) criteria. The minimum Beck Depression score was 23. Thus this large study took as subjects a group of patients whose neurotic depression was really quite severe. The controls against which cognitive-behavioural therapy was compared were excellent which adds to the robustness of the study. But what makes the study even more interesting is the comprehensiveness of its assessment procedures. These are detailed in Table 4.2. As

Table 4.2 List of variables assessed in McLean and Hakstian (1979)

Cognitive	*Social*
Memory	Arranging activity with others
Decision-making ability	Time/day with friends
Negative thoughts	Had friends over
	Went out with friends
Coping	Phoned a friend
Coping ability	Verbally praised someone
No. productive hours	People spoken to (excluding work)
No. wasted hours	
Procrastination	*Somatic*
	Hours of sleep
Personal activity	Fatigue rating
Working on hobby	Relaxation rating
Writing letters	
Watching TV	*Mood*
Doing paperwork	Depresive Adjective Check List
Home or car improvement	Laughing out loud
	Crying
Beck Depression Inventory	
Depression history (since age 16)	*Average satisfaction*
Depression history (this episode)	Satisfaction with job
Employment status	Satisfaction with housekeeping abilities
No. life events	
Eysenck Personality Questionnaire	*Marital satisfaction*
– neuroticism	Average complaint rating
– extraversion	Average goal attainment
	Negative thoughts re self
Age	Sex

can be seen, in addition to sociodemographic, life events and personality variables a large number of self-descriptive scales covered a large range of issues.

Ten categories were derived: cognitive, coping, personal activity, social, BDI, satisfaction, somatic indicators, mood, average goal attainment, and average complaint rating. In addition to their usefulness as outcome variables, some of these derived categories (pretreatment scores) could be combined with the demographic variables for cluster analysis. The results of this analysis will be mentioned later in connection with the question of 'what works best for whom?' Meanwhile, the main results on the efficacy of the treatment procedures can be reported. The first thing to note is that all groups improved markedly from pre- to post-treatment. It is impossible to say to what extent this was due to the efficacy of the individual treatments since depression tends to remit spontaneously after six to nine months, and the inclusion of criteria of at least two months' duration implies that some individuals would have been tending to recover anyway towards the end of a ten- or twelve-week therapy programme. Superimposed on this general improvement was a clear-cut tendency for behaviour therapy to be superior to the other three treatments. On the BDI, complaints, goals, social adjustment, average satisfaction and mood, behaviour therapy was superior to psychotherapy, and on all but BDI and social adjustment, was superior to relaxation and drug therapy as well. On six of the ten measures, psychotherapy scored most poorly. Pharmacological therapy did no better nor worse than the relaxation control treatment. This pattern of results was maintained at follow-up three months later. Although the scale of the differences was diminished, the behavioural therapy group was still superior to the others on seven out of ten outcome variables, and significantly so on social adjustment. On the mood variable, both behaviour therapy and drugs were superior to psychotherapy, with relaxation differing from neither. Interestingly, the dropout rate differed markedly for the different treatments; 5 per cent for cognitive-behavioural therapy, with the other three varying between 26 and 36 per cent.

The results showing unequivocal superiority of cognitive-behaviour therapy in this study gained a great deal of robustness from the careful way in which the study was constructed. Hollon's (1981) review applauded this aspect, but commented that the low dosage of drug used made it difficult to draw firm conclusions. In fact, Hollon's conclusion was based on false evidence. He said (p. 55) that McLean and Hakstian used 125 mg/day of imipramine, whereas in fact they used 150 mg/day of amitriptyline. The first would have been an inadequate dose, the second is not. It is a pity that Hollon not only made the initial factual error but then chose to comment upon it.

McLean and Hakstian's study was useful not only because of the care taken to ensure that the drug group really was taking the medication, but also because they included the psychological treatment groups to compare with the cognitive-behaviour therapy group. These other treatments were forcefully presented with a plausible rationale and one (relaxation) also involved homework assignments. Yet they did not produce as much improvement as the CBT. Thus these authors could not be accused of producing results which could easily be explained in terms of therapist attention and other non-specific effects. Of course, some non-specific treatment effects were inevitable, perhaps reflected in the fact that even the relaxation group improved to some extent. But they could not provide the complete answer and thus this study made an important point about the validity of the claims of cognitive-behavioural therapists to have collected together a set of techniques with active and incisive therapeutic potential.

Zeiss, Lewinsohn and Munoz (1979)

These investigators used recruited subjects for an interesting study which combined research on outcome with a study of process. Media advertisement of 'therapy for depression as part of a research project' elicited replies from a large range of individuals, of whom forty-four (aged nineteen to sixty-eight years, mean thirty-four) were admitted to the project on the basis of an MMPI(D) score greater than 80 and a structured interview. Subjects were allocated to one of four groups: cognitive therapy, interpersonal skills training, pleasant activity scheduling, or waiting list. In addition to using MMPI(D) scores as a general outcome measure, seven hours of comprehensive assessments were given every month (four occasions in all) to assess the specific subcomponents purported to mediate the efficacy of the various therapies. Thus three ratings (including one observer rating) of interpersonal behaviour were taken; four ratings (including an observer rating) of cognitive style were taken; and the Pleasant Events Schedule was used to assess frequency and subjective pleasantness of activities performed. Results showed no differences between the three active therapy groups, though they all produced more improvement than the waiting list controls. More significantly, however, all assessments improved equally in the three different types of treatments. It was not the case that each therapy had its effect by modifying the particular mediating variable purported to underlie its particular set of therapeutic strategies. Rather, the authors suggest 'the label of therapy does not ensure that the behaviours labelled will be those most directly affected', and conclude that psychological treatment may be producing 'non-specific' improvement no matter what treatment model is being tested.

There is little doubt that non-specific treatment effects are present in studies of the effects of cognitive-behaviour therapy but does this study constitute strong evidence for their involvement? I think not. Even accepting that the results may be generalized to clinically depressed individuals whose motivation is not perhaps as consistently positive as these recruited volunteers, there is evidence that none of the individual procedures used in the study are, by themselves, very effective treatments (e.g. Taylor and Marshall, 1977; Rotzer *et al.*, 1981). Under such conditions, a floor effect of noticeable though minimal therapeutic improvement might be expected which would not differentiate the treatments. However, it is not the outcome data which are damaging to those who wish to claim specificity for their treatments, but the process data. The lack of discernible difference between treatments in the processes they affected seems conclusive. However, the assessments of these variables were only made once a month, hardly frequent enough to justify such a general conclusion. The time scale over which cognitive changes, if present, would be expected to affect mood and behaviour would be hours and days, rather than days and weeks, and this could be said to be true of the effect of interpersonal skills training and activity scheduling on the other process variables. This makes the once-a-month monitoring seem very inadequate. Admittedly, the seven hours of assessment used each month in the study could not realistically have been programmed each day or even each week, but investigators might in future content themselves with less assessment of each variable at any one time, with more frequent assessments being scheduled. Furthermore, it is naive to expect that wholesale changes in one variable will occur prior to wholesale changes in the next. It is more likely that change will be interactive, with small changes in one variable predicting small changes in the next, and so on. There is a danger that we will find such a complex sequence of interactions impossible to map. This may be so, although the more experimentally based tasks outlined by Williams *et al.* (1988) may help. In any event, we are a long way from having done sufficient process research to justify giving up yet. Zeiss *et al.*'s study represents a first step on that road, but it is not the last.

Blackburn, Bishop, Glen, Whalley and Christie (1981)

It may not have escaped the notice of readers that virtually all of the outcome studies on the efficacy of cognitive-behavioural methods reviewed thus far were from North America. For some time, there was the suspicion that crosscultural differences between continents would make generalization to Europe difficult. Furthermore, cognitive therapy in particular had been subject to criticism on the grounds that, as a 'logical' therapy, it would not be suitable for the less verbally intelligent, less psychologically-minded patient. Blackburn *et al.*'s study was therefore very significant. First, it was the first outcome study to use a British population, and second, many of the sample were from a down-town end of the city.

Sixty-four primary major depressives (Research Diagnostic Criteria, Spitzer *et al.*, 1978), all of whom had a BDI score of 14 or more, were randomly allocated to receive maximum twenty weeks of cognitive-behaviour therapy, pharmacotherapy (mainly amitriptyline and clomipramine up to 150 mg/day, but at the doctor's discretion) or a combination of CBT and drugs. Assessment was made using the BDI, HRS(D), and Snaith's Irritability, Depression and Anxiety Scale (Snaith *et al.*, 1978). Twenty-four of the sample were patients attending their family doctor, and forty were hospital outpatients. The hospital sample had significantly more education, a higher socioeconomic level, longer duration of illness, greater number of previous episodes, a higher total psychopathology score on the Present State Examination (Wing *et al.*, 1974), and were less outwardly irritable than the general practitioner sample. (Where necessary these variables were partialled out for analysis of the main effects of therapy.) Importantly, there were no differences between hospital and GP samples in age, sex ratio, initial severity of depression (BDI, HRS(D)), presence of suicidal ideas and attempts (PSE: Item 24) or presence of endogenous features in the psychopathology.

Results showed that the GP sample required less of the combination treatment (approximately twelve sessions) than the hospital sample (approximately seventeen sessions). For the outcome results, Snaith's scale showed few overall changes, but the BDI and HRS(D) both revealed clear-cut effects. In the hospital sample, the combination of drugs and CBT produced greater proportionate changes in BDI and HRS(D) than either CBT or drugs alone, which did not differ significantly from each other except on anxiety where CBT produced more improvement than drugs. In the GP sample, on the other hand, the combination treatment and the CBT alone were both equally effective and considerably better than drugs alone. Both samples contained a large proportion of endogenous-type as well as non-endogenous-type patients (for the total sample, twenty-seven and thirty-seven respectively). Analysis of outcome as a function of endogeneity revealed no differences in response for any of the three treatments.

Commenting on the difference between this result, and that of Rush *et al.* (1977) who found CBT to be superior to drugs in mood and attrition rate, Blackburn points out that in their study, the drug regimen was tailored to the individual patient, thus presumably enhancing effectiveness. Patients were also still on drugs when assessed at the end of treatment, unlike those of Rush *et al.* Blackburn *et al.* did not consider another plausible alternative, that Rush *et al.*'s outpatient population may have been more comparable to Blackburn's GP sample, in whom the results were very similar. On the other hand, the important characteristic of Blackburn's GP sample was that it was drawn from a family practice serving a population of 6,633 in a largely working-class area of a large city. That drugs are ineffective for a group of people who may have major social problems is hardly surprising, but for many it will be no less surprising that individualized cognitive-behavioural therapy works so well in this context. Perhaps the emphasis in CBT on not minimizing real problems is an important component of its success.

Early follow-up studies

Until 1981, there had been few controlled studies which had followed up their patients adequately. McLean and Hakstian (1979) observed their group for three months, but the first study in which adequate time between discharge and follow-up was that of Kovacs *et al.* (1981) (a follow-up of Rush *et al.*'s patients). Thirty-five of the forty-six were followed up (eighteen CBT and seventeen drug). They found no significant difference between dependent measures at the end of one year from those taken at the end of treatment, indicating that treatment gains had been maintained. Despite this, they found considerable variability in the course of both cognitive-behavioural and drug groups' progress, and the difference between the two was not always apparent on the dependent measures. On the other hand, the comparisons always favoured the CBT group, and reached statistical significance at some points over the year. Defining 'relapse' as a BDI score of over 16 during the year at any time, receiving further psychological treatment (plus either of these or both of these), the drug group was found to have been twice as likely to relapse as the cognitive therapy group. It is apparent from these data that there is no evidence that any improvement brought about by cognitive-behaviour therapy is merely short-term, and that what differences there are suggest these methods of psychotherapy and behaviour change may be the treatment of choice for these patients. However, note that this study followed up both those who responded and those who did not respond to the original treatment. Thus it could not distinguish between 'non-responders' and 'relapsers' (those who did recover, but later became depressed again). Subsequent studies have made this distinction, and I shall describe these towards the end of the chapter.

Wilson, Goldin and Charbonneau-Powis (1983)

By the end of the 1970s, interest in cognitive therapy had spread, not only to the UK, but throughout the world. I shall mention, below, a study by Rotzer-Zimmer in Tübingen, Germany. In 1983, Wilson *et al.* published a study they had done in Sydney, Australia. Like Taylor and Marshall (1977), they were interested in comparing behavioural strategies with cognitive strategies. Whereas Taylor and Marshall had used solicited volunteers whose Beck Depression Inventory scores were greater than 13 and whose depression had lasted more than two weeks, Wilson *et al.*'s volunteers had to meet a cut-off of 17 on the BDI (be at least 'moderately depressed') and to have been depressed for at least three months. Consistent with their greater severity, Wilson *et al.*'s treatment was longer. Whereas Taylor and Marshall had used six forty-minute sessions over four weeks, Wilson *et al.*'s treatment consisted of eight one-hour sessions. Instead of a five week follow-up (Taylor and Marshall, 1977) Wilson *et al.* followed up their patients for five months. Twenty-five depressed people took part (twenty women, five men) mean age 39.5 years. Twenty had received previous treatment for depression and seven had been hospitalized.

Eight people received behaviour therapy based on Lewinsohn's model (see Chapter Two). Twenty-five items were selected for each person from the Pleasant Events Schedule. These were activities which the patient had rated as enjoyable but which had not or had only rarely been done in the previous month (e.g. contacting former friends, arranging joint outings, etc.). Patients made daily records of situations and activities associated with best and worst mood. In therapy sessions, discussions centred around these attempts to increase pleasant activities.

Eight people received cognitive therapy which was broadly Beckian without behavioural assignments. Negative thoughts were collected and scrutinized for evidence of distortion or irrationality. Parallel to the individualized construction of the activity assignment in behavioural therapy, twenty-five thoughts were collected and compiled to make 'thought schedules': those thoughts rated as most pleasurable but experienced rarely, and those rated most unpleasant but experienced frequently. Each session focused on countering the negative thoughts by employing positive statements. Patients were also encouraged to read the positive thought schedules three times a day before meals. Like the behavioural work, emphasis was placed on noticing the connection between mood and the occurrence of these thoughts.

Nine additional depressed patients were placed on a waiting list, and assessed after eight weeks as a control for spontaneous remission. The depression scores of these control patients (assessed with BDI and HRS(D)) did not shift at all in that time. By contrast, both behavioural and cognitive treatments shifted depression levels so that they fell within the non-depressed range of both measures. Neither was more effective than the other. This improvement was maintained in both groups at five months follow-up.

Consistent with the findings of Zeiss *et al.* (1979) both treatments brought about equal changes on the Irrational Beliefs Test (the target of cognitive intervention) and on the Pleasant Events Schedule (the target of the behavioural intervention). The only evidence for specificity was that, half way through therapy, the cognitive treatment had brought about significantly more change on a measure of the frequency and impact of positive thoughts such as 'I'm pretty lucky', 'This is fun', 'I feel energetic'. These differences, though still present, were not significant statistically at the end of treatment. This strengthened the conclusion that focusing on behaviour brings about cognitive change, and focusing on cognition (simply increasing positive and decreasing negative thoughts and becoming aware of thought-affect connections) brings about increase in frequency and enjoyability of pleasant activities. This conclusion was to become a recurring theme in later outcome studies. The studies were to conclude that there was little to choose between psychological treatments, and between psychological and drug treatments, either in outcome, or in the speed of change in the cognitive measures during therapy. Gradually therapists were to shift their attention away from acute treatments of the depressive episode and on to the prevention of relapse. But before discussing this shift there are five more studies to be reviewed – studies done in Oxford, St Louis, Tübingen, Pennsylvania and, the final study, divided between three sites: Pittsburgh, Washington DC and Oklahoma.

Teasdale, Fennell, Hibbert and Amies (1984)

Until this study, outcome studies had used either outpatients or volunteer depressives solicited by advertisement. Only Blackburn *et al.* (1981) had studied depressed patients in a family practitioner setting. However, some of the conclusions about the effectiveness of cognitive therapy in such a setting were weakened by the fact that the group receiving the antidepressants had been very small, and appeared to do unusually poorly in Blackburn *et al.*'s study. Despite the paucity of studies, general practice remains the setting where the vast majority of depressed patients are seen. Whereas three per 1,000 of the population are referred to psychiatrists for depression (two of the three being treated as outpatients and one out of three being admitted), 3 per cent of the general population are treated by general practitioners, ten times the number treated by psychiatrists. Does cognitive therapy have anything to offer?

Teasdale *et al.*'s study asked a simple question. Can cognitive therapy add anything to what patients normally receive? The study treated patients from practices in Oxfordshire, and the authors were careful to check that the class distribution of participants reflected the general population. (In fact, no University students or employees entered the trial.) The median social class was 3.

Thirty-four patients (two men, thirty-two women) were randomly allocated to receive either treatment as usual (TAU), or treatment as usual and cognitive therapy (TAU+CT). For admission to the trial, patients had to be between eighteen and sixty, have a Beck score of 20 or more and a Hamilton score of 14 or more. All patients had 'major depressive disorder' (unipolar, non-psychotic) on the Research Diagnostic Criteria and all but three were 'definite or probable endogenous major depressive disorder'. Beckian cognitive therapy was given and audiotapes made and rated for competence by the Center for Cognitive Therapy in Philadelphia. Patients received up to twenty one-hour sessions (the mean amount of treatment received turned out to be 15.2), plus two booster sessions six weeks and three months after the main treatment. Blind ratings by independent clinical assessors were made, using the Hamilton Rating Scale for Depression. Since it was equally likely that patients from either group would be taking antidepressant medication, there was less chance than in many studies of the independent assessor guessing (by observing side-effects) in which treatment group the patient belonged.

Results showed a clear advantage for the addition of cognitive therapy on both the Beck and Hamilton scales. At the end of treatment, fourteen out of the seventeen in the CT plus TAU group had a Beck score under 14, compared with only four out of the seventeen in the TAU group. However the TAU group steadily improved (as would be expected partly on the basis that depression is episodic), so that, after a further three months, the groups were equivalent in depression level (ten out of the seventeen being non-depressed in the CT plus TAU group, compared with nine out of seventeen in the TAU group). This outcome was only the first of a number of studies to raise an urgent question about the necessity of giving cognitive therapy if conventional drug and supportive treatment will work just as well, albeit in this study taking a further three months.

Murphy, Simons, Wetzel and Lustman (1984)

Murphy *et al.*'s outcome trial, conducted in St Louis, was to raise the identical question. They had set out to replicate the original Rush *et al.* (1977) study. Their study, published seven years after that of Rush *et al.*, was the first US study to do so. They used the same inclusion criteria as had Rush *et al.* (primary, unipolar, outpatient depressives on Feighner *et al.*'s criteria). Their depressed patients had to have scores of 20 or more on the Beck Depression Inventory and 14 or more on the Hamilton Depression Scale. In addition to comparing cognitive behaviour therapy with antidepressants, they (a) examined the combination of cognitive therapy and tricyclic antidepressants (TCA); and (b) examined the combination of cognitive therapy and an active placebo ('active' because it contained 5 mg of phenobarbitone and 0.05 mg of atropine sulphate to produce mild sedative and anticholinergic effects to simulate the side-effects of antidepressants). The other difference was that, whereas Rush *et al.* had used imipramine, Murphy *et al.* used nortriptyline. This drug had been argued to have a therapeutic window and blood tests were made to check that the plasma range remained within 50–150 ng/ml. A final difference was that antidepressants were not withdrawn until after the final twelve-week assessment. As I mentioned above, Rush *et al.* had started withdrawal of the drug at ten weeks so that the twelve-week comparison of cognitive therapy and drugs might have been affected by some patients relapsing in response to drug withdrawal.

Seventy patients were allocated to the four groups (TCA alone, TCA + CBT, CBT alone, CBT + placebo). Patients could receive up to twenty sessions in twelve weeks (twice weekly for the first eight weeks). The mean number of sessions actually received was 17.1. The TCA alone group was seen for twenty minutes once a week for twelve weeks.

Results showed no difference between the four groups. The suggestion from Blackburn et al.'s (1981) trial that the combination of CBT and TCA would do better than either CBT or TCA alone was not supported. All improved significantly, the final means for Beck and Hamilton scores being at or near the 'not depressed' level. Two-thirds of the seventy patients had 'recovered' as defined by a Hamilton score of 7 or less. The pattern of recovery was similar in all four groups, with 80 per cent of the change taking place in the first eight sessions (four weeks). Furthermore in an examination of some process data from this study, Simons et al. (1984) found no difference in the pattern or extent to which automatic thoughts, dysfunctional attitudes or cognitive responses were affected by cognitive therapy or drugs.

Murphy et al.'s conclusions were clear:

> While only a small number of studies attest to the efficacy of CT in comparison with other treatments, no negative study has yet appeared . . . . Regardless of how one views the evidence for the efficacy of TCA's in adequate dosage as a treatment for affective disorder of the type studied, cognitive therapy, either alone or in combination, performed as well and may be viewed as equally effective in moderately to severe depressed patients.
>
> (Murphy et al., 1984: 39)

I shall address, later, the question of whether economic arguments should now take over in making decisions about the management of depressed patients.

Beck, Hollon, Young, Bedrosian and Budenz (1985)

Blackburn et al. (1981) had found that combining CBT with TCA had produced a better outcome in outpatients than either treatment alone had done. Murphy et al. (1984) had found no such evidence. Beck et al.'s (1985) trial was designed to address this very question. Eighteen patients were given a maximum of twenty sessions of CBT over twelve weeks and a further fifteen had the same therapy plus amitriptyline (75–200 mg/d averaging 152 mg/d). All patients began therapy with Beck scores in excess of 20 .and Hamilton scores in excess of 14. All had a diagnosis of definite major depressive disorder by Feighner et al.'s (1972) criteria. The usual exclusion criteria were applied – no psychotic depression, no medical risk contraindicating the use of TCAs, no one with a history of schizophrenia, alcoholism, drug abuse, bipolar affective disorder, organic brain syndrome or antisocial personality disorder. In the end, the CBT alone group received a mean of 13.6 sessions and the combination group received a mean of 16.2 sessions. Dropout rates were comparable in the two groups (22 and 27 per cent in the CBT and combination groups respectively).

Both groups improved significantly, and there were no significant differences between them, despite a large apparent difference in the proportion of patients achieving a BDI score of 9 or less at post-treatment (71 per cent of CBT group and 36 per cent of the combination group, Table 4, p.146 of the study). At twelve months follow-up this trend was reversed: 58 per cent of the CBT alone patients were now in remission, whereas 82 per cent of the combination group were in remission. This reversal most likely occurred because patients in the combination group had received by that time, significantly more further sessions of CBT (a mean of 14.2 further sessions in the following year) than had the CBT alone group (a mean of 5.9 further sessions in that year).

Beck *et al.*'s conclusion (p. 146) was similar to that of Murphy *et al.* (1984): 'neither treatment proved superior to the other with regard to any of several types of outcome: the magnitude of acute symptom reduction; the acceptability of treatment (as indexed by drop out rates), or the stability of treatment gains'.

Rotzer-Zimmer, Axmann, Koch, Giedke, Pflug and Heimann (1985)

I alluded to this study from the University of Tübingen in the 1984 edition of this book. At that time, eighteen patients had been entered into a trial which was comparing three modes of cognitive therapy (activity scheduling (AS), AS plus self-regulation, AS plus positive self-description). This three-component cognitive therapy package was to be used alone or in combination with tricyclics (amitriptyline or maprotyline) and both would be compared with tricyclics alone. At that time, interest focused on comparisons between the three different subcomponents of cognitive therapy. As more patients completed the trial, it became clear that the three subcomponents each contributed equal amounts to the outcome (a conclusion by now familiar from the studies of Taylor and Marshall (1977), Zeiss *et al.* (1981) and Wilson *et al.* (1983)). By 1985, when the study was reported to the European Association for Behaviour Therapy, forty-six patients had been treated by this three-component CBT, CBT + TCA, or TCA alone. All of these patients met the usual admission criteria (BDI >20, HRS(D) >14 and unipolar, non-psychotic major depressive disorder on the RDC). All were aged between twenty and sixty. All groups improved significantly. Despite a tendency for more of the CBT and CBT + TCA to achieve remission than the TCA alone group (on the basis of Hamilton score of 6 or less plus two out of three self-report measures of improvement: 57 per cent, 65 per cent and 38 per cent of the CBT, combination, and TCA alone group respectively) these differences were not statistically reliable.

Patients were followed up at three, six and twelve months. The proportion of patients requiring medication during this twelve-month period was 20 per cent, 42 per cent and 50 per cent in the CBT, CBT + TCA combination, and TCA alone groups respectively. The equivalent proportion of patients needing further psychotherapy was 19 per cent, 30 per cent and 51 per cent. The suggestion that cognitive therapy might have effects beyond the acute treatment is one to which I shall return after considering the last major study of the 1980s – the NIMH multicentre trial.

Elkin, Shea, Watkins, Imber, Sotsky, Collins, Glass, Pilkonis, Leber, Docherty, Fiester and Parloff (1989)

Up until now, I have been reviewing studies which, though starting with behavioural treatments in the early 1970s, gradually focused more and more on cognitive-behavioural treatment of Beck. Other developments had been occurring in psychological treatments, which are beyond the scope of our review simply because this book is concerned with individual behavioural and cognitive treatment. As Beck *et al.* acknowledged, cognitive therapy was not the only psychological treatment which appeared to be effective in treating depression:

> those approaches that combine both cognitive and behavioural pro-
> cedures (e.g. Rehm's self-control or McLean's behavioural-cognitive
> marital skills training) along with cognitive therapy and the newly refined
> interpersonal psychotherapy (IPT) seem to be the most efficacious
> psychotherapy interventions for depression . . . . Yet another report by
> Bellack *et al.* (1981) presented further evidence of the relative efficacy of
> structured psychological intervention in comparison to standard anti-
> depressant drugs.
>
> (Beck *et al.*, 1985: 147)

This last comment was a reference to the use of social skills training, and meant that at least five types of psychotherapy were considered effective. Beck *et al.* (1985) concluded that 'the type of psychotherapy may not prove to be nearly so important as the extent to which it is adapted to a specific symptomatic focus' (p.147).

In 1989 Elkin *et al.*'s multicentre trial found results which reinforced this conclusion. Two hundred and fifty patients at three sites were randomly allocated to receive Beckian cognitive therapy, interpersonal psychotherapy (IPT, Klerman *et al.*, 1984), imipramine plus clinical management (CM) or placebo plus CM. To be included in the trial, patients had to be unipolar, non-psychotic, outpatients (Research Diagnostic Criteria, major depressive disorder), who had a score of at least 14 on the Hamilton Depression Scale. The usual exclusion criteria (bipolar, alcoholism, etc.) operated. The tricyclic used was imipramine (a mean of 185 mg/d with 95 per cent of patients having at least 150 mg/d). Careful guidelines were laid down, not only for the CBT and IPT therapy, but also the CM. Experienced psychiatrists conducted these twenty to thirty-minute weekly interviews (after an initial session of forty-five to sixty minutes). The guidelines for CM specified discussion of medication and side-effects, plus a review of patient's clinical status and provision of support, encouragement and direct advice if necessary. All treatments were planned to be sixteen weeks in length, with a range of sixteen to twenty sessions. The mean number of sessions for patients who completed treatment turned out to be 16.2. Each psychotherapy session lasted fifty minutes. The proportion of patients dropping out of various treatments was not significantly different between the groups: 32 per cent for CBT, 23 per cent for IPT, 33 per cent for TCA + CM and 40 per cent for placebo + CM.

All treatments made significant gains, though there was a treatment × site interaction for the more depressed/impaired patients (Global Assessment Scale score ≤ 50), such that IPT did very well on one site, CBT on another, with TCA + CM being more consistent throughout sites. The similarity of outcome of the four treatments was shown by the fact that of twelve primary statistical analyses, only four revealed any statistically significant results. Two of these were analyses of those patients who completed treatment (N = 155 in the analysis, though 162 had completed, data not having been obtained for seven subjects). These significant findings concerned the Hopkins Symptom Checklist 90 and the Global Assessment Scale (GAS) and showed tricyclics to be superior to placebo. No other comparison was significant. The two other significant effects were found in their analysis of all patients who had entered treatment (N = 239) even if they had dropped out immediately and were found on the Hamilton and the GAS. Post-hoc tests, however, showed that only on the GAS could any between-group difference be detected; again a significant difference between the TCA + CM group and placebo + CM group. Looking at the final scores (for completers) on the BDI (see Table 4.4) one can see why the analyses yielded so few differences. Outcome for all treatments (including the placebo + CM) was very similar.

A slightly different picture emerged from two supplementary analyses. The first examined the proportion in each group that achieved remission (a score of 6 or less on the Hamilton Rating Scale). These are shown in Table 4.3 for the completers (N = 155) and the total sample (N = 239) mentioned above. The pattern shown in Table 4.3 is for the three active therapies (TCA + CM, IPT, and CBT) to achieve generally higher proportion of remission

Table 4.3 Proportion of patients in remission at end of treatment (Elkin *et al.*, 1989)

	IPT	TCA + CM	CBT	Placebo + CM
Completer sample (N = 155)	55%	57%	51%	29%
Total sample (N = 239) (including dropouts)	43%	42%	36%	21%

than placebo, and not different from each other. However, the IPT and TCA + CM were sufficiently higher than the placebo + CM to achieve statistical significance.

The second supplementary analysis divided the sample into high and low severity (≥20 on the Hamilton; ≤50 on the GAS). For the less severe patients, the outcome for all four groups was indistinguishable. For the more severe patients there was a clear advantage for TCA + CM, placebo was worst with the two psychotherapies in between and not differing from each other. Once again, the TCA + CM and IPT groups, though not differing from CBT, were sufficiently different from placebo to achieve significance. In none of these supplementary analyses did cognitive therapy differ significantly from placebo + CM. Consistent with the conclusion emerging from the studies we have reviewed, whether one looks at completers or at the total sample in Elkin *et al.*'s study there was no evidence of a significant difference between the three active treatments.

Elkin *et al.* themselves conclude: 'in the major analyses in this study, there was no evidence that either of the psychotherapies was significantly less (or more) effective than imipramine + CM' (p. 977). And regarding the comparison between IPT and CBT:

> there is no evidence in this study of the greater effectiveness of one of the psychotherapies on measures of depressive symptoms and overall functioning (although . . . there was adequate power in the primary analyses for detecting any large effect size differences that might exist).
>
> (Elkin *et al.*, 1989: 979)

Although there was limited evidence of the specific effectiveness of IPT and no evidence of the specific effectiveness of CBT when compared to placebo + CM the authors discuss these findings in the light of the more surprising conclusion that there was only some, but not a great deal of evidence of the superiority of imipramine + CM over placebo + CM. The fact that only four out of the twelve primary analyses yielded significance was very puzzling given that it included a straight comparison of active antidepressants against an inactive placebo. Final assessment of each of these therapies must await the results of the follow-up study, some of which are described below and present a somewhat different picture, with cognitive therapy being most effective in the longer term.

Returning to the acute treatment trial, examination of the percentage change scores on the BDI (Table 4.4) shows that the three active treatments achieved levels of improvement broadly comparable with previous studies (with TCA + CM doing better than any previous study of TCA alone – presumably due to the carefully described and supervised clinical management component). What is striking is that the placebo + CM group did as well as active treatments have in previous studies. Elkin *et al.* also noted the fact that their placebo, for some reason, exceeded the performance of placebos

in standard drug trials presumably due, once again, to the clinical management. If we had become accustomed to finding that different *active*
treatments produced similar outcomes (Taylor and Marshall, 1977; Zeiss *et
al.*, 1979; Murphy *et al.*, 1984) it was unexpected that a placebo condition
should do so well. This was most surprising for patients with a Hamilton
score of less than 20, where there was no advantage at all for tricyclics or for
the psychotherapies over the placebo + CM (though it is important to note
that placebo did not do so well for the more severe subsample). This result
potentially threatens both advocates of drug treatment and advocates of
psychotherapy for less severely depressed patients. Further work is therefore
needed to understand what the therapeutic property of the placebo + CM
treatment was. Clearly *something* is happening here. Is it increased optimism
in the patients? Or increased courage to try and do things that they have been
avoiding doing, due either to the pill or to the advice? The theory on which
interpersonal psychotherapy is premised would predict that what was
happening was that somehow, this clinical management was allowing the
patient to get over grief, to handle role transitions, to resolve interpersonal
disputes and to make up for interpersonal deficits. The theory on which
cognitive therapy is premised would suggest that these patients recovered
because they were gaining distance from their negative thoughts, engaging
in activities to gain a sense of mastery and pleasure, and thereby being
enabled to challenge their dysfunctional attitudes towards themselves.
Returning to the parable of the mineshaft (Chapter One), these may have
been people who were predominantly active problem-solvers who simply
needed encouragement to use the skills that depression had temporarily
undermined.

My guess is that all of these things were happening: interpersonal, cognitive and behavioural changes. In the less severe patients, such changes were
more easily prompted. The findings for the more severe patients are less
clear-cut. There were consistent treatment × site interactions for these
patients. At one site, cognitive therapy did extremely well, producing results
comparable with imipramine. At another, IPT did well in a similar way. Only
further examination of the data will reveal whether it was patient, therapist
or situational characteristics which were the cause of this pattern of results.

SUMMARY OF THOSE STUDIES WHICH USE THE BECK DEPRESSION INVENTORY

Table 4.4 shows those of the studies which have used the BDI to evaluate a
package of treatments including both cognitive and behavioural components, thus enabling some interesting (if crude) comparison from study to
study. Several conclusions emerge from scrutiny of these data. Firstly cognitive-behavioural therapy is efficacious with a variety of populations of
depressives – clinical and subclinical, from a fairly wide range of social class,

Table 4.4 Percentage change scores on Beck Depression Inventory (for inpatient studies see Ch 8)

	Rush et al. 77 (outpatients)	Taylor & Marshall 77 (non-clinical)	Mclean & Hakstian 79 (outpatients)	Blackburn et al. 81 (outpatients)	Blackburn et al. 81 (GP patients)	Wilson et al. 83 (non-clinical)	Teasdale et al. 84 (GP patients)	Murphy et al. 84 (outpatients)	Beck et al. 85 (outpatients)	Elkin et al. 89 (outpatients)
Behavioural techniques alone	–	52	–	–	–	65	–	–	–	–
Cognitive techniques alone	–	49	–	–	–	67	–	–	–	–
CBT	81	72	64	48	84	–	–	67	72	62
CBT + placebo	–	–	–	–	–	–	–	73	–	–
Drugs	58	–	48	60	14	–	–	69	–	–
CBT + drugs	–	–	–	79	72	–	73^{1}	70	67	–
Drugs + clinical management	–	–	–	–	–	–	–	–	–	76
Others										
IPT	–	–	–	–	–	–	–	–	–	70
Psychotherapy	–	–	38	–	–	–	–	–	–	–
Relaxation	–	–	44	–	–	–	–	–	–	–
Wait list/TAU	–	–	–	–	–	10	36	–	–	–
Placebo + clin. management	–	–	–	–	–	–	–	–	–	61

1. Teasdale et al.'s CBT group also received Treatment as usual which often included TCAs

in both the Americas, Australia and Europe at least. Secondly, the combination of drugs and CBT is sometimes more efficacious than CBT alone; CBT alone is sometimes more efficacious than drugs alone; but drugs alone have not so far been found to be superior to CBT. Thirdly, the inclusion by at least one study (McLean and Hakstian) of two alternative psychological techniques each plausible in its theoretical basis, and with one (relaxation) involving homework assignments and the other (psychotherapy) practised by therapists for whom this approach was preferred, strongly suggests that the superiority of CBT when it occurs is not a function of non-specifically raised efficacy expectations. Focusing on outpatients, the mean percentage change across the six samples of outpatients who have received cognitive-behaviour therapy alone is 65.7. This compares with a mean of 63 per cent in the five samples of outpatients receiving TCA alone (including Elkin *et al.*'s TCA+CM group), and 72 per cent for the three samples of outpatients which have received a combination of tricyclics and cognitive therapy.

FOR WHOM IS COGNITIVE-BEHAVIOURAL THERAPY MOST SUITABLE?

Research so far has not established its usefulness with bipolar depressives, highly regressed patients, or patients with delusions or hallucinations ('psychotic'), but that is because the research has not been done, rather than because any studies have actually demonstrated its inefficacy. Endogeneity or chronicity seem not to predict outcome (Kovacs *et al.*, 1981; Blackburn *et al.*, 1981; Beck *et al.*, 1985). Personality characteristics seem equally irrelevant; neither McLean and Hakstian (1979) nor Kovacs *et al.* (1981) found that Eysenck's scales correlated with outcome. McLean and Hakstian's study of 178 primary depressives remains the most comprehensive study of predictive variables. A large number of variables were assessed including sociodemographic variables, number of recent life events, personality (EPI), number of social contacts, cognitive depression – negative thoughts, indecisiveness, poor memory, severity of depression, episode duration, employment status, as well as measures of coping ability. Four distinct groups emerged from a cluster analysis but none did any better with any of their treatment conditions than any other. A similar result has been reported by Shea *et al.* (1990). Although patients in their trial (NIMH) had a worse outcome on social functioning if they had a personality disorder, the *type* of personality disorder did not affect the outcome.

Some analyses have been done of response to treatment in general (i.e. including both drug and CBT groups). Blackburn *et al.* (1981) analysed the characteristics of those who did not complete treatment in their study. They were found to be significantly more severely depressed (higher BDI and HRS(D)), more irritable, more negative and less educated than completers, but none of these variables differentiated drug from CBT dropouts. Of those who completed, the worst outcome occurred for those with the longer duration of the current episode. By contrast, no variables at all (demographic characteristics, history of illness factors, pretreatment clinical or self-rating depression scales) could be found by Rush *et al.* which differentiated the patients who dropped out of their trial from those who completed the trial. On the other hand analyses of those who had the worst outcome by Hollon (cited in Fennell and Teasdale, 1982) found that four or more of the following predicted a worse outcome:

1. Beck Depression Inventory score ≥30
2. duration of current episode ≥6 months
3. inadequate response to previous treatments
4. ≥2 previous episodes
5. associated psychopathology
6. overall impairment as rated by clinicians (moderate or severe)
7. poor estimated tolerance for life stress

However these patients also did worse in response to antidepressant medication. When twelve-month follow-up assessments of those who did complete treatment were made, depression severity at that time was not predicted by history of illness, sociodemographic variables or pretreatment BDI score. The only predictive variables were patient age (BDI vs age: $r = 0.29$; $p<0.06$) and number of previous episodes (BDI vs no. previous episodes = 0.31; $p<0.04$). These are marginal correlations of little clinical significance, and in any case did not distinguish between patients who had received drugs from those who had received the CBT.

Psychologists' responses to this state of affairs have been of two types. On the one hand are those who continue to look for predictive variables so that the clinician may in future be able to make informed decisions on rational criteria. Others, such as Liberman, have scorned 'the happy day when (an) extended data base will permit conclusions about which type of treatment is best for specific diagnostic groups of patients', calling it 'fatuous and unlikely to come to pass'. This is because 'it overlooks the over-reaching importance of individual differences in depression' (Liberman, 1981: 231).

Perhaps it will help if the issue is divided into two separate questions: a) Given cognitive therapy, who will do best, i.e. what are the *prognostic* indicators? b) Given a certain patient, and a range of options for treatment, in what therapy will they do best, i.e. what are the *prescriptive* indicators?

The prognostic indicators appear similar to prognostic indicators for tricyclics. The more chronic and severe patients and those with other psychopathology do less well with all therapies including cognitive therapy (though Elkin *et al.* (1989) found a good response to imipramine amongst more severely depressed patients). But this does not imply that cognitive therapy is not indicated for such patients – other treatments may do even worse for such patients in the long run. We do not know because only a few adequate trials of medication and psychological treatments for these 'non-responding' patients have been done (see Chapter Eight). Certainly there will be other patients who respond better to CBT than these more severe and chronic cases, but they will respond to other interventions too.

Are there any additional hints as to which patients will do best with cognitive therapy. Fennell and Teasdale (1987) gave their patients at the outset of therapy a booklet 'Coping with depression' which described the cognitive model of depression and how cognitive treatment proceeds. Those patients who responded favourably to this booklet at the next session were found to do better after twelve weeks of therapy.

Are there any prescriptive indicators – variables which would help make a decision whether to give antidepressants or cognitive therapy? Murphy *et al.* (1984) found that patients who scored high on Michael Rosenbaum's Self-Control Schedule (see Chapter Five), a questionnaire measuring whether patients typically use their own resources in dealing with problems, did better with cognitive therapy. Those who scored low (which tends to suggest a passive style of coping with stress) did better with nortriptyline. That an active coping style, as assessed by the Self-Control Schedule, can act as a prognostic indicator too, is suggested by the outcome of a structured group psychotherapy – self-control therapy (Rehm *et al.*, 1987). They studied 104 women meeting Research Diagnostic Criteria for non-psychotic, non-bipolar major affective disorder who received one and a half hours' weekly therapy in group format for ten weeks. Self-control therapy was administered with either behavioural targets, cognitive targets or combined targets. Patients in all conditions improved significantly and equally on both self-report and clinician ratings of depression. Initial high self-control skills (as assessed by Rosenbaum's scale) were related to better therapy outcome in all conditions. These studies need replication, but they suggest that both prognostic and prescriptive indicators exist.

DRUGS, PSYCHOTHERAPY AND THE PREVENTION OF RELAPSE[1]

It is very tempting to conclude from the outcome studies reviewed above that, since the outcomes are so similar whether drugs or psychotherapy are used, one may as well use drugs since they appear cheaper. But the cost of any treatment must depend on how long-lasting its effects are. There is no reason not to apply the same criteria we apply in our domestic life. Buying a cheaper product is wasteful if it does not last. If cognitive therapy could reduce relapse, the long-term cost may be equivalent or even less than the apparently cheaper therapies which have to be applied again and again. It is now clear that depression is a chronic relapsing condition: ideally, management should take this into account from the outset.

When I came to review this literature recently (Williams, 1989), I found that the estimate of proportion of people who relapse following the initial response to treatment varies depending on the severity of patients in the sample, the length of the follow-up period and the definition of relapse (see Table 4.5). Klerman *et al.* (1974) found that 36 per cent of their predominantly neurotically depressed outpatients relapsed within eight months following initial response to four to six weeks of amitriptyline, 100–200 mg/d (if given no further treatment). The UK Medical Research Council Multicentre Trial (Mindham *et al.*, 1973) involved more severely depressed outpatients and found that 50 per cent relapsed within six months following initial treatment response if given no further treatment. The US National Institute of Mental Health Study (Prien *et al.*, 1974) examined more severely depressed patients and found that 92 per cent of a placebo group relapsed within the two years following successful response to initial active treatment. This pattern of results has been replicated in a further MRC trial of maintenance amitriptyline or lithium treatment (Glen *et al.*, 1984): six months after good response to initial treatment, 56 per cent of patients given no further treatment had relapsed; this figure had increased to 67 per cent after twelve months and 78 per cent after twenty-four months.

Each of these cited studies has also examined to what extent maintenance dosage of antidepressant or lithium can reduce the probability of relapse. Although absolute levels have differed depending on severity of condition, most have found that relapse rates can be (at least) halved by maintenance medication (from 36 to 12 per cent after eight months (Klerman *et al.*, 1984); from 50 to 22 per cent after six months (Mindham *et al.*, 1973); from 92 to 48 per cent after 24 months (Prien *et al.*, 1974)). The most recent estimate from the MRC trial (Glen *et al.*, 1984) is more pessimistic, however. They found that relapse rates at six months were reduced from 56 to 34 per cent; but at twelve months, 45 per cent, and at twenty-four months, 59 per cent of patients who remained on maintenance medication had relapsed. It seems that we have a major challenge to find a method of keeping patients well after they have responded during the acute treatment phase. Relying solely on maintenance medication for such prophylaxis has the disadvantage associated with long-term drug usage. It depends on patients continuing to take their drugs, carries the risk of overdose, may be dangerous for patients with heart complaints, and may involve unpleasant side-effects over prolonged periods. Can cognitive therapy help?

There have been four outcome studies (see Table 4.6) which, having compared tricyclic antidepressants with cognitive therapy in the initial treatment, have taken patients who initially responded and examined their outcome over the subsequent twelve or twenty-four months (Evans *et al.*, submitted; Blackburn *et al.*, 1986; Simons *et al.*, 1986; Shea *et al.*, submitted which is the eighteen-month follow-up of the Elkin *et al.* (1989) NIMH trial). Each of these studies has found that patients who have responded to tricyclic antidepressants have a probability of relapse equivalent to that seen in the groups who receive no maintenance treatment in the drug trials with moderately to severe depression cited above (Evans *et al.* 50 per cent at twenty-four months; Simons *et al.* 66 per cent at twelve months; Blackburn *et al.* 78 per cent at twenty-four months; Shea *et al.* 28 per cent at twelve months and 50 per cent at eighteen months[2]). These studies have also found, however, that the proportion of patients relapsing was substantially reduced if cognitive therapy had been added to tricyclic antidepressant medication during the acute treatment – Evans *et al.* from 50 per cent to 15 per cent at twenty-four months (cognitive therapy alone 20 per cent); this compares with a 27 per cent rate of relapse for medication plus maintenance medication for the first twelve months; Simons *et al.*, from 66 per cent to 43 per cent at twelve months (cognitive therapy alone 20 per cent); Blackburn *et al.* from 78 per cent to 21 per cent at twenty-four months (cognitive therapy alone 23 per cent); and Shea *et al.* found that cognitive therapy alone had a relapse rate of 9 per cent compared with the TCA + clinical management of 28 per cent at twelve months, and 36 per cent for CT alone compared with 50 per cent for TCA + CM at eighteen months.

The results of these studies conducted at different centres in both the US and the UK appear consistent. They are particularly interesting in that three of them (Evans *et al.*; Simons *et al.*; Shea *et al.*) found some differences in relapse rates despite having found no difference between tricyclic antidepressant and cognitive therapy or the combination of the two in the acute

Table 4.5 Percentage of patients relapsing following initial recovery after antidepressant acute or maintenance treatment

Study	Treatment	Follow-up (months)				
		% relapse (amongst initial responders)				
		6	8	12	18	24
Klerman *et al.* (1974)	TCA[1] (acute)		36			
	TCA (+ maintenance)		12			
Mindham *et al.* (1973)	TCA[2] (acute)	50				
	TCA (+ maintenance)	22				
Prien *et al.* (1974)	TCA (acute)[3]					92
	TCA + lithium (+ maintenance)					48
Glen *et al.* (1984)	TCA[4] (acute)	56		67		78
	TCA + lithium (+ maintenance)	34		45		59

1. 4–6 weeks amitriptyline, 100–200 mg/d
2. 3–10 weeks imipramine/amitriptyline
3. imipramine
4. amitriptyline

Table 4.6 Percentage of patients relapsing following initial recovery after acute treatment by antidepressants, cognitive therapy or the combination

Study	Treatment	Follow-up (months)			
		% relapse *(amongst initial responders)*			
		6	12	18	24
Evans *et al.* (submitted)	TCA				50
	TCA (+ maintenance for 12 months)				27
	CBT				20
	TCA + CBT				15
Simons *et al.* (1986)	TCA[1]		66		
	CBT		20		
	TCA + CBT		43		
Blackburn *et al.* (1987)	TCA[2]				78
	CBT				23
	CBT + TCA				21
Shea *et al.* (submitted)	TCA[3] + clinical management	11	28	50	
	CBT	9	9	36	

1. nortriptyline
2. amitriptyline and clomipramine
3. imipramine

phase of treatment. If these results are reliable, it will indicate an important advance in the management of chronically relapsing depressive illness. For example, Shea *et al.* found that over the eighteen-month follow-up period, recovered patients who had received CBT received an average of 4.2 weeks of further treatment. Recovered patients who had received imipramine received an average of 20.3 weeks of further treatment ($p<0.017$).

Can we predict who will relapse? People who have more severe depression at the outset of treatment are clearly more likely to become depressed again, but even controlling for level of depression, high scores on the Dysfunctional Attitude Scale contribute to the prediction of relapse (Rush *et al.*, 1986; Evans *et al.*, 1985; Simons *et al.*, 1986). I shall discuss these studies again in Chapter Ten when examining the data on vulnerability.

But even if drugs and cognitive therapy were comparable in relapse prevention, would this imply that cognitive therapy should be discarded? I concur with the comments of Murphy *et al.* (1984) who discussed this very issue at the end of their study (which was one of those to find no difference in the acute phase between antidepressants and cognitive therapy). I shall quote these authors in full:

> If treatments are equally effective, should the least expensive be the treatment of choice? For a number of reasons, the answer is not as simple as that. First, not every patient is psychologically disposed to accept medication as the appropriate treatment for his/her depression. Some will strongly prefer a psychological approach as shown by our intake attrition. Second, some patients tolerate the side-effects of TCA's poorly or not at all. Rejection of pharmacotherapy is a recurrent problem in outcome studies that include psychotherapy (Friedman, 1975; Rush et al., 1977; McLean and Hakstian, 1979; Bellack et al., 1981). Third, TCA's are potentially dangerous to patients with cardiac conduction defects. In addition, TCA's in overdose are cardiotoxic and therefore dangerous for the unsupervised suicidally depressed patient.
>
> (Murphy et al., 1984: 40)

Current research by Chris Freeman and his colleagues in Edinburgh is also challenging the economic argument by studying how many contact hours it takes to achieve remission criteria if optimal drug therapy, cognitive behaviour therapy, dynamic psychotherapy by a social worker or treatment as usual by a GP is used. The interesting fact to emerge is that whereas dynamic counselling took 20.9 hours to achieve criteria of remission (exceeding the twenty hours set at the outset for therapy), cognitive therapy took 14.6 hours and drug therapy eleven hours. The difference in time between drugs and cognitive therapy was only 3.6 hours. If this result proves reliable, it will cast the cost benefit argument in a new light.

My conclusion is that a comprehensive health service should always have available psychological treatments as an alternative to physical treatments. But these psychological treatments should have been found to be reliably effective in their own right. Cognitive therapy has been a pioneer in the empirical validation of structured psychological treatment for depression. No study has found it to be less effective than antidepressants, four have found it more effective in preventing relapse. It remains one of the most valuable contributions to the treatment of depression.

NOTES

1 'Relapse' in each of the studies cited implies that the patient had responded successfully to the treatment of their acute symptoms. Definition of such successful response varies from study to study, but usually consists of achieving a certain low score on a measure of depression such as the Hamilton (cut-offs of 6 or 7 have been suggested) or the Beck, where cut-offs of 15 or less (partial remission) or 9 or less (complete remission) have been used. 'Relapse' is then said to have occurred *either* if a person's score rises above a cut-off on such a scale (e.g. two consecutive weeks of a BDI score of 16 or more, Evans et al., submitted)

or if a patient returns for treatment for their depression. For a review of these issues of relapse and its definition see Belsher and Costello (1988).

2   These generally lower relapse rates of Shea *et al.* (submitted) most likely occurred because they used a more rigorous definition of recovery than other studies. For their patients to have been considered recovered they had to have eight consecutive weeks of symptomatic remission. Only 48 per cent of those completing treatment recovered on this definition (N = 78) (only one-third of the original sample), thus these recovered patients in this study were much more likely to be truly recovered than the recovered patients in other studies. Relapse in the Shea *et al.* study might more properly be recalled recurrence. In any event, in the Shea *et al.* study relapse was defined as meeting criteria for major depressive disorder for at least two consecutive weeks in the follow-up period. If relapse is defined as either meeting these criteria or receiving at least three consecutive weeks' treatment for depression, then 14 per cent of CBT patients relapsed in twelve months versus 50 per cent for TCA (IPT was 43 per cent); by eighteen months 41 per cent of the CBT group had relapsed compared with 61 per cent of the TCA and 57 per cent of IPT. In the first twelve months of the follow-up period, of those patients who recovered, only 5 per cent of the CBT group sought further treatment, compared with 38 per cent of the IPT group (χ^2 = 7.43, p<0.007) and 39 per cent of the TCA group (χ^2 = 7.3, p<0.007). The corresponding percentage of those seeking treatment over eighteen months is 14, 43 and 44 per cent from the CBT, IPT and TCA groups respectively (p<0.03 for each comparison with CBT).

Chapter 5

The assessment of depression
Some representative procedures

This section of the book aims to give details of enough aspects of assessment to allow the practitioner to make a comprehensive evaluation of various aspects of the patient's problems. After a brief general introduction, representative scales which include assessment of somatic, behavioural and cognitive variables are individually introduced. Each is printed in full as an appendix to the chapter. The literature already contains comprehensive reviews of assessment procedures (Kendall and Korgeski, 1979; Rehm, 1981; Hamilton and Shapiro, 1990). Because these are easily available, I have not attempted to repeat their work in this section. Rather, it seemed more useful to supply a representative sample of actual tests, chosen to be as comprehensive as possible, covering observational, interview and self-rating methods across the range of somatic, behavioural and cognitive variables. For the behavioural and cognitive components, techniques to assess both general and specific aspects are included.

The extent to which the practitioner wants to make use of this material will depend on whether they are interested in assessment which will guide treatment strategies and tactics, observing predominant problems and correlations between variables, or whether the interest is in evaluating treatment efficacy by examining general severity before, during and after therapeutic intervention. The questions asked in assessment can help the patient gain a greater understanding of their difficulties, which may prove therapeutically valuable. Two additional and less explicit purposes in assessment may be borne in mind. The first is that a thorough assessment, especially in the context of a structured interview, may communicate hope to the patient that their symptoms are frequent and understandable aspects of their emotional problems. This can help deal with a natural tendency to attribute their symptoms to 'laziness' or 'inadequacy'. The second implicit aim follows from the first: that because assessment techniques can help to objectify and distance some aspects of the problem for the patient, they may be used at any point in therapy as a therapeutic technique, and not just at the beginning, middle and end of therapy. For example, if the patient reports having had a bad week, detailed assessment of all aspects of the past few days may sometimes be an appropriate strategy, communicating to the patient that the reality of their problems is being taken seriously.

Most writers on depression emphasize the triad of somatic, behavioural and cognitive disturbances which are involved in the disorder. McLean (1976) suggests that there is a regularly observed sequence in the onset of depression, with negative and pessimistic thoughts occurring first accompanied by low mood. With increasing severity, these thoughts and feelings generalize to affect behaviour. If the depression becomes even more severe, then 'neuro-vegetative' systems (e.g. eating and sleeping) are affected as well.

Evidence supporting this suggestion comes not only from observation at the stage of onset of depression, but also at the stage of remission, where, according to many clinicians, the exact reverse order can be seen – appetite and sleep improving first, behaviour second, and thoughts and feelings last (Weissman *et al.*, 1979). Other evidence of the significance of somatic symptoms as an index of severity comes from the use of different types of depression scale. Scales which assess somatic aspects of depression (e.g. Hamilton) discriminate better between severely and moderately severely depressed patients than a self-rating scale (e.g. Zung) which places less emphasis on somatic items (Carroll *et al.*, 1973).

This, then, is the context in which the scales below are reproduced. I am grateful to Professor Max Hamilton, Professor Aaron T. Beck, Dr Arlene Weissman, Dr Margaret Bellew, Dr Michael Rosenbaum, Dr Ivy Blackburn and Mr Ian Wilkinson for permission to reproduce their scales.

THE ASSESSMENT OF GENERAL SEVERITY, INCLUDING SOMATIC ASPECTS

The Hamilton Rating Scale (1967) (see Appendix A)

This is an observer scale in which all known observations about the patient's current mental state are taken into account. These observations can also, however, be supplemented by a clinical interview, and some standard questions for this interview are reproduced in the Appendix A.

The scale includes assessment of cognitive and behavioural components of depression, but is especially thorough in assessing the somatic aspects. Its inter-rater reliability is 0.84 to 0.90, and it has consistently correlated highly with other widely used observer and self-rated scales of depression. (See Rehm (1981) for a more detailed discussion of its psychometric properties.)

Note (a) that the scale cannot be used to establish a diagnosis of depression but is designed to assess severity in patients already diagnosed as having the disorder; and (b) that items are individually scored by a rater during an interview, but the total score ranges from 0 to 100, representing the sum of two raters' scores or double the score for one rater. It has become more conventional, however, to report the scores from one rater, with 50 as maximum, and to see 14 or more as indicating a level of depression justifying treatment, and 6/7 or less as indicating remission (Ziegler *et al.*, 1976 and Knesevich *et al.*, 1977). Hamilton (1982) has suggested that when the HRS(D) score has been reduced to a third (or less) of its pretreatment level, patients feel their treatment has been successful.

The Beck Depression Inventory (1961) (see Appendix B)

The BDI was first developed as an interview scale where the interviewer read out loud each item to the patient while the patient read their own copy of the scale, and gave their choice. It is now more widely used as a self-rating scale.

It consists of twenty-one items, each containing four or five statements ranked in order of severity. The patient chooses the statement closest to their present state.

The split-half reliability is around 0.9, and its test–retest reliability is approximately 0.75. It has consistently been found to correlate well with clinicians' ratings of severity of depression, as well as with other scales of depression. It has the advantage of being useful across a great range of severity levels and in both clinical, subclinical and student populations.

Like the Hamilton, it cannot be used to diagnose depression in the absence of a prior diagnosis – it is only a measure of severity once the clinical diagnosis has been made. This is an important point, for people may have an inflated BDI score for a number of reasons (e.g. bereavement reaction, chronic low self-esteem) without a diagnosis of depression being warranted. In this sense the generalizability of many research findings in 'mildly depressed' students to clinically depressed populations may be called into question (see Depue and Monroe, 1978). However, this is a reflection on the use of the scale, rather than on the scale itself, which remains probably the best all-round scale of its type. A review of the use and the properties of the Beck Depression Inventory can be found in recent papers by Beck *et al.* (1988); Kendall *et al.* (1987) and Louks *et al.* (1989). Finally, the NIMH collaborative study (Imber *et al.*, 1990) identified a 'seven-item self-denigration factor' with good internal consistency. This consisted of items 2, 3, 5, 6, 7, 8 and 14.

THE ASSESSMENT OF THE COGNITIVE COMPONENT OF DEPRESSION

Cognitive Style Test (Blackburn *et al.*, 1986) (see Appendix C)

This scale consists of thirty short descriptions of everyday events. Subjects are asked to choose one of four possible cognitive responses to the situation.

It can be presented in written format or using a card format which enables randomization of the types of events. In the latter case, the experimenter reads the situation aloud and then presents the responses visually which are printed on the reverse side of the same card.

The events are classified into three themes which relate to Beck's cognitive triad of self (events of an interpersonal nature, relating particularly to self-image), world (situations which are more task orientated) and future (dealing with anticipated responses and plans). Within each of the three categories, half the items are pleasant/rewarding situations and half are unpleasant/punishing. Each positive item is roughly counterbalanced with a negative item. Thus the overall structure of the test yields six types of events with five items in each type.

The responses are chosen to represent degrees of depressive distortion. The extreme responses include cognitive errors listed by Beck – arbitrary inference, selective abstraction, overgeneralization, magnification, minimization, personalization – though not systematically, since in practice these categories are not independent of each other.

The statements are listed in random order for degree of positive and negative attitude: 4 = very negative; 3 = negative with some qualification; 2 = positive with some qualification; 1 = very positive.

The test in its present form is a further development of the test reported by Wilkinson and Blackburn (1981). The validity and reliability of both the original scale and the present version have been found to be satisfactory.[1]

Dysfunctional Attitude Scale (Weissman and Beck, 1978) (see Appendix D)

This instrument was developed in order to identify the assumptions which commonly underlie idiosyncratic thoughts typical of depression. Originally a hundred-item scale, two parallel forms of the DAS were developed (consisting of forty items each) and are reproduced in Appendix D. In each form, forty items 'elicit information on an individual's dysfunctional beliefs which act as schemas by which he constructs his world' (Weissman and Beck, 1978). Weissman and Beck report mean reliability (Cronbach's alpha) levels of 0.89 and above for both Form A and Form B. The correlation between Forms A and B (given to undergraduates in counterbalanced order, eight weeks apart) exceeded 0.81.

Hopelessness Scale (Beck et al., 1974) (see Appendix E)

This scale measures the patient's view of the future, or degree of hopelessness. A depressed patient or other potentially suicidal patient can tolerate his or her illness provided they have some hope for the future. When they begin to view the future in totally negative terms, life becomes pointless and intolerable, and the patient becomes a high suicide risk. This risk exists particularly if the patient is depressed, but occasionally hopelessness does occur in patients who do not have the physical symptoms of depression. (A further factor for the therapist to consider is whether the patient has an impulsive nature, which increases the risk of suicidal behaviour.)

Assessment of self-schema using memory for positive and negative words (Bellew, 1990)

It has been known for some time that the memory of depressed people tends to be biased so that they preferentially recall negative rather than positive items (see Williams *et al.*, 1988, Chapter 5, for review). If people read a list of words (some positive, some negative) those who are more depressed at the time of reading the list (or become depressed by the time they attempt to recall the words on the list) will remember more of the negative than the positive words. This technique can be adapted as a measure of vulnerability to depression, in those not already depressed.

In a recent study, Margaret Bellew, at the University of Keele, gave such a mixed list to 156 women who were between twenty-eight and thirty-seven weeks pregnant. Each word was presented for three seconds. There were thirty words in all, fifteen positive and fifteen negative (self-esteem threatening). The words were mixed together randomly, with the constraint that the first and last six words had equal numbers of positive and negative words. Immediately after seeing the complete list, the women were given five minutes to try and remember as many words as they could.

Out of 156, thirty-five women remembered more negative than positive words. Were these thirty-five women more vulnerable to later depression? Note that at the time that they were doing the task, these thirty-five were no more depressed (as measured by the Beck Depression Inventory) than the rest of the women.

The women were seen again three months after the birth of their babies. Bellew found that although these vulnerable women had not been more depressed at the time of their initial testing, if they had had a bad experience adjusting to the birth of their baby then their depression had increased. For all other women, depression had reduced from the time that they were first assessed. In those women who had an equally bad time since the birth of their babies, if they were not vulnerable prior to the birth (recalled more positive than negative words) they did not become depressed. It appears then that the extent to which one remembers the negative over the positive, may be a marker for vulnerability to later depression if one has a negative life event. The positive and self-esteem threatening words (balanced for frequency and length) which Bellew used are given below:

Positive	*Self-esteem threatening*
Joy	Degradation
Courtesy	Humiliation
Gentleness	Dishonour
Security	Failure
Euphoria	Desertion
Warmth	Ridicule
Sunshine	Disgrace
Rapture	Unpopularity
Adventure	Rejection
Excitement	Exclusion
Cheerfulness	Loneliness
Delight	Inadequacy
Contentment	Guilt
Laughter	Inferiority
Luxury	Shame

Self-Control Schedule (Rosenbaum 1980) (see Appendix F)

This scale was devised to assess 'learned resourcefulness', the extent to which individuals rely on their own resources when they have a problem, or prefer to remain passive in the face of such problems. More specifically it aims to measure: a) the use of cognitions to control unpleasant emotional and physical reactions; b) application of problem-solving strategies; c) ability to delay gratification; and d) self-efficacy about self-control. High scores on the original thirty-six item version (each item scored from +3 (very characteristic of me, extremely descriptive; to –3 very uncharacteristic of me, extremely undescriptive) have been found to predict a good response to cognitive therapy. Low scores on this scale predicted good response to antidepressant medication (Murphy *et al.*, 1984; Simons *et al.*, 1985).

A new, fifteen-item version (the Problem-Solving Scale) is currently being piloted. This uses items 1, 2, 7, 10, 11, 12, 20, 22, 26, 27, 28, 30, 32, 33, and 34. However, it is the thirty-six-item version which Murphy *et al.* (1984) used in their research trial and which is reproduced in Appendix F.

NOTE

1   Users may refer for use of the scale to Dr Ivy Blackburn at the Department of Psychiatry, Royal Edinburgh Hospital, Morningside Park, Edinburgh.

APPENDIX A – HAMILTON RATING SCALE FOR DEPRESSION

Summary sheet

Item No.	Score range	Symptom	Score
1	0–4	Depressed mood	
2	0–4	Guilt	
3	0–4	Suicide	
4	0–2	Insomnia: initial	
5	0–2	Insomnia: middle	
6	0–2	Insomnia: delayed	
7	0–4	Work and interests	
8	0–4	Retardation	
9	0–2	Agitation	
10	0–4	Anxiety: psychic	
11	0–4	Anxiety: somatic	
12	0–2	Somatic symptoms: gastrointestinal	
13	0–2	Somatic symptoms: general	
14	0–2	Genital symptoms	
15	0–4	Hypochondriasis	
16	0–2	Loss of insight	
17	0–2	Loss of weight	

Grading

0	Absent		0	Absent
1	Mild or trivial		1	Slight or doubtful
2 ⎫ 3 ⎭	Moderate		2	Clearly present
4	Severe			

Interview schedule

1. Depression (0–4)

Depressed mood is not easy to assess. One looks for a gloomy attitude, pessimism about the future, feelings of hopelessness and a tendency to weep. As a rule, milder depressive mood is relieved, at least in part, by company or external stimulation. When patients are severely depressed they may 'go beyond weeping'. It is important to remember that patients may interpret the word 'depression' in all sorts of strange ways. A useful common phrase is 'lowering of spirits'.

It is generally believed that women weep more readily than men, but there is little evidence that this is true in the case of depressive illness. There is no reason to believe, at the moment, that an assessment of the frequency of weeping could be misleading when rating the intensity of depression in women.

> Now, I would like to ask you about the way you have been feeling during the last month. Do you keep reasonably cheerful, or have you felt depressed or low spirited recently? How would you describe it? Moody? Downhearted? Dejected? Sad? How often? Does it come and go? Does it get better if you are with someone else? How long does it last? Have you wanted to cry? Does crying relieve it? Do you feel beyond tears? So bad it is excruciating or very painful?

0 = *Absent* or very mild or occasional feelings no worse than the patient's normal feelings when well.

1 = *Mild.* Persistent feelings described as moody, downhearted, dejected, or similar ways; more intense, occasional feelings; may be relieved by company, being at work.

2 = *Moderate.* Persistent or frequent feelings of depression, blueness etc.; often feels like crying, may cry occasionally; not easily relieved by company.

3 = *Marked.* More intense feelings; may be frequent tears; more persistent throughout the waking day.

4 = *Severe.* Persistent severe feelings; may be described as usually beyond tears, painful, little relief *or* extremely severe; excrutiating, agonizing, persistent, unrelieved feelings.

2. Guilt (0–4)

This is fairly easy to assess but judgement is needed, for the rating is concerned with pathological guilt. From the patient's point of view, some action which precipitated a crisis may appear as a 'rational' basis for self-blame, which persists even after recovery from illness. For example, the patient may have accepted a promotion, but the increased responsibility has precipitated breakdown. When the patient 'blames' himself for this, he is ascribing a cause and not necessarily expressing pathological guilt.

> Have you had a low impression of yourself? Have you blamed yourself for things you have done in the past or recently? Have you felt guilty about things? Have you felt you have let your friends and family down? Have you felt you are to blame for your illness? In what way? A little? A lot? Is your condition a punishment?

0 = *Absent* or very mild feelings of self-blame on borderline of normality.

1 = *Mild.* Lowered opinion of self with persisting feelings of regret about past actions which in themselves are not markedly unusual.

2 = *Moderate.* More intense or pervasive feelings of guilt or self-blame which are pathological in the rater's judgement.

3 = *Severe.* Pervasive feelings of self-blame, guilt, or worthlessness regarding many areas of patient's existence. This often leads to a feeling that the illness is a punishment for past misdeeds.

4 = *Delusions of guilt.* Incorrigible beliefs of pathological guilt, with or without hallucinations of voices emphasizing guilt.

3. Suicide (0–4)

This symptom covers a range of feeling, from life not being worth living to active suicidal behaviour. Note that assessment of intent needs careful investigation using instruments such as the Suicide Intent Scale (Beck *et al.*, 1974). Judgement must be used when the patient is considered to be concealing this symptom, or conversely when the patient appears to be using suicidal threats as a weapon, to intimidate others, obtain help and so on.

Have you felt that life was not worth living? Have you wished you were dead? Have you had any thoughts of taking your life? Have you gone so far as to make any plans to do so? Have you actually made an attempt on your life?

0 = *Absent.*

1 = Has felt life not worth living – a persistent thought, which recurs.

2 = Has wished they were out of it, dead, but no suicidal thoughts.

3 = Has thoughts of taking own life, which may include working out a plan, or has rehearsed plan (e.g. standing on a bridge, holding tablets in hand) or has made minor gesture, e.g. cut on wrists, taken up to two tablets.

4 = Suicidal attempt of any but the most minor kind.

Insomnia

Both severity and frequency should be taken into account. Middle insomnia (disturbed sleep during the night) is the most difficult to assess, possibly because it is an artifact of the system of rating. When insomnia is severe, it generally affects all phases. Delayed insomnia (early morning wakening) tends not to be relieved by hypnotic drugs and is often present without other forms of insomnia. If insomnia is not present every night, rate as present if it occurs at least every third night.

Have you been taking sleeping pills? Have you had any difficulty sleeping or getting off to sleep? When you do get to sleep do you sleep well? Are you restless, or do you keep waking?

4. Early insomnia (0–2)

0 = *Absent,* or occasional delay in falling asleep, no more than normally experienced.
1 = *Mild.* Delay of half to one hour in falling asleep. Recognized to be a change from normal by patient.
2 = *Severe.* Delay of one to two hours in falling asleep.

5. Middle insomnia (0–2)

0 = *Absent* or habitual nocturnal waking to void bladder.
1 = Wakes once or twice during the night but falls asleep again without undue delay.
2 = Wakes frequently, or wakes occasionally but has difficulty falling asleep again.

6. Delayed insomnia (0–2)

0 = *Absent.* Sleeps with usual time for waking.
1 = *Mild.* Regularly wakes half to one hour before usual time.
2 = *Severe.* Awake more than one hour before usual time.

7. Work and interests (0–4)

It could be argued that the patient's loss of interest in work and activities should be rated separately from decreased performance, but it has been found to be difficult to do so in practice. Care should be taken not to include fatigability and lack of energy here; the rating is concerned with loss of efficiency and the extra effort required to do anything. When the patient has to be admitted to hospital because symptoms render them unable to carry on, this should be rated 4 points, but not if they have been admitted for investigation or observation. When the patient improves they will eventually return to work, but when they do so may depend on the nature of the work; judgement must be used here.

The work of many women who are housewives can be varied, both in quantity and intensity. Women may not complain of work being an effort, but they may say they have to take things easily, or that they neglect some of their work. Other members of the family may have to increase the help they give. It is rare for a housewife to stop looking after her home completely. If she has an additional job outside the home she may find she feels she has to change it to part-time or reduce her hours of work or even give it up completely. For people who do not engage in hobbies frequently, loss of interest may not be as obvious. Patients may complain of inability to feel affection for their families. This could be rated here, but it could be rated under other symptoms, depending upon its meaning and setting. Care should be taken not to rate it in two places. It is a very valuable and important symptom if the patient mentions it spontaneously but could be very misleading as a reply to a question.

Have you been affected at all in your capacity to do your work and other activities? What have you actually been doing in work, housework, hobbies, and interests and in social life? Have you let your appearance go?

0 = *Absent*. Full normal activity.
1 = *Mild*. Definite but mild loss of interest or enjoyment in work, hobbies, housework, social activities. Essential tasks continue to be performed.
2 = *Moderate*. The patient reports the beginnings of impairment of performance as well as a more significant loss of interest. Leisure pursuits deserted.
3 = *Marked*. Loss of efficiency becomes impossible to hide, deficiencies occur at work leading to comment, household tasks are not completed, work disorganized, hygiene and self-care start to suffer, withdrawn from friends.
4 = *Severe*. Unable to carry on outside and admitted to hospital for protection (but not for investigation or observation) *or* off work because of illness. Relative or neighbour doing most of housework and shopping. Unable to care for self.

8. Retardation (0–4)

Severe forms of this symptom are rare, and the mild forms are difficult to perceive. Although some patients may say that their thinking is slowed or their emotional responsiveness has been diminished, questions about these manifestations usually produce misleading answers. Therefore, rate observed behaviour rather than what the patient claims.

0 = *Absent*.
1 = *Mild*. Distinct flattening of emotional response or fixity of expression.
2 = *Moderate*. Voice is monotonous, delay in answering, tendency to sit motionless.
3 = *Marked*. Slowness of response sufficient for the interview to be difficult and prolonged.
4 = *Severe*. Interview impossible owing to retardation; patient may be stuporose.

9. Agitation (0–4)

Severe agitation, when the patient paces up and down, picking at face and hair, tearing at clothes, is extremely rare. In milder forms the essential component is motor restlessness, coupled with some impression of tension or distress. Although agitation and retardation may appear to be opposed forms of behaviour, in mild form they can coexist.

0 = *Absent* or minimal, within normal limits.
1 = *Mild.* Fidgety, moving excessively in chair, tapping fingers, moving feet.
2 = *Moderate.* Pulling at hair, twisting handkerchief or clothes.
3 = *Marked.* Patient has to rise during interview, then may return to seat.
4 = *Severe.* Interview conducted 'on the run'.

10. Anxiety (psychic symptoms) (0–4)

Many symptoms are included here, such as tension and difficulty in relaxing, irritability, worrying over trivial matters, apprehension and feelings of panic, fears; difficulty in concentration and forgetfulness, 'feeling jumpy'. The rating should be based on pathological changes that have occurred during the illness and an effort should be made to discount the features of a previous anxious disposition. If a phobic patient has averted anxiety by restriction of activity to avoid the phobic stimulus this should be rated, based on the severity of restriction.

> Have you been feeling nervous, anxious, or frightened? Have you felt tense or found it hard to relax? Have you had a feeling of dread, as though something terrible were about to happen?

0 = *Absent.*
1 = *Mild.* Complains of out of the ordinary and inappropriate worries or tension states, which are mild but persistent thoughts not occupying most of the patient's time.
2 = *Moderate.* Persisting and fairly frequent symptoms of greater intensity, and concerning patient for much of the time.
3 = *Marked.* Phobias with avoidance and risk of panic.
4 = *Severe.* Persistent state of intense anxiety, or near panic, dominating patient's mental life and talk at interview. Frequent panic attacks or severe impairment due to phobic avoidance.

11. Anxiety (somatic symptoms) (0–4)

These consist of the well-recognized effects of autonomic overactivity in the respiratory, cardiovascular, gastrointestinal and urinary systems. Patients may also complain of attacks of giddiness, blurring of vision and tinnitus.

These last three symptoms appear to be more common in women than in men.

> Have you suffered from any of the following – trembling, shakiness, excessive sweating, feelings of suffocation or choking, attacks of

shortness of breath, dizziness, palpitations, faintness, headaches, pain at the back of the neck, butterflies or tightness in the stomach? How often? How badly?

0 = *Absent.*
1 = *Mild.* One or two physical symptoms definite but mild, occurring less than twice a week.
2 = *Moderate.* Increased severity, more symptoms, occurring more than twice a week.
3 = *Marked.* Persisting, and frequent, e.g. everyday. Occasional severe episodic symptom, which incapacitates while it lasts.
4 = *Severe.* Several persisting and very frequent symptoms, resulting in disabling attacks.

12. Gastrointestinal symptoms (0–2)

The characteristic symptom in depression is loss of appetite and this occurs very frequently. Constipation also occurs, but is relatively uncommon. On rare occasions patients will complain of 'heavy feelings' in the abdomen. Symptoms of indigestion, wind and pain, etc. are rated under anxiety. Note also that in mild depression, many people gain weight.

How has your appetite been? Have you suffered from constipation?

0 = Normal appetite for patient.
1 = *Mild.* Loss of interest in food averaged over period in question or change of bowel movement in direction of constipation.
2 = *Moderate to severe.* Noticeable diminution in food intake or definite constipation requiring unusual use of laxatives.

13. General somatic symptoms (0–2)

These fall into two groups: the first is fatigability, which may reach the point where patients feel tired all the time. In addition, patients complain of 'loss of energy' which appears to be related to difficulty in starting up an activity. The other type of symptom consists of diffuse muscular aches, ill-defined and often difficult to locate, but frequently in the back and sometimes in the limbs; these may also feel 'heavy'.

It is not uncommon for women to complain of backache and to ascribe it to a pelvic disorder. This symptom requires careful questioning.

Do you feel tired easily? All the time? Have you much energy? Is it an effort to do anything? Do you spend a lot of time resting? In bed?

0 = *Absent.*
1 = *Mild.* Definite disproportionate fatigue. More time than usual spent

sitting down leading to some interference with day-to-day activity. Diffuse physical malaise.

2 = *Moderate to severe*. Marked complaints requiring frequent rests after bursts of physical activity. Difficult 'to get going'. Body feels heavy. Exhausted.

14. Loss of libido (0–2)

This is a common and characteristic symptom of depression, but it is difficult to assess in older men and especially those whose sexual activity is usually at a low level, e.g. single people without partners. The assessment is based on a pathological change, i.e. deterioration obviously related to the patient's illness. Inadequate or no information should be rated as zero.

Has there been any change in your interest in sex during the past month? Have you lost interest in the opposite sex recently? Have you had less sexual drive than usual? Sexual relations less often?

0 = *Absent*. Normal level of activity for the individual.
1 = *Mild*. Some loss of interest, or decrease in activity.
2 = *Moderate to severe*. Total absence of interest or activity.

15. Hypochondriasis (0–4)

The severe states of this symptom, concerning delusions and hallucinations of rotting and blockages, are extremely uncommon in men. Excessive preoccupation with bodily functions is the essence of a hypochondriacal attitude.

0 = *Absent*.
1 = *Mild*. Excessive preoccupation with bodily functions or minor symptoms, e.g. patient talks in these terms when asked but does not return to topic spontaneously.
2 = *Moderate*. Much preoccupation with physical symptoms and thoughts of organic disease, which are volunteered.
3 = *Marked*. Strong irrational convictions of the presence of physical disease, accounting for the patient's condition.
4 = *Severe*. Delusions of disease (rotting, blockage, riddled with tumour).

16. Loss of weight (0–2)

The simplest way to rate this would be to record the amount of loss, but many patients do not know their normal weight. (It is assumed that most weighing machines are fallible.)

0 = *Absent*, or claimed loss of less than 4lb.

1 = *Mild*. 4–14 lb over previous eight weeks or clothes slack around waist.
2 = *Marked*. Over 14 lb in previous eight weeks or noticeable thinning.

17. Loss of insight (0–2)

This is not necessarily present when patients deny that they are suffering from mental disorder. It may be that they are denying that they are insane and may willingly recognize that they have a 'nervous' illness. In case of doubt, enquiries should be directed to the patients' attitude to their symptoms of guilt and hypochondriasis.

What do you think is the matter with you?

0 = Full appreciation of situation.
1 = *Partial loss*. Admits reluctantly to possibility of nervous condition.
2 = *Full loss*. Denies completely the possibility of mental illness or nervous disorder.

APPENDIX B – THE BECK DEPRESSION INVENTORY

The Beck Depression Inventory (BDI) is now available from the Psychological Corporation:

555 Academic Court
San Antonio
Texas 78204-2498

Its twenty-one items cover the following domains:

1. Sadness
2. Pessimism
3. Feelings of failure
4. Anhedonia
5. Guilt
6. Self-punishment
7. Self-disappointment/hatred
8. Self-criticism
9. Suicidal ideation
10. Tearfulness
11. Irritability
12. Loss of interest
13. Difficulty making decisions
14. Feeling unattractive
15. Lack of energy/drive
16. Sleep difficulties

17. Fatigability
18. Loss of appetite
19. Loss of weight (when not dieting)
20. Health-related concerns
21. Loss of interest in sex

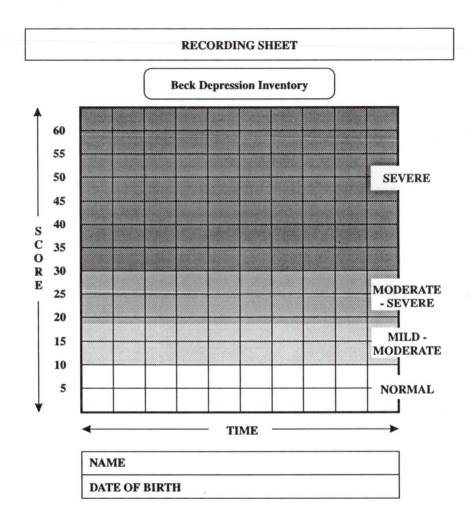

Figure 5.1 Possible format for daily or weekly recording of Beck Depression Inventory. Produced by the Psychology Department, Norwich Area Health Authority

The BDI is scored 0 to 3 for each item, minimum score 0, maximum score 63. Rush *et al.* (1977) and Murphy *et al.* (1984) used the following definition of severity levels:

0–9   Not depressed
10–15   Mildly depressed
16–24   Moderately depressed
25+   Severely depressed

Items 2, 3, 5, 6, 7, 8 and 14 have been found to constitute a coherent 'self-denigration' factor (Imber *et al.* 1990). For further information, and comparison with other assessment scales and schedules for depression, see the review article by Philip Snaith (1993) 'What do depression scales measure?' in the *British Journal of Psychiatry*, 163, 293–8.

APPENDIX C – THE COGNITIVE STYLE TEST

Instructions

On the following pages you will find a series of descriptions of everyday events. After each situation are alternative ways that people might think about it, marked A, B, C and D. I would like you to imagine that these events are happening to you. Then choose the alternative that best describes how you would think about the situation. (If your reaction is different from the alternatives provided choose the thought that is nearest to your own. If you agree with more than one, choose the one which would run through your mind most often.) When you have chosen the thought, put a circle around the letter next to it.

There are no right or wrong answers. Work through the questions quite quickly and try to pick the thought that is nearest to your *immediate* reaction to the situation.

1. You are about to go into hospital for an operation on your back which has been giving you pain.

I think: A. It may not work
          B. It should work, but there may still be some pain
          C. I don't think there's much chance of it working
          D. It will be a success and I will be able to do all the things I used to do

2. Some close friends will be moving away to a different town.

I think: A. With some effort we can still be friends
   B. It's likely that we won't be so friendly now
   C. It won't change anything
   D. I shall never see them again

3. You meet friends whom you haven't seen for a long time.

I think: A. I wonder if they still like me
   B. It's good to see old friends
   C. They won't like me any more
   D. They like me a lot

4. You manage to deal with a difficult problem at work.

I think: A. I am a capable person
   B. I wonder how I managed it
   C. I have some abilities
   D. This was just luck

5. Something goes wrong with your work.

I think: A. Nobody will mind, it happens to everyone
   B. This job is too difficult for me
   C. It was just a mistake, I can correct it
   D. I must be more careful

6. You are promised a large pay rise next year.

I think: A. I look forward to it eagerly
   B. It will probably not happen
   C. If it happens I shall be pleased
   D. It's better not to make plans as it might not happen

7. Next year you will have saved enough money for your dream holiday.

I think: A. It should be good fun
   B. I don't think it's going to be enjoyable
   C. It may be a disappointment
   D. I will have a fabulous time

8. You fall out with friends over some minor matters.

I think: A. They still like me
          B. I don't have the knack to keep friends
          C. I should be more careful with friends
          D. They probably won't mind

9. You attend a family reunion.

I think: A. It is nice to see some of the family again
          B. This may not be a good idea
          C. Family reunions are generally disastrous
          D. They are very happy to see me

10. You are told that you won't get a pay increase this year.

I think: A. I will probably lose my job
          B. I will get one next year
          C. I may not have one for a long time
          D. I wonder when I will get one

11. A person you admire tells you he/she likes you.

I think: A. I am glad he/she likes me
          B. People sometimes say that without really meaning it
          C. I am a very likeable person
          D. I cannot believe that I am likeable

12. You go out with some new people and you have a marvellous time.

I think: A. I did not contribute much
          B. It was all because of them
          C. I might have contributed something
          D. I helped to make it go alright

13. You cannot go on holiday because of unforeseen circumstances.

I think: A. This is an unfortunate coincidence
          B. Why do problems like this happen to me
          C. It really does not matter
          D. There are always obstacles in my way whatever I want to do

14. A close friend has an argument with you.

I think: A. This is a major blow to our friendship
          B. Our friendship will suffer a bit temporarily
          C. It won't make any difference to our friendship
          D. This friendship is ruined for good

15. The roof of your house starts leaking.

I think: A. There are too many problems for me to deal with
          B. It will be no problem to get it repaired
          C. This is another problem which I must try to deal with
          D. Maybe it could be repaired soon

16. You will have to meet some relatives whom you don't get on with.

I think: A. This is going to be absolutely awful
          B. It shouldn't be too bad
          C. We shall probably get on better this time
          D. This will be rather uncomfortable

17. You are unable to deal with a problem at work and have to ask for help.

I think: A. I often find it difficult to cope with problems
          B. I find it difficult to cope with some problems
          C. I am a failure
          D. These sorts of problems are always easier with help

18. You do not manage to finish a piece of work on time.

I think: A. I should have tried harder
          B. I am just lazy and inept
          C. I have tried my best
          D. Maybe I could have tried harder

19. Things are going well at work.

I think: A. This job is just right for me
          B. This job is not interesting
          C. This job may be right for me
          D. This job may be too easy

20. You are obliged to move out of your home and you are looking for a new flat/house.

I think: A. I shall soon find what I'm looking for
          B. I'll never find anything as good as what I've got
          C. I may have to settle for something less than I want
          D. It's unlikely that I'll find something suitable

21. You will be starting a new job which involves work you've always wanted to do.

I think: A. I will probably annoy people when I can't do it right straight away
          B. It may take a little while to settle in, but it will be OK
          C. I doubt that I will be able to do the work
          D. Everything should go smoothly

22. You help friends to do their garden. The next time you visit, they thank you enthusiastically.

I think: A. I am very good at this sort of thing
          B. They don't mean it
          C. Maybe I have some skills
          D. I don't deserve that much praise

23. A special dinner gets spoilt because the main dish is slightly burnt.

I think: A. Nothing ever goes right for me
          B. It can be easily remedied
          C. It had to happen today and nothing can be done about it
          D. Maybe it could be saved somehow

24. You invite some new friends round to your home for a meal.

I think: A. They probably won't enjoy it
          B. It may turn out well
          C. It will be nice to get to know them better
          D. It will be a good evening

25. You can at last make plans to redecorate your house.

I think: A. There are bound to be problems
          B. It will be beautiful when it's finished
          C. Something may interfere with the plans
          D. It should turn out nice

26. You try to make friends with some new neighbours, but they do not seem to care much.

I think: A. I may not be their type
          B. I have done all I can
          C. I am not a likeable person
          D. They may not like me

27. The other members of a local club choose you to be the new club secretary.

I think: A. This is a mixed blessing
          B. This is an impossible task/position
          C. It is an important and interesting position
          D. This position may be too difficult

28. You spill your drink over a friend's new carpet.

I think: A. I am always a clumsy person
          B. It could have happened to anybody
          C. I can be so clumsy at times
          D. I am not usually so clumsy

29. A surprise party is arranged by friends for your birthday.

I think: A. They meant well, but I have reservations
          B. This is a wonderful idea
          C. This is more trouble than it's worth
          D. Birthday parties are never enjoyable

30. You have planned to do certain jobs on Saturday and some old friends turn up unexpectedly to see you.

I think: A. This has completely ruined my plans
          B. This is great
          C. It is not a very suitable time
          D. It is a bit untimely but it's nice to see them

Scoring

The test consists of thirty statements: ten relating to view of the world, ten to view of self and ten to view of the future. Each group of statements consists of five pleasant and five unpleasant situations. The situations are randomly listed.

In the list below: S = self; W = world; F = future; U = unpleasant; P = pleasant

1. F/U	2. F/U	3. S/P	4. S/P
A. 3	A. 2	A. 3	A. 1
B. 2	B. 3	B. 2	B. 3
C. 4	C. 1	C. 4	C. 2
D. 1	D. 4	D. 1	D. 4

5. W/U	6. F/P	7. F/P	8. S/U
A. 1	A. 1	A. 2	A. 1
B. 4	B. 4	B. 4	B. 4
C. 2	C. 2	C. 3	C. 3
D. 3	D. 3	D. 1	D. 2

9. W/P	10. F/U	11. S/P	12. S/P
A. 2	A. 4	A. 2	A. 3
B. 3	B. 1	B. 3	B. 4
C. 4	C. 2	C. 1	C. 2
D. 1	D. 3	D. 4	D. 1

13. W/U	14. W/U	15. W/U	16. F/U
A. 2	A. 3	A. 4	A. 4
B. 3	B. 2	B. 1	B. 2
C. 1	C. 1	C. 3	C. 1
D. 4	D. 4	D. 2	D. 3

17. S/U	18. S/U	19. W/P	20. F/U
A. 3	A. 3	A. 1	A. 1
B. 2	B. 4	B. 4	B. 4
C. 4	C. 1	C. 2	C. 2
D. 1	D. 2	D. 3	D. 3

21. F/P	22. S/P	23. W/U	24. F/P
A. 3	A. 1	A. 4	A. 4
B. 2	B. 4	B. 1	B. 3
C. 4	C. 2	C. 3	C. 2
D. 1	D. 3	D. 2	D. 1

25. F/P	26. S/U	27. W/P	28. S/U
A. 4	A. 2	A. 2	A. 4
B. 1	B. 1	B. 4	B. 1
C. 3	C. 4	C. 1	C. 3
D. 2	D. 3	D. 3	D. 2

29. W/P	30. W/P
A. 2	A. 4
B. 1	B. 1
C. 3	C. 3
D. 4	D. 2

Norms

Depressed group (N = 20), (mean age forty-six years, s.d. 13.0), mean CST total = 70.3 (s.d. 10.8).

Non-depressed group (N = 20), (mean age forty-seven years, s.d. 13.0), mean CST total = 58.6 (s.d. 8.4) (Blackburn *et al.*, 1986)

APPENDIX D – DYSFUNCTIONAL ATTITUDE SCALE

Form A

Name: _____

Date: _____

This inventory lists different attitudes or beliefs which people sometimes hold. Read each statement carefully and decide how much you agree or disagree with it. For each statement, mark your answer using the number code given below that *best describes how you think*. To decide whether a given attitude is typical of your views, keep in mind how you think *most of the time*.

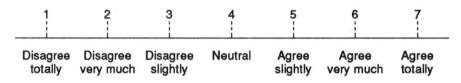

1	2	3	4	5	6	7
Disagree totally	Disagree very much	Disagree slightly	Neutral	Agree slightly	Agree very much	Agree totally

Statement   *Answer*

1. People will probably think less of me if I make a mistake
2. I must be a useful, productive, creative person or life has no purpose
3. I can find greater enjoyment if I do things because I want to, rather than in order to please other people
4. By controlling the way I interpret situations, I can control my emotions
5. If you cannot do something well, there is little point in doing it at all
6. What other people think about me is very important
7. People should prepare for the worst or they will be disappointed
8. I should be able to please everybody
9. Even though a person may not be able to control what happens to him, he can control how he thinks
10. It is shameful for a person to display his weaknesses
11. If a person has to be alone for a long period of time, it follows that he has to be lonely

12. A person should try to be the best at everything he undertakes
13. If a person is not a success, then his life is meaningless
14. It is not necessary for a person to become frustrated if he finds obstacles to getting what he wants
15. If I make a foolish statement, it means I am a foolish person
16. I should always have complete control over my feelings
17. I can enjoy myself even when others do not like me
18. If I do not set the highest standards for myself, I am likely to end up a second-rate person
19. If I do not do well all the time, people will not respect me
20. One should look for a practical solution to problems rather than a perfect solution
21. My value as a person depends greatly on what others think of me
22. A person should do well at everything he undertakes
23. If someone disagrees with me, it probably means he does not like me
24. I cannot be happy unless most people I know admire me
25. My own opinions of myself are more important than others' opinions of me
26. If I do not treat people kindly, fairly and considerately, I am a rotten person.
27. It is awful to be disapproved of by people important to you
28. If you do not have other people to lean on, you are bound to be sad
29. People will like me even if I am not successful
30. If other people know what you are really like, they will think less of you
31. Whenever I take a chance or risk I am only looking for trouble
32. If a person avoids problems, the problems go away
33. No one can hurt me with words. I hurt myself by the way I choose to react to people's words
34. Others can care for me even if they know all my weaknesses
35. If I fail partly, it is as bad as being a complete failure
36. People will reject you if they know all your weaknesses
37. I can reach important goals without slave-driving myself
38. My happiness depends more on other people than it does on me
39. If a person I love does not love me, it means I am unlovable
40. I ought to be able to solve my problems quickly and without a great deal of effort

Form B

Name: _____

Date: _____

This inventory lists different attitudes or beliefs which people sometimes hold. Read each statement carefully and decide how much you agree or disagree with it. For each statement, mark your answer using the number code given below that *best describes how you think*. To decide whether a given attitude is typical of your views, keep in mind how you think *most of the time.*

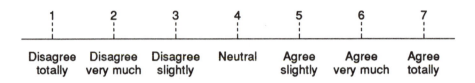

1	2	3	4	5	6	7
Disagree totally	Disagree very much	Disagree slightly	Neutral	Agree slightly	Agree very much	Agree totally

Statement   *Answer*

1. I can find happiness without being loved by another person
2. People who have the marks of success (good looks, fame, wealth) are bound to be happier than people who do not
3. I should be happy all the time
4. Turning to someone else for advice or help is an admission of weakness
5. If people consider me unattractive it need not upset me
6. I can be happy even if I miss out on many of the good things in life
7. If someone performs a selfish act, it means he is a selfish person
8. If I ask a question, it makes me look inferior
9. If a person is indifferent to me, it means he does not like me
10. Happiness is more a matter of my attitude towards myself than the way other people feel about me
11. People should have a reasonable likelihood of success before undertaking anything
12. It is possible to gain another person's respect without being especially talented at anything
13. You can be a happy person without going out of your way to please other people
14. It is not necessary to stop myself from doing something for my own welfare simply because it might displease another person
15. I can take responsibility only for what I do, not what other people do

16. People who have good ideas are more worthy than those who do not
17. If others dislike you, you cannot be happy
18. Taking even a small risk is foolish because the loss is likely to be a disaster
19. If I do not do as well as other people, it means I am an inferior human being
20. I may be able to influence other people's behaviour but I cannot control it
21. My life is wasted unless I am a success
22. If people whom I care about do not care for me, it is awful
23. If I fail at my work, then I am a failure as a person
24. A person should think less of himself if other people do not accept him
25. If I do well, it is probably due to chance; if I do badly, it is probably my own fault
26. People should be criticized for making mistakes
27. If I try hard enough I should be able to excel at anything I attempt
28. It is difficult to be happy unless one is good-looking, intelligent, rich and creative
29. I cannot trust other people because they might be cruel to me
30. I do not need the approval of other people in order to be happy
31. I should set higher standards for myself than other people
32. I am nothing if a person I love doesn't love me
33. A person should be able to control what happens to him
34. One can get pleasure from an activity regardless of the end result
35. A person doesn't need to be well liked in order to be happy
36. Being isolated from others is bound to lead to unhappiness
37. If a person asks for help, it is a sign of weakness
38. If I am to be a worthwhile person, I must be truly outstanding in at least one major respect
39. To be a good, moral person, I must help everyone who needs it
40. I must be a useful, productive, creative person or life has no purpose

Scoring

1. Every item on the DAS (Form A or Form B) is scored from 1–7. Depending on the content, items are scored in either direction (see below).

2. The following items are scored in the adaptive way if a response towards 'agree totally' is given.

   Form A: Items 3, 4, 9, 14, 17, 20, 25, 29, 33, 34 and 37

   Form B: Items 1, 5, 6, 10, 12, 13, 14, 15, 20, 30, 34, and 35

   That is, agree totally = 1; agree very much = 2; agree slightly = 3; neutral = 4; disagree slightly = 5; disagree very much = 6; disagree totally = 7.

3. All the other items on Form A and Form B of the DAS are scored in the reverse direction (ie: disagree totally = 1 . . . totally agree = 7).

4. If the individual omits a large proportion of the items, the test should be ignored.

Norms

Normal undergraduates (N = 355, mean = 119.4, s.d. = 27.2) (Weissman, 1979). DAS Form B endogenous depressives = 142.7 (39.7) non-endogenous depressives = 166.7 (38.1) (Robins *et al.*, 1990).

Major depressives (N = 35) in episode: mean = 147.45 and re-tested in remission, mean = 113.31 (Silverman *et al.*, 1984).

Major depressive group (N = 14) receiving cognitive therapy, before therapy = 160.3 (28.8) after therapy = 111.4 (44.6) (Simons *et al.*, 1984).

Group receiving tricyclic antidepressants (N = 14) before therapy mean DAS = 157.5 (29.2) after therapy 128.1 (51.3) (Simons *et al.*, 1984).

APPENDIX E – HOPELESSNESS SCALE

This questionnaire consists of a list of twenty statements (sentences). Please read the statements carefully one by one.

If the statement describes your attitude *for the past week, including today*, write down 'true' next to it. If the statement is false for you, write 'false' next to it. You may simply write T for 'true' and F for 'false'. Please be sure to read each sentence.

1. I look forward to the future with hope and enthusiasm
2. I might as well give up because there's nothing I can do about making things better for myself
3. When things are going badly, I am helped by knowing that they can't stay that way forever
4. I can't imagine what my life would be like in ten years
5. I have enough time to accomplish the things I most want to do
6. In the future I expect to succeed in what concerns me most
7. My future seems dark to me
8. I happen to be particularly lucky and I expect to get more of the good things in life than the average person
9. I just don't get the breaks, and there's no reason to believe that I will in the future

10. My past experiences have prepared me well for my future
11. All I can see ahead of me is unpleasantness rather than pleasantness
12. I don't expect to get what I really want
13. When I look ahead to the future I expect I will be happier than I am now
14. Things just won't work out the way I want them to
15. I have great faith in the future
16. I never get what I want so it's foolish to want anything
17. It is very unlikely that I will get any real satisfaction in the future
18. The future seems vague and uncertain to me
19. I can look forward to more good times than bad times
20. There's no use in really trying to get something I want because I probably won't get it

Scoring

One point is scored each time the respondent endorses the item in the following ways (maximum total = 20):

1.	F	8.	F	15.	F
2.	T	9.	T	16.	T
3.	F	10.	F	17.	T
4.	T	11.	T	18.	T
5.	F	12.	T	19.	F
6.	F	13.	F	20.	T
7.	T	14.	T		

Tentative cut-off scores

In Beck's clinic, each patient in a sample of suicide attempters was rated independently by a clinician for depth of hopelessness. This scale was also administered. The standard deviations and means for the groups categorized by clinician's ratings of hopelessness were computed, and the following tentative cut-off points for each category established.

0–3   = None or minimal
4–8   = Mild
9–14 = Moderate. May not be in immediate danger but requires frequent regular monitoring. Is the life situation stable?
15+   = Severe. Definite suicidal risk.

Beck, Weissman *et al.* (1974) reported a mean score of 9.0 (s.d. = 6.1) for 384 suicide attempters. Greene (1981) has reported a mean score of 4.45 (s.d. = 3.09) in a normal population (396 randomly selected adults). Further data are given in a paper by Nekanda-Trepka *et al.*, (1983).

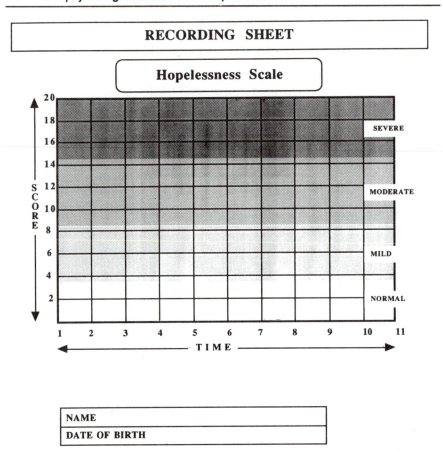

Figure 5.2 Possible format for daily or weekly recording of Hopelessness scores. Produced by the Psychology Department, Norwich Area Health Authority

APPENDIX F – SELF-CONTROL SCHEDULE

Indicate how characteristic or descriptive each of the following statements is of you by using the code given.

+3 very characteristic of me, extremely descriptive
+2 rather characteristic of me, quite descriptive
+1 somewhat characteristic of me, slightly descriptive
−1 somewhat uncharacteristic of me, slightly undescriptive
−2 rather uncharacteristic me of, quite undescriptive
−3 very unchatacteristic of me, extremely undescriptive

Statement   *Answer*

1. When I do a boring job, I think about the less boring parts of the job and the reward that I will receive once I am finished.

2. When I have to do something that is anxiety arousing for me, I try to visualize how I will overcome my anxieties while doing it.

3. Often by changing my way of thinking I am able to change my feelings about almost everything.

4. I often find it difficult to overcome my feelings of nervousness and tension without any outside help.*

5. When I am feeling depressed I try to think about pleasant events.

6. I cannot avoid thinking about mistakes I have made in the past.*

7. When I am faced with a difficult problem, I try to approach its solution in a systematic way.

8. I usually do my duties quicker when somebody is pressing me.*

9. When I am faced with a difficult decision, I prefer to postpone making a decision even if all the facts are at my disposal.*

10. When I find that I have difficulties in concentrating on my reading, I look for ways to increase my concentration.

11. When I plan to work, I remove all the things that are not relevant to my work.

12. When I try to get rid of a bad habit, I first try to find out all the factors that maintain this habit.

13. When an unpleasant thought is bothering me, I try to think about something pleasant.

14. If I smoked two packets of cigarettes a day, I probably would need outside help to stop smoking.*

15. When I am in a low mood, I try to act cheerful so my mood will change.

16. If I had the pills with me, I would take a tranquillizer whenever I felt tense and nervous.*

17. When I am depressed I try to keep myself busy with things that I like.

18. I tend to postpone unpleasant duties even if I could perform them immediately.*

19. I need outside help to get rid of some of my bad habits.*

20. When I find it difficult to settle down and do a certain job, I look for ways to help me settle down.

21. Although it makes me feel bad, I cannot avoid thinking about all kinds of possible catastrophes in the future.*

22. First of all I prefer to finish a job that I have to do and then start doing the things I really like.
23. When I feel pain in a certain part of my body, I try not to think about it.
24. My self-esteem increases once I am able to overcome a bad habit.
25. In order to overcome bad beliefs that accompany failure, I often tell myself that it is not so catastrophic and that I can do something about it.
26. When I feel that I am too impulsive, I tell myself 'Stop and think before you do anything'.
27. Even when I am terribly angry at somebody, I consider my actions very carefully.
28. Facing the need to make a decision, I usually find out all the possible alternatives instead of deciding quickly and spontaneously.
29. Usually I do first the things I really like to do even if there are more urgent things to do.*
30. When I realize that I cannot help but be late for an important meeting, I tell myself to keep calm.
31. When I feel pain in my body, I try to divert my thoughts from it.
32. I usually plan my work when faced with a number of things to do.
33. When I am short of money, I decide to record all my expenses in order to plan more carefully for the future.
34. If I find it difficult to concentrate on a certain job, I divide the job into smaller segments.
35. Quite often I cannot overcome unpleasant thoughts that bother me.*
36. Once I am hungry and unable to eat, I try to divert my thoughts away from my stomach or try to imagine that I am satisfied.

*Scored in reverse direction

Norms

Test–retest reliability: 0.86.

Internal consistency (alpha coefficients): 0.78 –0.81.

Normative data (Rosenbaum, 1980) for thirty-six-item version: Israeli students, means for five samples ranged between 23.1 (s.d. 21.4) and 27.2 (s.d. 25.1).

American students (males) 25.9 (s.d. 20.6) (females) 27.5 (s.d. 20.6).

Depressed patients (end of treatment scores for those who subsequently relapsed) mean = 3.9, N = 16 (s.d. 28.3) (end of treatment scores for those who remitted) mean = 35.96, N = 28 (s.d. 31.6) (Simons *et al.*, 1986).

For depressed patients N = 42 meeting criteria for major depressive episode in the DSM III diagnostic system (ninteen males and twenty-three females, age range twenty-two to sixty years), mean = 40.1. In episode Self-Control Schedule mean = 13.1 (22.69), then following nine two-hour group therapy sessions of cognitive therapy, mean = 6.17 (25.92) (Kavanagh and Wilson, in press).

Chapter 6

Treatment techniques I
Overview, basic behavioural techniques and symptom management

OVERVIEW OF THE COGNITIVE–BEHAVIOURAL THERAPY 'PACKAGE'

A large growth in interest in Beck's cognitive-behavioural therapy (CBT) took place in the 1970s. This is surprisingly late given the fact that Beck himself had been writing about a cognitive theory of affective disorders for some years (Beck, 1963; 1964; 1967). Many factors probably contributed to the sudden large growth of interest, but two seem to be of especial importance. Firstly, psychologists working with *anxious* patients had begun to describe the importance of taking the 'thoughts' or 'self-talk' of patients into account (Lang, 1971; Meichenbaum, 1974; Rachman, 1976), and cognitive behaviour modification for these patients became respectable (Meichenbaum, 1977). Secondly, Seligman's theory of learned helplessness, the origins of which had been animal experiments in 1967 (Overmier and Seligman, 1967; Seligman and Maier, 1967), but whose theory was most fully propounded in his book in 1975, gave a coherent 'cognitive' account of some depressive states. Most of Seligman's early work was experimental rather than clinical, and the clinical implications of helplessness theory poorly worked out. Suggestions such as giving patients a sense of control, through, for example, success experience, were made, but (a) much of the evidence was from studies using analogue student populations; (b) therapeutic strategies were not outlined in sufficient detail to be of practical use to clinicians and (c) none of the suggestions, if successful, would have uniquely supported the theory on which they were based, so the impetus to carry out detailed clinical anti-helplessness work was lacking. None of this hindered helplessness theory itself from becoming very widely known, accepted and extensively researched (see Abramson *et al.* (1978) for a review). Against the background of an attractive theory with few therapy strategies linked to it, psychologists were bound to look with greater urgency to existing approaches for the treatment of depression, and Beck's cognitive therapy was there to fill the vacuum. (See Seligman (1981) for his account of the overlap and differences between anti-helplessness interventions and CBT.)

The underlying assumption of cognitive theory of depression is that the patient's emotional disturbance follows from distortions in thinking, so that change in the patient will be long-lasting only if changes in thinking patterns occur during treatment. In other treatments, this change may occur incidentally (as a side-effect of psycho-dynamic or pharmacological intervention), but in CBT the thinking-style is met and dealt with 'head on'. A range of behavioural and cognitive techniques are used for this purpose. The term 'cognitive therapy' is misleading in that it sounds like one specific therapy; it is not. Many of the techniques are very familiar to the behavioural therapist (assertion training, task assignment). It is the way they are introduced to the patient and used in therapy which provides a common and distinctive theme to the therapy sessions and to the techniques which are to be reviewed here.

Several core techniques are used to serve the common purpose of: (a) eliciting the patient's thoughts, self-talk and interpretations of events; (b) gathering with the patient, evidence for or against the interpretations; and (c) setting up experiments (homework) to test out the validity of the interpretations and gather more data for discussion.

Particularly, CBT focuses on errors in thinking which habitually occur in depressives, for example:

1. Dichotomous thinking: black/white, all or nothing thinking, where there is no perceived middle path – just the extremes.
2. Selective abstraction: the selecting out of small parts of a situation and ignoring others. For example, a tutor's report on your essay gives much praise, but mentions at one point that the introduction was too long. 'He doesn't like my essay' would be selective abstraction.
3. Arbitrary inference: where a conclusion is inferred from irrelevant evidence. For example, you phone your girlfriend and no one answers. 'She's probably out with another partner' would be arbitrary inference (if inferred on those grounds alone).
4. Overgeneralization: to conclude from one specific negative event that another negative event is thereby more likely, e.g. failure at maths means failure at everything.
5. Catastrophizing: to think the very worst of a situation. Each of the above examples would suffice.

It is an active therapy in which the therapist deliberately seeks to collaborate with the patient, with therapy concentrating mainly on the 'here and now'. The past is introduced only so far as it helps to explain habitual modes of thinking and behaviour in the present.

INDICATIONS FOR USE

Beck *et al.* (1979) recommend standard physical treatments for bipolar depressives, highly regressed or highly suicidal patients. Early research in both the USA and UK (see Chapter Four) has so far concentrated on unipolar non-psychotic outpatients and primary care patients (though many of Blackburn's Edinburgh patients were 'endogenous' depressives by Spitzer's criteria). More recent research (reviewed separately in Chapter Eight) has extended cognitive and behavioural therapy to more chronic and severely depressed inpatients.

OVERALL STRATEGY

CBT for outpatients is normally limited to fifteen to twenty sessions of fifty minutes each, once weekly, though for more severely depressed patients sessions are held twice weekly for the first four to five weeks. It is interesting to note that in Blackburn *et al.*'s study, patients were considered 'non-responders' if their Beck *or* Hamilton Scores had not dropped by 50 per cent after twelve weeks of treatment.

OUTLINE PLAN OF THERAPY

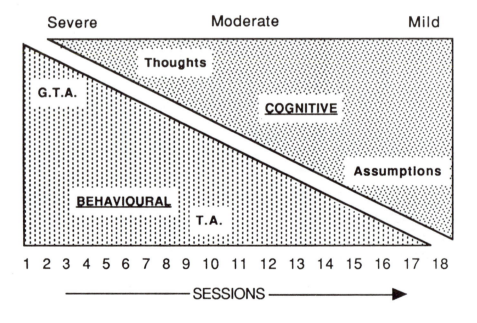

SEVERITY OF DEPRESSION

Figure 6.1 Diagrammatic representation of relative proportion of cognitive and behavioural techniques used as a function of stage in therapy and/or severity of depression

Note: G.T.A. = graded task assignment; T.A. = task assignment

Figure 6.1 shows a general treatment plan. It conveys the idea that the overall approach is partly behavioural and partly cognitive and that the more severe the depression at the outset of therapy (as defined by clinical judgement or questionnaires such as Beck or Hamilton), the greater weight is given to behavioural techniques. A less severe depression would start with both facets (e.g. equivalent of Session 6 in diagram). Finally, it illustrates that within each component, the progression is from the simple to the complex. Within the behavioural component, this involves grading tasks before assignment – splitting, for example 'housework' into cooking, dusting, ironing, mending, etc., and 'studying' into getting books together, allocating time for study, tidying desk, reading a limited number of pages, and so on. Even within this list, any one item may itself have to be split up into subcomponents. Within the cognitive component, the progression is from discussion of simple 'thoughts' and obvious interpretive errors to more complex 'assumptions' on which the patient's attitudes are premised.

In the sections that follow, specific techniques are described in detail. The clinician who is new to cognitive therapy might also like to look at Chapter Nine where some training exercises are presented for use by themselves or in training groups.

GENERAL CHARACTERISTICS OF THERAPY SESSIONS

There are certain general characteristics of cognitive therapy which give structure to each session.

First, the therapist establishes an agenda. The therapist reviews with the patient points that they wish to be discussed in that session. This may take up to ten minutes at the outset of the session, and may include review of previous week's homework. Substantive issues arising from homework may, however, form a major part of the entire session.

Second, the therapist structures the therapy time. This involves covering the issues on the agenda, and assigning time next session for discussion of those issues not discussed. The therapist attempts to keep a balance between central and peripheral issues so that the latter don't predominate.

Third, the therapist summarizes periodically during the interview, and elicits patient's reactions to the summary. The therapist deliberately seeks the patient's guidance on where he/she may have misinterpreted any aspect of the patient's problem.

Fourth, the session is dominated by a questioning approach by the therapist. Statements of fact or offering advice are not thought to be therapeutic.

Finally, the therapist does two things: (a) assigns homework based on topics that have emerged during the session as problematic; and (b) asks patient to sum up the session and go over what the homework assignment is. The patient is encouraged to indicate any points at which the topics discussed have been (in)appropriate, hurtful or helpful.

There are many techniques used in CBT which are used in other treatments – task assignment, assertive training, relaxation, role-play, reattribution training, etc. The distinctive thing about CBT is the way in which the techniques are used. Cognitive therapists call the overall strategy 'collaborative empiricism'. In reading through the techniques below, be aware of the ways in which the cognitive therapist attempts to keep the collaboration in the forefront of the discussion, and keeps the entire interaction empirical.

GETTING STARTED – CLARIFYING THE PROBLEMS

The aim of the first one or two sessions of cognitive behaviour therapy is to work with the patient in clarifying the nature of their problems, to agree on a formulation which will take account of past and present vulnerability, precipitating factors and maintenance factors. A second aim is to inform the patient about the therapy and agree on a treatment plan. As part of this assessment, many therapists make use of the scales and inventories given in Chapter Five. As I remarked then, such scales can be very useful in their quick but comprehensive review of a wide range of symptoms. Often they will refer to symptoms patients are experiencing (e.g. concentration problems), but which they have explained in terms of their own stupidity or in terms of an impending dementia. Such assessment can then allow the patient to become aware that these are common symptoms of depression. This itself may be a source of relief for them. It is surprising how little is explained to patients about the signs and symptoms of depression by professionals they have consulted. For this reason, even when questionnaires are not used, an important aspect of the initial sessions of cognitive behaviour therapy will be a systematic enquiry about symptoms, and asking the patient if there is anything they do not understand about their experience or behaviour.

GENERAL BEHAVIOURAL ASSESSMENT

The following assessment format may be used as a structured interview or as a checklist, and corroborative evidence may be sought from spouse, relatives or friends where necessary and appropriate:

1. Background data
   – Who lives with patient?
   – Previous psychiatric treatment (including hospitalizations) and results
   – Age, marital status, family status, social class
2. Problems
   – Onset, current frequency, intensity, duration, inappropriate form, inappropriate occasions
   – Behavioural excesses (motivation to reduce?)

    – Behavioural deficits (motivation to increase?)

    – Which of the last two aspects most bothers the patient? Which would they like to work on first?

3. Assets and strengths (now, in recent past and in distant past)

    – Appearance, dress, etc.

    – Self-help skills

    – Social (including conversation, recreation, friendship, clubs, church?)

    – Work

    – Educational, vocational training

4. Functional analysis of problems

    – What are consequences of current problems? What would difference be if problem did not exist? Therapist notes potential loss of rewarding consequences if problem removed.

    – Who persuaded patient into treatment? Or was it self-initiated? Does patient acknowledge problems and desire treatment?

    – What are the S^Ds (discriminative stimuli: conditions, settings) which serve as occasions for occurrence of problems? Where? When? With whom? (Alternative strategy: when does problem *not* occur? Where? When? With whom?)

5. Reinforcement survey

    – What does the patient find rewarding? People/places/things/food/activities (now-past)

    – What does patient find unpleasant? People/places/things/food/activities (now-past)

(NB. Take into account your own observations of patient and those of significant others and not only self-report.)

6. Medical

    – Medical/surgical problems and limitations to activity

    – Date of last physical examination

    – Name/address of general practitioner

    – Current medical treatment and drugs (psychotropic and others)

    – Family history of significant psychological problems

7. Social – interpersonal (recent and past)

    – Recent changes in milieu (change job, house, conflict in family)

    – Recent changes in social relationships (friend leaves area, etc. as well as separation, divorce), deaths

    – Other recent traumas and stresses

    – (What *losses* has the patient sustained in their own mind, even if not in reality?)

    – What changes were there when patient was a child/adolescent/young adult in environment (e.g. move house, school); in relationships inside/outside family?

    – How did patient react?

    – Other past stressors (and reactions to them)

8. Patient's own view of problems
   - How have they explained their problems to themselves? What is their theory? How have they come to that conclusion?
   - How much do they know about clinical depression? What has been their source of information – books, family, friends, voluntary agencies, GPs, former psychiatrists and psychologists? Evaluate extent to which patient is clinging to previous advice and formulations they have been given, e.g. that they have a 'biochemical depression'.
   - How much do they know about cognitive-behavioural theories and strategies? What are their expectations of therapy (style, length, outcome)?
9. Formulation of behavioural goals (be specific)
   - Which desirable behaviour to increase (include strengthening assets)? Short term (one month) long term (three months)?
   - Which undesirable behaviours to decrease (include self-talk component)? Short term/long term?
   - Treatment techniques and interventions
   - Recording and monitoring procedure: diaries, etc.; self-report inventories; observational (by therapist or spouse/friend)?

Clearly some of these issues will need to be explored more extensively than others, and supplementary questions asked. The nature of the questioning will vary depending on the psychological sophistication of the patient. To avoid seeming inquisitorial, the therapist may move freely between topics, rather than follow the scheduled questions in set order. However, it will be useful to check with this assessment format after assessment session(s) to see what has been missed and needs to be asked next session.

THE PROVISIONAL FORMULATION

One of the first collaborative exercises between patient and therapist is to produce a provisional formulation. Having asked questions about the past and current problems, and having asked the patient what his or her theory is, it should be possible to agree on a model which captures, fairly succinctly, what the problems are, and how they have developed and are maintained. If it is to be helpful, this formulation will include a description of most of the following:

1. Long-term vulnerability factors, such as temperamental factors (e.g. shyness, tendency to withdraw) and early experience (e.g. actual or threatened loss).
2. Short-term vulnerability factors, such as difficulty in relationships, jobs or housing problems.
3. Immediate precipitants, such as illness, job loss, separation.

4. Maintaining factors, such as low mood, lack of interest in social contacts, irritability with close family members, etc.

It may be helpful to use simple diagrams on which the important pieces of information are written. Such a diagram becomes the map to which both patient and therapist may refer in generating a treatment plan.

EXPLAINING THERAPY AND THE COGNITIVE MODEL

It is easy to forget that patients may know little or nothing about what to expect in psychotherapy. Most therapists see many patients; most patients see very few therapists and you may be their first. What would you want to know if you were embarking on such a novel and perhaps frightening experience? (Remember that most patients' knowledge of psychotherapy may have come from films, books, radio and television; not always the most helpful sources.) If you were the patient, you would at least want to know how often you will meet your therapist, for how long each time, for how many sessions. You would find it helpful to know what was expected of you. It would certainly help you to make a decision about the therapy to know that it emphasized self-help, that it was collaborative, emphasizing skills in solving problems, and that others who had similar problems had found it helpful. You would also find it helpful to know that homework and task assignments would be given to discover more about your problems and find out which approaches would work best for you to learn to cope with them.

In explaining the cognitive model of emotional problems to people, it is helpful to use examples from their own experience. It is also important to check often that the patient understands and has a chance to challenge what is being said if it doesn't quite fit their experience. You may like to start by saying that depression affects people differently, but there are often some common features. It affects your body (sleep, eating, sex, how much energy you have); it affects your behaviour (reluctance to join in anymore, losing interest in hobbies, friends); and it affects your mind (memory, remembering to do things, concentration). Check how much of this is true of the patient. But as if this wasn't bad enough, depression often affects the way people think about themselves and their world. It makes people interpret everything negatively. It is as if depression causes a steady stream of propaganda which convinces people it is their fault, that they are no good, that no one could possibly like them. Check for an example of these issues from the patient's own experience; explore these themes with their own examples; ask what their reaction would have been to these particular examples if they had not been depressed at the time to explore what difference depression makes.

The explanation may then continue as follows:

Psychologists and psychiatrists have known for a long time that when people get depressed their experience gets distorted in this way but it was always assumed that it was a mere symptom of depression. One just had to wait until the depression went away. Alternatively you could treat the depression with anti-depressants – this does indeed seem to get rid of the depression quite effectively for some people (though it often returns).

Recently however, it has been found that you don't have to wait for the depression to lift. Therapists have developed techniques called cognitive therapy ('cognitive' because it's about how we think). This therapy teaches people how to notice the negative propaganda. It teaches you how to tell which are accurate and which are just exaggerations. After a while it teaches you how to challenge the thoughts and begin to do again those things you have been avoiding doing. Different people find different things helpful, so we will need to work together to find what works best for you. It may be hard work, but it is worth it. Sometimes the depression has gone on for so long people can't imagine what it would be like to be free of it. (Ask about what it would be like for them to be free of depression. What would they do? How would daily life be different?).

We have already looked at some things in your life which have caused you problems (refer to formulations). At the end of this session (or next session) we shall work together to get a list of the problems you'd like to tackle during therapy. Therapy usually lasts twelve to fifteen weeks, but often we review things after four weeks so both of us can see how we're getting on.

The therapist should pause at appropriate points in the explanation to ask if the patient has any questions.

Finally, the therapist mentions again that the therapy teaches new skills and that this will involve homeworks as a centrally important aspect:

Much of this homework will need to be monitored by you in a simple way so that the ideas and difficulties you experience can be recorded when they occur. Don't rely on memory – it may forget something important. Each session we shall begin by setting an agenda for that session which includes a review of homework and anything else you or I want to bring up. Before each session finishes, we shall summarize what we've been doing and agree on homework for the following week. You can suggest ideas for homeworks. Indeed, it is better if they come more from you than me. But don't worry if you can't, there are things which others have found helpful that I can suggest that you try, but you may have to adapt it to your own situation.

Clearly, this information does not have to be given in one large chunk as I have reproduced it, but before therapy proper starts, it may be worth checking that the following has been done:

1. Assessment of background: problems; assets and strengths; functional analysis; reinforcement survey; medical aspects; social and interpersonal

(past); social and interpersonal (present); patient's own view of their problems.

2. Provisional formulation: long-term vulnerability factors; short-term vulnerability factors; precipitating factors; maintaining factors.

3. Explanation of therapy: specific problems to be tackled in therapy; patient's understanding of cognitive model of emotional problems and how it fits their own case; patient understanding of scope and type of therapy; number of sessions; length of sessions; need for targets and homeworks.

BEHAVIOURAL DIARY

Most cognitive-behaviour therapists find it useful to supplement within-session assessment by asking patients to keep a daily diary. The items to be included in such a diary will depend on individual therapist and patient. I have found the format in Table 6.1 to be useful because it includes self-ratings of feelings (Questions 1 and 2), somatic symptoms (3 and 4), and target behaviour (5–7).

Table 6.1 Diary (to be completed each night before going to bed)

Name .... Today's date ....

1. How anxious/tense have you been today?

0	1	2	3	4	5	6	7	8	9	10
Not at all				Moderately						Extremely

2. How depressed have you been today?

0	1	2	3	4	5	6	7	8	9	10
Not at all				Moderately						Extremely

3. How has your appetite been today?

0	1	2	3	4	5	6	7	8	9	10
Very poor				Moderate						Very good

4. How did you sleep *last* night?

0	1	2	3	4	5	6	7	8	9	10
Very badly				Moderately						Very well

5. How long did you spend .... today? ....
   (or) How many times did you .... today? ....
   How did you cope with .... today? ....%

6. How long did you spend .... today? ....
   (or) How many times did you .... today? ....
   How did you cope with .... today? ....%

7. How long did you spend .... today? ....
   (or) How many times did you .... today? ....
   How did you cope with .... today? ....%

Any other comments

MASTERY AND PLEASURE

In the case of any type of diary, it is often useful to ask the patient to rate each activity for how much a sense of mastery (M) or pleasure (P) they felt. 'Mastery' refers to a feeling of accomplishment, a sense that something has been achieved, even if the activity itself was not pleasurable. Often, activities such as mowing the lawn, clearing out a cupboard, writing a letter or paying a bill give very little pleasure in themselves. At the end of each activity, however, something in the world has changed by virtue of the action of the patient. If the patient is gradually to regain a sense of control over events (to reverse their learned helplessness), then there will need to be such activities scheduled into the daily routine. Activities which may give a sense of pleasure (walking, watching TV, talking to a friend) do not necessarily give a feeling of mastery. That is why it needs to be discussed and assessed separately.

'Pleasure' is easier for patients to understand. They are well aware that fewer activities give them pleasure now than used to be the case. But note the importance of the diary in rating this aspect. A diary allows them to rate activities for pleasure when they actually occur, rather than relying on memory for whether something was pleasurable. This is important because, later, depressed mood or negative experiences can overshadow and cancel out an earlier activity that was genuinely pleasurable. Often the person will rate an activity as not having been pleasurable when in fact it might have been. If there is a discrepancy between a patient's diary, and how they later report the event, then it is useful to use this as an opportunity to discuss how memory can be biased.

Note also that many patients report that something is not pleasurable simply because the good feelings they had when they were doing it do not last. This is an opportunity to encourage the patient to distinguish between feeling pleasure while doing the task (which is followed by depression when they stop) on the one hand, and not experiencing pleasure while doing the task, on the other. These are different problems, and will need different strategies. The first is often mistaken for the second.

I will now describe some basic behavioural techniques which can be used towards the beginning of therapy to get things started. In each case I shall give the rationale and overall aim of the technique before outlining what is actually done in therapy. Where relevant, I mention potential problems with the technique or a comment on it using case examples. Note that these techniques have been used by psychologists outside the cognitive therapy tradition, so I have decided to retain their original rationale. Some therapists may wish to adapt the technique so they more easily fit in with the cognitive framework.

TEACHING THE INDIVIDUAL TO SELF-REINFORCE

Rationale

Depression results where a person's behaviour has become ineffective in securing rewards from their environment, because of alterations in the reinforcement schedule or changes in significant discriminative stimuli under which behaviours were typically emitted. This leads depressed people to have overly high criteria for self-reward and too low criteria for self-punishment. However, with many individuals it is not possible to remedy this situation by changing their environment. The individual may have few friends or other people available, willing or able to give such rewards.

Aim of treatment

The aim is to teach the patient to self-administer rewards contingent upon performing a pre-established response, in the absence of direct social influence.

Procedure

1. Assessment phase:
   – Behavioural assessment (see p. 114).
   – List everyday tasks.
   – Select one item which is performed frequently and patient considers important.
2. Baseline phase (ten days) Instruct patient to keep three records (completed each night before retiring):
   – Total amount of time that day spent doing any subcomponent of selected task.
   – Rate depression according to patient's own criteria on a predetermined scale.
   – Record number of rewards patient self-administers for that task. (Definition of reward: 'praising yourself, doing something you like, feeling contented as a consequence of doing activity'.)
3. Treatment phase
   – Explain to patient the role of self-reward in general, and particularly its role in maintaining behaviour for which external rewards are available only infrequently.
   – Split up selected task into subcomponents – take each separately and help patient to outline what they want to accomplish. What does 'completion' of that component mean? How long do they estimate it will take?
   – Help patient to set appropriate (often lower!) goals, in order to

maximize the chances of successful completion.
- Encourage patient to write down each goal (being specific about what the performance criteria are) before starting the task (these diaries are useful for later reference by patient).
- Encourage patient to assess performance in light of what they had set out to do (see diary).
- If goals matched (or surpassed), tell patient to do something pleasant immediately. If there is a need to ensure that this self-reward takes place, give patient packet of counters or poker chips. Instruct patient to take as many as they feel they deserve up to ten, and to record number taken.
- Continue to monitor behaviour and mood (as baseline phase).
- Later sessions: generalize scheme to other behaviours. Drop use of counters/chips when patient efficient at self-evaluating and self-rewarding.

Example

Jackson (1972) gives the example of a twenty-two-year-old housewife, who, since getting married two years before had been depressed, and suffered feelings of worthlessness, had been inactive, and had constantly made self-derogatory statements. Despite this she was, by her husband's account, a 'meticulous housewife and excellent cook'. On questioning, the client herself 'knew' rationally that she did do things comparable to or better than her peers, but this knowledge was insufficient to shift her low moods. Even compliments by others had become discriminative stimuli for self-criticism. (Note here that a therapist might eventually wish to discuss with such a patient the extent to which her goals were being determined by her partner!)

The patient's list of activities to be increased were: relating to people; housekeeping; reading; talking to husband; watching TV; drawing.

She decided to select *housekeeping* as a *frequent* but *important* task. Splitting this up into subcomponents, she recorded how long she spent in washing dishes, drying dishes, dusting and so on for ten days. She also recorded frequency of self-reward, and the mood, each day.

In the treatment phase, therapist and patient decided that 'self-reward' should consist of doing something from a list of 'pleasant' or 'positive' things. For example she would compliment herself, or telephone an interesting friend, or have a cigarette. She was given a box of poker chips to start off with.

An appointment was arranged on Day 4 and Day 10 of the treatment phase to check progress. Gradually, the patient found that she was doing housework more efficiently, and had adopted a more easy-going attitude to it. This resulted in spending less time doing the housework. On her own initiative she started to apply the same principles of socializing, inviting friends to a meal, etc. by deciding exactly what goals she wanted to accomplish and then self-evaluating and self-reinforcing. At a follow-up two months later, the depression had subsided and the effects of the specific treatment technique had generalized to other areas of her life.

Comment

In the example given above, the problem involves a collusion between husband and wife to reinforce a passive, powerless role for the latter. This sort of issue occurs frequently in therapy and time should be set aside to discuss it. Nevertheless, it can be seen how the technique could be appropriate if clients live alone or the partner is unavailable or unable to dispense rewards appropriately.

Note that in Jackson's example, the self-monitoring (SM) phase (ten days baseline) did not itself produce any improvement in mood (though some clinicians would argue that SM is itself therapeutic). Of course, it is quite possible that the treatment phase would have been ineffective if it had not followed a period of SM.

Jackson considered two aspects of the treatment essential. First, requiring the person to administer the *tangible* reinforcer (points or tokens) at the same time as positive self-talk. He contends that 'it encourages the person to engage deliberately and overtly in the act of self-evaluation and self-reinforcement, and also provides the means of recording these behaviours'. Second, presenting ordered task assignments in which the probability of successful completion is maximized. In this respect, Jackson is following the behavioural therapists, though differing from the cognitive therapy approach somewhat which emphasizes the collection of thought data whether the task succeeded or failed.

One problem that often arises, not discussed by Jackson, is where the patient persistently refuses to self-reinforce, explaining away successes as being 'too easy', or 'anyone could have done that'. In these cases it is necessary to remind the patient that their goal was successful completion of that subcomponent. That is what then deserves the pre-arranged self-reward. It may be necessary to re-negotiate the tasks that are going to be attempted – re-specifying the behaviours so there is less room for ambiguity over the outcome. It may also be necessary to remind the patient that often depression affects these little tasks most, so that being able to improve them is an important step.

Finally, this technique is obviously more appropriate for those patients who have maintained some basic behaviours but who find them a great effort, rather than those who have stopped these altogether. For other techniques which aim to increase activity see Activity scheduling, Systematic resensitization, and Anticipation training.

ACTIVITY SCHEDULING – LEWINSOHN'S TECHNIQUE

Rationale

Depression is seen as being associated with schedules of positive reinforcement which are inadequate to maintain adaptive behaviour. Thus therapy needs to restore the level, quality and range of activities and interactions for the patient. Activity scheduling seeks to select carefully those activities of demonstrated reinforcement potential for an individual.

Aim of treatment

The aim is to increase the patient's frequency of engaging in activities that are likely to be reinforced by others or are intrinsically reinforcing for the patient.

Procedure

1. Assessment phase
   - Either ask the patient to list activities which were enjoyable, interesting, or gave a sense of accomplishment in the past; or use a previously derived activities list (see Table 6.2) or Pleasant Events Schedule (MacPhillamy and Lewinsohn, 1971). Alternatively, select targets from list used in assessment phase which the patient is able to endorse as having *once* been pleasant and enjoyable (Lewinsohn's own list may be particularly helpful here, see Table 6.3.)
   - Rate each item on list for pleasantness and frequency over past month
   - Select items from list which are rated as at least slightly pleasant, or use whole list if not too long
2. Baseline phase
   - Instruct patient to use list as basis of diary to be completed each evening before retiring, ticking each item which has been done if (and only if) it was at least slightly pleasant
   - Patient should rate mood at same time as completing diary
3. Treatment phase
   - Compute correlation between daily pleasant activity score and daily mood rating
   - Select those activities which are most frequently associated with good mood to use as targets
   - Instruct patient to engage in as many of these activities per day/week as possible

Table 6.2 Sample list of activities for activity scheduling

Activity	Past frequency	Past enjoyment	Present enjoyment	Present frequency
Buying new clothes				
Cooking a meal				
Gardening				
Going for bike ride				
Going for drive/ride				
Going for walk				
Going on the train				
Going out for a meal				
Going shopping				
Going to bingo				
Going to football match				
Going to pictures				
Going to pub/club				
Going to rugby match				
Jogging				
Knitting, sewing				
Playing musical instrument				
Reading				
Swimming				
Telling a joke				
Visiting friends				
Visiting relatives				
Watching TV				
Patient's own ideas for activities				

Table 6.3 Activities found by Lewinsohn to be associated with mood for 10 per cent of his sample (Lewinsohn and Graf, 1973)

Social interaction

Being with happy people
Having people show interest in what you have said
Being with friends
Being noticed as sexually attractive
Kissing
Watching people
Having a frank and open conversation
Being told I am loved
Expressing my love to someone
Petting, necking
Being with someone I love
Complimenting or praising someone
Having coffee, tea, a coke, and so on with friends
Being popular at a gathering
Having a lively talk
Listening to the radio
Seeing old friends
Being asked for my help or advice
Amusing people
Having a sexual relationship
Meeting someone new of the same sex

Incompatible affect

Laughing

Being relaxed

Thinking about something good in the future

Thinking about people I like

Seeing beautiful scenery

Breathing clean air

Having peace and quiet

Sitting in the sun

Wearing clean clothes

Having spare time

Sleeping soundly at night

Listening to music

Smiling at people

Seeing good things happen to my family or friends

Feeling the presence of the Lord in my life

Watching wild animals

Self-efficacy

Doing a project in my own way

Reading stories, novels, poems or plays

Planning or organizing something

Driving skilfully

Saying something clearly

Planning trips or vacations

Learning to do something new

Being complimented or told I have done well

Doing a job well

Miscellaneous

Eating good meals

Going to a restaurant

Being with animals

Comment

Activity scheduling of some sort is the most commonly used technique in cognitive-behaviour therapy. Notice how Lewinsohn and his colleagues take great trouble to establish the correlations between activity and mood before starting treatment.

For most clinical purposes it may not be necessary to go to such lengths, especially since it requires patients to go through a list of fifty activities each day, checking which they have done and found pleasurable. Over several days (Lewinsohn's baseline period is thirty) a computer or calculator is needed to give quick answers to the question of whether there is a correlation between mood and activity at all, and then, which activities are associated most with pleasant mood. There are usually only ten to twenty activities which are mood-related for any given subject. Lewinsohn reports that, in his studies, the average correlation between total number of pleasant activities and mood over a thirty-day period is about 0.3–0.4, but he also reports wide individual variation in the level of correlation from 0 to 0.75. Importantly, he then insists that increasing pleasant activity can only be expected to alleviate mood in those individuals in whom a reasonable level of activity/mood correlation has been found (Lewinsohn, 1975). What is the level at which one should proceed? Lewinsohn suggests levels of >0.3. But this is not the only restriction in using instructions to increase pleasant events as a treatment for depression. For clearly if someone is depressed and yet is engaging in a reasonable number of events from which they derive some pleasure, increasing these events may not have any effect. They already do these activities, yet their depression remains. In fact, Lewinsohn argues that increasing pleasant activities is only likely to work in those whose pleasant activities score emerges at 1 or 2 s.d. below the mean of a normal control group. Such a rule may be useful in research, but clinicians do not have normal data at their disposal with which to compare their patient's score. In any case, if the activity list is individually tailored for the patient, this precludes the use of any control data. Perhaps the clinician should take the message that if, in their judgement, their patient is engaging in very few pleasant activities, then the opportunity may exist to use Lewinsohn's technique in therapy.

A final word is needed about the activities list in Table 6.3. Lewinsohn has found these to be associated with mood for 10 per cent of his sample, and has observed that they fall into three categories – social, incompatible affect, and ego-supportive (self-efficacy). Note that some of these activities are essentially passive, e.g. 'being complimented'. It may be thought difficult for a patient actively to procure 'being complimented'. On the other hand, these items may lead to a discussion of where one is likely to be in a situation where one will be noticed, complimented, etc. 'Where did you use to go where you felt noticed?' Answers to this sort of question may lead to new targets being negotiated in order to maximize the chance of these events occurring. Secondly, other items on the list are not easy actively to procure, e.g. 'sleeping soundly at night'. Nevertheless this item is still useful as a diary measure. If it demonstrates a correlation with mood, it can show the patient how getting overtired can contribute to a problem, or how sleeping too much during the day often leads to bad nights which may lead to poor work next day.

ACTIVITY SCHEDULING – OTHER METHODS

Rationale

(as above)

Aim of treatment

The aim is as above, but often without the very careful baseline observations of Lewinsohn.

Procedure

Ask patient to provide lists of activities which they used to enjoy, or use lists in Tables 6.2 and 6.3. Choose, with patient, one or two activities as targets for the week.

The following method of generating pleasant activities from a patient's own experience was used by Anton *et al.* (1976).

Activity log

Name _____ Date _____

Direction: Take a few minutes and think back over what you did today. Select the eight most important activities of the day and list them below. If it seemed important to you, for whatever reasons, put it down. What seems like an important activity on one day may seem unimportant on another day. Don't worry about that. For each day, select the eight activities which seemed most important on that day, regardless of how they compare to activities on other days. After you have listed the activities, rate each activity using the seven-point scale: (extremely unpleasant) 1 2 3 4 5 6 7 (extremely pleasant)

Graded task assignment

Many therapy strategies urge caution in choosing activities as targets. Some suggest that targets be chosen to maximize the probability of successful completion. Grading tasks involves choosing targets in order of difficulty so that the patient starts with the easiest. However for some patients, even the most simple task seems too difficult, in which case the task must be split into subcomponents, with targeted activity being the completion of only one component. Ingenuity is often required to split tasks satisfactorily. In general, a task can be split in terms of *time* (e.g. only do ten minutes' work and then stop no matter how much/little you have done), in terms of *place* (only work in one place on that day); or in terms of *proportion* (don't try and do every assignment at one go).

It is sometimes useful for patients to write down the target just before starting the task, to reinforce the idea that they are to reward themselves following completion of a target as defined previously (rather than criticizing themselves for 'only' doing part of what they might have once considered an 'easy' task).

Cognitive therapy also makes use of graded task assignment to test out a person's negative thoughts (see p. 154).

SYSTEMATIC RESENSITIZATION (Sammons, 1974)

Rationale

Encouraging a patient to engage in a formerly enjoyable activity often causes *more* frustration and depression. This may be because the person has tried the activity while depressed and a counter-conditioning process has taken place so that the activity has become associated with depression. Indeed it may be that the more enjoyable an activity once was, the more *upset* an individual gets when they try to do it when depressed.

Aim of treatment

The aim is to *re*sensitize the individual to previously enjoyed activities in the same way as phobic patients are *de*sensitized to feared objects.

Procedure

1. Behavioural assessment – focus especially on previously enjoyed activities and feelings that result when any of these are tried.
2. Choose, with patient, one of these activities which is currently available to work on as a target.
3. Develop, with patient, a hierarchy of scenes associated with the activity – e.g. making plans to do it, getting dressed up, getting equipment (if sport, etc.), travelling to activity, meeting friend outside, going to door, entering, meeting one friend inside, meeting three friends inside, meeting crowd of friends inside, doing activity. Ask patient what was good about each stage of hierarchy.
4. Teach patient progressive relaxation.
5. Instruct patient to relax and form image of scenes at bottom of hierarchy. Attempt to get vivid image of anything that was good about this particular subcomponent – imagine pleasant feelings. Present scenes with a lot of 'positive suggestion' about 'feeling better'.
6. If at any stage the patient feels upset or uncomfortable about a scene, the imagining is stopped immediately, and the previous scene is imagined.
7. When patient can imagine the top of this hierarchy (i.e. the formerly *most* reinforcing aspect) without feeling uncomfortable, instruct patient to start *in vivo* work: first target: bottom of hierarchy, and so on up the hierarchy with instructions to leave the situation if there are any feelings of discomfort.
8. Continue to instruct patient to try activities for longer (etc.) up hierarchy until pleasant feelings are gained for activity.
9. Introduce other activities in same imagination – *in vivo* sequence.

Example

Sammons (1974) reports the use of this technique with a thirty-nine-year old depressed man. He had been hospitalized on five separate occasions with the shortest hospitalization being six months. During the past ten years, the patient had not remained out of hospital for more than nine months at a time. On initial assessment the patient was extremely lethargic, with no spontaneous speech and only seldom initiation of any activity.

Despite this he was able to list some things which had once been rein-forcing for him. These included 'shooting pool' and since there was a pool hall at the hospital, the therapist suggested he might attend on a couple of occasions. At the next session, the patient reported feeling worse after having tried to carry out the assignment.

Although the patient was reluctant to begin relaxation training, he agreed, and found he enjoyed it. It was at this time that Sammons decided to attempt to use the relaxation to 'resensitize' the patient to the previous reinforcers. Together they developed a 'pool shooting' hierarchy which ended with a scene of the patient having completed three consecutive games of pool. After inducing relaxation, these scenes were presented along with positive suggestions of 'feeling good, feeling better than he had in a long time'. If at any time the patient began to feel uncomfortable or depressed, the scene was terminated and the previous scene repeated. Gradually, *in vivo* ex-posure was introduced. The patient was invited to try to play the game for as long as he felt good, but to leave the area for at least thirty minutes if he felt at all uncomfortable or depressed. It was impressed upon him that the duration of contact with the activity was not as important as his participating in the activity only for as long as it was pleasant.

The first day the patient spent thirty seconds in the pool hall, then left. The second day he spent nine minutes. By the end of seven days, he was spending one hour a day playing the game. By this time, Sammons had started to use the same approach with the patient's television watching. General recovery was rapid, and the patient was soon discharged. After twelve months the patient was still well and out of hospital.

Comment

There is little doubt that Sammons' procedure contains an important insight – the inverse correlation that is found, for many patients, between former enjoyability of tasks and current enjoyability. This may be because non-depressed individuals tend to get most pleasure out of activities which take a lot of effort and concentration (two aspects which are most vulnerable to depressive breakdown). Or it may be that the more the expected enjoyment, the greater the frustration, which then becomes a contributor to the low mood. In any event, it is not an uncommon phenomenon, and because it baffles patients, deserves to be explained to them. One patient of mine had loved knitting before she became depressed, but as for sewing – she could 'take it or leave it' – finding it rather a bore. When I met her as a depressed inpatient, she found sewing her greatest ally – it was the only activity she found she could do. She reported that even looking at her knitting bag made her feel very low, and on the few occasions she had attempted to start knitting she had given up after a very few minutes, extremely frustrated and upset. Another patient, a young man who suffered bouts of severe depression and had made a very serious attempt on his life (it had failed only by accident), gave the following as his previously enjoyed activities: academic discussion (6), electronic gadgetry (4/5), travelling (10), countryside (8), special friend (8), girlfriend (10), being in good company (10), guitar (4/5), art in general (10).

The numbers in brackets represent a rating on a ten point scale of how much pleasure he used to get out of each. When asked to rank the activities for how much he felt able/willing to do each *now*, the rankings showed a strong inverse correlation. When asked which of these he currently did, the answer was playing the guitar and fiddling with electronic gadgets. Note again how the activities most easily performed are the ones which were previously the least rewarding.

In both cases the individuals were very relieved to know that this was quite common – for they had both felt hopeless about ever getting better partly on the grounds that if they didn't even enjoy their favoured activity, what hope was there of getting pleasure out of anything else.

So systematic resensitization contains a useful element. Furthermore this useful element may be exploited even if the patient does not find relaxation helpful. The hierarchical organization of targets is reminiscent of graded task assignment (though GTA does not advocate leaving the situation if unpleasant feelings arise), and the suggestion of pleasant feelings while covertly rehearsing the target activity is reminiscent of Beck's cognitive rehearsal. It may be the way in which these techniques overlap which explains why systematic resensitization has not, to my knowledge, been subjected to an extensive clinical study.

ANTICIPATION TRAINING (Anton *et al.*, 1976)

Rationale

Although increasing the quantity of reinforcement may be achieved by increasing the number of pleasant events the person experiences, depressed patients very often anticipate a negative outcome of such experiences, and direct their attention to the negative side of otherwise potentially pleasant events.

Aim of treatment

The aim is to modify the negative anticipations of depressed patients.

Procedure

1. First session
   – Behavioural assessment (see above).

– Give 'activity log' to the patient to be completed each night before retiring (see above, p. 128).

2. Second session
   – Focus on arranging for pleasant activities to happen. Patient to select six pleasant activities to be performed over the next two weeks. Three to involve the patient alone, three to involve other people. Each task to take at least ten to fifteen minutes to perform. Each task to be able to be performed most days.
   – Patient then to construct three positive anticipation statements for first scheduled activity (see Table 6.4). Instructed to close eyes, relax, imagine activity as if it were actually happening. Rehearse in mind three statements and create a vivid image of the feelings associated with the statements.
   – Continue repeating imagery and statements (covertly) until patient can identify a positive feeling while doing so.
   – Encouraged to do this for Activities 1 and 2 at home. Activity 1 scheduled to occur before third session.

Table 6.4 Activity schedule

---

1. Select six pleasant activities. The aim is to do these over the next two weeks. Three of these must be activities you do by yourself, and three activities you will do with someone else. Each should take more than ten to fifteen minutes to perform, but should be easily performed within the day.

2. Complete the following form for each activity.

   Activity planned: ....

   Date planned for: ....

3. Now complete the following sentences with three different statements.

   I will enjoy ....

   I will enjoy ....

   I will enjoy ....

4. Three times a day (morning, afternoon and before retiring), find a comfortable quiet place, relax, and imagine doing the planned activity. Say each of the three statements to yourself, and create a vivid image for each statement. Do this every day until the activity has been performed.

---

3. Third session
   – Activity 1 discussed and any problem associated with anticipation sequence reviewed.
   – Schedule Activity 3 and discuss anticipation statements. Patient to construct statement for Activity 4.
   – Activities 2 and 3 occur before Session 4.

4. Fourth session
   – Activities 2 and 3 anticipation practice reviewed.

- Activity 5 scheduled; patient to construct own anticipation statements for Activities 5 and 6, and actually schedule Activity 6 without assistance.
5. Fifth session
   - Review of anticipations and scheduling. If difficulty in motivation, instruct patient to image task *completed* and associated feelings.
6. Sixth session
   - Review of progress and of generalization of anticipation training to other behaviours.

Anton *et al.* provide some examples of the use of this technique with some depressed women. It may be interesting to see their examples of activities planned by their clients during treatment.

Alone	*With someone*
Have hair done	Go to a film
Spend an afternoon in town	Phone parents
Browse in antique shops	Take a friend to lunch
Spend three hours reading	Play tennis
Prepare a Chinese meal	Go out to dinner
Buy new towels	Have friend to dinner
Ride bicycle	Visit an art museum
Work in the garden	Go to the city
Drive to the beach	Take children to the zoo
Go to a lecture	Go to a concert
Buy a new plant	Spend an evening playing with
Browse in a bookshop	the children
Take a long walk	Go to a Health Club

Other activities, should the patient not be able to select any, could be selected from Lewinsohn's list, above.

Example

This is how a colleague of mine introduced anticipation training to a patient. He was a twenty-six-year-old chartered surveyor who had been referred specifically for cognitive-behavioural therapy for depression. His Beck score was 22, and he had particular problems with sleeping, loss of energy, fatigue, psychomotor agitation, loss of interest in sex, hobbies and social contacts, and a diminished ability to concentrate.

Therapist What I'd like you to do first is to make a list of things you used to do that you got pleasure from – that you're not doing now. Let's choose some in which your pleasure doesn't depend on other people getting pleasure from it – we can't control how other people will react.

Patient The first thing is going out for a drink in the evening. I used to do it a lot when I was a student.

Therapist That's a good one.

Patient I find I can't sit down and relax to watch TV – I do, but I can't switch off my negative feelings.

Patient and therapist finally decide on three activities for next week: a night in with my wife – just spending some time together; a night out at the cinema; go out to a local football match.

Therapist What I would like you to do is to prepare yourself for these activities – so that you set yourself up to enjoy them rather than setting yourself up not to enjoy them. Let's think about the football match (scheduled first). You've mentioned two things that could dampen it; one, you feel you ought to be working for your exams, and two, you feel bad about going out without your wife. Have there been any other negative thoughts about going?

Patient Yes. The two friends who've invited me have already passed the exam I'm struggling with – I've thought that I hope they don't talk shop.

Therapist What I want you to do with this first activity is to practice a technique that I'd like you to apply to the other two activities later on. First of all, can you list three things that you will enjoy about going to the match. Start off with 'I will enjoy'.

Patient The company of friends; watching the football.

Therapist Finally, 'I will enjoy . . . '

Patient An evening away from work.

Therapist Now what I'd like you to do in the next five minutes is to get as relaxed as you can – and to imagine all the things that are going to happen tonight. At any point when you get to any of the things that you've listed you will enjoy (being with friends, watching the football and not thinking about your work) let it enhance the scene. Imagine feeling the pleasure.

The patient was encouraged to use the technique at home, and it was discussed at subsequent sessions. Over the ensuing weeks, the following activities were successfully instituted using this method – three enjoyment statements listed in each case.

1. To go out for a drink with wife
   – I will enjoy the company of just the two of us.
   – I will enjoy being able to relax.
   – I will enjoy a change of environment.
2. To stay in one night with Frances – just spend the evening in each other's company
   – I will enjoy an evening in with Frances.
   – I will enjoy her company and she mine.
   – I will enjoy making love.

3. Staying in to watch TV – no revision
   - I will enjoy doing nothing that evening.
   - I will enjoy watching TV without thinking about work.
   - I will enjoy being able to relax with just my own company.
4. Going to a film with Frances
   - I will enjoy an evening out of the house.
   - I will enjoy getting absorbed in the film.
   - I will enjoy Frances being with me.
5. Going to football match
   - I will enjoy the company of friends.
   - I will enjoy watching the football.
   - I will enjoy the novelty of doing something other than work.

Comment

The problem with this strategy is what to do if the patient continually can't find the motivation to do the actual targeted behaviour. This may need discussion in itself though some therapists have suggested making therapist time contingent upon completion of activities.

Anton *et al.* themselves point out that it is better to choose activities which do not rely too heavily on other people's reaction in order to be pleasant for the patient. Furthermore, the patient must be able to be fairly sure that the activity itself is one that has given pleasure in the past, rather than choosing something which they are not sure will be pleasurable. However, in Anton's group of depressed patients (mean Lubin DACL score 66) a shift over six weeks to 49 (within nondepressed range) was noted.

It is doubtful whether anticipation training by itself would be sufficient to alleviate depression. In Anton *et al.*'s paper, many depressed clients asked for further counselling, despite the fact that the outcome measures showed a favourable response. It is not that such training is too short (though it may be) but that it is uncommon for the behavioural analysis (done at the assessment stage) to reveal no other problem than anticipation of events.

DESENSITIZATION

Rationale

Depression is sometimes associated with phobic reactions, and anxiety about certain situations may block progress by preventing the patient from engaging in activities which are potential reinforcers. Desensitization may thus be useful in conjunction with other techniques.

Aim of treatment

The aim is to alter phobic response patterns which restrict the patient's progress, by pairing feared situations (in imagination or *in vivo*) with relaxation.

Procedure

1. Behavioural assessment, as before, with the addition of a fear survey schedule which patient can use to list fears and phobias (see Table 6.5).
2. Select target situations which are to become focus of treatment, and discuss *in vivo* vs 'imagination' options with patient.
3. Construct hierarchy of anxiety-provoking situations or subcomponents/ aspects of situation.
4. Teach relaxation method.
5. Present situations/scenes in imagination or *in vivo* telling patient to relax when they signal experiencing any anxiety and continue imagining scene until patient can successfully imagine coping with the scene.

Table 6.5 A fear survey schedule

Leaving home or travelling
Going into the street or open places	Travelling by bus
Going shopping	Travelling by car
Travelling by tube train	Travelling in aeroplane
Travelling by surface train	Other situations (specify)
Travelling by ship	

Crowded or confined spaces
Crowded shops	Lifts
Cinema, theatre or church	Going to the hairdresser
Tunnels	Other situations (specify)
Football match	

Heights and water
High places	Having a bath
Bridges	Other situations (specify)
Deep water	

Animals
Dogs	Rats or mice
Cats	Spiders
Snakes	Birds
Worms	Other animals (specify)
Bees or wasps	

Social situations
Speaking or acting to an audience	Signing your name in front of someone
Being stared at	Going to parties

Meeting someone of the opposite sex
Meeting authority
Arguing with someone
Being criticized

Illness, injury, disease
Hospitals
Germs
Surgical operations
The sight of blood
The thought of dying
Sharp objects – needles, knives, glass

Other fears
Thunder and lightning
Strong winds or storms
Darkness
Being left alone for a few hours

Eating or drinking with other people
Talking to someone you don't know well
Seeing others vomit or vomiting yourself
Other situations (specify)

Being mentally ill
Fear of suffocation
Going to the dentist
Fear of fainting
Fear of certain illness (specify)
Fear of heart stopping
Other situations (specify)

Failing in some task or exam
Urinating in a public toilet
Other situations

Comment

Many variants of these procedures have been developed, some emphasizing the induction of anxiety followed by practising the management of that elicited anxiety. Others emphasize the importance of only allowing a minimal amount of anxiety to be experienced at all. There is no general rule to help choose between them. Some researchers maintain that neither relaxation nor the hierarchy are essential requirements for successful treatment. On the other hand, many therapists prefer to use both, since they seem very plausible to the client (and may thereby enhance expectancy-based improvement). In addition, relaxation training may have more general benefits for other aspects of the patient's functioning (e.g. sleep).

It must be said that there is no good evidence that relaxation treatment is by itself effective as a technique for primary depression. McLean and Hakstian (1979) in a very careful evaluation of behavioural and drug treatment in depression, used relaxation as a 'no treatment' control, and the results seemed to justify this decision. Many therapists who have vainly tried to relax depressed patients would agree with this conclusion. Nevertheless, there is little doubt that some patients do benefit (see Sammons' procedure above), so it ought to be kept in mind if the behavioural analysis reveals avoidance of anxiety-provoking material as a major component of the problem.

THE TREATMENT OF INITIAL INSOMNIA (Borkovec and Boudewyns, 1976)

Rationale

Although some sleep disturbance associated with depression is undoubtedly biochemically based, sleep disturbance may, once initiated, be maintained by the maladaptive strategies the patient uses to try and cope. These may be amenable to psychological intervention.

Aim of treatment

The aim is to teach patients methods of coping (a) to bring sleep under appropriate stimulus control; (b) to distract them from interfering thoughts; and (c) to decrease arousal.

Assessment procedure

First, assess alternative explanations for sleep disturbance – life crises, primary depression, fears and phobias, etc. Then, to assess the sleep pattern, use questionnaire or structured interview to ask about the following:

1. Background
    – Duration of disorder – when first noticed?
    – Life circumstances at that time
    – Previous attempts to control sleeping: activities during day; activities when retiring; medication past and present
    – Any ideas as to what might be causing current problem
2. Actual sleep
    – No. of nights per week initial insomnia experienced
    – How long does it take to fall asleep?
    – No. of nights per week middle insomnia experienced
    – How many times in night?
    – What proportion of times is there difficulty in getting back to sleep?
    – Rate (ten-point scale) difficulty of getting off to sleep
    – Rate (ten-point scale) how rested you feel in the morning
    – How often do you feel tired during the day because of poor sleep on the preceding night?
    – Specify disruption in daily living caused by insomnia.
3. Situational factors
    – Time of retiring
    – Time of awakening (self or alarm)
    – Bedroom (own or shared)
    – Bed (own or shared)
    – Noise/light level during the night

- Use of bed for other activities: studying, eating, listening to music, reading, resting during day, watching TV, listening to radio
- Taking of naps during the day – how often, where.

4. Cognitive/physiological problems
   - Intrusive or repetitive thoughts – specify content
   - Recurring dreams/nightmares
   - Bodily sensations (heartbeat/muscle tension)

Treatment (ten weekly fifty-minute sessions)

The purpose of the assessment is to build up a picture of the factors preventing sleep, especially the environment in which the patient attempts to sleep and the cognitive and physiological events which distract from sleep. Often, individuals (perhaps as an earlier attempt to cope with insomnia) take snacks to bed, or watch TV, or read. These then become conditioned to the bedroom and distract from sleep. A similar outcome follows changing hours of retiring and arising too often.

Treatment strategy 1

Instruct the patient to:

1. Stop all other activities in the bedroom or on the bed (if in a bedsitter). If they must be in the bedroom during the day for a long period, avoid visual or physical contact with the bed if possible . . . 'beds are for sleeping'. (Borkovec goes further and asks the patients to start treatment by rearranging the bedroom furniture to create stimulus conditions which are different from their past insomnia).
2. Keep to fixed retiring and arising times, and to change daytime schedules to fit in with their new sleep schedule.
3. Avoid taking naps during the day. Relax by reading or listening to music instead, but do not lie down.
4. Reduce external distractors – noises and lights – which may maintain insomnia.

In conjunction with this, the therapist should use Strategy 2.

Treatment strategy 2

This is to teach progressive muscular relaxation and encourage twice daily practice at home over the ten weeks of treatment, the second practice session to be on retiring (when there will be no need to get up again). Emphasize to the patient (a) that 'overarousal' is often associated with insomnia, and that a specific means of relaxing is required to combat this; and (b) that concentrating on pleasant internal sensations will help to distract from intrusive and repetitive thoughts which are often associated with insomnia.

Treatment strategy 3

This accompanies the above, and may be used specifically for those who are mainly bothered by worrying or repetitive thoughts. Many patients find themselves going over the events of the day in their mind, or planning tomorrow, or next week, or are just bombarded with random thoughts.

1. Instruct patient to leave the bedroom if they have not fallen asleep after ten or fifteen minutes. The aim of this is to associate the bedroom with the rapid onset of sleep (Bootzin, 1973).
2. Allocate 'worry time' to solve problems, plan next day, etc., at a separate time (from bedtime) and a separate place (from the bedroom). Teach the rule to engage in such planning/worrying activities at this scheduled time and place. Do not retire until this activity is complete, and a specific time has been set aside for the same activity the next day.
3. Use desensitization for worrying in bed. Imagine lying on a bed and the mind begins racing. Imagine switching off the thoughts and concentrating on relaxing (Geer and Katkin, 1966). Desensitization may also be used to combat recurrent nightmares, with components of the nightmare forming the hierarchy.
4. In my own clinical practice, I encourage patients to combat intrusive thoughts and plans by writing them all down so that there is less need to rehearse or remember them for the following day. Then, in bed, under the breath, count from one to ten fairly steadily, but pausing after one of the numbers. The number after which to pause is increased by one each time:

     1 – (pause) 2 – 3 – 4 – 5 – 6 – 7 – 8 – 9 – 10
     1 – 2 – (pause) 3 – 4 – 5 – 6 – 7 – 8 – 9 – 10
     1 – 2 – 3 – (pause) 4 – 5 – 6 – 7 – 8 – 9 – 10 and so on

   The rationale for this procedure is that it combines the distraction effect of counting with a slight memory-load (having to remember which number to pause after). The memory-load appears just sufficient to block intrusive thoughts, plans and memories.

Finally, treatment progress is monitored with daily diaries completed on rising from sleep. Monitor time taken to get off to sleep and middle of the night wakening; presence of distracting stimuli, internal or external; and degree of success at practising relaxation and distraction techniques.

Example

Mrs S. was thirty-five years old, married with one son, aged eight. Her husband worked night shift, so that the time she went to bed each night was under her own control. Even though her depression had responded to pharmacological treatment, she was referred for psychological assessment and treatment for initial insomnia. This insomnia (lying awake for two to three hours after her first attempts to go to sleep) was controllable with hypnotic medication, but she sought psychological help because she was afraid of long-term dependency on the sleeping pills.

Initial assessment revealed a very maladaptive pattern of behaviour. Because her husband was out she would often retire to her bedroom just after she had put her son to bed (about 8 p.m.) and would sew, knit, read, watch television or listen to the radio in her bedroom. She would also have mid- and late-evening snacks in her bedroom. At 10.30 p.m. she would put off the light and lie down, to try and sleep.

Treatment consisted of three components: (a) explanation of the probable cause of her present insomnia problems; (b) behavioural management – staying downstairs until bedtime being the main change initiated; and (c) relaxation training. The hypnotic medication was gradually reduced as the patient became more accomplished at relaxing.

At the end of eight weeks of treatment she was symptom-free and not dependent on hypnotics. She had also allowed her son to stay the night with a friend (unthinkable previously) and she coped well by herself.

Comments

In Borkovec and Boudewyns' original paper, they do not address the question of sexual activity. Instructions to the client will depend on whether sleep disturbance is associated with sexual activity or not, on assessment. If it is unreasonable to suggest a different time (e.g. mornings) or place for sex to take place, then therapy will have to concentrate on the other potential distractors, such as eating and watching TV, and ignore the sex 'distractor'. It is still possible to instruct the patient to do the relaxation and distraction practice following sex, rather than before.

As for using relaxation techniques, the comments made when these techniques were discussed above are relevant here. There is not a great deal of optimism that depressed patients find relaxation a useful technique in general. However, several workers have found it useful for some patients and some stages in the treatment programme, so it ought to be borne in mind.

The caveat about the insomnia being secondary to life crises or primary depression, implied at the start of Assessment procedure above needs emphasizing. To treat the symptom of insomnia without enquiring about other symptoms of depression or life circumstances is very bad therapeutic practice. Nevertheless, this book assumes that depression has already been identified as a major problem, and will probably be under active pharmacological and/or psychological treatment when the question of treating the insomnia is raised. In any event, it is worth bearing in mind that insomnia, however initiated, may thereafter become established and hard to eliminate because of 'bad habits' acquired by the patient, which these strategies aim to treat.

Finally, therapists who have worked long in this area advise never to instruct patients to suddenly give up their medication. First, withdrawal effects will almost certainly be evident, and disrupt the treatment progress. Second, drugs may form a useful aid to psychological treatment methods in the early stages, and can be reduced gradually as sleep patterns respond to psychological strategies. Third, the patient's doctor may be using a psychotropic medication for a dual purpose. For example, amitriptyline, taken before retiring, has a hypnotic effect although its primary action is antidepressant. If the therapist is not responsible for the patient's drug regimen, it is essential to consult the physician who is before recommending changes. On the other hand, putting sleep back into the patient's own control, without the use of drugs, is the ultimate aim of these treatment strategies.

Chapter 7

Treatment techniques II
Cognitive strategies

In this chapter, I shall discuss several cognitive techniques. The basic cognitive technique is thought-catching, which elicits the patient's self-talk and interpretations and (later in therapy) the long-term attitudes and assumptions on which self-talk is based. Having elicited the thought or image, the patient is taught the principles of reality-testing, encouraged to see thoughts and interpretations as 'hypotheses' to be tested out. They will be tested out against the patient's current experience and against their past experience. Homework assignments will be used to gather further data for or against the 'hypotheses'. If there is a problem remembering what has occurred, or imagining what might occur, cognitive rehearsal is used. The aim is that patients will eventually learn to notice when they are thinking or imagining in ways which are unhelpful; to distance themselves from their thoughts sufficiently so that the evidence can be more reliably assessed; and to think of ways of solving their problems (particularly interpersonal problems) in adaptive ways. Alternative therapy is used to help this problem-solving component.

LINKING THOUGHTS WITH FEELINGS AND BEHAVIOUR

It is important, before introducing cognitive techniques, to explain the cognitive model (see the beginning of the previous chapter) and particularly to explain the links between thoughts, feelings and behaviour.

Patients who have long believed that they have a biological depression may be surprised and threatened to find a therapist encouraging them to record and modify thoughts. For these patients, the way in which their thoughts and interpretations *maintain* the depressive cycle, no matter what initiated it, may need to be carefully explained. But even then a patient may not be able readily to identify 'thoughts' as separate entities. Beck *et al.* (1979) find it useful to use a patient's thought as they waited in the waiting room before their first appointment as an example. The question would be: 'what was running through your mind just before you came in to see me?' The patient may well reply 'I thought you might say I was unsuitable for treatment', or 'What am I doing here seeing a psychotherapist!' The therapist may then ask 'What did you feel when this was going through your mind?' From this situation, the therapist extracts a model for other situations. But the identification of the patient's self-talk as 'thought' rather than as 'reality' may have to be constantly made throughout the early sessions. When a person has been feeling for a long time that they are 'pathetic', 'useless', and that 'no one could possibly love them', they see these conclusions as true, not as thoughts or beliefs they happen to hold strongly. There is little point in asking patients to catch their thoughts until they have shown, within the therapy session, some evidence that they have understood the purpose of so doing. One method is to ask patients about the effect that certain recurrent thoughts have on their feelings and behaviour. Consider the following interchange: the patient is upset and puzzled by her failure to overcome her procrastination:

> *Patient* I always put off and put off until there's just no . . . I can't be bothered.
> *Therapist* You *always* do that?
> *Patient* Yes – I didn't used to.
> *Therapist* Or you *feel* like doing that?
> *Patient* Oh, I feel like doing that, yeah. And that's wrong. To me it is wrong. But I still do it.
> *Therapist* What do you feel like when you say 'it's wrong'? What does that make you feel?
> (Therapist attempting to identify 'it's wrong' as a 'thought' rather than 'reality', to draw out thought and affect connections)
> *Patient* That I should pull my socks up.
> (Patient replies with another thought).
> *Therapist* OK. Well what do you feel when you say 'I should pull my socks up?'
> *Patient* Ashamed of myself.
> *Therapist* What about your feelings? What does it make you feel?
> *Patient* Guilty, ashamed, depressed.
> *Therapist* Would you like to change those things? Would you like to do something in the morning instead of the afternoon, or the afternoon instead of the evening?
> *Patient* I'd just like to keep on doing things instead of having to make such a tremendous effort – supreme effort – all the time.
> *Therapist* You'd like to keep 'ticking over'?
> *Patient* Yes I would, but at the moment I'm just not.
> *Therapist* How likely is it that you'll keep 'ticking over' when you feel guilty?
> *Patient* From past experience, no likelihood at all, but it's the guilt that drives me on.

Therapist The guilt drives you on, but it also inhibits you – is that what you're saying?

Patient (After a pause) It inhibits me, yes.

Here the therapist, through questions, attempts to make the relationship between thoughts, feelings and behaviour the central subject of the discussion. The question is not whether it actually *is* wrong for the patient to procrastinate, but what effect that thought has on her feelings (guilt, shame, depression) and behaviour (procrastination followed by intense activity).

THOUGHT-CATCHING

Rationale

By recording thoughts the connection between thought, feeling and behaviour will be demonstrated. The act of recording will itself help to break the thought-affect link by making the thought seem less real. It will also provide data for therapist and patient to formulate hypotheses for reality testing.

Aim of technique

The aim is to enable patients accurately to monitor and record their own self-talk whenever they feel upset in any way.

When the therapist feels that the patient is able to begin to identify such thoughts within the session (the thought list in Table 7.3 may help in this process), the patient can be asked to monitor their own thoughts between sessions.

Example of introducing 'thought-catching'

Therapist In the session today we've talked about several recent situations which have made you feel upset or depressed. In these cases, we saw how the things that ran through your mind at the time seemed to make things worse. In fact, it is rare that people feel upset without there being thought behind it. Between now and next session I want you to be on the lookout for feelings of upset and depression and 'catch' the thoughts that go along with these moods.

A form (see Tables 7.1 and 7.2) is given to the patient on which they may complete date, situation, feeling, and thought. They may complete it in the actual situation, or later when alone. If later, it is useful to advise the patient to note down the thought on a scrap of paper as soon as possible after it has occurred. If this is not done, valuable data may be lost; nor will there be the opportunity for the technique of thought-catching to help to 'distance' the thought itself in a therapeutic way.

Table 7.1 Thought diary

Date	Situation	Emotions	Negative thought(s)	Rational response	Outcome
	Describe (1) Actual event leading to unpleasant emotion, or (2) Stream of thoughts, daydreams or recollections, leading to unpleasant emotion.	(1) Specify sad/anxious/ angry, etc. (2) Rate degree of emotion, 1–100.	(1) Write automatic thought(s) that preceded emotion(s). (2) Rate belief in automatic thought(s) 0–100 per cent.	(1) Write rational response to automatic thought(s). (2) Rate belief in rational response, 0–100 per cent.	(1) Re-rate belief in automatic thought(s), 0–100 per cent. (2) Specify and rate subsequent emotions, 0–100.

Thought forms

Tables 7.1 and 7.2 give two examples of forms which can be used by patients. The first is based on Beck *et al.*'s (1979) Dysfunctional Thought Form, and asks patients to list the situation, the emotion, the negative thought, a rational alternative thought and emotional outcome. Beck *et al.*'s form also asks patients to rate on a scale 1–100 how much they believe in the negative thought and its rational alternative and to re-rate belief in the original negative thought when re-rating the emotional outcome. Patients are asked to fill the form in whenever they have a negative thought, or whenever they feel low.

There is no doubt that some patients find the full version of the form difficult to complete, and therapists may need to tailor the form to individual requirements. For example, rating strength of belief may be difficult at the early stages of treatment. Similarly, finding alternative explanations and interpretations may be too hard a struggle at the outset and ought to be left until patients are familiar with the practice of thought-catching for their negative thoughts. Some colleagues have also pointed out that since the essence of the diary is to 'catch' the negative thought, perhaps the thought or the emotion ought to be noted first, with details of the situation noted afterwards. It is worth stating here, though, that unlike therapy for anxiety and phobic states in which competence at diary-keeping may be assumed from early on in therapy, such competence at thought diary-keeping cannot be assumed for many depressed patients. In fact competence at filling in the full thought form may be conceived as a reasonable *goal* of therapy, since the aim of therapy is to make patients more objective about their self-talk, in a way which should make the form-filling easier.

Table 7.2 Activity and thoughts diary

We would like you to complete this diary during the next week. Fill out a diary page each day, preferably a little bit at a time, several times during the day. Indicate the major activity you were doing within each two-hour block.
PLEASE EXAMINE THE EXAMPLE ILLUSTRATED
In the activity section please indicate what you have been doing during the time indicated. Write down M (for mastery) if you got any sense of accomplishment, and/or P (for pleasure) if you obtained enjoyment during the time concerned. In the thoughts and feelings section write down how you felt during the period and what thoughts have been going through your mind.

	Activity	M or P	Thoughts and feelings
12–2 a.m.	Sleep		
2–4 a.m.	Sleep		
4–6 a.m.	Woke up at 4.15 a.m. and got up to let cat out	M	Felt half-awake and unreal
6–8 a.m.	Woke hour before alarm		Worrying about Len's (son's) problem with his boss
8–10 a.m.	Made breakfast, woke family (burnt toast)	M	Why can't I do anything right?
10–12 a.m.	Took bus to town shopped in market. Bought flowers	M P	Managed to shop without feeling anxious like I normally do
12–2 p.m.	Had lunch in town with Vera (friend). Window-shopped	M	Enjoyed Vera's company at first but then had argument about her children's behaviour. Made me miserable.
2–4 p.m.	Took Metro home. Sat and did nothing		Wished I didn't always brood after arguments
4–6 p.m.	Collected Sara from school. Made her tea. Prepared Joe's (husband's) meal	M	Felt empty even though I did everything right
6–8 p.m.	Had meal with Joe and Len. Talked about moving	M	I wish he would listen for once to my point of view
8–10 p.m.	Watched TV for hour, after reading story to Sara	M	Wish my life was like these stories
10–12 p.m.	Crocheted shawl for niece's christening. Bed at 11.00 p.m.	M P	Made good progress. Joe in a good mood and this helped me

The second form (Table 7.2) is an activity, thoughts and feelings diary developed by Stephen Tyrer in Newcastle. It has the advantage of simplicity and understandability. Beck's concept of mastery and pleasure is included. No attempt is made to separate thoughts from feelings, but since many patients themselves do not easily make this distinction, especially at the start of therapy, this is not necessarily a disadvantage of the scale. It has the advantage of covering twenty-four hours, which is important in view of the idiosyncratic sleeping patterns of some patients with early, middle or late insomnia.

Its lack of specificity which allows it to be straightforward may also be a disadvantage later on in therapy when therapist and patient need to be more precise about thought/affect connections and rational alternative explanations. It may be appropriate therefore to use the Tyrer scale early on in therapy and introduce the Beck *et al.*'s form after patients have shown themselves able to complete the simpler scale competently. In any event, no diary at all should be given to patients until they have shown themselves able to grasp, within the session, what counts as an 'activity', 'thought/feeling', 'mastery' and 'pleasure'.

Rating frequency of negative thoughts

Table 7.3 lists sample negative thoughts in the patient's day-to-day experience. This is especially useful if the patient finds it difficult to identify spontaneously when a negative thought occurs. The patient may not clearly recall having had a depressing thought in the past hour, session, or day, yet may recognize having had a particular thought if it is shown to them.

The clinician may ask the patient how frequently each thought has occurred in the past hour, day, few days or week. If the precise frequency is difficult for the patient to estimate, then a card with a five-point scale written on it may be shown: 0 - not at all; 1 - sometimes; 2 - moderately often; 3 - often; 4 - all the time.

Comment and problems

The patient may feel that it will make them worse to concentrate on their negative thoughts. From the patient's perspective this seems a very reasonable prediction, especially if they have been consciously trying to put some thoughts out of their head. The therapist may ask whether trying to exclude the thoughts has worked, or whether they just pop up again regardless of the patient's attempts. In this case the therapist may point out the possible advantages of meeting the thoughts 'head on', so to speak, and to deal with them directly. Another useful strategy is to admit that it may cause some distress or it may not; that some find it surprisingly therapeutic, and that there is no way of knowing which category your patient falls into until they try it. This approach emphasizes the collaborative and experimental nature of the therapy, in which the therapist is seen by the patient not as somebody who knows the answers, but as a collaborator in finding the answers.

Alternatively, the patient may believe they have no thoughts. In this case, it may be possible to use the thought list (Table 7.3). Some patients are

Table 7.3 List of negative thoughts for frequency ratings

It seems such an effort to do anything
I feel pessimistic about the future
I have too many bad things in my life
I have very little to look forward to
I'm drained of energy, worn out
I'm not as successful as other people
Everything seems futile and pointless
I just want to curl up and go to sleep
There are things about me that I don't like
It's too much effort even to move
I'm absolutely exhausted
The future seems just one string of problems
My thoughts keep drifting away
I get no satisfaction from the things I do
I've made so many mistakes in the past
I've got to really concentrate just to keep my eyes open
Everything I do turns out badly
My whole body has slowed down
I regret some of the things I've done
I can't make the effort to liven myself up
I feel depressed with the way things are going
I haven't any real friends anymore
I do have a number of problems
There's no-one I can feel really close to
I wish I were somebody else
I'm annoyed at myself for being bad at making decisions
I don't make a good impression on other people
The future looks hopeless
I don't get the same satisfaction out of things these days
I wish something would happen to make me feel better

unable to recall negative thoughts on demand, but can easily recognize them. An example of using this technique follows.

Miss H. was a forty-one-year-old shop assistant who lived with her married sister and family. She first presented three years before with 'depression in the context of a chronically anxious personality'. She had been admitted five times and had received a large number of medications to no effect. She was the least attaining member of her family (of which she was constantly reminded by living with her sister) and seemed to feel that life had passed her by in her prime. On assessment, her responses revealed her attempts to ignore any thoughts she might have 'There is nothing', 'I've trained myself to feel nothing', 'I'm cut off from everything', 'I can smile, but it means nothing'. Interestingly, although she *thought* she was feeling nothing, and thinking nothing, she was clearly being very upset by something. Sixteen items from the list of self-statements (Table 7.3) were used, and she was asked to rate frequency of occurrence over the last twenty-four-hour period on a ten-point scale (0 – not occurred at all; 10 – occurred almost constantly). She found she could rate the frequency of the thoughts. Indeed, five of the sixteen she rated as 'very frequent', and she was able to appreciate that, in fact, far from blotting out thoughts, she was bombarded with them for the most part of the day.

Giving specific examples of thoughts was an aid to identifying naturally occurring depressive cognitions in a patient unable or unwilling to do this for herself.

Some patients find that negative thoughts come so fast and with such intensity that they feel unable to write them down. Beck *et al.* recommend that if thoughts are just too intense to 'catch', then short-term *distraction* techniques are appropriate. Such diversionary tactics may consist of focusing all attention on some object in the immediate environment and describing it to themselves in great detail, counting numbers of marks, scratches, patterns, etc. Some patients find it helpful to count backwards from 100. If this does not demand all available attention, then the patient may count backwards in threes or sevens. Of course, there are some general diversionary tactics like reading or taking a walk which can be advised, but many patients may have tried these to no effect. In general, emphasize that mood alleviation due to distraction may only be shortlived in the first instance, but they will become more practised. Patients may like to note down how long it worked for, and discuss this in the next therapy session.

Another problem may be that the recording of thoughts, feelings and situations in 'essay' format makes it difficult to clarify things in the following session. For example, here is the diary of a patient who is afraid to send invitations for a party for fear no one would come (a major issue for her in her depression):

I wrote party invitations feeling excited and cheerful, then panicked a bit – wondering if anyone would come. Thoughts such as 'if they do come it will be because they don't know how to say no' or 'they'll come for a party rather than for me'. In the end I dreaded sending the invitations in case no-one wanted to come. The first two responses were negative but I realized they were genuine reasons and not excuses. I told myself that people would come – because they really wanted to! Several phone calls later from friends pleased to be coming made me realize that I'm not so awful after all! I've used the party to contact people I have not seen for quite a while and they seem really pleased to hear from me. Apart from the usual fear of anyone hosting a 'do', I'm looking forward to Sunday.

Note that this document can be a valuable source of information. This diary provides a great opportunity for exploring the links between thoughts, feelings and behaviours. It may be worth going through it with the patient spotting thoughts and feelings and behaviours and distinguishing between them. Second, it may be possible to work together to transfer these thoughts and feelings on to a more formal diary within the therapy session. So long as this is not done in a way that makes the patient feel that they have failed, it can be helpful in clarifying the distinctions that need to be made in cognitive therapy between situations, interpretations and resulting feelings and behaviour. Third, it will then be possible to see if there are any additional ways of challenging the thoughts that were present (for example, the thought that 'they'll want to come to the party rather than to see me'). It may be important to see if the patient can challenge this particular thought (e.g. by specifically asking *which* friends would be likely to think this). It may provide an opportunity for the patient to notice how depression and anxiety were loading their predictions.

REALITY-TESTING–WITHIN SESSION

Rationale

Testing out thoughts may help patients to see them as 'psychological' phenomena, not identical with reality, and to recognize that many reactions are based on interpretation rather than fact. Making patients aware of, and distanced from their erroneous thinking style may make them hesitate before making a similar error in future.

Aim

The aim is to seek, with patient's help, evidence for and against the negative thoughts and assumptions.

Procedure

1. Identify thoughts and statements made by patient which are negative or associated with bad feelings.
2. Ask patient how much they believe that statement is true, or how likely it is that this negative event will come about.
3. Check feelings associated with statement, 'When you say that to yourself, what does it make you feel?'.
4. Leaving the validity of the statement as an open question, gently probe the evidence, e.g. past outcomes of similar situations; alternative outcomes and their frequencies, times when same situation has had (a) worse consequences than at present envisaged (note here a sometimes useful therapeutic technique of being prepared to consider worse situations than the patient, to get away from the 'I'm sure it's OK really' attitude); or (b) better consequences than envisaged.
5. If patient catastrophizes about the future, ask them to rate actual

probability, e.g. if patient says 'I'll never find another friend like him', ask them how probable that state of affairs actually is – one chance in a million, one in a hundred, 10 per cent or 40 per cent chance.

6. Throughout the interchange, emphasize that it is not a glowing positive interpretation which is being encouraged, but challenging thoughts with *reality*.
7. Check how much the patient now believes the original statement is true.

One patient had the habit of biting her nails down to the quick, when she felt very stressed and upset. This in turn upset her, even after the precipitating event had passed, when she saw what she had done to 'her appearance'. She believed everyone would immediately notice that her nails were bitten, that they would know that she was 'still a child' (she was twenty-eight years old). After a nail-biting bout, she said in one session, 'my whole life is affected', 'I can never pull myself together at all after doing this'.

Therapist When you say to yourself 'my whole life is affected', how does it leave you feeling?
Patient Helpless and depressed.
Therapist How true do you think it really is that it affects everything in your life?
Patient It always affects everything. It takes me ages to get over it.
Therapist So if I asked you to rate your percentage belief in those statements 'it always affects everything' and 'it takes me ages to get over it', what would your rating be?
Patient One hundred per cent.
Therapist Can you tell me about a time when you bit your nails and it seemed your whole life fell apart?
(Note here that the therapist does not ignore patient's claim that everything is affected. The patient gave such a description.)
Therapist Can you remember a time when you bit your nails when it hasn't been quite so bad afterwards?
Patient Well, I suppose there have been times, at home, not this year, but at other times when I've pulled myself together.
Therapist Well, give me a couple of examples . . . remind me of a couple of times when you've bitten your nails, been really down, and then you've recovered quite quickly.
(Interestingly, at this point in the interview, the patient can remember that there *have* been times when the consequences haven't been so catastrophic, but struggles to find particular examples (see p. 261).)
Patient There have been times . . . (pause)
. . . nothing shines up, but there have been times when I have got really low, and I've just decided the next morning that I've got to make the best of this bad situation.
Therapist Do you remember such a time?

Patient Well . . . there was that . . . Oh, I know!

(At this point the patient's mood rapidly lifted, as she went on to recall an *actual* event. Her mood had not lifted when she merely remembered *that* such events had occurred. This illustrates the fact that recalling specific incidents is an important part of the reality-testing procedure.)

Therapist (after discussion of this event) So it seems that when you've been biting your nails, you feel pretty fed up and depressed, and much of the time this seems to get you right down, but at other times you manage to cope pretty well. You know at the start of the discussion you said 'It *always* affects everything' and 'It takes me ages to get over it'. How much do you now believe that that statement is true?

Patient Well it's pretty bad. Well, about 60 per cent.

Note that reality-testing within the session rarely allows a patient totally to reject their negative thoughts. Furthermore, the therapist will have to go through a similar procedure again and again throughout therapy before the patient starts to do the same thing spontaneously.

Problems

The patient does not understand 'rating degree of belief as a percentage'. Because some patients think in extremes ('It's either true or false') it may be difficult for them to understand the request to rate degree of belief. Drawing out a scale on paper or a blackboard, using analogues such as temperature on a thermometer, reducing the scale to five points and putting words to each point, may be useful, e.g.:

Thought	Disagree strongly	Disagree	Neutral, uncertain	Agree	Strongly agree
So far in my life everything's gone wrong for me	−2	−1	0	1	2

The patient gets depressed when thinking of good times. Some patients constantly remind themselves of when times were better and become upset in so doing (the upset being perhaps caused by the focusing on the loss of past rewards, and the implicit or explicit thought, 'I'm never going to have such happiness again' or 'I shouldn't be like this when I've got such a good home and family', etc.). Note how thoughts about 'good times' are themselves ambiguous. They may be associated with a preoccupation with loss, or used by the therapist and patient to challenge current feelings of hopelessness. In either case, the therapist and patient may collaborate in an attempt to identify what is different about current circumstances or attitudes – what is the 'roadblock' which prevents the patient getting the rewards which they once obtained.

The patient cannot think of better times. If a patient says that nothing gives them satisfaction at present, it may be little use challenging the notion by mere argument. A therapist who says to patients 'You're wrong, surely. There must be something which gives you pleasure', will quickly lose the patient's trust. If the patient feels the therapist is belittling the problems in some way, they are less likely to collaborate. Instead a therapist may ask about things the person did when they were young, members of their family or friends with whom they were close, hobbies or pastimes they may have had (did they ever have a pet?). The therapist may re-phrase the questions to ask about the times when the depression was not so intense (it is sometimes better to ask about specific times, e.g. last month, last week or yesterday). Finally, the therapist can ask the patient to keep a diary of activities for the next week marking with an M (for mastery) anything which gives a slight sense of accomplishment and a P (for pleasure) anything which gives a sense of pleasure. As I pointed out in Chapter Six the idea of rating both M and P is that some tasks (e.g. clearing out a cupboard, mowing the lawn) may give little pleasure but some sense of accomplishment. By contrast, other tasks (e.g. watching TV) may give pleasure without accomplishment. The therapist and patient may discuss how to increase both facets. The less depressed or more 'rating conscious' patient may rate M and P on a five- or ten-point scale. The next session may be taken up with discussion of the diary and to what extent the patient's prediction that 'nothing gives me pleasure' has turned out to be true.

REALITY-TESTING BY TASK ASSIGNMENT

Rationale

Virtually all cognitive-behavioural approaches to depression incorporate task assignment in one form or other as a means of increasing the patient's activities, interactions and range of rewards. In CBT, the role of task assignment is extended to that of 'data collection' as a means of confirming or refuting an hypothesis based on a negative thought. So in addition to the beneficial effects of activity *per se*, the aim is also to make the patient view their thoughts as hypotheses to be tested out – something which initiates and stimulates action rather than inhibits it.

Aim of technique

The aim is to come to agreement with the patient regarding between-session targets which will test out a negative thought as if it was an hypothesis ('hunch', 'idea').

Procedure

1. Identify within session an idea or thought which is upsetting – ask patient to rate degree of belief.
2. Define, with the patient, the implications of the statement – what does it predict will happen?
3. Discuss ways of testing out the truth of the statement.
4. Set up a between-session 'homework' to test out statement – agree on criteria by which homework will be evaluated.
5. Emphasize a 'data gathering' approach to task assignment rather than 'success/failure' approach. 'Try it out, see how far you get, and keep a note of your thoughts and feelings for us to talk about next time.' 'It doesn't matter how far you get – if you come across a "roadblock" we can talk about it next time – just note down what happens.' The implicit emphasis of the therapist is not 'You can do it if you try' (relatives and friends may have been saying that for some time to no avail). Rather it is: 'You may find it *more* difficult than you imagine or *less* difficult than you imagine, I don't know. So let's try it out to see exactly what the difficulties are, then we can discuss them next time and get to work on them.' The therapist shares his/her ignorance of the outcome with the patient, thus subtly challenging the patient's view that 'it's bound to make me feel worse'.
6. Next session, discuss the outcome of the homework, remembering to come back to the specific purpose of the assignment, i.e. to test out a negative thought.

Example

This patient had said during one session 'my friends are sick of me'. Within that session the therapist had discussed this thought and discovered that the evidence on which it was based was that she and her friends had not been in contact with each other for two or three weeks. In fact, when examining the reason for this, it had occurred to her that she had been out of the area for three weekends out of four. Despite this evidence, she still felt they were probably sick of her. Patient and therapist discussed how it could be tested out between sessions. She decided she would phone some friends and, together, therapist and patient made up a list of people to contact.

In discussing the homework in the next session the following interchange occurred:

Therapist What was the point of doing this?
Patient To find out whether my friends were sick of me or not.
Therapist Why should we want to find out whether your friends were sick of you or not? Why did we select that as being something we should look at?

(Note, here, the therapist is trying to remind the patient that this thought was selected because it was upsetting her and they wanted to test out the upsetting thought.)

Patient Because I had not heard from them for two or three weeks.

Therapist And why had you not heard from them?

Patient Well (a) I had been out of the district, and (b) I'd just lost confidence altogether.

Therapist OK. So you'd been out of the district and you'd lost confidence and you hadn't heard from them. What were you saying to yourself?

Patient That I really am an awful person to be with.

Therapist So what did you decide to do to test it out?

Patient Well first of all, I rang Marilyn, no, I rang Simon, but he was at work, and it wasn't convenient. And then I rang Marilyn, a girl I got to know through church and she lives near the hospital and she said 'Bring Veronica along'. So we went to see 'The Jazz Singer', and I really enjoyed it; I was glad of the company.

Therapist So what was the target, what was the homework to do?

Patient It was to see if my friends were sick of me. Now Marilyn wanted to go out, she desperately wanted to go out with me . . . we had quite a nice evening actually . . . she wasn't sick of me.

Problem

One of the most frequent problems that therapists report is that the patient fails to carry out the assignment or keep a record of any attempts to do so. A blank form. No diaries. Failure to do assignments. Since progress in therapy is often speedier if such assignments are completed, it is worth specifically assessing why they are not being done. Remember that completing diaries and thought forms is a *skill* which many patients may not have at the outset. A consistent theme emerging from our own research at Cambridge and Newcastle (e.g. Williams and Scott, 1988; Moore *et al*, 1988) is that depressed people have difficulty focusing on specifics. Keeping a diary relies to some extent on memory: memory to complete the diary; memory of events to write in the diary. Remember also that completing assignments takes effort. It is instructive for therapists themselves to try and keep a diary of their thoughts and experiences. I have tried it and it is not easy at all. Add to this the hopelessness of many depressed patients: that everything else has failed, why should this succeed and it becomes surprising that any patients complete assignments! How to shape up the skill of doing assignments, whether tasks or diary-keeping, will depend on your analysis of the problem. Beck *et al.* (1979) list possible 'reasons for not doing self-help assignments' in the form of a questionnaire for patients to complete. The main themes covered there (which could form the basis of a structured interview) are the following:

1. Patient too hopeless: thinks nothing will help.
2. The connection cannot be seen between this particular assignment and 'getting better'.
3. Negative thoughts get in the way.
4. Forgetfulness.
5. Business.
6. Patient wants to be independent, 'unique' and not classified as a typical patient.
7. Patient feels the therapist will disapprove or criticize their homework.
8. Patient is afraid of novel or unfamiliar situations.
9. Patient feels that these things haven't worked in the past.
10. Patient may prefer a more passive approach. 'There must be some therapy or some pill that would make me feel better without having to do these things?'
11. Patient feels it is too simplistic.
12. Embarrassment about keeping diaries and doing assignments because someone may notice.
13. Insufficient guidance or training on how to do them.
14. Therapist has not emphasized that homework is a part of the treatment, not an 'optional extra'.
15. Therapist has not explained the reason for that particular assignment (get patient to restate reasons and assignments in own words).
16. Therapist has not allowed enough time during session in which the homework was set up for patient to voice objections to it.
17. Task too complex – needs to be graded.
18. Patient did not understand the 'try anyway' message.

These reasons for not doing assignments can perhaps be categorized into three. First, the patient is questioning whether 'merely doing it' will help the depression. This is a common underlying feeling. It may be explained to the patient that concentrating on the smaller simple parts of a task is an important preparation for some complex activity. Mountaineers often plan their climb by a series of 'camps'. At any one time, all effort will be concentrated on getting to the next camp. Straining to see the summit, the eventual goal, might be a dangerous distraction. So what are the patient's 'camps' on the way to the solution of this or that problem? It may also help to explain that depression is a disorder which affects ability to carry out minor tasks as much or more than the major ones.

Second, the patient is feeling that the therapist is trying to control them. Emphasize the patient's freedom to choose the methods used to help them. Discuss a range of homeworks and let the patient choose.

Finally, the patient may be feeling that the depressed behaviour is inevitable. Discuss depressive behaviour and its effects on mood. Discuss alternative strategies and their probable consequences. Emphasize that the patient is free to choose, and set up homework instructing them to choose the strategy and to follow it through. For example, Beck *et al.* quote the case of a patient who went back to bed and stayed there for long periods every time her boyfriend left her following a visit. Attempts to schedule alternative activity seemed to have been unsuccessful. The therapist suggested to the patient that she could operate Plan A (going back to bed) *or* Plan B (getting up and doing a, b and c). The between-session instruction was to choose one of the strategies on future occasions, and follow it through. In this case, the depressive behaviour actually became part of the homework assignment, but by 'free choice'. In such cases, once the patient believes that the behaviour (whichever is chosen) is under their own control, the thought 'I am the victim of my moods' becomes less of a burden and the more adaptive strategy may be selected. See Premack principle (Chapter Eight) for the use of high frequency (depressive) behaviours as reinforcers for low frequency (constructive) behaviours.

REALITY-TESTING – BY FINDING ALTERNATIVE RESPONSES TO NEGATIVE THOUGHTS

Rationale

A major problem with automatic negative thoughts is that they seem indisputable and incontrovertible. If the patient learns to write them down, this may itself lessen their impact because it makes them seem like 'thoughts' rather than 'reality'. Producing alternative, realistic responses is a further stage in weakening the hold the automatic negative thoughts have on a person's mood and behaviour.

Aim of technique

The aim is to teach the patient to answer their own automatic thoughts with believable rational responses.

Procedure

1. After discussing the automatic negative thoughts the patient has collected between sessions, ask them for other possible interpretations of the situation.
2. Collect and write down other interpretations (but without regard at this stage for whether they would upset the patient *more* or *less*).
3. Demonstrate the range of alternatives in order to show that the original interpretation was one among several.
4. Begin testing the evidence for or against the alternatives – keep an open

mind on which alternative the evidence will turn out to support.

5. If the evidence supports the more negative alternatives, review with patient 'Is it as bad as it seems?'
6. Give patient full 'thought record form' (see Table 7.1) and ask them to note down situation, emotion (rate intensity), negative thought (rate belief), alternative thought interpretation (rate belief), subsequent emotion (rate intensity) plus rate final belief in negative thought. (If all these ratings overcomplicate matters for a particular patient, then they may be omitted, but careful demonstration, with examples, will help to alleviate confusion.)

Problem

Very often the patient can't think of any rational responses. This problem is not resolved by the therapist merely suggesting that the negative thought is wrong, and suggesting alternatives. More realistic responses may have to be *shaped* (i.e. therapist gradually rewards for successive approximation to a realistic response). The therapist must ensure that the rational responses are as empirical as the negative responses. That is, if the patient's only rational response is 'It'll all turn out right in the end', there may be as little evidence for this overoptimistic view as for the pessimistic view it is supposed to replace. Try evaluating the evidence for things turning out alright in the end.

Another approach is to ask the patient what they would say to a friend with a similar problem. This may take the form of a more formal role-play in which patient and therapist take on different roles. Or the therapist may ask the patient what they would say to themselves 'on a good day'.

Alternatively, the therapist may suggest that the patient concentrates attention on the negative thought itself, analyses it, makes sure it truly represents the situation, categorizes it (overgeneralization, selective abstraction, etc.). If it is a statement about the past, has there *never* been a counter-instance? If it is a statement about the future write down the *actual* probability. If it is a general statement like 'I always . . . ', 'I can never . . . ', and if this is based on valid evidence, then the statement may be changed to 'In the past, I have been unable . . . '. This ties the statement down more to a specific time period and makes it easier to evaluate.

Finally, the therapist may suggest a number of possible alternative thoughts and ask the patient to choose one which is least inappropriate. Ask how much they could believe in that. Remember that small belief in the rational response is most unlikely to shift the belief in the negative thought, leaving the mood just as intense. So if someone says that writing alternative rational responses 'doesn't work', examine the responses to see how believable they really are. Bland expressions of optimism are rarely sufficient to reduce the impact of a negative automatic thought (see Training exercise, Chapter Nine).

COGNITIVE REHEARSAL

Rationale

If a patient has stopped many activities they used to perform, it sometimes becomes difficult even to imagine doing the task successfully. The entire task (even the simplest) seems a great effort without the patient being aware of what it is about the task that they find difficult. Cognitive rehearsal provides useful data on these questions. Each newly discovered 'roadblock' may become a target in itself. Furthermore, if the patient can imagine successfully completing the task, and something of the feeling of accomplishment that this involves, it may enhance motivation to attempt the task or some aspect of it between sessions (see also Chapter Six: Anticipation training and Systematic resensitization).

Aim of technique

The aim is to identify 'roadblocks' in progress and thoughts/feelings associated with doing activities by imagining doing them in every detail during the session.

Procedure

1. Identify a task with which the patient has particular difficulty, or that they used to do but say 'I couldn't possibly do that now'.
2. Check whether it is the sort of activity which would give mastery or pleasure to them if it could be done.
3. Check that initiating the task or its successful completion is not crucially dependent on anyone or anything other than the patient (e.g. I can only decorate that room when we can afford it, or when my wife/husband chooses the wallpaper), though these 'reasons' in themselves may be the subject of enquiry and challenge in some cases.
4. Ask patient to imagine doing the activity starting with planning stage, buying, preparing any materials/ingredients, starting activity, middle of activity, end of activity, immediately afterwards, own feelings, others' reactions, etc.
5. During cognitive rehearsal, identify points which patient finds difficult, ask patient to imagine all aspects of that difficulty, then suggest that any particular 'roadblock' is passed so they may continue the task. Do this with each block until patient imagines successful completion.
6. Discuss with patient roadblocks and/or whole task with a view to setting up between-session assignments.

Example

This patient was a twenty-six-year-old secretary who had been referred for psychological treatment of depression and failure to cope at work. It became clear during therapy that a major underlying problem was the patient's inability to deal with her mother, who lived elsewhere in the locality, and whom she felt to be imposing on her. She was also concerned about, though jealous of, her brother who still lived with the widowed mother, but who himself got very anxious and disturbed at times. The patient felt duty-bound to phone her mother each week. She found that this left her feeling upset, but she did not know why. Cognitive rehearsal was used for this situation. The patient closed her eyes and imagined vividly going to the telephone, and dialling her mother's number. She was instructed to talk aloud her thoughts as the phone call progressed. These are extracts from what she said:

It's mother on the line.
He's been getting at her again.
Why should she suffer this again?
She's upset.
She's alone – she can't escape – she's a bit paralysed.
My mind builds this image – my mind has a field day with the most . . . .
This is silly, I shouldn't be reacting like this.
It's absolutely true.
How long before Martin (brother) really cracks up!
I feel churned up. I can't talk about nice things.
Giving her suggestions doesn't help. I can't make her feel good.
I can't tell her about me. It doesn't help.
For God's sake shut up, I can't stand listening.

A number of issues emerged from this session of cognitive rehearsal. On reviewing the statements made, the patient was able to clarify the reasons why she found the phone situation so upsetting (e.g. having to listen to mother's problems, having to listen to mother's preoccupation with brother (jealousy?), feeling there was nothing she could do about mother's situation, being reminded that she couldn't confide in mother because her mother was not strong enough, being reminded of the apparent insolubility of her own problems). Note the statement 'I can't tell her about me', this was seen by the patient to explain a lot of her feelings.

In this way, a great number of thoughts were brought to the surface and examined. Those that were seen to be important formed the basis of further discussion. Meanwhile the difficulty of the phone situation itself was not lost sight of, and a search for alternative strategies (see next section) was implemented to enable the patient to have some tactics for coping. Methods of closing the telephone conversation (she felt particularly guilty about closing conversations) were practised, and between-session homework was set up for her to practise phoning her mother up for a short conversation which the patient herself would terminate. The next session revealed that she had been able to terminate such calls more easily than anticipated, using some of her strategies, and had not felt so guilty or upset after the phone call.

Comment

The way in which cognitive rehearsal is used depends upon therapist preference and upon characteristics of the patient and the situation being imagined. Sometimes it is used as a more formal procedure where the aims and rationale are explained, and the patient is instructed to relax and/or close their eyes and attempt vividly to imagine being in the particular situation. Alternatively, the technique may be informally applied as a component of a normal therapy session. Here the therapist merely asks the patient (for example) 'If you were now, at this moment, sitting at your desk trying to work – what thoughts would be going through your mind – what would you be feeling – what would you do?' The latter procedure is more appropriate if the patient is more restless and agitated, or for some other reason may find relaxing and closing eyes very difficult. There is no definite prescription for how formal to be. It is a matter of judgement for the therapist.

The therapist uses all their skills to elicit from the patient an entire range of real and imagined roadblocks to progress. For some patients, this is a very easy process – it will be obvious what the proh' `ms are, and these can be the subject of individual task assignments. For others, it will not be at all clear. Some, for example, say 'I should be able to get to the shops without any bother – I'm so stupid' or 'I have a lovely home and family – there's no reason for me to be depressed' or 'There's lots of people worse off than I am'. Individual therapists have their own way of dealing with this sort of comment. Some may ask what the patient *feels* when these responses occur. The therapist may point out how such thoughts seem themselves to lead to feelings of depression and try to raise the patient's curiosity as to why thinking a seemingly *positive* thought, (like 'I've got a lovely home') leads to feelings of depression. Are there any other examples of remembering or imagining positive events which lead to bad feelings (e.g. I used to be athletic, I had such good times at school, my family believe in me)? In what situations do these thoughts occur? (A further opportunity for cognitive rehearsal.) Follow through the sequence of thoughts and feelings. It will often be the case that it is not the 'lovely home' thought itself that causes the dysphoria, but rather the subsequent thought 'I should be grateful' or 'I should not feel like this'. The patient may be reassured to know that many people feel this way when they are depressed. It may help to demonstrate how such thoughts bring to mind the discrepancy between the patient's ideal and what they think they really are, and the thought of the discrepancy itself produces a negative mood. A similar effect is discussed in relation to systematic resensitization (Chapter Six) where it is recognized that the enjoyment a depressed patient obtains from current activities is often inversely related to the pleasure obtained before the onset of depression. Thus the woman referred to earlier who had loved knitting, but had always found sewing rather a bore found that, when depressed, all she could do was sew, whereas even *looking* at her knitting bag made her feel drained and hopeless.

Each of the thoughts, feelings and situations reported by the patient may become the target for formal or informal cognitive rehearsal within the therapy session to enable therapist and patient get a clearer idea of the context in which the thoughts and feelings occur, and the blocks which inhibit behavioural progress.

THE SEARCH FOR ALTERNATIVES (ALTERNATIVE THERAPY)

Rationale

Inducing depressed mood under controlled conditions of therapy may itself distance and objectify the depressing situation, allowing the patient to feel more in control of their mood. Searching for alternative behaviours increases possible response options allowing patients to feel more in control of their environment.

Aim of technique

The aim is to ask the patient to imagine being in a situation likely to induce depressed mood, then to generate alternative solutions to the situation.

Procedure

1. Ask patient to imagine a typically desperate situation (perhaps one that has actually occurred in the past week or is likely to occur in the next few days).
2. Encourage patient to experience, right now, the usual despair; the whole range of negative thoughts and feelings.
3. Attempt to collaborate with patient in generating solutions to the situation. During or after generating some options, develop each possible course of action in great detail to discover roadblocks.

Example

This twenty-three-year-old patient, married, with no children, was attending weekly sessions for relaxation treatment, in addition to regular cognitive behaviour therapy. While attending one such relaxation session she had felt very depressed and hopeless and took an overdose.

In the session which followed, and after some initial general discussion, it was decided to use 'alternative therapy'. After the situation had been graphically described, patient and therapist went through some of the apparent alternative strategies. The therapist then asked the patient to summarize these alternatives by writing them down. This is what she wrote:

Options	Consequences
Stayed at hospital	
Remained in day room	Inability to talk to other members of group. Did not want them to realize how desperate I felt.
Gone to recreation room	Someone would probably have come to find me, either staff or group member. Did not want to draw attention to myself. Did not want to remain alone, yet at same time I could not cope with other people. I remember that this choice did occur to me.
Talk to a member of staff	No one I feel at ease with, unable to confide in them. Would have to seek them out. This has gone on for three years – continuing 'nuisance value' to others. I repeat myself and feel that doctors and nurses would say the same old things which offer neither solution nor help.
Continue with the day	Probably one of the easiest options. Could not do it feeling as I did – could not keep up appearance – this eventually becomes such a strain that I just crack.
Left hospital	
Rung GP	Have done this before – means putting strain on her. Last time she felt obliged to contact other agencies – don't want to put her in that position again. I feel I am burdening her with my problems.
Gone to see Priest	Again the feeling of his reaction being 'Not again' – I will appear a failure because I can't cope again. I should be able to cope.
Gone home	If Mike (husband) at home. Don't want to upset or annoy him. If Mike not there – lonely – wouldn't have helped. Same end result.
Gone for a walk/drive	But feeling the way I did (or worse) I would have wandered, thinking, getting more upset – trying to find answer, solution, way out.
Gone shopping	No spare cash. Already done weekly shopping. Don't particularly enjoy shopping – especially when depressed. Need to be organised to shop don't like seeing all the other shoppers coping quite adequately.

Notice here how the therapist has not just encouraged the patient to list all the options, but also to list reasons why they might not have seemed genuine options at the time. For example, on first generating options, 'shopping' appeared a clearly available choice. It was only after going through 'cognitive rehearsal' strategies to examine this seemingly viable option that some obvious roadblocks became evident (e.g. 'I'd already done the weekly shopping', 'I had no money', etc.).

Thus the search for alternatives is a technique used in close association with cognitive rehearsal in which the apparent options are explored. The reader may find it instructive to go back to this patient's 'options' and think about what their own therapeutic strategies would have been.

Problem

The patient may fail to generate alternatives – believes nothing will help the situation. The therapist's own ideas may be of little use here, merely serving further to alienate the client. Instead, the therapist might (a) list advantages of behaviour, and (b) ask about the sort of options available if the patient were not depressed. Consider this example of another patient:

Patient I went back home to my parents to sort out some of my stuff. I couldn't face it. I felt so depressed.

Therapist Has this happened before when you've tried to sort it out?

Patient Oh yes, it happens all the time. I get so low. It's no use.

(Therapist asks more questions to make situation clear. It becomes evident that being in the family home is rather difficult anyway, but that attempts to sort out belongings have produced depressed mood of suicidal proportions).

(Therapist decides to focus on task.)

Therapist You mention that you need to sort out your stuff because of moving into this new flat. Let's list all the reasons why it might be good to sort it out – what would the advantages be? (List written on paper/ blackboard.) And now what are the disadvantages/problems? (Patient lists, e.g. 'too much stuff to go into new flat', 'my clothes won't fit now I've put on weight', 'my new flatmates might not want to use my cups and plates'.)

Note how this procedure elicits negative thoughts which tend to occur when the patient thinks of clearing up her belongings. The therapist may also bear in mind less explicit thoughts which may be affecting patient's mood, such as 'If I move all my stuff out, I won't have anything left in my old home' (i.e. guilt and anger about abandonment of (and by) parents). Each of these thoughts may need to be subjected to reality-testing. If there seem to be too many to test individually, the therapist may identify a theme (e.g. possible rejection) to discuss with the patient, or may select one salient thought to test out.

Therapist Now, we've got a list of reasons for sorting out your stuff and some disadvantages too. Let's take these disadvantages – these road-blocks – one by one and see if we can think of a way of coping. Imagine, for example, that the only problem was that your clothes might not fit, everything else is O.K., but you're really worried about the clothes not fitting.

Patient It's such a long time. I've put on so much weight.

Therapist So nothing will fit you?

Patient Well there may be some things.

Therapist Give me an example of something you know won't fit you – definitely – without doubt.

Patient My blue skirt – it was always a bit tight.

Therapist And is there anything which you're fairly sure will still fit?

Patient I made a large cape for myself when I was at college. I suppose that would fit me.

Therapist So it seems likely that some clothes won't fit, and others will. What proportion of your clothes do you think won't fit you anymore.

Patient About 60 per cent.

Therapist Now let's suppose you weren't concerned about anything else but your clothes not fitting. How would you cope with sorting out your stuff?

Patient I suppose I would get a couple of boxes and a suitcase, and sort it out.

Therapist And then?

Patient Well, one box could go to a jumble sale – another could stay there in case I lose weight again – and I could take the suitcase back to the flat.

Note how already the patient begins to think about practical coping strategies. She seems to be beginning to think through the problem, imagining herself up in the attic with the boxes. In the same way the therapist may take her through the other 'roadblocks'. In each case a coping strategy may suggest itself. At the end of the session, therapist and patient may end up with a short list of possible strategies which could form the basis of a homework assignment. At this point, before terminating the session, the therapist may wish to return to the patient's belief that 'there is no solution', and discuss the homework targets as an attempt to test this idea out.

RE-ATTRIBUTION TRAINING

Rationale

Following a stressful experience, an individual will attempt to explain the occurrence, i.e. to attribute the event to various causes. It has been suggested that depressed individuals tend to have biased attributional styles in which adverse events are attributed to internal, stable and global causes, and positive events to external, unstable and specific causes (see Chapter Three).

Aim of treatment

The aim is to help the patient identify their maladaptive causal attributions and then to make more realistic and appropriate attributions of causality.

Procedure

1. Assess attributional style. Seligman *et al.* (1979) devised a questionnaire measurement of attributional style – a sample item from which is reproduced below.

   You have been looking for a job unsuccessfully for some time:
   a) Write down one major cause.
   b) Is the cause of your unsuccessful job search due to something about you or something about other people or circumstances? (circle one number).

   | Totally due to other people or circumstances | 1 2 3 4 5 6 7 | Totally due to me |

   c) In the future when looking for a job will this cause again be present? (circle one number)

   | Will never again be present | 1 2 3 4 5 6 7 | Will always be present |

   d) Is this cause something that just influences looking for a job or does it also influence other areas of your life? (circle one number)

   | Influences just this particular situation | 1 2 3 4 5 6 7 | Influences all situations in my life |

   e) How important would this situation be if it happened to you? (circle one number)

   | Not at all important | 1 2 3 4 5 6 7 | Extremely important |

Alternatively, the cognitive style measure given in Chapter Five could be used, with particular attention being paid to those items which reveal maladaptive attributional styles.

2. Explain the importance of attribution to the patient. An example such as the following (Cleaver, 1981) may be used:

> Consider the case of an individual who fails a maths exam and attributes the failure to the fact that 'I am useless at everything I attempt?' This is an *internal* attribution because it relates failure to *personal* incompetence; it is a stable attribution because it relates failure to an *unchanging* or *constant* feature of his functioning, namely, uselessness. And it is *global* because it may be used to explain failure in a wide range of situations (e.g. the individual might use the attribution 'I am useless at everything I do' to explain why the supper got burnt).

Such an attribution pattern would (if widely applied) tend to magnify all failures, and lead to hopelessness and depression, especially if the event was important. The example continues:

> Imagine that the individual had passed the exam, and had attributed it to the fact that the questions were particularly easy. Such an attribution is external because it relates success to a characteristic of the exam, not to a characteristic of the individual; it is unstable because easy questions cannot be regarded as a constant feature of exams, and it is specific because it cannot be used to explain success in any other setting.

Such an attribution pattern (if widely applied) would tend to minimize all successes, and act to maintain hopelessness and depression.

3. Choose a hypothetical example and get patient to work out maladaptive and adaptive attributional style.
4. Find a particular example from the patient's recent past (preferably last week) and discuss attribution for that event.
5. Examine with patient links between attribution for an event and mood.
6. Discuss alternative attributions for the event in question.

Re-attribution training using hypothetical situations

Cleaver (1981) devised a re-attribution training technique which worked from discussion of hypothetical situations to actual situations explicitly within the framework of Abramson *et al.*'s (1978) attributional reformulation of learned helplessness. That is, she attempted to teach patients what internal, stable, global attributions were, and how they could be modified.

Stage 1 The patient is asked to imagine that:

1. A friend has passed you by in the street and ignored you.
2. You're in a group learning to do something new and everybody seems to get the hang of it faster than you.

3. You write to a friend asking if you can stay with her for a few days and you don't get a reply within a fortnight.
4. You're in the pub with a group of friends and no one is talking to you.

In each case, the patient is asked: 'What would it be most natural for you to think was the reason for this happening?' Their answers are then analysed on the three dimensions of internality, stability and globality. For each dimension, the patient is praised for employing the 'adaptive' attribution, and it is pointed out what they have done. Alternatives are called for and suggested if the 'maladaptive' attribution is offered. As follows:

1. If an internal attribution is given, the therapist invites the patient to try and think of some other reasons which suggest that it is something about the other people not something about themselves. For example, the friend who passed by in the street was day dreaming at the time or not wearing his glasses.

   If an external attribution is given, the therapist can say: 'Good, that's just the sort of thing we're looking for. Some other reasons you could have given are . . . .'
2. If a stable attribution is given, the therapist invites the patient to try and think of a reason which suggests that things could change – could be different on another occasion.

   If an unusable attribution is given, the therapist can say: 'That's good, you've chosen something which suggests that things would be different on another occasion. Some other things you could have thought of are . . . .'
3. If a global attribution is given, the therapist points out that it is the sort of reason which could explain why things go badly on another occasion, and asks the patient to think of a reason which applies only to the situation in question.

   If a specific attribution is given, the therapist can respond: 'Good, you've chosen a reason which can only apply to this particular situation. Other suitable reasons would have been . . . .'

Stage 2

The patient is asked to describe real negative events with a view to discussing and changing maladaptive attributions for them. Go through same procedures as above using patient's own examples. Cues: rejection, snubs, disappointments, accidents, etc.

Stage 3

Hypothetical 'success' situations are discussed, e.g.

1. You've been invited out to supper by a couple you know.

2. You've been successful in completing the crossword puzzle in a newspaper.
3. You've been complimented on your appearance by a friend in the pub.

Analyse attributions as before, encouraging internal, stable and global attributions.

Stage 4
The patient is asked to recall real positive events with a view to discussing and changing maladaptive attributions.

Comment

There have been few systematic investigations of re-attribution theory as a treatment of depressed patients in its own right, though both Seligman (1981) and Beck *et al.* (1979) claim that it is an important component of psychological treatment. It must be said that the theory on which it is based is constantly shifting, so it would be unwise to think that the attributional styles outlined here are always maladaptive and that modification of them will necessarily be beneficial. Many of these issues are discussed by Cleaver (1981) and referred to in Williams (1982b) as well as in other chapters in Antaki and Brewin's book *Attribution and Psychological Change* (1982).

A useful strategy may be to incorporate some elements of attributional modification into cognitive-behavioural therapy where it becomes clear that constant misinterpretation of events is a problem for the patient. In such cases one could encourage them to keep a diary of their interpretations of events (perhaps taking one attributional dimension each week as a 'theme', e.g. look for internal attributions one week and stable attributions the next) and challenging themselves to try out other interpretations. Another useful strategy may be to encourage the person to see the consequences of attributions on behaviour, and how the behaviour then brings its own consequences. For example, if people aren't talking to you in a pub, and you think this is because they don't like you, you may turn away slightly, making it even less likely that they will talk to you. The attribution may in this way become a self-fulfilling prophecy. Role-play may be used in the sessions to allow the person to practise acting on the consequences of alternative attributions (e.g. they're too shy to talk, so how can I break the ice). In these ways re-attribution training may become a useful adjunct to psychological treatment. It needs a great deal more systematic investigation, however, before the extent of its usefulness may be properly assessed.

DEALING WITH UNDERLYING FEARS AND ASSUMPTIONS

Rationale

Automatic negative thoughts and low mood are often produced by a stressful situation 'activating' long-held fears or assumptions.

Aim of treatment

The aim is to make explicit these long-term dysfunctional attitudes, beliefs, fears, and assumptions, and to challenge them by (a) recalling how they arose, (b) discovering how they have been maintained; and (c) bringing to mind contrary evidence from the past and present.

Procedure

1. Assess
   - By asking patient to count the number of times they find themselves saying or thinking 'should', 'must', and 'ought' as they go about their daily activities.
   - By noticing times when the mood disturbance they experience appears out of proportion to the thought or picture in their mind. Use 'inverted arrow' technique to follow through consequences of thought (see below).
   - By using the Dysfunctional Attitude Scale (see Chapter Five) either formally in the therapy session, or informally as a thought checklist between sessions.
2. Discuss the origins of the idea: when did the patient first remember coming to that conclusion? At what age? What else was happening? Was anyone else in the family depressed or under stress? How might things have been different? Be specific. Talk about actual situations. Discuss also the effect that the attitude or fear has had on situations throughout life. Take a few concrete examples and discuss how they might have been different. In other words, how has the attitude/fear been maintained? In what way has the person been afraid to challenge it? Look at evidence that contradicts the attitude (which may have been ignored in the past).
3. Challenge the attitude by examining specific ways in which the patient is still acting on it in their day-to-day life. Work together to think of the assumption as a hypothesis and find a way in which this hypothesis can be tested.

Here is an example of using 'shoulds' to detect underlying beliefs and assumptions. This patient was reading from her diary of the previous day when she became upset. When a patient becomes upset in this way, it is often helpful to ask 'What went through your mind just then?' During such a line of questions, the following interchange occurred.

> *Therapist* And now you're reporting – you're reminding yourself of the feeling you had yesterday – and what is happening, now you're reminding yourself?
> *Patient* I'm getting all upset again.
> *Therapist* And why are you getting upset do you think? What thoughts are going through your mind that are making you upset?
> *Patient* Because I feel an adult person should know what they want out of life and what they are capable of doing – what they are capable of.
> *Therapist* And when you reminded yourself about saying those things today, when you started reading out from your book – what did you start to think here and now?
> *Patient* My goodness, I'm still a child, I'm not grown up yet.
> *Therapist* And what did that make you feel when you said that to yourself?
> *Patient* Very frightened, very insecure.

Note that the 'should' gave a hint that there was an underlying assumption being expressed. In this case it was that 'an adult person should know their own mind'. Like many dysfunctional assumptions, this belief is not particularly depressing in itself, but in a situation in which she felt she did not know her own mind (and she felt she had been indecisive about something), it allowed her to reach the conclusion that she was not an adult, she was a child.

Inverted arrow technique (consequential analysis)

This is particularly valuable when someone seems more upset than the thoughts they are reporting would seem to justify. This may be because the mood is being disturbed by the underlying belief, assumption or fear; and not by the thoughts or images of which they are most aware. Here is an example:

This forty-two-year-old engineer had been off work for four months because of his depression. He was due to start work again in two weeks. He came to a therapy session in deep distress because the previous weekend he had 'fallen apart'. He'd been 'back to square one' having spent all weekend 'lying on the couch feeling low'. We were able to trace the beginning of the downswing in mood to a moment when he was helping his wife move some boxes in the loft of his house.

Therapist What was going through your mind when you were moving the boxes?

Patient Well we were just shifting some things. Everything seemed OK. Then I felt a little tired and I thought I'd better stop. Then I suddenly began to feel terrible.

Therapist Can you recall anything else that might have gone through your mind?

Patient No it just hit me.

Therapist You mentioned you felt tired. I wonder if we could just follow that up. If you had carried on feeling tired, what would have happened?

Patient Well, if I felt tired of doing that little job, how am I going to cope when I go back to work?

Therapist What do you feel about that?

Patient Well, the bosses have been very good in the past but they are bound to lose patience sooner or later.

Therapist You think you may need more time off you mean?

Patient Well if I get tired just moving boxes around in the loft, maybe I'm not ready for work.

Therapist And if you're not ready for work, what do you think may happen when you go back?

Patient I'll only last a few days, then I'll be off again (gets upset). They'll not stand for any more. I think that'll be the end of it.

Therapist The end of the job?

Patient Yes, the job, me, my family – I don't know how we'd keep going if I can't work. It will be the finish.

Therapist (After some silence) Do you remember you said you felt a little tired when moving things around in the loft – then felt really bad?

Patient Yes.

Therapist Do you think the feeling tired might have triggered off all these feelings and worries about work?

Patient That's maybe what happened. I was dimly aware of a sort of picture of me not coping at work – just everything going wrong – but then I just felt so depressed I went to lie down and didn't get up at all all weekend.

Therapist I wonder if we could look to see if there have been other times when this deep fear about the future has affected you?

Therapist and patient continued to try and identify other such situations. It is important to assess fully the times when underlying assumptions and fears are affecting thoughts and mood before proceeding to challenge them. The inverted arrow scheme could be written out during or after this sort of interchange. It would look something like this:

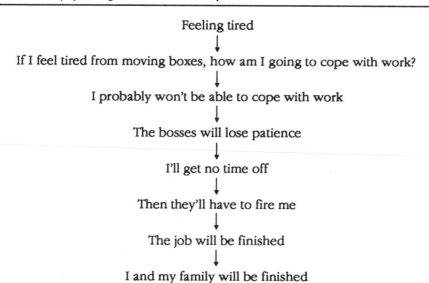

Feeling tired

↓

If I feel tired from moving boxes, how am I going to cope with work?

↓

I probably won't be able to cope with work

↓

The bosses will lose patience

↓

I'll get no time off

↓

Then they'll have to fire me

↓

The job will be finished

↓

I and my family will be finished

As with thought-catching and reality-testing, described earlier, until the patient understands that their assumptions and fears *are* assumptions and fears, they will find it difficult to convert them into hypotheses to be evaluated. Here is another brief example of using this analysis of consequences:

This patient reported that after the session a week before she had felt very apprehensive for a long period of time. When asked to try and remember what had been going through her mind at that point she said: 'I was not sure I'd like what I found out about myself.' At first this appeared to be doubts about the psychotherapy, but the apprehension seemed deeper than was justified on the basis of this thought. So the therapist asked the question: 'What would happen if you did find out something about yourself?' The patient replied: 'I'd have to leave college, it would show that I had no vocation to be a social worker.' When asked what would happen then, the patient replied that her parents would be disappointed, that she would have to live at home. After a while she said: 'There would be nothing left of my life.' It is now easier to see why this patient's apprehension had been so deep. There was in her mind a fairly direct link between finding out something about herself in therapy that she didn't like and there being nothing left of her life.

Assessing assumptions

There are two ways of assessing beliefs and assumptions: cross-sectional assessment (how are they affecting current day-to-day life) and longitudinal assessment (their origins and how they have affected life between the time they started and the present). Evaluating their current influence is relatively easy if the patient has become adept at catching thoughts. They simply move to 'catching assumptions' using the same thought forms. The Dysfunctional Attitude Scale (Chapter Five) may be used as a checklist to help this. Or the patient may prefer to count 'shoulds', 'musts' or 'oughts'. The therapist tells the patient that every time a 'should' occurs there is likely to be an 'eleventh commandment' lying beneath the surface; e.g. 'a person must be liked by everybody', 'a person who is not successful in absolutely everything cannot be happy'.

Longitudinal assessment is more difficult. The aim is to discover the origins of the assumption without spending so much time talking about the past that it begins to set up a new dysfunctional belief that 'my past is so terrible I cannot possibly be happy in the future'. The aim is to describe the situation out of which the belief arose in sufficient detail that the patient can reattribute the dysfunctional belief to the *situation*, rather than continue to think that the assumption reflects reality. For example:

A patient discovered that his work as a lab technician was being affected by his depression and tension. He became especially low when he felt he had a deadline on building a piece of equipment. There was always too much to do, and he felt he would fail and others would notice. During therapy, he noticed that the assumption 'you must be successful in absolutely everything or you cannot be happy' was ruling his everyday life. He realized that he had always separated his work into 'success and failure', there was no 'in-between'. He never succeeded in meeting deadlines because of the nature of the work. So he always failed. We wanted to assess this assumption longitudinally.

> *Therapist* Can you remember when you first became aware of this idea that you had to succeed?
>
> *Patient* Well . . . it must be a long time ago. I remember at school . . . no, before that . . . I remember when I was about seven – I changed schools. The teachers were OK but the other kids were a bit big for me.
>
> *Therapist* When did you feel you had to succeed?
>
> *Patient* I remember not wanting to go and my Dad saying that I had to. He said I had to just get on with things – ignore the change. I remember him getting really angry with me once because I was upset when I came home from school. He said I had to keep trying – work – or I'd never be happy.
>
> *Therapist* What was your Mum's reaction?
>
> *Patient* Well she wasn't around much of the time. She was in hospital having my little brother and it went wrong. She nearly died. That's why I moved school, so we could live near my Gran so she could help look after us when it was all over.
>
> *Therapist* That must have been very difficult for you.

Patient I haven't thought about it much 'cos it still makes me feel sad.

Therapist What happened then?

Patient Well, things sorted themselves out. My brother was OK. Dad was never quite the same – he seemed more quiet. I think he missed a promotion during all the commotion. After that he was always going on at me about being successful, about working hard.

Therapist So you began to believe that success was very important for happiness? Did this help or hinder you in your schoolwork?

Patient Both. I worked hard – but I'd get terribly upset if anything went wrong. I wasn't all that bright, and so there was always something to correct. Whenever I got something wrong I'd always feel really upset inside.

Therapist Had you been like that before all this happened?

Patient I can't remember, but I don't think so.

Therapist What do you think was going on in your Dad's mind at this time?

Patient He was worried about my Mum. She nearly died. He had to look after us. He had to arrange the house move. It was only a few streets, but it was a new borough – that's why I changed school.

Therapist Was success important to him?

Patient Well he lost promotion. I think he thought if he'd worked harder things might have been different. His father had been a real tyrant. I think that affected him. Actually, now I think about it, his father died only one year before all this happened, when I was five or six.

Therapist It was a bad time for him? Do you think it was all this that made him take that attitude with you, you know, 'success and happiness go together'?

Patient I think it must have been, 'cos when you think about it – it's not really how it is, well it wasn't for him. Perhaps that's why he was so strong on it, he wanted to persuade himself.

Therapist I think you may be right. What would things have been like for you if you'd not felt that any small failure was catastrophic?

Patient Well I may have been less intense – I've always been so intense. Finishing a job on time is really important to me. The trouble is, in my job, it just can't be done. No-one else expects it – that's how the job is. And I end up getting miserable.

This interchange illustrates the way in which the therapist may use the past to investigate assumptions, but always with the intention of discovering origins, of examining the effects they had at that time and thereafter, and loosening the hold the idea has on the person. In further discussion, the therapist will need to summarize what he has been doing, so that the patient is aware that the assumption has an origin, that it was the result of certain specific difficult situations which might have been different. Together, patient and therapist will need also to examine the actual evidence for and against the assumption, using the techniques of reality-testing described above.

CONCLUDING REMARKS

Beck *et al.* (1979) take pains to point out that cognitive therapy techniques must be used in the context of a therapy session in which the patient is offered empathy and warmth. The therapeutic strategies are not 'mechanical devices' in which the turning of a particular screw has predictable consequences. Rapport between patient and therapist in which collaboration and mutual understanding are the keynote is essential.

As emphasized in Chapter Four, cognitive therapy has used a blend of cognitive and behavioural techniques. Prospective users may refer to that chapter to find information on which techniques have been found most useful in what combinations. (That chapter also has a section on drug interactions which may be of interest.) The cognitive-behavioural therapist does not attempt to stick rigidly to any one technique, but will select from a range of techniques the one which seems most appropriate at any time. The range is large, but the evidence suggests that the core techniques here described, when taken together with some core behavioural techniques (e.g. task assignment) should form a sound basis on which to proceed with many depressed patients.

Chapter 8

Treatment techniques III
Behavioural and cognitive therapy for chronic and unremitting depression

Six out of ten people who become depressed find that their depression tends to lift spontaneously after some time. It used to be thought that once the depression had lifted, the person could return to a normal life without any great fear that they would become depressed again. It is now clear that this is not the case. Depression tends to be a chronic relapsing condition. A typical depressed outpatient can be expected to have a new episode approximately every three years (Lavori *et al.*, 1984). Over half of those successfully treated with antidepressant medication will relapse over the following two years (see Chapter Four). Added to these are the people who never responded to the treatment. Weissman *et al.* (1978) found that 25–30 per cent of patients have long episodes or do not benefit from treatment. Keller *et al.* (1984) found a 20 per cent rate of chronicity in patients with major depressive disorders. Many of these patients are admitted as day-patients or inpatients, and some will have many such admissions. These patients appear not to respond to physical or psychological treatment. Some become long-stay patients. Indeed between 5 and 15 per cent of new long-stay patients in England and Wales are there because of chronic affective disorders (Mann and Cree, 1976).

Has psychological treatment a role to play? The evidence suggests that it has. Of course, it is clear that these patients may not respond to psychological treatment as quickly as many other patients. It is interesting that the variables which predict nonresponse to psychological treatments are also those that predict nonresponse to physical treatments (see Hollon's Global Chronicity/Severity Index (179). But it still may be the case that, for most of these very difficult patients, psychological treatment will ultimately be an essential component of effective clinical management. In some cases it may even prove to be the only intervention that will succeed.

Because such treatments often require changes to the ward milieu, managers of hospitals and units (both administrative and clinical staff) may need to be involved in the planning stage together with the would-be therapists. Whether or not this is the case, it may be helpful to evaluate the results of introducing behavioural and cognitive therapy into inpatient or daypatient settings not only by examining changes in Beck or Hamilton scores for the patient, but also in terms of the number of days a patient spends on the unit, staff morale, job turnover, and in terms of how much patients and their families feel supported by the service being offered.

But in the end, it is the clinical case for the use of psychological treatment for these patients which is the core issue. To make such a case, we need a thorough knowledge of the particular problems these patients are likely to have experienced, an awareness of what clinical research has been already done, and some specific proposals for what can be done for such chronic patients. This chapter will examine each in turn.[1]

FACTORS ASSOCIATED WITH CHRONICITY

One in every seven people (15 per cent) who have been hospitalized for major depression will eventually die by suicide. Such a statistic lends impetus to the search for factors which contribute to chronicity, and to the search for those factors about which we may be able to do something. Let us start at the most general level. Hollon found seven factors in patients who had been included in Rush *et al.*'s (1977) outcome trial of cognitive therapy (cited in Fennell and Teasdale, 1982) which predicted response to treatment. These factors together accounted for 39 per cent of the variance in response to treatment (both tricyclic antidepressant and cognitive therapy). They were:

1. Beck Depression Inventory score >30
2. duration of current episode > six months
3. inadequate response to previous treatment
4. two or more previous episodes
5. associated psychopathology
6. overall impairment (rated by clinician) moderate or severe
7. poor estimated tolerance for stress

If patients had four or more of these characteristics they tended not to respond to either treatment. One can readily see that a large component of this Global Chronicity/Severity Index refers to the patient's history (previous episodes, response to previous treatment and duration of current episode). This is consistent with independent evidence (Keller *et al.*, 1984) that the most powerful predictor of chronic course is the long duration of the episode prior to assessment and treatment. Many of the other items on the Chronicity Index may well be secondary to these aspects of the patient's own history.

What then are the core differences between chronic and non-chronic patients, if number of prior episodes and length of current episode are matched? Two studies have included sufficient patients to match in this way and have converged on the same conclusion. In a longitudinal prospective study which was part of the NIMH Clinical Research Branch Collaborative

Program in the Psychobiology of Depression, Hirschfeld *et al.* (1986) compared nineteen patients with a diagnosis of major depressive disorder who had not recovered at two-year follow-up with nineteen who had recovered less than one year from initial evaluation and had remained well for two years. Patients were matched for age, sex, primary/secondary status, and, importantly, duration of prior episode. The patients did not differ on educational level, marital status, social class, number of children at home, age of first hospitalization, overall severity or number of hospital admissions. Patients were given a life-events interview to assess frequency of life events before onset of depression, but were found not to differ on that either. The only differences emerged on some personality scales reflecting neuroticism and what was termed 'ego resiliency', thought to be closely related to neuroticism.

Weissman *et al.* (1978) had reached a similar conclusion in a four-year follow-up of 150 depressed women. A large number of variables were examined to see if they predicted chronicity: age, race, social class, marital status, religion, number of previous episodes, suicide attempts, diagnosis, history of death or separation, presence of neurotic traits as a child, amount and type of stress prior to onset, and severity of pretreatment symptoms. None of these predicted chronicity. However the neuroticism scale of the Maudsley Personality Inventory did predict chronicity.

More recent studies are consistent with those of Keller *et al.* (1984) and Weissman *et al.* (1978). Scott *et al.* (1988) found that increased neuroticism score on the Eysenck Personality Inventory was one of a number of factors differentiating chronic from episodic depressed patients.

What can we conclude from these studies? First, that when all possible controls for sociodemographic factors and diagnosis are made, a psychological attribute differentiates the groups – a personality trait. Second, that although scores on this self-rated trait are almost certainly inflated by the questionnaire being completed when patients are depressed, nevertheless the scores cannot merely reflect severity of depression since severity was controlled for. Therefore, thirdly, the high neuroticism score probably reflects long-standing personality difficulties of which the most prominent is likely to be hypersensitivity to affective stimuli in the environment arising from other people, objects, or one's own bodily sensations. Such people may selectively attend to emotional stimuli (Williams and Nulty, 1986; Bentall and Kaney, 1989) and selectively remember unpleasant self-referent material (Martin, 1985).

What we cannot conclude is that, because neuroticism emerges when other factors are controlled, these other factors are 'secondary' in the sense that they make no contribution to outcome of treatment. Psychological treatments may take some encouragement from the fact that, underneath all the other stresses and difficulties lies a psychological, personality problem. The encouragement will be shortlived unless we develop some strategies to cope with all the other problems these patients have.

What are these other problems? The list is long (Scott, 1988a; Scott *et al.*, 1988). First, these patients come from families where there has been a greater than normal incidence of unipolar depression. This may suggest a genetic component (it is known that neuroticism has a high heritability factor). But it also suggests that patients have often been exposed to depression in the family and may have learned negative ways of looking at the world, or failed to learn coping skills from an early age.

But problems in the family are not confined to the patient's childhood. Vaughn and Leff (1976), Campbell *et al.* (1983), Hooley and Teasdale (1988) and Brown (1989) are just some of the investigators who have found that current close family members play an important role in the maintenance of depression. Partners of patients often themselves show a mixture of anger and despair when new treatments are suggested. They often, wittingly or unwittingly reinforce the patient's low self-image.

Second, these patients tend to have an increased number of stressful life events both before their depression and since its onset. Often this second set of life events has meant that they are denied support just when they need it most.

Third, they have had chronic low self-esteem prior to the onset of depression. They have rarely, if ever, given themselves adequate reward for their own efforts; they have dropped out of relationships; they see no hope or point in restoring these relationships. They show the signs of learned helplessness (Seligman, 1975). Consistent with such helplessness, Scott *et al.* (1988) found that chronic patients' score on the Hopelessness Scale (see Chapter Five) was very high (16.3, the maximum being 20). To put this in context, our own research finds the mean level of hopelessness to be lower than this, even in patients who have recently attempted suicide. (The means were 11.8 in Williams and Broadbent, 1986a and 9.9 in Williams and Dritschel, 1988).

Fourth, these patients show deficits in information processing skills. The difficulty that depressed and hopeless patients have in recalling specific personal memories (Williams and Scott, 1988) is exacerbated in chronic depressives (Brittlebank *et al.*, in preparation). This has two serious effects. First, it prevents them from identifying specific links between thought, feeling and behaviour. Second, it reduces their ability to generate solutions for current problems, since retrieval of possible solutions must heavily depend on effective access to past episodes when a similar problem occurred (see Chapter Eleven).

Fifth, these patients have such a long experience of low mood that fluctuations in current state may be ignored. Scott (submitted) studied sixteen inpatients undergoing treatment with cognitive therapy. She found that reductions in independently rated symptoms (Hamilton Rating Scale for Depression and a Nurse's Observer Scale) occurred before self-rated mood (Beck Depression Inventory and overall mood self-rating). This was found to be true within therapy sessions as well. Every ten minutes, a mood thermometer was used to check transient mood shift. Even when there had been a shift in belief in an automatic thought sufficient to affect mood in less chronic patients, these patients reported feeling no change in their mood.

Finally, these patients have an inevitable ambivalence to trying any new treatment. Their prediction that 'nothing will help' is appropriate given their history. This makes it extremely difficult to build up a collaborative relationship. I have yet to meet a therapist who does not, to some extent, blame themselves for this inability to help such patients. The guilt is often mixed with anger and frustration, and, in the end, it turns to hopelessness and despair in the therapist about their prospects of ever being able to help this chronic patient.

If anything is to be done for such patients, we therapists need to do something about our own despair and tendency to give up in the face of the enormous problems they have. We need to look to see what strategies are available. We need to set realistic goals for ourselves, for our patients and for their families. We need to be clear about which problems are the focus of treatment and which are not and assess the frequency and severity of these problems throughout the intervention period. We must expect that any change noticed by others may not be reflected in the patient's own self-ratings for some considerable time. We must expect that a patient's learning in one situation will not necessarily generalize to another – that many learning trials may be necessary. In the terminology of learned helplessness, the patient may need to be repeatedly exposed to success experience – to the contingency between action and outcome – before he or she will learn or relearn that control is possible. All these point to the involvement of as many people as possible. Where only one therapist is available, communication between therapist and nursing staff who have more hour-by-hour contact with the patient is essential. But ideally, the entire milieu of the unit will be orientated along behavioural/cognitive lines.

CAN SUCH TREATMENT WORK?

The application of any therapy to a new area proceeds slowly. First, individual case studies are done to show that such a treatment can at least be used with this particular type of patients. Second, a series of patients receives the treatment to check that the individual case studies were not 'one-offs'. Third, controlled trials are carried out, to judge the effectiveness of the treatment compared to existing standard treatments. Finally, long-term studies are done to study how each treatment fares in reducing the probability of relapse. To date, only one relapse study has been done for this group of patients; but good progress has been made in evaluating acute treatment effects.

Fennell and Teasdale (1982) published a paper called 'Cognitive therapy for chronic drug refractory outpatients: a note of caution' which was, as the title implied, cautious. They found only very modest results with five treatment-resistant patients. Although these were outpatients they scored between 4 and 7 respectively on Hollon's Global Chronicity/Severity Index. After twenty sessions, these five patients' Beck Depression Inventory scores had shifted from a mean of 30.8 to a mean of 21.4 (a change of 30 per cent). Three patients needed further therapy. At follow-up (mean eight months) the Beck Depression score was 15.6. Consistent with these results, Blackburn *et al.*'s (1981) study of outpatients had also found that the most chronic patients responded least well. There was a mood of pessimism about extending cognitive therapy to inpatient settings.

There had been some signs of hope, however. Shaw (1980) had used cognitive behaviour therapy with eleven drug-free depressed inpatients, and found significant reduction in their symptoms. And in 1985, Miller *et al.* published a paper with a title which mimicked that of Fennell and Teasdale (1982): 'Cognitive behaviour therapy and pharmacotherapy with chronic, drug refractory depressed inpatients: a note of optimism'. Their small clinical series consisted of six inpatients (who had each had multiple hospitalizations for depression). Patients received either cognitive therapy plus tricyclic antidepressants, or social skills training plus tricyclic anti-depressants. At the end of treatment, two out of three patients in each small group had complete remission of depressive symptoms. The other two had partial remission. A similar outcome was reported by de Jong *et al.* (1986), who found that cognitive-behavioural therapy reduced depressive symptoms and increased social skills in depressed inpatients. Blackburn (1989) has extended the use of cognitive therapy not only to inpatients, but to an inpatient who was psychotically depressed. The Research Diagnostic Criteria diagnosis was major depressive disorder, psychotic, endogenous, recurrent unipolar depression. This patient believed that 'people are talking about my secret affairs', 'people are following me', the 'CID are watching me'. Hamilton Rating Scale for depression score fell from 27 at the outset to 6 at discharge. This was seven weeks (twenty-six sessions) later. The Beck Depression Inventory fell from 22 to 9 (a 59 per cent change).

Scott (submitted) reports the findings of two separate clinical series. The first (eight inpatients, of whom five were women) used fifteen sessions of cognitive therapy over twelve weeks together with lithium, phenelzine and L-tryptophan. The mean age of the patients was forty-eight years. They had been depressed for an average of 4.6 years and all had failed to respond to previous adequate treatment. In each case the current episode had lasted two years or more, and at least one had been hospitalized for five years prior to treatment. After twelve weeks, their Hamilton scores had fallen from 22.5 to 13.1, and their Beck scores from 38.3 to 22.3 (a percentage change on the

Beck of 42 per cent). While these shifts are statistically significant, and indeed clinically significant for these patients, these patients were by no means 'recovered'.

Scott's second series of sixteen patients were admitted to a special unit where the entire milieu was orientated to behavioural and cognitive intervention. The same antidepressant medication was used concurrently. Details of the milieu therapy are given below so will not be given here. Twenty-six sessions of cognitive therapy were given over twelve weeks, with initial emphasis on action orientated behavioural work. Hamilton scores fell from 24.5 at the outset to 10.6 after twelve weeks. The Beck scores fell from 38.7 to 14.7 (a 62 per cent change). Eleven out of the sixteen rated themselves as 'much improved' or 'back to my normal self'. The remaining five reported 'minimal change' or 'no change'.

Miller *et al.* (1989) reported a six- and twelve-month follow-up of depressed inpatients who had been given standard hospital treatment alone (pharmacotherapy using at least 150 mg/d of desipramine (with no upper limit on dosage) plus clinical management) *or* standard hospital treatment with the addition of cognitive-behavioural treatment (either cognitive or social skills treatment). Ten patients out of seventeen completed the standard treatment (i.e. 41 per cent dropped out); twenty-three patients out of twenty-eight completed the combination treatment (18 per cent dropped out). Patients were seen daily while inpatients (mean length of stay = 23.4(8.2) days for standard and 27.3 (8.6) days for combination treatment) and weekly for twenty weeks thereafter as outpatients. Although there were no significant differences between the groups at the point of discharge, at the end of the treatment (twenty weeks later), analysis of covariance showed that BDI scores were lower in the combination group. In the group of completers, BDI scores had changed by 74 per cent (62 per cent if patients who had dropped out were included). In the standard treatment group, BDI had changed by 60 per cent (35 per cent if dropouts were included).

A naturalistic follow-up over twelve months showed that more patients in the combination treatment remained well. Relapse was defined as 'recovery' followed by either re-hospitalization or Hamilton score >17, or BDI score >16, or Scale for Suicidal Ideation >7. Of the twenty-six patients who recovered during the treatment phase, seven (27 per cent) relapsed. Three of these had received standard treatment (out of six 'recovered' = 50 per cent) and four had received combination treatment (out of 20 'recovered' = 20 per cent). The most striking finding was the overall treatment response. When all patients who entered treatment were considered, a significantly higher percentage of patients given additional CBT achieved remission (i.e. recovered and stayed well): 54 per cent vs 18 per cent for the standard pharmacotherapy group. (The percentages for those thirty-one who completed treatment are 68 per cent and 33 per cent for combination and standard treatments respectively.) Although the numbers in this study were small, as for most inpatient studies to date, the fact that the results were comparable to outpatient treatment and follow-up studies (see Chapter Four) suggests that the results are reliable.

Finally, Bowers (1990) conducted a controlled trial in which TCA alone (nortriptyline; initial dose range 25–75 mg/d; the dosage rising to 100–200 mg/d) was compared with the same dose of TCA combined either with CBT or with relaxation. There were ten inpatients (age eighteen to sixty years) (DSM III unipolar depressives) in each group. The psychotherapy was conducted daily for twelve days. The mean number of days in hospital was 31.9 days for the TCA alone group, 29.4 for the CBT + TCA group and 27 days for the relaxation plus TCA group. Independently rated Hamilton Rating Scale for Depression scores shifted from 22.1 to 8.5, 20.7 to 6.6 and 16.5 to 7.3 in the TCA alone, TCA plus CBT and TCA plus relaxation respectively. The corresponding Beck scores were 31.2 to 19.6 (37 per cent); 24.2 to 10.1 (58 per cent) and 25.8 to 9.3 (64 per cent) respectively. These results were very encouraging for the addition of psychological treatment to the TCA. Even more encouraging was the analysis of the proportion in each group who achieved the criterion of 'remission' (Hamilton score of 6 or less). Whereas eight out of ten patients in the TCA + CBT group had a score of 6 or less, only one out of ten of the TCA + relaxation group and only two out of ten of the TCA alone group achieved remission.

These studies suggest that a range of behavioural and cognitive procedures, applied systematically, may have a significant effect in combination with antidepressants. No study has yet compared psychological treatment alone and in combination with antidepressants, with antidepressants alone. However, the evidence from clinical trials with outpatients (reviewed in Chapter Four) suggested that the combination of psychological and drug treatments has never been found to be less effective than either alone. So although we await controlled trials to examine this specific question, there appears no reason to stop one treatment while the other proceeds, except for the evident advantages of giving patients who may have been on psychotropic medication for a long time a chance to come off their drugs in the protected environment of an inpatient unit and while alternative psychological treatments are available. It is to a more detailed description of these alternative psychological treatments that we now turn.

OVERVIEW OF TECHNIQUES

When the cognitive therapy package was introduced earlier (Chapter Six) I pointed out how, for the more severely depressed patients at the outset of therapy, it was more appropriate to focus on behavioural targets using behavioural techniques, rather than on cognitive aspects. Behavioural approaches are often criticized for being too objective and unfeeling, for not taking into account the personal experience of the client. But in some contexts, this may be its strength. After a long period of depression and after many periods in hospital, the patient, their family, the therapists and staff find it difficult to be objective about the situation. Because behavioural approaches so clearly try to stand outside personal experience, it may lay essential foundations on which relationships and self-esteem may be rebuilt. Patients, staff and family members who have agreed simply to count the number of times a certain objective 'behaviour' occurs, can find this a very liberating experience. Consistently defining these behaviours as the central aspect of depression to be changed encourages all concerned to see things more clearly. There is a greater chance that all involved will be able to agree on what changes need to be made. The irony is that ignoring personal experience may sometimes be the best way to change it.

This section gives information about techniques that have been used successfully with people who are more severely and more chronically depressed. Generally, the number of sessions is greater than conventional cognitive therapy, though the total number of weeks in therapy may not be longer. Shorter sessions are held two or three times a week and wherever possible the whole milieu of the unit is used to promote awareness of cognitive and behavioural principles of coping with depression.

CONTINGENCY MANAGEMENT

Rationale

Depressive behaviours *per se* constitute the disorder. They can be manipulated by encouraging the performance of positive behaviours (by a token economy or contingency management scheme) which are incompatible with symptomatic manifestation.

Aims of treatment

The aim is to increase frequency of 'work behaviour', coping strategies and interpersonal efficiency which will be incompatible with depressive behaviour.

Procedure

Because the treatment is usually carried out in an inpatient or daypatient setting, staff can observe and interact with patients over a long period each day. Many of a patient's 'daily-living' activities, such as cooking, cleaning, personal hygiene and social interaction, can be made the focus of treatment. Typically, the patient consents to participate in a scheme which is running for a whole ward or unit. (Some therapists maintain that programmes for individuals within a normal ward are impractical, noncost-effective, and more difficult to control. However, there is nothing in principle to stop therapists from adapting these procedures for use with individuals in normal inpatient or daypatient settings.)

In introducing the patient to the scheme, a great deal of didactic explanation of its underlying principles is thought to be essential. Some patients and relatives will readily accept the philosophy, others may not. Liberman and Roberts (1976) give the following written information to patients participating in the Coupon Incentive Scheme at their day treatment centre.

1. The emphasis is on active participation in the programme as the 'best therapy'.
2. A brief description of way the unit is run – meals, recreation, therapy, etc.
3. Introduction to 'token economy' concept – tokens given on predetermined basis at a set rate for jobs around unit.
4. Procedure for exchange of tokens (snacks, coffee, recreation, etc.).
5. Procedure for monthly renewal of tokens and 'fresh start'.
6. Management of token economy by patients themselves chosen by all patients weekly, with staff members in support.
7. Patients are asked to sign a consent form.

These details give something of the 'flavour' of the coupon incentive scheme, and although not appropriate for many settings, it may be modified for use in other centres. Note that it is explicitly behavioural-educational, but that the patients run many aspects of the scheme themselves. One important aspect of the approach in Liberman and Roberts' centre, was that the token economy was not the only therapy strategy operating. Each patient was assigned to a therapist (nurse, psychological technician, rehabilitation worker – ten in all) who worked out individual strategies for each patient, including homework assignments.

Other activities during the day included workshops (with the emphasis again on education) which taught skills in community living and personal finance, as well as conversational skills, use of public agencies, etc.

Example of contingency management in a daypatient setting

Liberman and Roberts (1976) describe the case of Sarah Jane, a thirty-year-old married ex-secretary with three children. On admission to their day treatment centre she had a history of loss of interest in everything, 'feeling like a nothing', staying in bed for long hours, failure to cope with housework and childcare. On previous admissions to other units she had been described as agitated, tremulous and apathetic. Her diagnosis was 'neurotic depression'. Psychotherapy had been tried during a previous admission to no avail.

Table 8.1 gives a specification of problems and goals for Sarah Jane.

The staff at the centre where Sarah Jane was a daypatient were encouraged to ignore her negative self-reference and give social approval for

Table 8.1 Specification of problems and goals for Sarah Jane

Problems	Goals
Deficits	**Behaviour to strengthen**
Fails to perform housework and childcare	Cleaning, clothes washing, making beds, going shopping, cooking meals, making snacks for children.
Poor grooming	Fix hair more stylishly, wear more colourful clothes, iron clothes so they are not baggy or wrinkled.
Infrequent conversation with husband and children	At least fifteen minutes of conversing with husband each day, read to children in evening
Excesses	*Behaviour to decrease*
Complains about helplessness and worthlessness	Verbalizations about feeling sick, helpless, worthless, 'like a nothing'
Retreating to bed	Time spent in bed during daytime and before 11 p.m. each evening

her improved personal appearance (as per specification). The treatment of the excess sleeping and 'deficient housework' was carried out by pairing the two in a contingency self-management programme which will be described in a later section. Sarah Jane was taken off the medication she had been taking on admission (doxepin and chlorpromazine) (on the grounds that 'the scientific literature reveals no clear benefit of medication in neurotic depression'). She and her therapist met daily to review the contents of her daily diary. During these sessions also, the therapist ignored remarks about how difficult her housework duties were, and instead enquired further into the details of Sarah Jane's accomplishments in her assignments.

After one month of this intensive day treatment, conjoint marital therapy (one session per week) was started, though it seems that the patient continued to attend the centre on some days until three or four months later – by which time she was doing a three-day-a-week volunteer job. A three-year follow-up revealed that she and her husband had decided to separate by mutual consent. She was leading an extremely happy and fulfilled life.

Comment

A number of things are notable about the original contracts that were made. Firstly, many may object that it is sexist. 'Adaptive' behaviours seem to be geared to increasing comfort with the housewife and 'sexually attractive wife' role. This may be so, though it is very important to achieve a negotiated contract between therapist and patient, with neither side being able to impose a philosophy on the other. (In fact, the authors were well aware that the causes of this patient's depression had much to do with her husband's behaviour, and arranged for marital therapy to take place.) Secondly, in common with much behaviourist formulation, there is no place for 'reasons'. 'Verbalizations about feeling sick' are to be decreased with, it seems, scant regard for what prompts such talk (e.g. actually *feeling* sick). On the other hand, the indications are that such contracts are willingly negotiated and in some patients there is *relief* that the focus of treatment is so observable. No therapist would wish to impose such a programme on an unwilling party.

Note also, that in this case the token economy scheme was very much a 'background' against which these other treatments were implemented. The coupons were given for helping out around the unit, but the modification of particular depressive behaviours (e.g. unkempt appearance) were individually tailored for each patient. This individually specific assessment and treatment formulation differs from other token economy programmes. In that of Hersen *et al.* (1973), for example, patients were awarded blue index cards contingently upon completion of target behaviours in four categories – personal hygiene, responsibility, occupational therapy attendance and work (all off the ward). These assignments were administered by hospital personnel, nonpsychiatric staff. Even within this more rigid system, however, individuals took responsibility for planning their day each morning during the unit's 'banking hours'. The indications are that both practices can work well. It is up to individual practitioners to decide which approach they prefer.

APPLICATION OF PREMACK PRINCIPLE

Rationale

For people who have been severely depressed for a long time, there often seems to be nothing which is rewarding, nothing which can be used as 'reinforcement' in contingency management. The Premack principle (Premack, 1959) states that the 'occurrence of high frequency behaviour should have reinforcing value for low frequency behaviours'. That is, it starts with the assumption that whatever the patient does most of the time is reinforcing for them and can be used to reinforce behaviours they do least frequently.

Aim of technique

The aim is to draw up a plan with patient, family and staff (where relevant) to 'make the occurrence of a high frequency behaviour contingent upon a low frequency behaviour'. That is, to allow the person to do what they normally do most of only if they have done (initially a small amount of) what they do least.

Procedure and examples

When therapist controls contingency

Lewinsohn *et al.* (1969) present the case of a twenty-two-year-old divorced male who was in financial difficulties, would ruminate on his marital and other failures, feeling suicidal and ignoring his personal appearance.

The first step was to identify high frequency behaviour to be reduced (depressive talk). The next step was to identify low frequency behaviour to be increased and to establish a series of targets which the patient agreed were achievable in principle (talking to tutor, making arrangements to recover from his financial plight, making enquiries into availability of various jobs). The therapist then made available more time to listen to depressive talk (if patient wished to talk) only if some prescribed positive steps were taken between sessions. Each interview began with a report on progress the patient had made. If all targets had been met, a full hour session was made available. If little had been accomplished, the therapist was polite but brief, and ended the session within ten or fifteen minutes, suggesting that the patient return three or four days later.

Within a few weeks the patient had made and acted upon many decisions, had found a job and arranged a loan to ease his financial embarrassment.

Comment

There are several points that deserve comment. Firstly theoretical: given that all behaviours have multiple causes, it is doubtful whether a clear contingency between the high probability behaviour and low probability behaviour was established in this case. Activity scheduling itself has been used clinically without making opportunity for occurrence of depressive talk contingent upon it, and may thus have been the effective component. Secondly practical: many therapists would be unwilling (a) to terminate a session prematurely for any reason other than by mutual agreement of both parties; or (b) to let the longer session wander aimlessly, directed only by the patient's wish to discuss self-critical topics. Nevertheless, for some patients who seem to find therapy sessions an end in themselves, and in whom there is evidence of low motivation to pursue targets because of a fear of termination of therapy, this principle may be applicable. In these cases, it can be made clear to the patient that you want to meet weekly to monitor midweek progress, and that there is no point in meeting for long if no homework has been attempted.

When patient applies Premack principle to self

In Liberman and Roberts' treatment of Sarah Jane, they included a self-managed Premack technique which the patient operated herself when on leave from the unit. Together, the therapist and patient prepared a notebook for use as a behavioural diary, dividing each page into two columns. One column was headed 'constructive activity' (low frequency behaviour which they had decided to try and increase). The other column was for recording the particular depressive high frequency activity they had decided to try and decrease – in Sarah Jane's case, the time spent lying down during the day (approximately five hours at the outset). The patient was urged to go to bed during the day only after she had completed a predetermined amount of adaptive, constructive activity (e.g. housework, shopping, interactions with children). Sarah Jane herself produced the list of constructive activities which would be subject to this scheme. The idea is that as the frequency of constructive activities increases, they gain their own reinforcing qualities independently of the inappropriate activities. This, it is hoped, will improve mood. Gradually the desire to take to bed will decrease. This is what occurred in the case of Sarah Jane. By the end of seven weeks the 'time in bed' earned by the completion of constructive activities consistently exceeded the time in bed actually taken up.

Comment

The use of the Premack principle in this way seems to avoid the disadvantage of the use of the principle by the therapist. It is self-managed and is therefore easier to make plain to the patient exactly what the purpose of it is. Furthermore, it gives permission for the depressive behaviour to take place. My own impression is that depressed patients have often become very immune to attempts by partners, family and friends to spur them into action. Often partners have tried both positive and negative approaches in attempts to prevent the patient lying down on the bed (for example) for a great part of the day – to no avail. Patients themselves are often extremely frustrated and puzzled by their own lack of energy and listlessness. A therapy which allows any amount of this to happen, so long as some (at first) minimal constructive activity has taken place has a lot to commend it. It is this which makes the technique particularly useful in an inpatient setting. If therapist, nursing staff and patient can agree on what small amount of constructive activity on the ward will 'buy' what amount of 'depressive behaviour' (e.g. lying in bed), this allows all concerned to reduce the unsystematic and frustrating interactions between staff and patients that otherwise often occur.

A variant of the Premack principle is used in *covariant conditioning*. In this procedure, a list of positive self-descriptions are drawn up by the patient with the therapist's help. The items are written on cards, and the patient is instructed to read through the list before engaging in a high probability behaviour (e.g. smoking, drinking coffee or tea, using the toilet, etc.). The aim is an increase in spontaneous use of such positive verbalizations as a result of these 'conditioning' trials, but no attempt to decrease the high probability behaviour itself is implied.

COGNITIVE-BEHAVIOURAL MILIEU THERAPY

Rationale and aims

Chronic patients take longer to engage in psychological treatment, and their problems are multiple, severe and complex. Psychotherapy must reflect this complexity by (a) being multifacetted; (b) by all members of the clinical team being consistent in reinforcing the behavioural and cognitive approach; and (c) by engaging close family members as part of the collaborative team alongside staff and patient.

Procedure

The following outline is based on procedures at the Affective Disorders Unit, Newcastle upon Tyne (Scott, 1988b). Patients are admitted to a specialist unit in which biological aspects of their depression can be closely monitored, previous drugs 'washed out' and new medications tried where appropriate. The unit is staffed by psychiatrists, psychologists and nurses who are all aware of, or trained in, the theory and practice of cognitive-behavioural therapy. Twenty-six sessions of cognitive-behavioural therapy are given over a twelve-week period (the mean length of stay on the Newcastle unit was fourteen weeks). Initial sessions are shorter but more frequent (twenty minutes, three times a week) so that the total, one hour per week, is the same as conventional cognitive therapy but split into manageable units. The initial emphasis is on 'action-orientated' behavioural work and specific attention is given to engaging the patient in psychological treatment.

Each patient has a key worker who coordinates their therapy. Members of staff (not necessarily the key worker) spend periods of five to fifteen minutes at various points during every day seeing the patient, and encouraging them in therapy. Because of shift changes, *roles* are defined, so that the same people can take on different roles, or different people can take on the same role on different days. There are six roles defined so that each patient will have at least this number of periods of time spent with them each day:

1. *Activator:* the person in this role, usually the key worker, helps the patient plan their activity schedule for the day.
2. *Reinforcer:* the person in this role encourages the patient during the day, looking out for when they have achieved a task on their activity schedule.
3. *Motivator:* the person in this role deals with those thoughts and

experiences a patient may have during the day which make them feel hopeless and that 'nothing will help them'.

4. *Collaborator*: the person in this role looks for opportunities to collaborate with the patient in finding ways around difficult problems that occur in carrying out assignments.

5. *Observer*: the person in this role monitors the behaviour of the person during the day.

6. *Evening therapist*: the night staff spend a short time with the patient talking over the day (see below). The aim is to remind the patient of positive or neutral things which have happened during the day, which the patient might normally ignore when encoding the events of the day into long-term memory.

After three weeks (nine sessions), the frequency of sessions is reduced to two (half-hour) per week. By the end of treatment sessions are scheduled for once a week.

Three sessions are scheduled for close family members. The aim is:

1. to explain the cognitive-behavioural approach
2. to involve them as co-therapists
3. to examine their own cognitive distortions about themselves and the patient
4. to encourage them to reduce any negative attributions and behaviours which arise from these distortions
5. to re-integrate the depressed person into their family

As soon as possible, inpatients are encouraged to go home for weekends as part of the re-integration with the family, and to encourage the cognitive-behavioural principles to generalize from the ward to the home setting.

Comment

The fact that eleven out of sixteen patients who experienced this milieu therapy in Scott's series reported that they were either much improved or back to normal implies that this approach is worthwhile. These were patients with very severe and chronic problems. The cost of the treatment package must be offset against the cost of future inpatient treatment for these people. As with most milieu therapies, the greatest effort is setting them up in the first place. Once in place, nurses typically find that they spend no more time with patients than they did before, but now their time spent with patients has greater purpose. This increases the staff morale, and with it there is more optimism about the possibility of change which communicates itself to the patients and their families.

Defining the roles to be taken up with respect to each person each day helps to overcome problems associated with shift changes and changes in personnel. Where this is not done, individual staff bear all the responsibility for an individual patient, but when that staff member is off shift or away on leave there is often no one who takes over responsibility. Treatment is then put on 'hold' and the patient may well become very pessimistic again. By contrast, the shared responsibility in the Newcastle unit ensured that treatment did not come to a standstill when staff were away or on another shift.

EVENING THERAPY (Benatov, 1981)

Rationale

Memory is a basic determinant of consciousness, behaviour and future expectations. Many events each day do not pass the 'barrier' or 'filter' into long-term memory. This filter is biased negatively in depressed patients so that only depressive events tend to be remembered. This biasing maintains the disorder.

Aim of treatment

The aim is to redress the bias in what is selected from everyday events to pass into long-term memory.

Procedure

Time is set aside each evening or at least four times a week. A quiet room and a comfortable armchair (back to therapist) is the setting in which the patient is instructed to recall every detail of that day. Benatov talks of the 're-activation of short-term memory', the aim being to 'restore STMs of the day in all details'.

The patient is led to concentrate on information from 'perception' rather than 'interpretation'. In early sessions, patients tend to begin with an 'ego-centric structure of the facts', but later are able to pay more attention to all details of daily experiences.

Comment

This is an interesting procedure which seems to share the aims of reality-testing of cognitive therapy. It is simple in concept, and has, of course, a great deal of experimental evidence to back up its rationale. Depressed individuals do tend to select out the negative feedback. Of course, the terms STM and LTM should not be taken as referring to the same constructs as in most cognitive psychology theories. If so, there would be some difficulty in the 'recovery' of material which was supposed to be 'lost'. Nevertheless it is true that for all people (depressed or non-depressed) remembering everything we have done in the last twenty-four hours is difficult, and this common frailty allows a great deal of negative bias to creep in for a depressed individual who can easily believe that a long sequence of unpleasant things has happened to the exclusion of all else.

Because it needs to occur daily, if possible, it seems very suitable for inpatient work. The role of therapist could perhaps be played by any one (or more) members of the multidisciplinary team – nurse, psychiatrist, social worker or psychologist (see milieu therapy above).

INTERPERSONAL ISSUES FOR THE CHRONICALLY DEPRESSED PATIENT

So far, a number of techniques to use with inpatients or daypatients have been described. A consistent theme has been the need to take account of the family of the patient. There has been a burgeoning interest in the use of cognitive-behavioural therapy in treating relationship problems, such as Beck's book *Love is Never Enough* (1988). Readers particularly interested in marital work will find Beck's book very helpful both for themselves and for their patients to use. In the section which follows I bring together one or two basic behavioural techniques for use when one partner has been severely depressed for a long time.

The general aim of such therapy techniques is to improve skills in interacting, and to increase the extent to which patients and partners accept themselves and each other. The particular communication skills to be improved includes the expression of and response to wishes, anger, disappointment, anxiety and positive emotions – happiness, joy, interest, surprise, contentment. Some therapists suggest that a central difficulty for couples is to maintain a balance between distance and closeness. Conflicts often occur when one partner wants more distance and the other wants more closeness. Strategies must be developed for coping with these competing needs.

USING PARTNER AS SOURCE OF REINFORCEMENT

Rationale

Depressive states are associated with a failure to control one's interpersonal environment (McLean *et al.*, 1973) with the result that adaptive ('performing') behaviour is extinguished and depressive behaviour is reinforced (Burgess, 1969).

Aim of treatment

The treatment aims to reverse (using partner as ally) the progressive extinction of 'performing behaviours' and reverse the acquisition/maintenance of 'depressive behaviour'. This is attempted by teaching both patient and partner about reinforcement principles, instructing the partner to selectively ignore and reinforce aspects of the patient's behaviour (Burgess, 1969; Lewinsohn *et al.*, 1969) or by modification of the verbal interaction style between partners (McLean *et al.*, 1973).

Procedure

Assessment takes place according to principles outlined in Chapter Six at an initial interview. Emphasis is on discovering the things which the patient is *not* now doing that they used to do; finding out what they used to find most rewarding and which of these activities are still currently available (see Chapter Six); specifying ways in which the depressive behaviours are being inadvertently maintained and reinforced; getting a complete description of symptoms, and a breakdown of any recent life events.

Burgess (1969) emphasized to her patients that a major effect of depression was its tendency to inhibit the completion of tasks. These little failures themselves arouse further mood disturbance and also represent an interruption in the smooth flow of behaviour, a disruption which is often socially reinforced (e.g. someone else finishes the task, sympathizes with the patient, etc.).

At the most straightforward level, treatment consists of selecting simple, easily executed tasks for which the probability of completion is high, and encouraging the partner to reward completion with attention and praise. Note that in this treatment, the couple is told that successful completion of a task is in itself the goal, and that the nature and value of the task itself does not matter. It is important to encourage the partner to give reward only according to prescribed contingencies – for completion of tasks, not for complaints of how difficult the task is (see Chapter Six for activity scheduling procedures).

Burgess gives two examples of patients whose spouses were involved in treatment. Both found the simplest tasks very difficult, showed sleep disturbance and decreased sexual interest, they failed to attend work, had little interest in interacting with others, and ruminated about their own worthlessness and the possibility of suicide. The first was a twenty-six-year-old graduate who, having recently changed his job, was having difficulty adjusting. He blamed all of these difficulties on to his own failures and deficiencies. Task assignment started at the most simple level with making telephone calls, mowing the lawn, drying dishes, etc. and progressed to complex tasks such as job interviews, taking employment tests, and writing CVs. The patient's wife rewarded him only for completion of a prescribed activity with attention and praise, and ignored the depressive behaviour. Burgess reported very quick improvement (two weeks) although it is to be noted that the patient was seen daily for the first week, thus demanding a great deal of therapist time.

The second was a forty-year-old sociologist who had recently lost his job and was in the process of selling two properties. Again he was seen daily at the outset. His assigned tasks included receiving telephone calls, reading twenty pages of a textbook, eating dinner with the family and keeping a log of tasks performed (time spent, others reactions, his own level of mood disturbance). Husband and wife were subsequently seen together once a week. It seems that instructions to the wife about rewarding, ignoring and coping with depressive behaviour respectively had not been sufficient to change the wife's negative style towards him, or the family's reinforcement of his depressive behaviour. Follow-up data suggested that this treatment was producing gradual changes in the desired direction.

CONJOINT THERAPY – MUTUAL REINFORCEMENT BY PATIENT AND SPOUSE

Procedure

Assessment is done by a one-hour session conducted at the outset in the patient's own home with all the family present (there is a similar session conducted at the middle and end of treatment). During this home session, the behaviour of the patient, and its consequences, are carefully monitored. Lewinsohn has produced a manual for how to do this ('*A manual for instructions for the behavioural ratings used for the observation of interpersonal behaviour*, unpublished MS, University of Oregon). McLean *et al.* (1973) adapted these assessments for twenty couples with the following form (see Table 8.2):

1. Instruct the couple to conduct a conversation, at home, about some of their problems, lasting half an hour, and to tape record it (by themselves).
2. Analyse the tape recording by splitting it up into sixty thirty-second intervals.
3. Code the interaction according to whether, during that period, an individual was *initiating* or *reacting to* conversation in a *positive* or *negative* manner.
4. Average the scores across patient and partner.
5. Express negative interaction score as the proportion of total interaction for each tape session.

McLean *et al.* (1973) report inter-scorer agreement between 73 and 97 per cent (average 88 per cent).

Table 8.2 Subcategories of verbal interactions

	Action	Reaction	
Negative	a	b	a & b
Positive	c	d	c & d
Total	a & c	b & d	a & b & c & d

Clearly, one can concentrate either on total negative actions and reactions within an interaction, or only on the actions and reactions of the patient.

(Lewinsohn then uses the interaction data to define treatment goals. Such analysis following home observation may reveal very one-sided interactions or that the patient does not reinforce behaviour directed at them. It may also become clear that the topics of conversation in the home are of little interest to one or other partner.)

McLean *et al.* (1973) focus explicitly on the relationship. They emphasize to patients the punishment aspect of these interactions, and how, very quickly, depressed behaviour by one partner leads to (and is then further caused by) ignoring or criticism of a behaviour. It is explained how couples often take appropriate behaviour for granted, and reserve feedback for behaviour which is not appreciated. Eventually, the couple may decide that 'it doesn't pay to talk about it' and thus condemn each other to continue to make the same mistakes.

Treatment consists of eight one-hour weekly conjoint sessions with male and female co-therapists. At the outset, depression is explained to the couple in social learning theory terms. Three aspects are emphasized:

1. Alienation and apathy can grow up in a relationship over a long period due to the couple not rewarding each other for appropriate behaviour. If one individual does not behave in a way which elicits a positive reaction from the other, a downward spiral in the relationship may begin.
2. As the level of adaptive, appropriate behaviour gets less and less, the couple will tend to turn to coercive techniques to try and produce the desired behaviour. The coercive techniques tend actually to lower the probability of the very behaviour it aims to increase, in the long run. This leaves both partners feeling powerless. (Seligman's learned helplessness theory is used here to illustrate the wide-ranging effect of such feelings of powerlessness.)
3. Such a sequence of events may lead to cognitive, somatic and behavioural manifestations of depression in one or both partners. In the early stages, there are payoffs for depressive behaviour which reinforce the non-coping behavioural style – sympathy, lessening of criticism by spouse, etc.

A ban is put, by the therapists, on 'blameful' statements by either partner. The therapists emphasize the importance of avoiding 'bringing up the past' to explain or justify the current situation.

The differential effect of positive and negative reinforcement on behaviour and emotions is discussed. Emphasis is placed on being specific about behavioural goals each wants to achieve or wants their partner to achieve. The therapy consists mainly of the use of reciprocal behavioural contracts, practised throughout the eight sessions (for further details of this approach see Patterson and Hops (1972)). In this scheme, partners are taught to make specific requests about the behaviours they would like the other to change. If it is agreeable to the spouse, each requests the change in the other's behaviour. An example of reciprocal contracting is given in Table 8.3, from the case of Sarah Jane.

Table 8.3 Reciprocal contracts negotiated by Sarah Jane and her husband Jack during marital therapy (Liberman and Roberts, 1976)

Sarah Jane's responsibilities	Jack's responsibilities
Contract I	
Sit and talk with husband during breakfast, Monday to Friday	Arise from bed by 10 a.m. on Saturday and Sunday
Clean the living room for two hours each week	Engage in some mutual activity with Sarah Jane 10–11 p.m. on Tuesday, Thursday, Saturday and Sunday
Contract II	
Same as above plus the following:	
Dress in clothes that appeal to husband	Arrive home by 5.30 p.m. each day
Initiate affection (kisses, hugs, hand-holding, caresses)	Avoid expressing hostility or 'uptightness' (coldness, rejection, annoyance, silence, withdrawal) when
Reward husband	wife asks not to pursue sexual relations

Comment

Note that Liberman and Roberts were implementing this strategy following Sarah Jane's progress in making use of behavioural contracts as part of the day unit. It was explained that, though the receipts were very artificial, they at least kept both partners aware of the contractual agreement into which they had entered for the purposes of therapy. It also represented some observable reminder to give more general reinforcement (attention, praise, etc.) to the other. The couple is assured that the receipts will be dropped when both feel settled in the new pattern of interacting.

In McLean's use of this technique, the couple are instructed to comply with their side of the bargain whether or not their own requests are being met, for the first three weeks of the eight-week treatment. Thereafter, they are obliged only to carry out their behavioural target (e.g. coming home on time) if their partner carries out theirs (e.g. dressing attractively).

CONCLUDING REMARKS

Most clinical research trials of psychological treatments come to the same conclusion as clinicians who work with depressed patients: that there are some patients who respond very poorly, if at all, to psychological treatment. I mentioned at the outset Hollon's list of factors which are associated with such 'nonresponse': high Beck score, current episode longer than six months; inadequate response to previous treatment; two or more previous episodes; other psychopathology apart from depression; impairment across a wide range of psychological functioning; and poor tolerance of stress. But I also pointed out that these (and other chronic factors – most notably a high score on neuroticism) predict poor response to any intervention, physical or psychological. So the conclusion that 'chronic patients do not respond so well to cognitive-behavioural therapy' is perfectly consistent with the proposition that cognitive therapy may be better than any other approach for such patients. The therapy will be delivered differently from the standard one hour per week treatment over three to four months. But the studies reported at the start of this chapter, and the techniques detailed in the latter part, should give us hope that some of the most difficult and intractable problems known in psychiatry and psychology may now be treatable: that some people who previously could not be helped may now be able to work alongside their family and therapist to achieve some more lasting progress.

NOTE

In writing this chapter, I am greatly indebted to Dr Jan Scott of the University Department of Psychiatry, Newcastle upon Tyne whose pioneering clinical work in this area has given hope to many patients and clinicians where there was little hope before.

Chapter 9

Training exercises

There are probably as many ways to improve one's skills in therapy as there are trainers and trainees. Whether one is fairly new to the practice of psychological treatment of depressed patients or has a great deal of experience, the improvement of skills remains an important component of one's job. To some extent we may apply the same model to our own skills as we ask our patients to apply in coping with their lives: we may learn to determine appropriate *goals* for our therapeutic practice, then decide what *strategies* will make those goals more likely. Within each general strategy, there will be specific *tactics* which will be optimal in attaining the desired goals. In order to improve these skills we shall need to do what we require of our patients: to self-monitor, self-evaluate and self-reinforce. The first of these is easy to arrange. We can tape our interactions with some patients some of the time, and it may be useful to be specific in scheduling this into our therapeutic practice. This can be a very revealing exercise. There is often no harsher critic of one's practice than oneself. On the other hand it has its drawbacks. We may be better at spotting our faults than knowing how to put them right. In this respect, it is often useful to hold group discussions on a regular basis with close colleagues who are grappling with the same issues. Such regular discussions will help the self-evaluation and self-reinforcement aspects of skill development. This section of the book aims to provide some material which individuals or groups may find helpful in their own skills training. Part I contains some case descriptions together with questions to direct the attention to certain aspects of the material. The focus is on determining general therapeutic strategies. Part II becomes more particular, focusing on determining strategies within the therapy session. Part III is similarly specific, but focuses on between-session homeworks, diaries and thought forms. Part IV gives some suggested techniques for role induction, should a group wish to use role-play format as a training exercise. Finally, Part V gives hints on dealing with common frustrations in therapy.

None of this material is an adequate substitute for the reader's own clinical case material. Rather the material included raises issues and illustrates points which may remind individuals and groups of patients they have seen to whom the same questions could be applied and with whom the course of therapy has raised similar issues.

Finally, in reading this material, guard against the assumption that the cases you read are 'obviously suitable for such and such an alternative therapy'. In many patients, alternative therapies will have been tried, and they are being referred for cognitive-behavioural therapy precisely because the alternatives have not been successful.

PART I: DECIDING GENERAL THERAPEUTIC STRATEGY

Read the following case descriptions as if you were to decide which therapeutic strategy you would prefer to use. It may be helpful to bear in mind two specific models and compare what further information you would need in order to initiate either. Let us therefore focus on contingency management and reality-testing. What contingencies would you want to manage? What strategies of reality-testing would you employ and what aspects of reality would you seek to test? To what extent do both techniques assume that the objective reality for the patient is benign. If 'reality' is genuinely stressful, what follows for your therapeutic practice?

Case 1

Stephanie is a twenty-three-year-old woman, who lives with her mother and father in a small private house near the city centre. She is their only child. She did moderately well at school until in her mid-teens when she got bored, and left at the earliest opportunity without taking any exams. She moved from job to job, never settling at anything for very long. She is now unemployed in an area where jobs are scarce, even for qualified youngsters.

The home situation has always been tense. Her mother and father have violent arguments. She takes her mother's part in these – feels she needs defending. Her passion is dressmaking. Although limited by lack of finance she takes great care about selecting patterns and has done some designing herself.

Stephanie has always been a loner, but now she has been referred by her GP for treatment of depression. She lacks interest in anything except dressmaking; she cannot get to sleep at night and finds it difficult to get up in the morning. She eats very little. She feels life is not worthwhile and has considered suicide.

Recent incident: an interesting-looking job prospect has fallen through.

Case 2

John is a thirty-four-year-old man, married with two children, aged six and four. He is referred for treatment of depression of three years' duration, the main characteristic of which is bouts of severe lethargy and depression (lasting two to three weeks) separated by up to a week of feeling 'perfectly OK'. During these 'good spells' he is not 'high', and shows no signs or symptoms of mania or hypomania.

Antidepressant drug and lithium therapy have had no effect.

He was trained as a junior school teacher. The depression came to the attention of health care professionals when he took a large overdose and was admitted to general, then psychiatric hospital. Since then there have been three further overdoses.

He has quite a few friends through the children's school, and through church, but feels he is a burden to them. He often thinks of suicide, and sometimes drives out by himself intending to 'do something', but ends up feeling angry that he hasn't got the courage. 'They would be better off if I wasn't there.' The mornings are especially bad. He is tired, irritable and depressed.

The evenings are not much better – he often lies on the couch listlessly, or watches the television without really taking it in. On these occasions he finds it difficult to get to sleep, and the four-year old often wakes them in the night anyway, having recently started to wet the bed.

Recent incident: wife went out for night class and children were both ill and bad-tempered.

Case 3

Carla is a twenty-nine-year-old unmarried woman who has been referred for psychological treatment of her depression. Before admission to the psychiatric unit she had lived in a flat with workmates (she is a trained physiotherapist). Her work had been punctuated by frequent absenteeism due to unspecified illnesses. She had found work stressful and had several times left the flat to go back to her family home. (Indeed, she had started training at a college away from home, but had returned after only two weeks, and completed her training from home.) She was a 'good worker' but her frequent absenteeism meant she could not be given responsibility, and juniors were promoted before her. Her absenteeism increased and she took three moderately severe overdoses during a four-year period.

Her mother and father and younger sister still live at home. When she goes home she gets frustrated and her mood is extremely volatile. She feels she has no personality, that she has no 'guts' or 'stickability'. 'Everyone else is so composed.' 'My friends are sick of me.' 'I can't even hold down a job.'

Recent incident: phoned home and parents too busy to talk, on same day as a friend did not keep a coffee appointment.

Case 4

Patrick was referred for psychological treatment of depression, secondary to bouts of panic and anxiety he had suffered for some time. At the time of referral he had difficulty sleeping, had loss of energy, and increased tiredness, psychomotor agitation, loss of interest in usual activities including social contact and sex, and a diminished ability to think and concentrate.

He trained as a veterinary surgeon (the same profession as his father). He took a year out due to excessive anxiety which failed to respond to pharmacological treatment. He moved back to his home town where, as an inpatient he was successfully treated by relaxation methods, after which he moved back to college to finish his training.

After qualifying he started to work in his father's surgery, but missed the college social life and felt isolated in a country practice. He married and moved back to the city in which he had trained. The anxiety symptoms returned and he also became very depressed. He was referred for assessment for individual psychodynamic therapy but was felt to be too overcompliant/dependent and started in group psychotherapy instead. He felt uncomfortable with this arrangement and discharged himself after a few weeks, after which he was referred for cognitive-behaviour therapy.

Recent incident: wife, who has been very supportive up until now, says she is getting tired of his behaviour. He feels she may get bored with him and leave.

PART II: CHOICE POINTS WITHIN THE THERAPY SESSION

When you listen to a tape of your therapy sessions you may be able to identify various points during the session where the course of therapy could have travelled in a number of directions. It becomes an interesting exercise for a therapist (perhaps with a group of colleagues) to listen to a tape and identify these choice points. Once these have been identified, you may discuss the range of options and why one was chosen rather than another. In this way, group members can sensitize themselves to the process of therapy interchange.

In the transcript that follows, I have cut up the session. At each stopping point, the reader may consider which way they would have directed the session, or whether they would have attempted to allow the patient to decide. If you are doing this exercise in a group, each member may first make their decision, after which differences in members' conclusions may be discussed. If you find this particular transcript is not satisfactory for your group's needs, use one of your own tapes or transcripts and stop it at various intervals to try the same exercise.

The transcript extracts which follow were from a twenty-two-year-old man who had been depressed since his final year at school. He had then given up his A level course but had now gone back to a technical college to do some less advanced exams – to 'get back into the swing of it'. By the time this session was held, considerable progress in therapy had been made, though the patient believed this was due to a 'biochemical depression' which had now lifted. The therapist was concerned to investigate the patient's attribution of his success (biological factors vs learning coping strategies) in order to discover his level of vulnerability to possible future stresses. The patient believes that everything he has achieved has been really quite easy since his biological depression lifted. What would your strategies have been at the choice points I have indicated?

Therapist So this is what you filled in two weeks ago. And we were doing this to see what activities you are involved in now. (Patient brought in two weeks' activity schedules.)

Patient Well I think it was to compare with the one I did right at the beginning.

Therapist That's right. Yes.

Patient I don't know how accurate the times are, because I tended to find I got to the end of the day and couldn't remember.

Therapist So you were filling it in at the end of the day retrospectively. It seems a lot busier, a lot more full than the other one we had, which we've got here (earlier activity schedule). The pleasure scores are quite high as well.

Patient Some are, some aren't, it depends.

Therapist There are quite a few over 5, 5 out of 10.

Patient Oh yes.

Therapist Before you were finding things had little pleasure, or enjoyment, is that right?

Patient I think some did, probably not everything.

Choice point

Therapist How's it been about getting up in the morning?

Patient OK.

Therapist What sort of times have you been getting up?.

Patient Well it depends what time I have to get up. If I'm going to college for nine, I get up around seven.

Therapist And is there any problem getting up at seven?

Patient No.

Therapist You don't find the old problems creeping back of lying in bed, thinking about getting up and not being able to do it, putting it off.

Patient Not if I have to go to college for nine. If, say, I don't have to go until the afternoon, sometimes I do.

Therapist What sort of thoughts do you have, if you've got college at nine; when you wake up, what thoughts run through your mind then?

Patient Just that I'm going to college and I have to get up, and that's it. It isn't really all that difficult actually.

Choice point

Therapist How do you actually get up, how do you decide to get up? If you're thinking – there's nothing to get up for, it doesn't make any difference what time I get up, so I might as well lie in a bit longer – where does the change come before you actually decide to get up?

Patient Possibly in the time. If it gets toward ten o'clock – I feel I ought to get up.

Therapist Um – so as it's getting later you feel slightly obliged?

Patient Yeah.

Therapist And that time's about ten o'clock.

Patient Yeah.

Therapist Whereas before you were saying it could be midday, one o'clock in the afternoon, that you were lying in till, and you still didn't want to get up.

Patient Yes, but I still might not want to get up at 10 o'clock.

Therapist But you do.

Patient But I do, yes.

Therapist So that's a big contrast, isn't it?

Patient Also I think, possibly, there are more things that I want to get done.

Therapist There are more things to get up for?

Patient Mmm.

Therapist Can you give me an example of what some of those things are?

Patient Uhm, well I might have essays to write, I might have a book I've started, or I haven't taken the dog out – which I could put off, but the more you put them off, there's probably things that I'd want to do then anyway. I suppose there's less empty space.

Choice point

Therapist Yes. So some of the things are the same things that you used to do before which seem to have a bit more meaning, like walking the dog or reading, they were the sort of things you were doing beforehand but you couldn't be bothered so much about.

Patient Yes, I think I could put them off longer.

Therapist And other things that you are doing are actually new things, that are part of your life now, that weren't before, to do with college. And they actually encourage you to get on with the day?

Patient Well I have to get them done, so – yes.

Choice point

Therapist It seemed, at one stage, when we were talking about the problem of getting up, that you thought you believed it to be insurmountable, and that there was no way round it.

Patient It depends on how I was feeling. If I was feeling very depressed, I think I would still see it like that. But I feel alright.

Therapist So you're saying that when you're OK, when you're not depressed, it's not a problem. But if . . .

Patient If I became depressed, it wouldn't bother me, not going to college, it wouldn't be worth getting up then.

Therapist So there's always the chance, that if you become depressed, it all might shatter again.

Patient It might.

Therapist And you might be back at square one?

Patient Possibly.

Choice point

Therapist What could you do to stop that happening?

Patient I don't know.

Therapist How have you stopped it happening in the past?

Patient You can ignore it.

Therapist So you just put up with it and carried on.

Patient I tried to for a while.

Therapist And then what makes it change?

Patient I start doing more.

Therapist And what makes it change when you start becoming better and start being more active, like you have done in the last six weeks?

Patient I start feeling better and I start wanting to do more.

Therapist So your mood improves.

Patient Yes and that makes me feel like I want to get up and do something.

Therapist Does it ever work the other way round? That you do something and that makes your mood improve?

Patient Don't think so. Maybe a little bit. Not to a great extent. It certainly feels like I don't have any control. I mean, I can sort of manipulate it – if I feel a little bit depressed I can ignore it or do something I like, things like that. But if I'm going to get *really* depressed, I don't think there's anything I can do.

Choice point

Therapist How did you feel when we set the first target of getting up, in the mornings at nine o'clock? Do you remember when we set that first target five weeks ago and beforehand you were having the problem of staying in bed indefinitely throughout the morning and rising fairly late morning or early afternoon?

Patient Uh-huh.

Therapist You had quite a lot of negative thoughts about that.

Patient Uh-huh.

Therapist But you did try and do the target, and you succeeded, didn't you?

Patient Mostly.

Therapist In the majority.

Patient Yes.

Therapist So how does that make you feel about how much control you have over what happens to you?

Patient But it still wasn't a very big target. And, I wasn't all that depressed at the time.

Choice point

The session continues with discussion of the extent to which the decision to go to college has helped his motivation to do other activities. The therapist then reviews another area the patient had found difficult.

Therapist Yes – how do you find your decision making is generally, because that was something that used to worry you, wasn't it?

Patient Yes, it's OK.

Therapist It's improved?

Patient Yeah.

Therapist In what sort of ways? What sort of things are easier to decide about?

Patient Well, I can't think of anything that's not improved, but I mean I haven't had any major decisions to make.

Therapist No, but it was small decisions that were . . .

Patient Everyday things are alright.

Therapist Yes, it was the everyday decisions that were difficult, weren't they?

Patient Yes.

Therapist What do you put that down to? What do you see as being . . .

Patient Feeling better, not feeling depressed.

PART III: STRATEGIES FOR BETWEEN-SESSION THOUGHT-CATCHING

In this section, samples from patients' thought-diaries are presented. Look particularly at the differential effectiveness of the 'rational response' category in alleviating the original emotional disturbance. Why do these responses sometimes work and sometimes not? A possible reason may be that the 'rational response' represents a 'vain hope'. If there is no evidence for the rational response the optimism is empty and may not effectively challenge the validity of the negative thought (e.g. 1, 3). A second possible reason is that the rational response represents a 'must' or 'ought' or 'got to' statement which merely increases pressure on the patient (e.g. 8, 9). A third important variable is degree of belief in the response (e.g. 7). In each case the intensity of emotion and degree of belief are rated on a 1–100 scale where high scores represent greater disturbance and greater belief, respectively.

1. Situation: Watching holiday advertisements on television
   – Emotion: Hopeless (80)

- Negative thought: I've been in this mess for a year – I'll never travel again (95)
- Rational response: I managed to cope before. I could do it again (20)
- Emotion: Sad (50)

2. Situation: Watching group of students talking
   - Emotion: Sad (100)
   - Negative thought: I don't think things will ever be the same again (60)
   - Rational response: Things are gradually getting back to normal. Just wait a little longer (80)
   - Emotion: Sad (50)

3. Situation: Trying to plan day, one morning
   - Emotion: Frustration (80)
   - Negative thought: My friends are all living their own lives and I can't break out of this prison (80)
   - Rational response: This time next year my life will be moving again (20)
   - Emotion: Frustration (80)

4. Situation: Just returned from evening with friend
   - Emotion: Sadness (100)
   - Negative thought: I hate being myself, I wish I could escape (50)
   - Rational response: This is just reaction against knowing I must change (70)
   - Emotion: Sadness (50)

5. Situation: Waking up (in dressing gown)
   - Emotion: Despair (80)
   - Negative thought: This is going to go on forever. I wish I were dead (40)
   - Rational response: I recognize this early morning feeling. It will go on for the next hour at most (80)
   - Emotion: Anxiety (50)

6. Situation: Thinking about old friends
   - Emotion: Loneliness (80)
   - Negative thought: I've made a terrible mess of my life (90)
   - Rational response: I've made a mess of the last year, perhaps (10)
   - Emotion: Loneliness (70)

7. Situation: Drinking with friends
   - Emotion: Rejection (80)
   - Negative thought: I feel distant from those around me. People can't like me (40)
   - Rational response: I'm expecting too much attention (unrated)
   - Emotion: Rejection (80)

8. Situation: Thinking about my situation
   - Emotion: Hopelessness, despair, feeling of failure (90)
   - Negative thought: There's no way out. There's no reason for

continuing. I'm tired of struggling to keep up appearances. I'd like to just drive away (95)
- Rational response: I've got to keep trying to overcome this (60)
- Emotion: Hopelessness – worse because I can't think of a rational response (95)
  (I know what to do but seem unable to do it)

9. Situation: In office, sitting looking busy but not working
   - Emotion: Despair (100)
   - Negative thought: I am a burden to my husband, children and everyone (100)
   - Rational response: I must attempt to get back the fight – the will to survive (unrated)
   - Emotion: Continuing desperation (100)

Now you have read them through, how useful do you think the technique was with these patients? What do you think accounted for the difference in effectiveness of rational responses? To what extent are the rational responses only helpful when they represent attempts to modify the factual basis of the negative thought (e.g. 5, 6)?

Finally, consider the following sequence:

- Situation: At home, sitting thinking
- Emotion: Nervy, anxious (70)
- Negative thought: I'm getting hooked on my pills. Joan (friend) said last night 'once you're on pills, you're lost'. I always used to think like that (70)
- Rational response: (I hate doing this bit; it makes me feel worse)
  1. I've mown the lawn today and talked to three interesting people
  2. I've made dinner, and done some reading – the normal things of life (20)
- Emotion: (unrated)
  (I find it difficult to think of rational responses. When I do, I don't believe them. It's very demanding.)

Why might this patient be finding it so difficult to generate rational responses? How representative of your own patients is this patient? At what point would you want to give up this approach and try an alternative strategy? What alternatives would you consider? (For a discussion of some aspects of this problem, see p. 159.)

PART IV: TECHNIQUES FOR ROLE INDUCTION FOR TRAINING WORKSHOPS

As in the course of cognitive behaviour therapy, so in training in therapeutic skills, the use of role-play is often beneficial. On many occasions it will be sufficient for a group to assign therapist and patient roles to two of its members, using pen portraits such as those in this chapter or other case histories. Occasionally, however, the group may wish to concentrate more attention on getting into the role of the patient – to attempt to experience something of the feelings that depressed patients feel. There is now an extensive research literature on mood induction procedures (see Goodwin and Williams, 1982; Clark, 1983), and in this section I want to describe two such procedures in enough detail to be usable in the role induction context. Specifically, I suggest that half the members of a group use the mood induction procedures to induce the role, which, together with some pre-prepared biographical outline, will form the basis of their role-play of the patient. The other group members, the therapists, have access to the bio-graphical information, but are not present at the mood induction. Therapists have prepared instructions to conduct, for example, an 'initial session' (in which part of their agenda will be to explain the principles on which therapy will be based), or to focus on explaining and using a particular technique. Role-plays are then conducted in pairs, with the group coming together again after a predefined interval to discuss their sessions. At other training sessions, the roles may be reversed.

Mood induction I – Negative self-statements

The following is a list of negative self-statements of the type used in mood induction research. They are divided into self-devaluative statements and statements reflecting somatic concern or fatigability. You may select some from each list or use each separately. Select twenty to thirty items and type each on a card. The procedure for mood induction has varied from study to study, but a powerful procedure is for the 'subject' to study the cards, one by one, spending longer on the statements which are felt to be particularly meaningful and less on those which are not felt to be disturbing or ap-propriate. Continue this for seven to eight minutes, if necessary looking through the statements for a second time. The individual is encouraged to identify with the mood associated with the statement. Some biographical detail will have to be supplied before or after the role induction procedure. For example:

> You are a thirty-three-year-old mother of three children. Your husband works shifts in a factory. The money is adequate but the shift times are inconvenient, and leave you having to look after the house and children without much support. (Coming off shift-work would mean less money.) Recently you have lost contact with several friends, and lost interest in hobbies inside and outside the home. Things look very hopeless.

Here is the list of self-statements:

1. Somatic statements
   - Other people seem so much more lively than I am
   - I really can't be bothered to do anything
   - I don't feel very energetic
   - My whole body feels worn out
   - I do feel ready for a good rest
   - I do seem to get tired very easily
   - I feel heavy and sluggish
   - It seems such an effort to do anything
   - The mere thought of exercise is appalling to me
   - I feel as if it would take me twice as long to do anything
   - I feel so tired that I would rather just sit than do anything
   - I haven't even the energy to keep a conversation going
   - I just can't make the effort to liven myself up
   - I just feel drained of energy, worn out
   - I feel as if my whole body has been slowed down
   - I feel as if I haven't had a proper sleep for a week
   - I don't think I could exert myself even if I wanted to
   - I'm so tired I don't want to do anything at all
   - I just want to curl up and go to sleep
   - I feel absolutely exhausted
   - Sometimes it's just too much effort even to move
   - I'd like to go to sleep for a very long time
   - I'm so tired, my thoughts keep drifting away
   - I have to really concentrate to keep my eyes open
   - I'm having difficulty stopping myself from just falling asleep
   - I feel absolutely shattered

2. Self-devaluative statements
   - I have too many bad things in my life
   - I often wish that I were somebody else
   - I have very little to look forward to
   - I am less successful than other people
   - I feel disappointed the way things have turned out
   - I don't get much pleasure about being with my friends
   - I am annoyed at myself for being bad at making decisions
   - I don't think I make a good impression on other people
   - I'm not too hopeful about the future
   - I don't get the same satisfaction out of things these days
   - There are things about me that I don't like
   - Everything I do seems to turn out badly
   - I regret some of the things I've done in the past
   - I know I've made mistakes in my life
   - I'm very aware of my faults
   - I often feel ashamed of things I've done

– There are things about me that aren't very attractive
– Some people don't have a very high opinion of me
– Life seems boring and uninteresting
– I feel lonely and isolated
– The future seems just one string of problems
– I'm miserable, and there's no way for things to get better

Mood induction II – taped depression story

The following story, developed by D. Rosenhan and his colleagues at Stanford in their studies on affective determinants of altruism, is also a powerful mood induction procedure (Williams, 1980). It is tape-recorded, and played to the 'subject' who is asked to identify with the story. As with the self-statement role induction, the person role-playing the patient will need to be given some biographical detail, following the mood induction, onto which the disturbed effect may be 'attached'. For example:

It is now three months after your friend's death. You have become tired and listless, and lost interest in your work. You don't go out much now, and your former hobbies are of no interest to you whatever, even the thought of them makes you feel drained of energy. You are thinking of giving up college, but on the advice of your tutor, have come to see a psychotherapist, though you doubt it will make any difference.

Here is the mood induction story:

Sit back, and close your eyes. Relax. Let yourself sink into the chair. Focus all your attention on my voice. Let yourself relax and become absorbed completely in the things I am telling you. What I would like you to do is use your imagination. Put yourself into the situation I will describe. Feel the same feelings.Think the same things. Experience the situation as if you were in it. Let yourself relax and react to your feelings. Picture the events happening to you. See yourself going through them. Try to create in yourself the emotions and thoughts that I describe to you. Imagine that you have a very good friend who is attending college with you. Imagine that you and your friend are very close – and that you like and respect her a great deal. When things go well in your friend's life you are happy for her, and when things go badly, you suffer nearly as much as she does. You and your friend have been through a lot together, and that has helped you to get to know each other very well. Lately, you've become aware that your friend has not been feeling well. She's been dragging around – not doing much of anything. She seems to have lost her enthusiasm for course-work, and has become grumpy and irritable. She's really annoying, and you're upset because you don't know what's wrong. One day she confides in you that she's been having a chronic series of headaches and has not felt well for almost two weeks. You are afraid that she might really be sick. At your urging, she goes to the student health centre, but the doctors there find nothing wrong with her, and suggest she might just be overworked. Taking the doctors' advice, your friend drops two of her courses, and cuts back on all of her extra-curricular activities. But this does not help. As several days go by, you notice that your friend seems to have less and less energy and her headaches become increasingly severe and frequent. She looks terrible, and she's always irritated with you. Finally you convince her to return to the health centre and this time the doctors take her complaints more seriously. When your friend doesn't come back from the health centre after three hours you call the centre to see if she's still there, and learn that your friend has been taken to the hospital where the doctors want to perform a series of tests immediately. The next evening you go to visit your friend at the hospital during visiting hours and to your surprise find your friend's parents in the waiting room outside her ward. They've driven up from their home that morning. They look keyed up and anxious. You realize that there must be something really wrong with your friend. They don't know what the problem is yet, but the doctors' tests have eliminated all but the most serious possibilities. You think back, and remember all the good times you and she have had together. They all seem so far away. It hurts you to see her so ill, but it hurts even more to think that those good times may never come again.

As the next few days pass, you live with constant depression, trying to be near a phone, spending all your spare time at the hospital and hoping for some change.

You think of all the worst things that could happen. She could die and you would lose her, never be able to talk to her again. Or worse, she could die slowly. Every minute with her could be your last time together. For months you would have to be cheerful for her while you were sad. You would have to watch her die in pieces, until the last piece finally went and you would be alone.

You know the tests are getting more painful. The spinal tap. The bone marrow extraction. The test in which she has to swallow a radioactive solution that leaves her ill for days. No one has said it yet, but as every other possibility gets eliminated, you come to suspect cancer. That's a thought you don't want to have. It would hurt too much to lose her. Only old people get cancer – not people you know. It's often a long and painful disease with no cure. So you think; and worry; and try and keep it out of your mind as the tests continue.

Finally, the uncertainty ends. The doctors determine that your friend has lymphoma, an incurable cancer of the lymph nodes.

Your worst imaginings are now real. You are despondent and shocked. She has a year or two to live at most, and her death will be slow and painful.

You feel that it's so senseless and so unfair to end this way – she will be gone so fast. All the time you spent with her – all the crazy plans you made together are over. She will leave you alone; and constantly asking yourself what went wrong. You can feel some empty space inside you that will take a long time to fill. But the thought is too much to bear. You are hurt, and helpless, and upset that you will lose someone close to you to a disease that is so arbitrary and cruel.

Note: When the story is taped, the friend may be male or female.

PART V: TROUBLESHOOTING

Psychotherapy with people who are depressed is emotionally demanding. Cases reported in the literature almost invariably recover marvellously. Your own patients may seem more reluctant to show such miraculous change. Furthermore, if you have read the outcome literature, you will have in your mind some impressive looking graphs, with smooth slopes heading gently downwards from left to right. Yet these are averaged results, and not a single patient in any outcome trial necessarily follows that pattern. Most patients at several points say they are 'back to square one'. On such occasions it is difficult not to feel at least a little guilty for not helping them, angry, depressed and hopeless about their prospects. It is difficult at that moment not to think 'if only I was more skilled, I'd know what to do'. Of course, experience will help: but one of the most important things that it will help with is learning to accept the setbacks, rather than responding to them by giving up.

So how can one learn to accept the setbacks? First, by preparing both yourself and the patient for them. Remind yourself and your patient that the course is not smooth and that the 'back to square one' feeling will occur. Second, by setting up therapy at the outset to focus on some specific problem which both you and the patient agree needs to be solved. Solutions will not come easily and the setbacks are often opportunities to learn exactly what the difficulties are. Which were anticipated, which were not? Separate the two. But bring the discussion back to the specific problems to be solved. Keep in mind that if the formulation was accurate, solving these problems will indeed have a beneficial effect on mood, but this will take time.

Third, you may find it helpful to use assessment instruments (such as the Beck Depression Inventory) regularly, at the start of each session. If this is too long, work together with the patient to select some of the items which seem most relevant, and compile your own 'short form' for regular use. Then you can map the score on to a graph such as that shown on page 94.

Finally, a hint about what to do when feeling completely lost in therapy. When this happens, try summarizing what has been said, as a prelude to obtaining further information. If possible, make what has been said into the first of a list of things. So, for example, if someone says: 'I feel completely useless, everything has fallen apart this week', you may ask 'What has happened this week which has made you feel like this?' If only one thing emerges (e.g. 'My husband threatened to leave') there may seem nowhere else to go in the therapy session. In this case it is nevertheless important to ask if anything else has happened which has contributed to this feeling (there may be something even more significant that you might miss if you do not). Continue asking whether there is anything else until the list has come to an end. You will then have a much better notion of where it is important to start.

Sometimes there will not seem to be many events in the list, and then it may be possible to return to the initial expression, 'I feel completely useless', and make this feeling into the first of a list. For example: 'You said that when this happened, you felt completely useless. Did you have any other re-actions?' This may then show that the person did indeed have other reactions such as anger and hopelessness or suicidal feelings. When this list is complete, you will again be in a better position to discover which of these thoughts and feelings was the most upsetting. The inverted arrow technique (page 172) may be used to discover more information, or talk about other things that the husband has threatened, or other things that have made her feel this hopeless. You may talk about how to cope, based on what has worked in the past.

In any event, gaining more information and listing the situations or listing the feelings deals with the therapist's own feeling of being completely stuck. Containing their own feelings of hopelessness on behalf of the patient, will allow the therapist to maintain a problem-solving attitude which can en-courage the patient. I believe myself that this is because such listing, though it elicits more negative information, can allow a slight distancing to be attained from the problems that are being listed. It may also give the patient the idea that their problems are not infinite – the list has an end.

IRRATIONAL BELIEFS OF THERAPISTS

It is worth becoming aware of the beliefs and 'oughts' that you have as a therapist. There are many of these which will affect how you feel about your patients. You may find it helpful to discuss these and other beliefs you have about yourself as therapist in training groups with other therapists. It will be helpful then to analyse the common problems in therapy that you share. The sorts of beliefs that therapists may have are as follows:

1. I have to be successful with all my patients.
2. If I fail, it is because I don't know enough.
3. Every session must go well.
4. It is my responsibility to make the patient feel good.

5. I have to be respected and loved by all my patients.
6. I must be a better therapist than anyone else.
7. As therapist, I should always know what to do in therapy.
8. I should not have any emotional problems of my own.
9. I must not dislike my patients.
10. My patients must never see me make a mistake or misjudgement.

In your training groups you may find it useful to include this sort of idea while discussing other problems that occur in therapy that all therapists share. These problems tend to fall into three categories: characteristics of the patient, characteristics of the patient's situation and the management of the session.

If you find that problems occur in therapy, you are not alone. Discuss with colleagues or your training group what alternative ways may exist to cope with them. Rehearse some of these alternatives. Become aware of how these difficulties are exacerbated by the thoughts they create and the assumptions they activate in you as therapist.

Chapter 10

The cognitive theory of depression revisited

Although it was not until the late 1960s and 1970s that experimental clinical psychologists started seriously to develop theories about the onset and maintenance of depression, even from these early theoretical writings there emerged a controversy about the necessity to postulate cognitive mediators. There are two forms of this debate, the first, with which we shall not be concerned here, is the philosophico-theoretical issue about the status of 'private events' and their explanatory power.

The other debate is that between those who believe that cognitive events precede and cause the emotional disturbance, and those who believe that the emotional disturbance can be explained on other grounds (biological or behavioural) and see cognitive distortions and negative self-talk as a product or correlate of the emotional disturbance.

Now this debate is crucial. If cognitive events are an epiphenomenon, accompanying though not playing a causal role in affective disorders, it would make less sense to devote years of research to how best to change cognitive styles or habitual self-talk strategies. Like ointment on a chicken-pox rash, such treatment may soothe but have little prospect of treating the underlying disorder. Of course cognitive therapies do work (see Chapter Four) but it may be that they are inadvertently affecting other more significant subsystems. Let us then examine the status of the aetiological cognitive thesis.

Just to complicate matters further there are also two forms of the aetiological thesis. Let us call them the 'precipitation theory' and the 'vulnerability theory'. The first is a 'state' theory and argues that moment-to-moment fluctuations in mood may in part be accounted for by the thoughts, images, and memories that occur to the individual. Controlling the nature, frequency or intensity of these thoughts and images will thereby affect the mood that is consequent upon them. The vulnerability theory argues that long-lasting styles of thinking (e.g. attributional style, tendency to selectively abstract or think dichotomously) occur prior to and render a person vulnerable to depressive breakdown in the face of stress. Although often confused under the general title of cognitive theory of depression, these theories are quite distinct and ought to be discussed separately. We shall consider the evidence for each in turn.

THE PRECIPITATION THEORY

There are two types of evidence in favour of the theory that thoughts and images may precipitate moment-to-moment fluctuations in mood. The first evidence comes from studies of experimentally induced mood. These studies provide particularly useful evidence because, using experimental manipulation of mood, they can eliminate other variables which might otherwise be important contributory factors to disturbed mood (e.g. individual differences). The second type of evidence comes from experiments which attempt to reduce the frequency of negative thoughts in depressed people, and observe the effect of so doing on their mood.

Mood induction research

Six forms of mood induction procedures (MIPs) have been used.

Self-referent mood statements are the most widely used MIP. First described by Velten (1968), the method involves reading aloud sixty negative self-referent statements, e.g. 'I'm discouraged and unhappy about myself' or 'I feel worn out, my health might not be as good as it's supposed to be'. The statements progress from relative mood neutrality to dysphoria, the overall tone being that of indecisiveness, tiredness, unhappiness, inefficiency and pessimism. Investigators agree that this general procedure is a potent manipulator of mood, as assessed by visual analogue scales (e.g. Teasdale and Fogarty, 1979), the Depressive Multiple Adjective Checklist (e.g. Hale and Strickland, 1976; Brewer *et al.*,1980), the Personal Feeling Scale (e.g. Frost *et al.*, 1979), and the Wessman and Ricks' Elation vs. Depression Scale (Coleman, 1975). Furthermore, independent ratings of general demeanour and 'mirth' outside the experimental situation (just having completed the experiment) have been found to differentiate between MIP and control groups (Coleman, 1975).

The *Autobiographical Recollections Method* was used by Brewer *et al.* (1980) in a comparison with Velten's MIP and various control conditions. Subjects were asked to close their eyes and recall three autobiographical mood-evoking events that made them feel lonely, rejected, defeated or hurt. The entire MIP lasted eleven minutes, the three events being spaced in time according to prerecorded instructions. Subjects had to try and recall three events which were progressively sadder and more unpleasant. The results showed that this method strongly affected mood, giving more affective disturbance on the DACL and Beck Depression Inventory than the Velten MIP. Spielberger State Anxiety scores were also affected by this MIP.

A taped depressive story has been developed as an MIP by D. Rosenhan and colleagues at Stanford, and subsequently modified for use with a British population by myself (Williams, 1980) (Chapter Nine). The taped story, with which subjects are asked to get involved, lasts approximately ten minutes. It asks the subject to imagine a friend becoming ill and eventually being diagnosed as having incurable lymphoma. The tape focuses on the subjects' own feelings of helplessness and loneliness. I found that this MIP significantly raised anxiety, despondency, irritation and frustration levels, and significantly lowered relaxation and happiness levels, when compared to a control condition.

Failure feedback has been used in a large amount of research on the learned helplessness and test anxiety phenomena. These have been comprehensively reviewed elsewhere (e.g. Abramson *et al.*, 1978; Weiner and Heckhausen, 1972). Although most studies have not aimed solely at manipulating depressed affect, many of the studies reviewed by these authors report affective changes following failure experience, or exposure to non-contingency.

Hypnosis has been used by Gordon Bower in his studies of state-dependent mood-memory effects. He asks subjects under hypnosis to induce a sad mood by imagining an episode in which they had been grievously sad. If they could call up no such scene from their life, the experiment helped them construct an imaginary one that 'would have the intended emotional impact'. Subjects were told to adjust the emotion until it was intense but not unbearable. Bower *et al.* (1978) report that their sad subjects were long-faced, morose, slow to respond, and often on the verge of tears. No objective measure of mood intensity was taken, nor any subjective ratings by the subject used, so it is difficult to establish just how effective the procedure was. Bower *et al.* used only subjects who had demonstrated good hypnotic facility, which, although suggesting that the mood induced would have been subjectively intense, is also a drawback in generalizing from these results.

Finally, several investigators have used *music* as a mood induction procedure (e.g. Sutherland *et al.*, 1982; Teasdale and Dent, 1987; see Clark (1983) for a review of the procedures involved). Sutherland *et al.* gave subjects a choice of music selected as having sad associations. They found the MIP more successful than that of Velten in changing subjective ratings of anxious, sad and happy moods, though ratings of 'apprehension', 'despondency' and 'tiredness' were not affected. Over the years, Teasdale and colleagues have increasingly used musical induction in preference to the Velten technique in their studies of the effect of mood on information processing (e.g. Clark and Teasdale, 1985; Teasdale and Dent, 1987). In this procedure, subjects listen to a depressing piece of music ('Russia under the Mongolian Yoke' by Prokofiev). This music is played at half-speed for seven minutes, and subjects are instructed to try hard to get into a depressed mood. An indication of the size of the effect produced by this procedure can be seen in the group of 'never depressed' subjects (N = 21) who took part in the Teasdale and Dent experiment. On a 100-point visual analogue scale labelled at 0, 'I do not feel at all depressed/anxious/happy', and at 100 'I feel extremely depressed/anxious/happy' subjects changed from 2 to 24 on depression (t = 3.62, p<.01) from 72 to 43 on happiness (t = 4.81, p<.001). The change on anxiety (from 16 to 19) was not significant which suggests some specificity for the procedure.

All these procedures provide strong evidence that asking subjects to voluntarily create images, thoughts or memories which are unpleasant or unhappy, affects mood. Nor can it be argued that subjects are only pretending to be depressed. Coleman (1975) asked observers to rate subjects after they had left the experimental situation. Reliable differences were found in blind ratings of observations of 'mirth' between the subjects who had and those who had not undergone the experimental induction of mood. Coleman also found, as Velten (1968) had done before, that subjects differing on the Harvard Scale of Suggestibility did not differ in intensity of mood disturbance reported following mood induction. Finally, Polivy and Doyle (1980) actually told subjects that they would feel the mood opposite to the depressive statements by a 'comparison' effect (the more they read, the more they would feel happy that they did *not* feel like this). Despite this very heavy counter-instruction, half the subjects still felt the mood suggested by the statements. Other investigators' have used a control group who are told to try and behave throughout as if they were depressed and have found that the quality and intensity of mood disturbance thus induced cannot match that obtained when a mood induction is carried out. The combined evidence in favour of the precipitation theory is very strong.

Reducing negative thoughts in depressed patients

The other strategy for examining the connection between depressive thoughts and negative mood is conceptually the opposite of the mood induction work: to block or reduce negative thoughts and examine whether mood can be affected. This has been done in a series of studies (Teasdale and Rezin, 1978; Davies, 1982; Fennell *et al.*, 1987). Negative thoughts are reduced by distraction procedures such as shadowing random digits, letter cancellation, or, more simply, asking patients to focus on a series of coloured slides for five minutes and describing them in detail to themselves. The common finding is that such procedures do indeed reduce the frequency of negative thoughts and that this does have a beneficial effect on mood. These studies have also converged on the conclusion that this effect is more marked for patients at the non-endogenous end of the endogeneity spectrum as assessed by the Newcastle Scale (Carney *et al.*, 1965) or, in the case of Davies (1982), using Spitzer *et al.*'s (1978) criteria. Even when high endogenous and low endogenous patients are carefully matched on the degree of reduction in negative thought frequency brought about by distraction, the impact on negative mood is less marked for the patients with the more endogenous symptoms. Fennell *et al.* (1987) explain this difference by saying that in high endogenous patients 'the main determinant of depressed mood is some internal, endogenous, biological factor' (p. 449), and it is clear that, at least for low endogenous patients, mood is quite closely linked with the frequency of depressive ruminations. These depressive ruminations appear to be mostly 'memory derived . . . related to losses, disappointments and problems in patient's lives' (p.449).

For these patients at least, the precipitation theory holds up well – negative thoughts activate and maintain negative mood. The theory has not, however, been proved for the more endogenous patients. However, no research has yet looked in detail at cognitive processing in these patients. Measures of frequency of explicit negative thoughts are unlikely to show all the information being processed by a person at any given moment. This information includes not only memories, judgements, plans, etc. which could in principle be made explicit but are not currently in consciousness, but also general themes and implications of current conscious thoughts which may remain even though the current thought is blocked. Until such research is done, there remains no evidence for the precipitation of mood by *conscious* thoughts and images in endogenous patients. This makes all the more striking the finding (reported in Chapter Four) that endogenous patients fare no less well with cognitive therapy than non-endogenous patients (although the Newcastle Scale has not itself been used in these studies to separate the groups). Perhaps different patients are responding to different aspects of the treatment. Or perhaps the precipitation of mood by moment-to-moment negative thoughts is not the main sense in which cognitive factors are important in depression. I mentioned that there were two aspects to the cognitive theory; it is now time to turn to the second way in which cognitive processes are thought to be important: that they render people more vulnerable to depression.

THE VULNERABILITY THEORY

The notion that clinical depression of at least some subtypes is preceded by personality traits, self-esteem deficits or cognitive distortions which render the person vulnerable to emotional breakdown is certainly not new in clinical psychiatry and psychology. Just three current exponents of the view will be mentioned; Beck, Seligman and Brown.

The vulnerability of the depression-prone person, according to Beck, is

attributable to the constellation of enduring negative attitudes about himself, about the world, and about his future. Even though these attitudes (or concepts) may not be prominent or even discernible at a given time, they persist in a latent state like an explosive charge ready to be detonated by an appropriate set of conditions. Once activated, these concepts dominate the person's thinking and lead to the typical depressive symptomatology.

(Beck, 1967: 227)

The idea that these may be 'latent' should sound a note of caution for the experimentalist. A model which includes such variables is often hard to refute.

In stating the reformulated hypothesis, Abramson *et al.* (1978) state that a persisting tendency to attribute negative events to internal, stable and global factors renders a person prone to depression, should they be exposed to non-contingent negative outcomes. Seligman (1981) has further argued that the maladaptive cognitive style detailed by Beck is reducible to the central tenets of the reformulated learned helplessness theory.

Brown and Harris (1978) argue that the factors which render women vulnerable to the effects of life events (loss of own mother before eleven years, no job, three or more children under fourteen at home, no confidante) are associated with low self-esteem. Self-esteem has a 'transitional position' in their account of the social origins of depression: 'as a background factor, low self-esteem can both predispose a person to a depressive reaction . . . (and can) . . . therefore become a prominent feature of the depressive disorder itself' (p. 265).

In reviewing the vulnerability model, it is helpful to see how the evidence has gradually accumulated over time. I shall therefore review the situation as it was in the early 1980s (up to 1983), identify what questions were raised by that early research, and then show how recent studies have helped to answer them. There are several separate questions for which this chronological approach is appropriate. First, are cognitive distortions actually found in patients when they are depressed? We shall see that the evidence was ambiguous in 1983 but is now less so. Second, in 1983 there was as much evidence against the vulnerability thesis as for it, but I identified two possible 'let out clauses' for the vulnerability theory (Williams, 1984a). Each of these has now been examined by more recent studies. Third, does the vulnerability theory require that an actual aversive event occur in order to turn depression proneness into a depressive episode? Once again, the evidence for this was ambiguous until the mid-1980s and now more evidence has become available.

Cognitive distortions in currently depressed patients

It may be thought odd that this issue needs raising at all. Is it not an essential prerequisite of a diagnosis of depression that such distorted thinking is shown? The answer is that it is not. If a person has dysphoric mood, early morning wakening, diurnal mood variation, retardation or agitation, weight loss and inability to concentrate, in the absence of prior diagnosis of alternative disorders the person will almost certainly be diagnosed as depressed. They may not show clear evidence of distorted thinking styles or misattribution. Research on mildly depressed students bears out possible dissociations between depressed mood and distorted thinking. Hammen and Peters (1978) found that, among high Beck scorers, there was an inverse relationship between cognitive distortion and number of recent life events. Depressed subjects with low levels of life stress were more distorted; those with high levels of life stress were less distorted. Gong-Guy and Hammen (1980) reported that a depressive attributional style was associated with depression only when attribution for the more stressful life events was taken into account and more trivial events excluded. So maladaptive style of thinking is not a general and universal accompaniment of depression. More recent work in Newcastle bears out this conclusion at least for attributional style. In one study Cleaver (1981) found that although there was some evidence that attributions co-varied with mood within individuals, there was little suggestion that these depressed patients showed a depressive attributional style in general. In a second study Davies (1982) found no evidence of a depressive attributional style in a group of eight endogenous and twelve neurotic depressives (Spitzer criteria). A more extensive study by Hargreaves (1982, 1985) comparing fifty depressed patients with fifty matched controls found no evidence that the groups differed in attributional style. By contrast, Raps *et al.* (1982) found the predicted attributional style in depressives, but not in hospitalized schizophrenics. They concluded that such a style is specific to depression and is not associated with psychopathology in general. That is a fair conclusion, but only up to a point, for current depression levels of the patient groups were not given although the schizophrenics were referred to as 'non-depressed'. If we suppose then that the depressed subjects were indeed more depressed, then the groups differ on two variables; diagnosis and mood level. So if the schizophrenics had also been dysphoric, they might have shown a depressive attributional style as well. Although this result helps to establish that maladaptive attributional style is not a correlate of schizophrenia; it does not establish that it is uniquely associated with the diagnosis of depression, only with depressed mood.

The studies in the later 1980s, however, have come to a different conclusion. These have used the Dysfunctional Attitude Scale (Weissman and Beck, 1978) and compared patients while depressed, with the same patients when in remission. Each has found that scores while depressed were significantly higher than when not depressed (Eaves and Rush, 1984; Hamilton and Abramson, 1983; Reda *et al.*, 1985; Silverman *et al.*, 1984; Simons *et al.*, 1984). I and my colleagues have recently obtained similar results using a Dysfunctional Attitude Questionnaire (Burns, 1980) in a group of (mostly endogenously) depressed inpatients (Williams *et al.*, 1990). Patients were tested on admission when their Hamilton scores averaged 28.6. At this time their mean DAQ score was 123 (possible range = 35–175). After six months, twenty-one patients had recovered (Hamilton score of 7 or less). The mean DAQ score of this subsample, which had been 124 on admission, was now 100 (t = 4.58, p<0.001). By contrast, the patients who remained depressed (whose DAQ scores had averaged 120 on admission), now had DAQ scores of 114 (a non-significant reduction).

In this study we also used a measure of negative self-schema. Patients rated themselves on twelve adjectives such as 'deficient', 'failure', 'inadequate' a task which had been found to predict persistence of depression in a community sample of women (Dent and Teasdale, 1988). When depressed, patients endorsed an average of six out of the twelve negative adjectives as describing themselves. However, six months later, those who had recovered endorsed an average of 1.4 (t = 4.45, p<0.001) whereas those still depressed endorsed slightly more (7.1) than they had before. Given the fact that these recent studies using a wider range of questionnaires and assessments have converged on the same conclusion that depressed patients (both endogenous and non-endogenous) show elevated cognitive distortions when depressed, this conclusion now appears more firmly established. The question then arises how much of the distortion observable when people are depressed occurs *before* the onset of depression and can therefore claim to represent a vulnerability factor.

Few clinicians would disagree with the contention that some people are vulnerable to depression, but the thesis to be discussed here concerns the nature of that vulnerability. For at least Beck and Seligman and their co-workers suggest that this vulnerability involves maladaptive thinking styles, and these styles are not far from Brown and Harris's concept of low self-esteem. Correlations between current depression and current distorted thinking establish neither that one variable preceded the other in time nor the direction of cause when both occur together. Until 1983–4 the evidence was very mixed. Before reviewing it, let us pause for a moment to consider the different research strategies that might be used to examine these issues.

Possible research strategies

The first strategy is to study *recovered depressed patients*. It is known that such people are vulnerable to further episodes of depression (see Chapter One). The probability that they will have an episode in the next two years exceeds 50 per cent. The argument is that they should thus show evidence of such vulnerability in measures of cognitive distortion compared with 'never depressed' controls.

A second strategy is the *prospective study*. Attempts are made to predict depression levels at Time 2 on the basis of cognitive distortion measures at

Time 1, after the effect of depression at Time 1 is partialled out. Three types of prospective methodology are available: Taking non-depressed people and predicting onset; taking recently remitted patients and predicting relapse; and thirdly, taking currently depressed people and predicting persistence.

A third strategy is to use *cross-sectional regression methodology*. Depression levels are assessed at the same time as dysfunctional attitudes and, for example, reported recent life events. Multiple regression statistics are used to 'predict' depression scores on the basis of either dysfunctional attitudes or life events alone, and then on the basis of the interaction of the two. This is the easiest strategy to use, but also the most difficult to interpret because of the cross-sectional nature of the data collection (e.g. life events may be affecting depression levels, but equally, depression levels may be causing selective recall of life events).

In evaluating research, it is worth bearing in mind that conclusions reached by convergence of different methodologies – remission, prospective, and cross-sectional methodologies, are likely to be more reliable than those reached on the basis of one methodology alone.

Evidence for and against the vulnerability theory – pre-1984

O'Hara *et al.* (1982) used a prospective methodology to try and predict depression in women who were going to have a baby. In their study, 170 women were assessed in the second trimester of pregnancy on the Beck Depression Inventory and measures of attributional and cognitive vulnerability. They were followed up between five and a half and twenty weeks (mean twelve weeks) after the birth of their babies, and depression levels were assessed. Results showed that all scales correlated with each other and with post-partum Beck score. However, most of the variance of the post-partum depression was accounted for by initial depression level, the cognitive style measures only accounting together for a further 4 per cent of the variance. Since there was no control group of women who had not had a child, or any life event, it was impossible to say to what extent this result was due to the stress of childbirth acting upon vulnerable personalities.

A similar problem arose in the interpretation of an interesting study by Golin *et al.* (1981). They used a cross-lagged panel correlational analysis to examine 'the causality of causal attributions in depression'. They found that the level of correlation of attributional vulnerability at Time 1 with depression level at Time 2 (one month later) significantly exceeded the level of correlation of depression at Time 1 with attributional vulnerability at Time 2. That is, people who were more depressed at Time 2 had shown greater attributional vulnerability (e.g. tended to attribute failure to stable and global factors, and success to unstable factors) one month before, but people who showed this vulnerability on second testing had not been more depressed one month before. They claimed that these results showed that such attributions 'may act as causes of depressive symptoms', although they admitted that the statistical method used acted as an indicator of temporal precedence rather than positive proof of causation. Their caution in this regard was entirely justified. The overall level of depression over the time interval remained constant, and no record was made of whether individuals suffered a life event during that month. Analogous results to these from a medical setting may clarify why a causal conclusion is not justified. In a measles attack, the rash is often preceded by some symptoms of a common cold. A cross-lagged correlational analysis might show cold symptoms at Time 1 correlating with severity of rash at Time 2, but no correlation between severity of rash at Time 1 with cold symptoms at Time 2. However, it would be wrong to conclude that the cold symptoms caused rash. It would be fair, however, to say that something interesting had been documented about the temporal sequence of a measles episode. And it is this aspect of Golin *et al.*'s result which is important. For they showed that, in some depressions at least, there was evidence of attributional distortion prior to the manifest depression. Their results tell us something about the time course of depression at its early stages. Earlier in this book mention is made of McLean's view that a common course for depression to follow is for cognitive symptoms to precede behavioural disturbance which is followed in turn by somatic symptoms if the depression becomes severe. Golin *et al.*'s results expanded on knowledge about this temporal sequence. They did not establish the causal status of the vulnerability thesis.

Metalsky *et al.* (1982), did, however, claim to test the causal thesis directly by carrying out a prospective study. They gave a measure of attributional vulnerability to 227 undergraduate students prior to taking their mid-term examination. They studied the correlation between this measure and how upset the students became following receipt of their results. Success and failure were defined by the students themselves who had declared beforehand what result they would be unhappy with, and what result they would be happy with, (this level of aspiration, was, incidentally, not correlated with attributional style). Fifty-three students fell at or below a grade with which they were unhappy. Their subsequent mood disturbance correlated significantly with greater tendency to make internal and global attributions for bad outcomes. Twenty-eight students fell at or above a grade with which they were happy. Their subsequent mood disturbance was not significantly correlated with attributional style, though attributing bad outcomes to stable causes tended to correlate with upset mood even in these 'successful' students. The actual correlations are shown in Table 10.1.

Like the results of Golin *et al.*, this study provided evidence of a correlation between cognitive vulnerability at Time 1 and mood disturbance at Time 2. But did they show what they claimed to have shown – that is, that 'in the absence of negative life events people exhibiting . . . depressogenic attributional styles . . . (were) no more likely to develop depressive reactions

Table 10.1 Correlations of attributional style subscales for negative outcomes with degree of mood disturbance (MAACL) following mid-term exam results

Attributional subscale	'Successful' students (N = 28)		'Unsuccessful' students (N = 53)	
	r	p	r	p
Internality	0.12	ns	0.34	0.01
Stability	0.36	0.06	0.04	ns
Globality	0.22	ns	0.32	0.05

ns = not significant; r = correlation; p = significance level

than people not displaying these attributional styles'? Note that a critical test of their hypothesis was not the correlation within the 'unsuccessful' group, but the difference in correlations between this group (who had suffered the stress of failure) and the other group of twenty-eight (who had not) (Williams, 1985). The authors did not test the significance of the difference in correlations. Table 10.2 shows the results of such a comparison, using Z transformation of the r-values. None of the differences was significant. This implies that mood disturbance was no more related to attributional vulnerability when students suffered the stress of exam disappointment than when they suffered no such stress.

So although there was accumulating evidence for the correlation of depressed mood and cognitive style, and for the fact that this cognitive style might be assessable some time before the depression is manifest, the evidence for the causal vulnerability theory from these studies was weak.

Table 10.2 Comparison of correlations between attributions and subsequent mood disturbances with or without exam disappointment

Attributional subscale	'Successful' students N = 28 Z_1	'Unsuccessful' students N = 53 Z_2	$Z_1 - Z_2$	Critical* ratio	p
Internality	0.121	0.354	−0.233	−0.95	ns
Stability	0.377	0.040	0.337	1.38	ns
Globality	0.224	0.332	−0.108	−0.44	ns

ns = not significant

$$* \ CR = \frac{Z_1 - Z_2}{\sqrt{\frac{1}{n_1 - 3} + \frac{1}{n_2 - 3}}}$$

An alternative to the correlational approach had been taken by Wittenborn and co-workers (Altman and Wittenborn, 1980; Cofer and Wittenborn, 1980). They studied women who had recovered from a depressive episode and compared their personality characteristics with a control sample of 'never depressed' women. They found that a large number of individual self-report items distinguished the recovered group from the controls. These items, when factor analysed, yielded such factors as low self-esteem, preoccupation with failure, pessimistic outlook, narcissistic vulnerability and general sense of incompetence. Unfortunately it was unclear from these studies how the initial diagnosis of depression was made during the prior episode, but the mean age of the women studied was thirty-seven. Paykel's (1971) analysis of 165 depressed patients suggested the existence of a 'moderately severe' cluster who were middle-aged, had a greater number of previous 'illnesses', and in whom there was a strong mixture of anxiety and additional neurotic manifestations (e.g. obsessional symptoms, depersonalization, etc.). If the vulnerability factors found by Wittenborn's group were attributable to associated neurotic traits, then although this might have explained this particular group's vulnerability, it may not be generalizable to other subgroups of depression.

We now turn from the early studies which purported to support the vulnerability theory, to those which purported to weaken it. Lewinsohn *et al.* (1981) carried out a large scale prospective study in the community. They gave 998 individuals various cognitive measures one year apart. These measures included a locus of control measure, a measure of expectation for positive and negative outcomes, an irrational beliefs questionnaire, a measure of perception of control and a measure of self-esteem. They hoped to identify those who became depressed during the year, then check back to see if these showed any differences on the cognitive measures. Of the 998, eighty-five became depressed during the follow-up period who had not been depressed at pre-test. So these investigators were able to compare the relationship between current depression and current cognitive style, as well as the relationship between cognitive style and future depression. Their results were clear-cut. Currently depressed subjects differed on all measures except the attributional assessment. They expected less positive and more negative outcomes, were more irrational, perceived themselves to have less control and had lower self-esteem than people who were not currently depressed. However the 'to-be-depressed' group did not differ from controls on any measure. Indeed the only evidence for the effect of antecedent cognitions on future depression was that depressed subjects with the worst cognitions as assessed by the 'expectation of positive outcomes', and 'perception of control' questionnaire showed poorer subsequent rates of improvement. In the light of these results showing no prospective effect for cognitions, Lewinsohn *et al.* concluded that depressive cognitions are consequents of depression, rather than antecedents.

An alternative approach to the same problem was to identify those who would be considered vulnerable to depression. Two studies which took this approach were Campbell, working in Oxford, and Wilkinson and Blackburn, working in Edinburgh. Campbell (1982) used a cross-sectional methodology and identified a 'vulnerable' group by selecting, from a community sample of women, those who had Brown and Harris's vulnerability factors (lack of confidante, three or more children under fourteen years at home, no job, loss of own mother before the age of eleven). Women were interviewed one year apart using the Present State Examination, Brown and Harris's Life Event Inventory, the Rosenberg Self-Esteem Scale, and a number of measures of cognitive distortion. She found that the vulnerability factors were associated with increased levels of non-specific neurotic symptoms and impoverished material resources, but not associated with low self-esteem (as Brown and Harris would surely have strongly predicted) nor with a negative cognitive style. Campbell concluded that the cognitive style results suggested a need for the modification of Beck's model of cognitive predisposition to depression. There was, however, evidence which undermined to some extent Campbell's conclusion. She examined 'vulnerability' as defined by Brown and Harris. But what if Brown and Harris's vulnerability factors were not universally applicable? Costello (1982) conducted a procedural replication study of Brown and Harris in Calgary, Canada, and found that neither social class, nor loss of mother, nor three children (of any age) nor lack of employment were vulnerability factors. Only 'lack of intimate relationship with a confidante' emerged as rendering women more vulnerable to depression following a life event – and this item is, of course, not independent of the individual's 'pre-morbid' personality nor of her current depression. Costello concluded 'the role of social factors is community specific and the causal roles of events and difficulties in relation to depression remain uncertain'.

So it is possible that the women Campbell studied were not actually vulnerable. On the other hand, one might still have expected an association between cognitive style measures and some of the vulnerability factors (e.g. lack of confidante), so her evidence remained damaging to the vulnerability theory.

Wilkinson and Blackburn (1981) approached the same issue by studying recovered depressives. They argued that 'patients who have recovered from a depressive illness can be defined as depression-prone individuals and . . . should still exhibit the typical thinking which made them vulnerable to depression', that is they should still show negative bias, typical logical errors in the interpretation of events and in their basic assumptions about the world. Fifteen patients (Beck score <8) who had undergone routine psychiatric (drug) treatment for unipolar major depression and had recovered at least three months (mean forty months) prior to the study, were compared with ten currently depressed (unipolar major) patients under inpatient or outpatient treatment. In addition there were two control groups: 'recovered other patient' (N = 10) and 'normal' (N = 15) recruited through newspaper advertising and matched with the recovered depressed group for age, sex, social class and educational level. All subjects completed the Beck, the Middlesex Hospital Questionnaire, Beck et al.'s (1974) Hopelessness Scale, a Cognitive Response Test (CRT 36) (Watkins and Rush, 1978) and a new Cognitive Style Test developed by the authors (see Chapter Five). It was found that the currently depressed group differed from the other group in having more distorted cognitions. These individuals were more hopeless, had more negative interpretations and non-self-attributions for positive events, more negative interpretations and self-attributions for negative events and more irrational negative responses. However, the recovered depressives showed none of these cognitive distortions, obtaining scores comparable to those of a sample who had never been clinically depressed. These results appeared contrary to the vulnerability theory. The authors conclude: 'cognitive distortions would appear to be specific to the illness phase of depression and not to depression-prone individuals . . . a state not a trait'.

Taken together, the Lewinsohn et al., Campbell and Wilkinson and Blackburn studies constituted impressive evidence against the vulnerability theory. Although there were some question marks against each study (we have already discussed the shortcomings of the first two, and Wilkinson and Blackburn admitted their numbers were small – and because of this there could be no attempt to divide the groups into those whose depression had been preceded by a provoking agent and those which had not), the studies gained strength because each was conducted in very different ways and yet converged on a similar conclusion.

Later studies of vulnerability

There have been many more studies published since the early 1980s. Those which have simply continued to test the vulnerability theory using similar methodology have continued to produce mixed results. Ingham et al. (1986) attempted to discover whether women who are more vulnerable on the basis of Brown and Harris's vulnerability factors actually suffer low self-esteem. They studied a randomly selected community sample of 493 non-depressed women from North Edinburgh, and interviewed them to establish whether they had suffered early loss, were employed or not, had children under fourteen years and had a person in whom they could confide. They found that lower self-esteem was significantly associated with lack of confidante and separation before eleven years but not with the other vulnerability factors.

Parry and Brewin (1988) also used a cross-sectional design to examine self-esteem, depression and life events in 193 women. They found that depression levels were higher in response to life events for those women who also had low self-esteem. They interpreted this to mean that women with low self-esteem reacted to a smaller number of life events with a greater amount of depression. However, a measure of the tendency to attribute negative events to oneself failed to interact with life events and depression in the way that the vulnerability theory would have predicted. The evidence from this study remains mixed for the vulnerability theory.

Similarly, later studies of attributional style have been mixed. First, the Attributional Style Questionnaire has been criticized. Robins and Block (unpublished paper) found that the internality scale had very low internal consistency. They also found that although stable attribution for hypothetical negative events and a stable attribution for real negative events both correlated with depression, these two forms of stable attribution did not correlate with each other! They found that the globality attribution was the only dimension to correlate with depression consistently across both real events and hypothetical events.

Robins and Block had used a cross-sectional methodology to study attributions and depression. It could thus be criticized on the basis of not being able to say which was cause and which was effect. Clearly a prospective study such as that done by Metalsky *et al.* (1982) is preferable, but I criticized this (Williams, 1985) for not proving what it purported to prove. Metalsky and colleagues later published another study (1987) which attempted to deal with these criticisms. Once again they measured attributional style in students who were about to take an examination and looked to see whether attributional style predicted the level of mood disturbance after the students had got their results and particularly amongst those students who had been disappointed by their results. The design of the study was strengthened by taking account of the initial level of mood disturbance, and by more carefully looking for differences in the correlation between attributional style and the change in mood disturbance as a result of being disappointed. Interestingly, they failed to replicate the results that they had found in their earlier study. Attributional style had no effect on mood disturbance following their results. However, they did find that four days after people had received their results some were still disturbed while others had recovered in their mood. A maladaptive attributional style did predict *how long* this mood persisted.

In a similar study Hunsley (1989) also looked to see whether attributional style predicted mood disturbance following disappointing exam results. He also found that attributional style did not predict mood disturbance at this time. What he did find, however, was that those students who were later disappointed with their grades, had been more disturbed following the actual exam (before they got their results) and the students with the maladaptive attributional styles were most disturbed by the event of the exam itself. Both these prospective studies cast doubt on the simple prediction that attributional style renders people more vulnerable to greater mood disturbance following a stressful life event, but they open the possibility there may be some more complex time-dependent effects which will need further research.

Meanwhile two different studies using recovered depressed patients produced mixed results for the attributional vulnerability theory. Eaves and Rush (1984) found attributional style was still significantly maladaptive when patients had recovered, but the patients in this study were tested very soon after recovery and remained mildly depressed. This makes the result difficult to interpret. Fennell and Campbell (1984) examined the attributional style of people who had been in remission for longer and compared them with people who had never been depressed. They found that there was no difference between the attributional style of the two groups.

In summary, research on attributional style as a vulnerability for depression has not yet settled to produce a clear-cut picture either for or against the vulnerability theory.

Turning now to studies examining wider measures of dysfunctional attitudes, at first sight these have also seemed to continue to produce a mixed pattern of results. Blackburn and Smyth (1985) and Hollon *et al.* (1984) found no difference between normal and recovered depressives in various measures of cognitive distortion (e.g. the Cognitive Style Test). Similarly, using the Dysfunctional Attitude Scale (DAS), Eaves and Rush (1984), Hamilton and Abramson (1983), Reda *et al.* (1985), Silverman *et al.* (1984) and Simons *et al.* (1984) all found that when patients had recovered, mean levels of dysfunctional attitudes were no different from control groups. The only exception was, once again, the study by Eaves and Rush which used the DAS in addition to the Attributional Style Questionnaire, but I have already mentioned that there are some doubts whether the patients were truly recovered in this study.

Prospective studies of the DAS have been a little more supportive of the vulnerability theory. Rush *et al.* (1986) found that dysfunctional attitudes assessed at Time 1 predicted depression at Time 2 six months later for at least one of three measures of depression. Barnett and Gotlib (1988) found that although DAS measured at Time 1 did not by itself predict depression at Time 2, nevertheless the combination of dysfunctional attitudes at Time 1 and a measure of social support at Time 2 did account for a significant proportion of the variance in Time 2 depression levels after controlling for Time 1 depression levels. However, Barnett and Gotlib comment that generally the depressive symptoms improved over the course of their study between Time 1 and Time 2 so it may be that the DAS may be predicting recovery only under certain social conditions.

If we had to rely on these studies alone, the picture would be no clearer now than it was in 1983. At that time, as we have seen, there was as much evidence against the vulnerability theory as there was for it. However, at the time of my 1984 review of the early studies, I suggested that there were two let-out clauses which remained for the vulnerability theory. One was that the sensitivity of measuring instruments used to assess cognitive distortions may not have been adequate. The second let-out clause was that the depression-prone individual may show such cognitive distortions only when under some sort of stress. I wish to take each of these points in turn and carefully evaluate some research which has been done since 1984 on each of them which, I believe, has allowed the field to progress substantially.

Problems in measuring dysfunctional schemas

There are two issues here. First of all it is possible that the questionnaires that have been used so far are simply too general to pick up the particular schemas on which depressed people are vulnerable. It is extremely likely that there are large individual differences in the particular schemas which render different people vulnerable, and yet research had up to this point tended to concentrate on relatively general questionnaires. There are in fact at least three studies which suggest that it is necessary to look for more specific measures of vulnerability.

Reda *et al.* (1985) examined sixty patients who were treated with amitriptyline. They gave each patient an Italian version of the DAS (a thirty-seven-item version). These patients had a mean age of thirty-seven years and were in hospital for an average of thirty-five days, being treated with 75–120 mg per day of amitriptyline. Following recovery, they were discharged on the maintenance dose of 50 mg per day. So these authors were able to examine these patients both at admission and at discharge. Thirty of the patients were followed up after one year. As others have found, the mean level of dysfunctional attitudes fell from admission to recovery. Both at discharge and at one year follow-up, the overall level of dysfunctional attitudes was no different from a non-depressed control group.

However, Reda *et al.* also examined the DAS item by item. They found that although the mean level of DAS was not significantly different from normal at discharge there were some individual items which remained significantly elevated. On examining the DAS scores again one year later in the thirty patients that they followed up, they found that these same items were still elevated despite the fact that these patients were symptom-free. Table 10.3 shows these 'peculiar persistent cognitions'. They claimed that the following traits could be observed to be persistent even after the general level of dysfunctional attitudes had come down:

1. A pessimistic view towards reality: 'I always see the negative aspect of everything'
2. In order to cope with negative experiences the patients must have complete control over the situation and over their feelings: 'people should have a reasonable likelihood of success before undertaking

Table 10.3 Beliefs that persisted after recovery from depression treated with amitriptyline

DAS item	Sample
I feel well only when I have complete control over the situation	M & F
Turning to someone else for advice or help is an admission of weakness	F
If you cannot do something well, there is little point in doing it at all	F
People should have a reasonable likelihood of success before undertaking anything	M
I should be able to please everybody	M & F
It is shameful for a person to display his weakness	M
If a person is not a success, then his life is meaningless	F
If I do not do as well as other people, it means I am an inferior human being	F
I should always have complete control over my feelings	M & F
If I fail at my work, then I am a failure as a person	F
My happiness depends more on other people's judgement than it does on me	F
I ought to be able to solve my problems quickly and without a great deal of effort	M & F
I always see the negative aspect of everything	M & F

Note: M & F = shown by both male and female recovered patients; M = shown by male recovered patients; F = shown by female recovered patients

anything' and 'If you cannot do something well there is little point in doing it at all'

3. A great deal of attention is directed towards other people's judgement: 'I should be able to please everybody' and 'It is shameful for a person to display his weaknesses'

4. The idea of commitment and fatigue is connected to the idea of duty: 'I ought to be able to solve my problems quickly and without a great deal of effort'

These particular items may be interpreted in various ways. Barnett and Gotlib (1988) suggest that they represent two dimensions: the need to please others combined with an attitude of perfectionist self-reliance, and conclude that this may represent an apparent conflict concerning dependence and autonomy. However they are interpreted, Reda *et al.*'s results raise an important issue about the specificity of the assessment used to look at dysfunctional attitudes as a whole.

In a prospective study, Segal *et al.* (1989) studied whether congruence between a person's schemas and type of life event was important in predicting depressive relapse. They examined the course of forty-six patients who had recently recovered from an episode of depression. They used the DAS (Form A) (see Chapter Five) and identified ten ex-patients who scored high on the items reflecting dependency and sixteen ex-patients who scored high on the items reflecting self-criticism. Over the following six months they assessed these patients and asked them to report any occurrence of life events. They had a list of sixty-six life events, half of which were achievement-related 'self-critical' events and half of which were personal 'relationship orientated/dependency' events. People who scored high on the dependency items were those who needed positive interchange with others, acted in ways to please others, and if depressed, tended to have feelings of helplessness, abandonment, feeling uncared for, unloved and needing to be protected. The patients scoring high on self-criticism are those who said they needed independence and goal attainment and were motivated to find ways to enhance their control over their environment, being highly concerned about the possibility of personal failure. These patients if they became depressed tended to feel inferior, guilty, worthless and have a sense of failure to live up to expectations. If at any time during this six-month period the Beck score of these patients exceeded 16 then they were given a telephone interview to establish whether their depression would meet the Research Diagnostic Criteria for depression. (Note the importance here of categorizing not just the dysfunctional attitudes but also the life events.) Looking at the correlation of the *uncategorized* life events with Beck Depression Inventory scores in the *dependent* subjects yielded a non-significant correlation of -0.15. The same correlation of uncategorized life events with the Beck Depression Inventory in the *self-critical* subjects was also non-significant at 0.24. Then the life events were divided between 'interpersonal' and 'self-critical' events. This categorization made no difference for the 'self-critical' patients. Depression levels and life events continued to be uncorrelated. For self-critical patients neither the interpersonal negative life events nor the self-critical life events correlated with the average level of depression over the course of the study. By contrast for the *dependent* subjects, there was a significant correlation between the number of *interpersonal* life events experienced and the level of depression ($r = 0.62$). These same subjects, however, were not responsive to self-critical events. These results partially confirmed Segal *et al.*'s 'congruency hypothesis' but only for the dependent subjects.

Finally Robins and Block (1988) used a cross-sectional regression design to examine differences in vulnerability. They were also concerned that the measures of dysfunctional attitudes that had been used were not sufficiently specific. In their study they used Beck's Sociotropy-Autonomy scale. The sociotropy dimension refers to a person's investment in positive interchange with other people, and therefore reflects a very similar construct to the dependency items on the DAS. These people are said to be very much in need of acceptance, intimacy, understanding, support and guidance. The autonomy scale represents a person's individuality, their investment in preserving and increasing independence, mobility and personal rights. They are motivated to increase their freedom of choice, action and expression and the protection of their own domain. It therefore appears to reflect the achievement orientated self-criticism dimension of the DAS. Like Segal *et al.*, Robins and Block divided a life event inventory into twenty negative 'sociotropic' items and fifteen negative 'autonomy' items and asked subjects to report how many of each of these items had occurred in the last three months. Ninety-eight undergraduates were tested once, and, on the same occasion, completed the Sociotropy-Autonomy Scale and the Beck Depression Inventory. Multiple regression analysis was used to try and predict Beck Depression Inventory scores on the basis of the different sorts of events that people had experienced and the different sorts of personality style that they showed. The results were similar in some respects to those of Segal *et al.* Like Segal *et al.* they found little evidence for correlations between autonomy scores and depression. When they examined the subjects who had the highest sociotropy scores they found that these subjects were indeed more depressed if they had experienced more negative sociotropic events. However these subjects were also more depressed if they had suffered more 'autonomy threatening' events. Robins and Block's conclusion was that although being more specific about people's personality clearly helped to make predictions about the way in which life events might contribute to increases in depression, the specific hypothesis of matching up type of personality with type of event could not be supported.

These studies suggest that one needs to look further than the overall mean derived from a questionnaire such as the DAS. All of these studies come to similar conclusions that looking more precisely at individual schemas assessed by these questionnaires is likely to yield more reliable predictions. Other studies which have adopted more personality-based psychodynamic approaches converge on similar conclusions. For example, Hirschfeld *et al.*, (1977) developed the Interpersonal Dependency Inventory to look at thoughts, feelings and behaviours associated with the need to interact and rely on others. Barnett and Gotlib (1988) review four studies by Hirschfeld and colleagues in which this measure has been used in recovered depressives. The results of these studies are consistent. 'Compared with never-depressed control subjects, remitted depressives report high emotional dependency and low social self-confidence. In addition, and consistent with the cross-sectional findings, autonomy scores did not differentiate recovered depressives from control subjects' (p.108). It is clear that as our understanding of the different domains in which people are vulnerable increases the assessment of these is likely to become more refined and the interaction with life events able to be assessed more precisely.

However, there is a basic fault in questionnaire measures of cognitive distortion that no amount of adding or subtracting items, or factor analysis of questionnaires, can easily overcome. That is their confounding of distortion (errors of induction or deduction) with hedonic tone (the positive or negative valence of the item). The Cognitive Style Test illustrates the problem. Consider this item:

A close friend has an argument with you.
A. This is a major blow to our friendship
B. Our friendship will suffer a bit temporarily
C. It won't make any difference to our friendship
D. This friendship is ruined for good

In this case, endorsement of item D would fall into Wilkinson and Blackburn's most extreme category, 'strong negative emotional attribution to self'. Note that the item which represents most distortion is also the most negative.

The problem is not that this is a bad scale for assessing distortion in currently depressed individuals. The problem is that when people are no longer depressed (or not yet depressed) they may fail to endorse the extreme items because they are too negative in tone for their current mood. These people may show logical errors and distortions, yet these may be masked by making a decision on the basis of the hedonic tone of the item. A very similar problem arose in relation to Rotter's Locus of Control Scale. Abramowitz (1969) found that this scale correlated with depression, a finding which has been taken by some to suggest that depressives are by nature more 'external' (believing that they have no control). However, it has since been pointed out that these typically weak correlations (0.25–0.30) may be due to the fact that the external items are themselves (independently) rated as more 'dysphoric' in tone than the internal items. Depressed subjects may be responding to the tone of the item rather than to its logic.

How can one separate an item's logic from its tone? Maybe instead it will be necessary to turn to an information processing view of cognitive distortion. After all, 'distortion' consists of biases in selection of certain material, due perhaps to the differential salience for the patient of that stimulus material in the environment. It may then represent biases in how the selected material is encoded, how much weight is given to various items in the stimulus complex, and what categorizations are made. Perhaps, then, these errors in processing are too subtle to be assessed by questionnaire. What alternatives are there?

Problems in measuring dysfunctional schemas: alternatives to questionnaires

The most commonly used alternative to questionnaires is an adjective self-rating in which positive or negative adjectives are presented, and subjects are first asked to rate them (e.g. 'does this describe you?') and are then given a test to see how many of the adjectives they can recall. Davis (1979) had been one of the first to use such a task to study self-schemas in depression, but he had only used positive words. On the basis of his results he had proposed a developmental theory that, on becoming depressed, a person changed from positive, then to mixed, finally to a stable, negative schema. Derry and Kuiper (1981) criticized this approach, arguing that depressive schemas were content specific. They found that whereas non-depressed subjects re- membered positive words best, mild to moderately depressed people remembered both negative and positive equally, but clinically depressed people's self-schemas were dominated by memory for negative concepts. Subsequent research has been done on vulnerability using this measure by Hammen and colleagues, and by Teasdale and colleagues.

Hammen *et al.* (1985) conducted a prospective study of 375 students. They measured depression levels using the Beck Depression Inventory and anyone with a score of 14 or more was allocated to the depressive group and anyone with a score of 7 or less allocated to the non-depressive group. They also gave subjects the negative and positive adjective task and used the proportion of 'yes-rated' negative words to diagnose people as 'schematic' or 'non-schematic'. They were able, in this way, to form four groups: depres- sed schematic (N = 28); depressed non-schematic (N = 13); non-depressed schematic (N = 11); and non-depressed non-schematic (N = 30). They followed up subjects for four months, giving monthly assessments to measure episodes of depression and the number and impact of life events. The results showed that whereas initial levels of depression and the occur- rence of life events predicted the number of episodes of depression over the four-month period, self-schema did not (neither did the interaction of life events and negative self-schema). (This study also attempted to assess self- schemas by asking subjects to list recent behavioural examples of adjectives that described them, up to a maximum of ten examples. This task fared no better in predicting depressive episodes.)

In another study, Hammen *et al.*, (1986) used the same negative self- rating memory task in a more limited prospective study over one week (in a sample of 106 undergraduates) and over one month (in a second sample of 124 undergraduates). They were interested not only in current and future depression levels in this study but also in subjects' history of depression over the past six months. Although they found that negative self-schema was raised in people currently depressed, they once again found no predictive effect on future depression. Interestingly though, they found the strongest bias for those who were currently depressed was for those who had also been depressed in the past six months. Currently depressed patients who had no history of prior depression in the past six months together with those who were currently non-depressed, showed less evidence of depressive self-schema.

A similar pattern emerged when they looked at the results of the behavioural examples test. The mean number of examples produced in response to positive words relative to negative words was high in the non-depressed (9.2 to 1.3) but very similar in those currently depressed who had *not* been depressed in the past (a mean of 9.4 examples to positive words versus 1.7 examples to negative words). However, those who were equally depressed now, but had *also* been depressed in the previous six months showed a very different pattern. To the positive words they produced slightly less examples (N = 6.5) and more to the negative (7.8). The correlation between duration of recent prior depression and the number of negative behavioural examples was 0.56 (p<.001) and, importantly, remained significant even after current depression level was partialled out (r = 0.47; p<.001). This pattern of results may simply be due to there having been less positive and more negative things happening in these people's lives. But in the next chapter I shall present much more evidence that suggests that the autobiographical memories of depressed patients suffer relatively enduring dysfunctional biases which reduce problem-solving capacity and exceed anything that can be explained merely on the basis of the positive and negative experience of the person.

However, returning to our major point, neither of these tasks were *predictive* of depression. If this result were to be true in samples other than college students, we should have good reason to doubt the vulnerability thesis as currently formulated.

But Dent and Teasdale (1988) produced different results. They screened a community population of women for the presence of depression. Fifty-seven women entered their final sample of mild to moderately depressed women. Each completed the Beck Depression Inventory and was assessed on an interview rating scale of depression. They also completed the negative self-rating scale (twelve negative and twelve positive words). Subjects were asked 'Does this describe your personality?' Although the incidental recall test was given, the correlation with yes ratings for negative words was so high (in excess of 0.8) that only the self-rating measure was used. The question was whether this measure would predict level of depression in five months' time. The results showed that it did. Multiple regression analysis found that the largest proportion of variance of Time 2 depression was accounted for by Time 1 depression but negative self-rating contributed significantly and additionally to the variance.

Why was there a discrepancy between this study's results and that of Hammen and colleagues? First, Hammen used college students whereas Teasdale used a community sample. It is possible that Hammen's subjects were not as depressed as Dent and Teasdale's, many of whom met Research Diagnostic Criteria (Spitzer *et al.*) for depression. Second, Dent and Teasdale were concerned with predicting the persistence of depression in people who were already depressed at the outset, whereas Hammen was attempting to use the schematic responding in people who were non-depressed people to predict the onset of depression. We shall see later that this is an important consideration: recent formulations of vulnerability have accepted that it may not be possible to measure vulnerability when people are not already a little depressed. A final difference is that the type of negative words differed between the studies. Whereas Hammen's list included words representing negative mood (e.g. blue, weary) or general negative concepts (e.g. unlucky), Dent and Teasdale only used words representing global, negative self-description (e.g. incompetent, inferior, pathetic). It is possible that it is only the activation of such global, negative, self-concepts which enters into a vicious circle with mood. Simply concluding 'I feel blue, I feel weary', may not start such a vicious circle. Indeed, some people use such self-diagnosis as part of their strategy to assist them when they feel low. It is unlikely, by contrast, that anyone finds that the thought 'I am pathetic' makes them feel better. Is there any further evidence bearing upon this point?

Margaret Bellew (1990) at Keele University has been studying exactly this issue. She reasoned that heightened recall of words that were simply negative would not render people vulnerable to depression unless they were words which were self-esteem threatening. In some mood induction experiments she was able to demonstrate that it was only biased recall of self-esteem threatening words which rendered subjects susceptible to the behavioural effects of a mood induction procedure.

She then used these self-esteem threatening words, and some matched positive words, in a prospective study of post-partum depression. Unlike Hammen, who used words as part of a depth of processing task, or Teasdale who asked 'Does this describe your personality?' she simply presented the positive and negative words (e.g. *joy, courtesy, gentleness*, or *degradation, humiliation, dishonour*) (see p.82 for the full list) for three seconds at a time with instructions to imagine the feeling. She then asked subjects to recall as many as possible over the next five minutes, and took the balance of positive versus negative words recalled as a measure of depressive susceptibility. (Taking the balance in this way has the advantage of correcting for those subjects who have generally poorer memories.)

She tested women who were between twenty-eight and thirty-seven weeks pregnant, measuring Beck Depression Inventory as well as using the self-schema task. She identified 112 subjects who were non-schematic (recalled more positive than negative), and thirty-five who were schematic (recalled more negative than positive). The mean level of depression scores on the BDI at the time of first testing was 6.3 and did not differ between the groups (the Beck scores were 6.4 and 6.3 for the non-schematic and schematic subjects respectively).

Three months after their babies were born she interviewed the women again, this time investigating life events and the positive or negative impact of the baby. The scores on the Beck Depression Inventory on those who were non-schematic fell from 6 to 2.4 where the impact of the baby had been positive and from 6.7 to 4.2 in the case where the baby had had a negative impact. However, for the schematic women, only if the baby had been positive did the Beck score fall (from 5.9 to 2.1). The combination of negative impact and having been schematic was to increase depression (against the trend of all the other groups) from 6.7 to 8.6.

Why did this study succeed in its assessment of vulnerability? It is very likely to be the careful development of self-esteem threatening words, which, like the global negative self-descriptions of Teasdale, are more likely to be an important aspect of the vicious circle which ensues when any mood disturbance occurs. We ought to add the caveat that both Dent and Teasdale's work and that of Bellew studied women. There is reason to believe that the association between mood and such global negative self-descriptors is much closer for women than for men (Clark and Teasdale, 1985).

But there is another difference between the Hammen studies and those of Dent and Teasdale and of Bellew. Hammen attempted to predict future depression on the basis of depressive schemas measured when non-depressed. By contrast, Dent and Teasdale subjects were already mildly depressed, and Bellew's subjects were showing slightly elevated depression scores compared to those obtained after the baby was born. Could it be, then, that vulnerability is best measured when the person is at least under some minimal stress? This brings us to the second 'let-out' clause for the vulnerability theory which was identified in 1984.

Stress-testing for vulnerability

In the 1984 edition of this book, I wrote:

A depression-prone individual may be prone to show such cognitive distortions when under some sort of stress, but the distortions themselves are latent and/or inactive during nondepressed periods. At first sight this seems far too lenient a theory. If something is latent, how is it to be assessed at all, and if nothing emerges on closer examination, is that because it is *too* latent? Does 'latent' imply literally 'hidden' (but existing all the time) or nonexistent between depression phases? And does this theory say any more than that there are certain individuals who are prone to get depressed, and who, when depressed, will show this pattern of distorted thinking? It may be helpful to look at an analogy from biochemical phenomena in depression. Although it has long been suspected that the adrenocorticotrophic hormone system is at fault in some depressive states, in general, measuring *levels* of cortisol in the blood has not proved conclusive. Yet Carroll has over the years developed the Dexamethasone Suppression Test as a way of probing the efficiency of the hypothalamo-pituitary-adrenal (HPA) axis (Carroll, 1982). The test introduces a dose of dexamethasone, which mimics the biochemical effect of cortisol. If the HPA axis is working efficiently it should, in order to restore equilibrium, suppress output of cortisol. The body thinks it has too much cortisol, it therefore 'shuts down the system'. At least, that is the normal response shown by 96–100 per cent of normals and nonendogenous depressives. By contrast, about 60 per cent of endogenomorphic depressives fail to suppress cortisol levels when assessed seventeen and twenty-four hours later (Carroll, 1982). Note here how measurement of levels of a substance failed to be sensitive to a demonstrable disorder – a major biochemical subsystem. Is there a sense in which, then, the measure of 'levels' of logical distortion in individuals fails to demonstrate a real disorder of 'thinking under stress'? If so, what would the appropriate 'stress test' be, and would it even be ethically justifiable to use it? One obvious manipulation is the mood induction procedure, another is the use of speed tests (e.g. Nufferno) with 'IQ' type instructions. Researchers using these techniques have found marked individual differences in nondepressed student volunteers in the extent to which they respond to these procedures, but it is not at all clear what these individual differences reflect. The speculation could be made that had Campbell given a mood induction procedure or stress test to her sample of women, the most 'vulnerable' identified on other grounds (e.g. Brown and Harris) would have evidenced the greatest degree of cognitive distortion.

Perhaps then, the vulnerability theory may be prevented from disappearing down an inaccessibility 'black hole'. If a person differs from another in 'proneness', and this difference is something to do with a tendency to react illogically under stress, it should be a demonstrable tendency. If it is not, we had better settle for the idea that cognitive distortions are only shown during or just prior to a depressive episode, and admit that it may be difficult or impossible to finally establish the causal primacy of either.

(Williams, 1984: 186–8)

In 1985 Blackburn and Smyth published an attempt to implement just such a procedure, giving Velten's mood induction procedure to people who had recently recovered from depression. Unfortunately, the recovered depressed patients did not shift their mood in response to the MIP, so the hypothesis could not be tested. Perhaps the Velten was too close to the thoughts these patients had recently experienced so they did not try to get into the mood.

However in 1987, Teasdale and Dent published a very similar experiment. They contrasted the effect of mood disturbance induced by music, on recovered depressives, with the effect on people who had never been depressed. They gave the negative self-description task and examined the number of negative words recalled following mood induction procedure. Recall levels were very low, so they divided subjects into those who recalled one or more negative words versus those who recalled none. Twenty-eight per cent of the previously depressed subjects recalled one or more, compared with only 5 per cent of the never depressed. These results, though tentative, are very suggestive of the need to assess vulnerability not when subjects are non-depressed, but when they are mildly dysphoric.

Although there are no other comparable experimental studies, there is one cross-sectional study and several prospective studies which suggest a similar conclusion. They suggest that there are individual differences in people's reactivity to mood. These individual differences may arise partly from long-term temperamental characteristics or early experience. But they may also arise from having had previous depression episodes however these were caused. That is because, during a prior depression, they will have built up associations between negative mood and global negative concepts (e.g. pathetic, stupid) and dysfunctional attitudes. If this is the case, then dysfunctional attitudes will (a) be more reactive to mood when there has been a previous history of depression; and (b) be able to predict future depressive onset and persistence when measured under at least mild mood disturbance.

· Miranda and Persons (1988) used a cross-sectional design to examine the first of these propositions: the reactivity of dysfunctional attitudes to depressed mood. They measured dysfunctional attitudes, current depression and assessed past history of depression. The best prediction of dysfunctional attitude score was the interaction of current depression and past history of depression. For those who have no history of depression, increased depression made no difference to dysfunctional attitudes. By contrast, for those with a previous history of depression, attitudes became more dysfunctional the more depressed these people were. The fact that dysfunctional attitudes were not simply reactive to depressive mood under any circumstances is significant. It is consistent with the theory that there are individual differences in degree of cognitive distortions which come about in response to the same degree of mood change. In order to observe these differences one is required to assess people when at least a small amount of mood disturbance has distinguished the 'reactive' and 'non-reactive' individuals.

Note that this is not simply saying that mood is primary and cognitive changes secondary or epiphenomenal. For if that were the case, the individual difference in reactivity would have no predictive power in itself. Yet, in contrast to the disappointing results of trying to predict depression from dysfunctional attitudes when people are not depressed, many studies have concluded that *cognitive distortions measured when activated by mild mood disturbance* do indeed predict relapse and in the case of those who already are clinically depressed, do predict how long the depression will last.

For example, in reviewing the early evidence against the vulnerability theory, I mentioned Lewinsohn *et al.*'s (1981) community study of 998 people. They found that the assessment of cognitive distortion in the non-depressed people at Time 1 did not predict onset of depression between Time 1 and Time 2. Despite this, they did find that, in those who were already depressed at the start of the study, those who were more cognitively biased (had lower expectancy of positive outcomes; perceived themselves to have less control) were more likely still to be depressed at the end of the study eight months later. This was true even after initial depression was partialled out. Once again, cognitive distortions measured when people were depressed, predicted further course of depression.

Steinmetz *et al.* (1983) assessed expectancies of positive outcome (expected depression level after group psychotherapy treatment) and perceived control in depressed patients undergoing psychotherapy. Once again, after initial depression was partialled out, these cognitive measures predicted the extent to which depression improved. More recently, in the study to which I have already referred by Dent and Teasdale (1988), a community sample of depressed women were assessed using the negative self-referent assessment of dysfunctional schemas. Multiple regression analysis found that depression after a five-month interval was predicted by initial depression, but after taking account of this, a significant additional proportion of the variance was accounted for by negative self-description. The theory that was now emerging could be summarized thus:

> Two individuals at a given point in time may have identical depression severity scores but quite different patterns (and magnitude) of activation of negative thinking. This is because overall severity is a composite measure of a number of factors, of which the contribution from depressive thinking need not necessarily be high or, indeed, present at all – it is possible to receive an RDC diagnosis of major depression in the absence of any features of negative thinking.
>
> (Dent and Teasdale, 1988: 33–4)

How far can this theory extend? The studies reviewed thus far have used community samples where the depression is likely to be less severe than for patients who most clinicians deal with: outpatients or inpatients. Can cognitive measures help predict persistence in these more severely depressed patients? Equally significantly, can they help predict relapse in those patients who are being discharged from treatment? The first of the questions has been answered in a recent study we have completed in Cambridge (Williams *et al.*, 1990). I have already mentioned some of the results of the study when discussing the extent to which dysfunctional attitudes and negative self-description change with recovery. However, in the study we were primarily interested in how such cognitive measures taken at admission would predict persistence in a group of severely depressed (mostly endogenous) inpatients, most of whom were undergoing antidepressant treatment. We found that a questionnaire measure of dysfunctional attitudes (Burns, 1980) did indeed predict persistence of symptoms in the face of treatment. Six weeks after admission, of sixteen patients who had shown high dysfunctional attitudes, six (35 per cent) had not recovered. By contrast, of seventeen patients who had been equally severely depressed at admission but who had low dysfunctional attitudes, only one (6 per cent) had not recovered. Regression analysis converged on the same conclusion. Only the DAQ scores on admission predicted depression level at six weeks. Another study has recently been published which came to an identical conclusion. Peselow *et al.* (1990) examined the role of maladaptive thinking patterns, administering the DAS to 112 depressed patients before and after three to six weeks of treatment with antidepressants or placebo. The mean pretreatment DAS in those patients (N = 41) who *responded* to antidepressant drugs was 140. The mean pretreatment level of those who *failed to respond* to antidepressant drugs (N = 36) was significantly higher at 171. Thus these results are exactly in agreement with those of Williams *et al.* (1990). These are the only two studies which have looked at whether dysfunctional attitudes predict persistence of depression in the face of treatment. It appears that they do.

· Can dysfunctional attitudes predict relapse following successful treatment? At discharge, most patients, although symptom-free, have some mild residual mood disturbance. If one assesses their cognitive distortions at this time one may be able to differentiate the 'reactives' from the 'non-reactives'. Three studies have used measures of dysfunctional attitudes at discharge and then tried to predict relapse. Rush *et al.* (1986) followed patients up for six months; Simons *et al.* (1986) for twelve months; Evans *et al.* (1985) for twenty-four months. The results were strikingly similar. In each study, those who had higher dysfunctional attitude scores at discharge were more likely to relapse, even after the effect of residual depression was partialled out.

CONCLUDING REMARKS

Teasdale has summarized the evidence for this differential activation theory of vulnerability as follows.

> Once a person is initially depressed, an important factor that determines whether their depression remains mild or transient, or becomes more severe and persistent, is the nature of the negative cognitive processes and constructs that become active and accessible in the depressed state. These interact with the nature of environmental difficulties, available social support, and biological factors, to determine whether a depression-maintaining cognitive-affective vicious cycle will be set up.
>
> (Teasdale, 1988: 247)

So, was Beck (1967) right when he said that although schemas may be latent at a given time, they are activated by particular kinds of experience and consequently may lead to a full blown depression? Yes and no. They are 'latent' in the sense that, when not depressed, dysfunctional attitudes are almost indistinguishable from those of people who have never been depressed and who are not vulnerable to depression. Between-episode vulnerability does not consist of having a higher level of dysfunctional schemas, but in being extra-sensitive to the effects of small amounts of mood disturbance. Vulnerable people are more reactive. To see who is vulnerable and who is not, it is necessary to see who reacts to mood disturbance and who does not. Clearly then, vulnerable people do differ in some permanent characteristics, between episodes of depression. This difference does indeed involve cognitive distortion as Beck claims. It is also likely that people differ in the aspects of their life in which they feel most vulnerable (Segal *et al.*, 1989; Robins and Block, 1988; Segal *et al.*, in press; Robins, 1991).

But the evidence on whether a specific event is necessary – an event which matches the theme of the vulnerable schema – is still unclear, especially for 'achievement' events and 'autonomous/self-critical' schemas (Robins, 1991). In fact, it may be that matching of life experiences and vulnerabilities, when they occur and lead to depression, do so because they more potently disturb mood and activate any schemas (see Segal, 1988). As Segal *et al.* (1989) point out, the experience of dysphoria following exposure to congruent life events activates the cognitive affective schemas which then begin to assert an increasingly intrusive influence on the information processing of the person. The conclusion of Segal *et al.* (1989) agrees with that of Teasdale (1988) that, under these circumstances, individuals' negative appraisal of the life events become more difficult to undermine, people have less energy to disconfirm them, everything seems more aversive and more uncontrollable, and everything seems hopeless.

In writing this chapter on cognitive vulnerability, I am aware that there are many others factors which might have been taken into account: social factors, interpersonal relationships, marital problems, etc. Each of them is important (Billings and Moos, 1985; see Barnett and Gotlib, 1988 for a comprehensive review) but it would take us too far from the central theme of this book. Each component (social, interpersonal, cognitive) which contributes to vulnerability to depression deserves detailed attention in its own right, for it is likely that each interacts with the others. So, for example, the finding that recovered depressed people have fewer friends and social contacts one year after admission and discharge (Billings and Moos, 1985) very likely contributes to, and is partly caused by, the excessive emotional reliance on others and lack of social self-confidence consistently found to follow a depressive episode (Hirschfeld *et al.*, 1977). In a similar vein, Hooley and Teasdale (1988) examined marital relationship factors which predicted relapse in thirty-nine unipolar depressed patients. Over a nine-month period, 51 per cent relapsed. Although 'expressed emotion' in the spouse and marital distress in general predicted relapse, the best predictor was the patient's answer to a question about how critical they considered their spouse to be of them. In other words, the perceived criticism (a cognitive variable) was a better predictor than the carefully measured objective variable. The point is not to see objective and cognitive variables as running a race against each other to see which can predict best. They interact so closely, such a race would be meaningless. Social support and interpersonal therapy will also be an important aspect of helping the depressed person. But, as we have seen, cognitive variables, both those which are part of the precipitation theory (the moment-to-moment interaction of mood and cognition) and those which are part of the vulnerability theory (the excessive reactivity of some people, responding to minor fluctuations of mood with large cognitive distortions) have an important role to play. In reviewing the outcome studies in Chapter Four, I mentioned how the literature was settling down to a stable pattern in which cognitive therapy, although faring no better than antidepressant medication in treating the acute phase of depression, was consistently able to reduce relapse rates. At one time this was a puzzling phenomenon since the levels of cognitive distortions appeared to be identical at the end of treatment whether people had received drugs or cognitive therapy. Now that we know that relapse is significantly predicted by dysfunctional attitudes when measured under conditions of mild dysphoria, it strongly suggests the possibility that cognitive therapy works by changing the extent to which people react to changes in their mood with cognitive distortions. Cognitive therapy does no better than drug therapy in changing the level of cognitive distortion at the end of treatment, but it may well be doing better than drugs in changing the pattern of association between changes in mood and cognition; the extent to which distorted thinking is recruited by any disturbance in mood. This is precisely the issue which I shall discuss in the next, and final chapter.

Chapter 11

Cognitive-behavioural therapy and the process of change

At the beginning of this book I mentioned that cognitive-behavioural therapy was only one amongst a number of structured psychotherapies which had proved to be effective in the acute treatment of depression. This has led some investigators to suggest that the changes brought about by structured psychotherapies are non-specific; they all share a common core of features which are the ones which matter. For example Goldfried (1980) says that most therapeutic strategies involve the following: (a) they provide patients with new corrective experiences; (b) they offer patients direct feedback; (c) they induce in patients the expectation that therapy will help them; (d) they create a therapeutic relationship; and (e) they provide patients with repeated opportunities to test reality. Focusing more specifically on depression, Zeiss *et al.* (1979) outlined the factors which were common to the therapies which are effective in treating depression. First, these therapies have an elaborate, well-planned rationale which provide an initial structure that guides patients to the belief that they can control their own behaviour and thereby their own depression. Secondly, therapy which is effective provides training in skills that patients can use to feel more effective in solving problems in their life. Thirdly, such therapies emphasize the independent use of these skills by the patient outside the therapy context, and provide sufficient structure so that the patient can attain the independent use of them. Finally, such therapies encourage patients to attribute improvement in their mood to their own increased skilfulness and not that of the therapist.

These accounts all claim that, by some means, different therapies bring about increases in self-efficacy and problem-solving abilities. But because they do not describe the mechanisms that bring about such an outcome, they do not help orientate the therapist whose patient becomes stuck and cannot increase their feelings of self-efficacy, learn skills, or solve their problems. The lack of detail occurs because such accounts are 'final common pathway' explanations. These may be accurate accounts of why change finally occurs in psychotherapy, but if so, they need not imply that the same mechanisms of change are always involved in bringing about the final outcome (Hollon *et al.*, 1987). It is equally likely that the same result can be produced by many and various specific factors, all of which may have a final common pathway. There are many examples in physical medicine where the same pathology can be treated by different methods with similar outcomes, but it is not suggested that they must share a common pathway to cure.

However, the evidence on specificity of change processes in different methods of treatment appears to give little grounds for supposing that such specificity exists. The evidence is overwhelming that, when a person recovers from depression, they differ from when they were depressed in all aspects of cognition: they have fewer negative intrusive thoughts (e.g. Simons *et al.*, 1984); they believe themselves to have more control over their environment (e.g. Lewinsohn *et al.*, 1981); they have fewer dysfunctional attitudes (e.g. Williams *et al.*, 1990); and they are less biased in information processing (e.g. Fogarty and Hemsley, 1983). It is also clear that levels of depressive negative thinking and dysfunctional attitudes appear to be equally affected by different modes of treatment whether one considers behavioural versus cognitive (Wilson *et al.*, 1983; Zeiss *et al.*, 1979); whether one considers cognitive therapy versus antidepressant medication (Simons *et al.*, 1986; Imber *et al.*, 1990); or whether one considers cognitive therapy versus interpersonal psychotherapy (Imber *et al.*, 1990).[1] Does not this evidence suggest that the specificity issue is dead and should be buried?

Unfortunately not. Let me take, for example, those results showing equal effectiveness for different treatments (see Chapter Four). It is true that it seems more parsimonious to conclude that they are all affecting the same variables. But as this evidence favouring 'no difference' has accumulated (Robinson *et al.*, 1990), so has evidence concerning differential relapse rates after different treatments, even when these treatments have had identical effects in the acute phase of treatment. Thus it is becoming clear that cognitive therapy is more successful than antidepressant medication and possibly more successful than interpersonal psychotherapy in preventing subsequent relapse (Evans *et al.*, submitted; Simons *et al.*, 1986; Blackburn *et al.*, 1986; Shea *et al.*, submitted). None of this follow-up data was taken into account by Robinson *et al.* (there are too few studies to subject to meta-analysis), yet these results need to be kept in mind when evaluating whether cognitive therapy has some specific effect. For if people treated by cognitive therapy and by other methods differ in relapse rates, then it appears either that existing methods of measuring outcome are not sensitive enough to pick up these differences in patients, which will later become clear in relapse rates, or we are using the measures in the wrong way. As Robinson *et al.* imply, it is important for those investigators who are interested in cognitive therapy to give as coherent an account as they can of the possible cognitive mechanisms which bring about change. Only then will it be sensible to discuss how best to measure these mechanisms.

However, cognitive accounts are themselves extremely diverse. As

Brewin (1989) has pointed out, cognitive psychotherapies use very diverse theoretical constructs: causal attribution, internal dialogue/self-statement, basic or irrational assumptions, personal constructs, problem-solving strategies, self-efficacy, and automatic thoughts. The only thing these different cognitive psychotherapies share is a general commitment to a cognitive mediational view of behaviour. At its simplest, this cognitive mediational view states that emotional reactions depend not on external reality, but on some mediating interpretations.

The word 'cognitive' has many meanings. It is worth tracing some of these strands of meaning because each has been woven into the current usage of the term. In this chapter I will therefore start by outlining four different ways in which the word 'cognitive' has been used in the literature. I will then review three recent attempts to say how cognitive therapy might work: those accounts given by Teasdale (1985), Barber and DeRubeis (1989) and by Brewin (1989), drawing out of each the component which seems to be most likely to help us understand the processes of change in cognitive therapy.

FOUR MEANINGS OF 'COGNITIVE'

Let us start by giving an illustrative example of a patient who came to a therapy session and described an event which had occurred during the previous week. She had been feeling low one day, and a friend dropped in to ask if she was intending to go to a mutual friend's birthday party that evening. Despite her mood, she thought it might do her some good to get out of herself, so she decided to go. She did not, however, brighten up on the way there. Her mind was dominated by such thoughts as: 'I'm not going to enjoy this'; 'There'll be a lot of people there I won't know'; 'I'll only spoil things for everybody'. She remembered other parties that had gone badly, which did not help her mood! When she arrived, she said later, the first thing she noticed was that everyone already knew each other. No-one came up to talk to her and at that point she concluded that her misgivings had been right all along; no one wanted her around.

Let us look at four different aspects of her account on which cognitive theorists in different traditions would concentrate.

Negative intrusive thoughts

According to one tradition, the 'cognitive' component here is the presence of negative intrusive thoughts, negative self-talk. This definition appealed to behaviourally oriented psychologists, for whom the negative thought could be viewed as internal noxious stimuli equivalent to the external noxious stimuli (e.g. spiders, supermarkets) which had been extensively studied. For example, Rachman (1971), in his analysis of intrusive thoughts in obsessional patients, defined obsessional ruminations as 'noxious stimuli' to which the patients had failed to habituate. Applying a similar principle to depression in the patient described above, the main unit of analysis would be the individual thoughts such as 'I'll only spoil things for everybody'. 'Cognitions' in this sense may be fleeting, but they are conscious. There are many interesting questions to be asked of this type of thought. Why are they so adhesive? How frequent are they? What are the discriminative stimuli associated with each of them? If they could be prevented from occurring, would mood lift? (Teasdale and Rezin 1978; Fennell *et al.*, 1987).

Computation of probabilities

A second use of the word cognitive occurs in the writings of those learning theorists who stand in the tradition of Tolman. This uses 'cognitive' to refer to expectancies built up from past experience; expectancies of future response–outcome contingencies. The most well-known recent example of this approach can be found in the pre-1978 theory of learned helplessness (see Chapter Two). According to this theory, a major determinant of motivation to respond in any environment is the balance of two probabilities: (a) the probability that an action will be followed by a certain outcome against (b) the probability that the outcome will follow even if the action is not performed. If these two probabilities are perceived as equal then the organism learns that it is helpless, and may come to expect that in the future they will be helpless ('no action of mine would affect the outcome'). If the event in question is aversive (as the party that our patient was attending was perceived to be), then this learned helplessness – the expectation of response–outcome independence – will result in symptoms of depression (cognitive, affective and behavioural changes).

These theorists would concentrate a) on the patient's expectation that the party was going to be aversive (and try to reduce the expected aversion); and b) on their expectation that there was nothing that could be done about the situation (and try, through social skills training, for example, to increase the person's self-efficacy beliefs). Note, however, that in contrast to the first definition of cognitive above, there is no assumption that the person's expectation is conscious or has to be made explicit. Indeed, the strength of learned helplessness theory has been its generalizability across the animal kingdom.

Attributions, assumptions and beliefs

The third use of the word cognitive is most clearly represented in Kelly's Personal Construct Approach, Beck's underlying Assumptions and Rules and in Abramson *et al.*'s Reformulation of Learned Helplessness (see Chapter Three). Each of these different theories suggests that a person has permanent trait-like structures which, though they may not be aware of them, affect their day-to-day reactions to events. Note that these assumptions and beliefs, though not usually made explicit, are nevertheless in principle accessible to introspection. Having said that, they may need careful monitoring within or between sessions to make them explicit. More formal methods exist for making them explicit, such as repertory grid technique. This is a good illustration of the fact that the assumptions, beliefs and construct systems are in principle accessible, though not commonly accessed. For in the grid technique, patients are asked to make a series of individual judgments, none of which demand access to unconscious information, but which, after grid analysis has integrated the information, can be fed back to the patient and produce genuinely new insights. A similar point can be made about the assessment of attributional style. This too can make patients aware of aspects of their thinking which, in principle, they might have noticed before but did not. Returning to my patient who went to the party, a clinician using this definition of 'cognitive' would wish to tackle her attribution of the fact that 'people were talking to each other' to mean that 'everyone knew each other' and the interpretation when she arrived of 'no one coming to talk to me' as 'no one wants me around'. The clinician might want to ask about how much these are habitual responses to similar situations, and follow up (using the inverted arrow technique, p. 172) what the implications of such rejection would be.

Information processing

The final use of the word cognitive is to refer to biases in information processing. There are many possible processes which may be involved. There may be bias in the processes by which information is registered, encoded, stored and retrieved; biases in how inferences are made to construct 'models' of the world; bias in how reality is distinguished from such inferences; and biases in the processes underlying judgements. Research conducted in this area has burgeoned in the past decade. Williams *et al.* (1988) review a great deal of experimental work on general processing deficits, attention and memory biases, thoughts and images, schemas, judgements and the relation between conscious and non-conscious processing. A clinician who used these experimental cognitive frameworks in addressing the needs of the patient who had been at the party, would attend to those aspects where information processing bias was evident. For example, on the way to the party she had remembered other previous parties which had been unpleasant, and the clinician might want to explore the extent to which these memories were state-dependent (c.f. Teasdale and Fogarty, 1979). This clinician might also wish to discuss the fact that the patient had, as soon as she arrived, noticed the people who were standing in groups talking to each other, and might not have attended to several people who were standing by themselves.

Having clarified the different ways in which the word 'cognitive' is used, we can assess the different accounts that have been given for how cognitive-behavioural strategies may overcome depression.

PROCESSES OF CHANGE: SOME POSSIBILITIES

I shall consider three models which have been proposed to account for change in cognitive therapy. First, it has been suggested that therapy breaks the reciprocal link between mood and cognition (Teasdale, 1985). Second, it could be that therapy mainly brings about change in the way information is processed (Brewin, 1989). Third, it could be that the patients learn coping strategies to compensate for the information biases and mood disturbance (Barber and DeRubeis, 1989). I shall describe each of these in turn.

Teasdale (1985) starts from the observation that depression brings about a shift in the relative activation of positive and negative cognitions. This implies that, in addition to any major life events and difficulties which depressed people have, even minor difficulties (such as minor marital disputes or difficulties in managing children) come to be interpreted as major difficulties. The bias in information processing makes these more minor difficulties seem more aversive and more uncontrollable than they would have seemed otherwise. Added to this is the fact that patients are often depressed not only about things that are happening in the outside world but about the state in which they find themselves when they are depressed. He points out that most symptoms of depression are themselves aversive and uncontrollable (dysphoric mood, loss of pleasure, irritability, lack of energy, concentration difficulties, indecisiveness and guilt). On the basis of these symptoms it is relatively easy for the depressed person to come to negative conclusions. For example, the mother who finds it difficult to get up in the morning may conclude that she is a selfish, good-for-nothing, poor mother. These conclusions add to the aversiveness and uncontrollability of the experience and so maintain the depression. Teasdale suggests that the explanations which are given to patients of their symptoms early on in therapy, together with some symptom management techniques, can result in speedy reductions in the perceived aversiveness and uncontrollability of the symptoms and bring about relatively rapid change in levels of depression.

Although this paper concentrates on using therapeutic strategies to reduce depression about the depressive symptoms themselves, the more general point that Teasdale wishes to make is that cognitive therapy works by breaking the reciprocal link between affect and cognition.

Major and minor life difficulties interpreted as highly aversive and un-controllable should be identified and modified by active problem solving strategies, and/or re-appraisal to counteract the effects of the depressed state negatively biasing the processing of information; the opportunity for depressive ruminations should be reduced, and the content of recurrent ruminations re-appraised; depression about depression should be reduced.

(Teasdale, 1985: 160)

Note that this model has some components of each of the definitions of the word cognitive given above. It aims to reduce perceived aversiveness and uncontrollability (the learned helplessness model) by encouraging re-interpretation and re-attribution (the beliefs and attributions component) and by reducing the opportunity for depressive ruminations (the intrusive thought component) and finally it puts these in the context of information processing biases, the fourth meaning of cognitive that I outlined.

Brewin (1989) starts by distinguishing between two cognitive systems, the first for information transmission and the second for conscious experience. The distinction between these is reminiscent of a distinction between rela-tively automatic aspects of information processing and relatively strategic aspects often made in cognitive psychology (see Williams *et al.*, 1988, Chapters 2 and 10). The automatic processing system is rapid, relatively inflexible, difficult to modify, requires minimal attention, and is activated without intention or awareness. Its function is to store the sum total of previous experiences. Its output depends on new situations matching some old situation. Under such circumstances such matching will elicit physio-logical responses similar to those that occurred in response to the original learning situation, but it requires no conscious deliberation. In the case of this cognitive system no account can be given by the person of the reasons why they are responding in this way.

The second cognitive system is limited by attention span and strongly influenced by *a priori* expectations and by simple rules and heuristics. It exists to calculate future consequences of possible actions, using knowledge of present situations. In contrast to the first cognitive system the contents of this can be verbally described.

Emotional memories may be coded by both cognitive systems. In the case of the former, they will be accessed by matches between current and past situations (they are 'situationally accessible'). In this case the process is not accessible to introspection although one may, on the basis of one's physical responses, infer something about what memories are stored. The example that Brewin gives of this mechanism in operation is irrational fear responses. Although the spider phobic 'knows' that the spider will not harm them, nevertheless they react very strongly when they see a spider in front of them. The flashbacks of traumatic experiences experienced by people who have post-traumatic stress disorder are also seen as due to the activity of this sort of situationally accessible memories, as are automatic thoughts that come unbidden into the mind in depression.

In contrast to these unconscious and inaccessible processes, emotional memories may also be coded by the second cognitive system. In this case they can be accessed verbally, by strategic, conscious strategies. This implies that people will be more likely to understand why they are becoming upset, for these memories are available to introspection. It is these conscious processes which will form the basis for further metacognitive analysis: labelling and attribution, the generation of coping options, evaluation of such options, the monitoring of change when any action is taken, and self-reinforcement that may or may not follow. Similarly these cognitive processes are involved in the selection of coping responses (e.g. distraction, providing positive self-statements, avoidance, self-medication, relaxation and exposure). In summary, this processing system is involved whenever particular labels, attributions or coping options are considered.

Brewin concludes that there are two different ways in which cognitive therapy is likely to work for depression:

1. Therapists' attempts to verbally isolate, identify, and challenge negative or dramatic thoughts may be seen as disrupting the feedback loop whereby upsetting (automatic) images and thoughts pervade consciousness . . . re-access the situational memories, and maintain the depressed mood.
2. Therapists may be seen as altering the contents of verbally accessible knowledge in order to counter inappropriate stimulus classification and avoid initial accessing of non-conscious situational memories.

(Brewin, 1989: 388)

Whereas the first of these options is brought about by the patients being instructed about the links between thoughts and affect and being trained to question and argue against them, the second is achieved by the deliberate focusing on upsetting experiences, examining the evidence for different interpretations and by the systematic reality-testing and re-labelling of events and experiences. In other words, Brewin concludes that cognitive therapy for depression mainly 'modifies access to non-conscious situational memories'. Those memories may still exist unmodified, but are not accessed because either they have been overlaid with newer memories which are preferentially accessed, or newer semantic categories and rules have been generated for interpreting current experience. Brewin's account can be seen as an attempt to specify in greater detail than Teasdale the nature of the vicious spiral between mood and information processing, particularly focusing on the information processing side of the equation. It shares with Teasdale the conclusion that cognitive therapy modifies these information processes. It is a conclusion that is not shared by Barber and DeRubeis.

Barber and DeRubeis (1989) attempt to describe where the action is in cognitive therapy for depression. They consider three possibilities: accommodation, activation/de-activation and compensation. 'Accommodation' refers to changes in the schematic processes or in the content of the schemas. 'Activation/de-activation' implies that there is no change in the content of the underlying attitudes and schemas but that the negative ones are less activated and the positive ones are more activated. 'Compensation' refers to the possibility that there is little initial change in either the schemas themselves or in their balance of activation, but the person learns some sets of skills to compensate for the schemas. In this case the individual learns to cope with negative thoughts which, it is assumed, still exist (at least for most of the time during short-term cognitive therapy). They reject the first two models in favour of the third. The evidence they bring to bear against the accommodation model is those studies using the DAS (reviewed in the previous chapter) which show that DAS levels are equivalent at the end of treatment whether the person has received cognitive therapy or antidepressants. They also find no convincing evidence that the cognitive processes which underlie the schemas are changed during therapy. They argue that it is the content of the schemas which is at the origin of the patient's problem rather than the mechanics of the information processing system. These appear to operate normally. 'What may at first appear to be an aberrant process may indeed be better characterized as aberrant content' (Barber and DeRubeis, 1989: 449).[2]

Barber and DeRubeis reject the activation/de-activation model on the basis of the same evidence. They point out that if there was less activation of negative schemas and greater activation of positive schemas one might expect there to be a difference between drugs and cognitive-behavioural therapy in DAS levels at the end of treatment, especially given the fact that the people who have undergone cognitive therapy are less vulnerable to relapse (see Chapter Four). They conclude that what happens during short-term cognitive therapy is that the patient remains with the same balance of negative and positive schemas, but learns meta-cognitive, planning and problem-solving skills to deal with them. They become more able to generate alternative accounts and explanations for their events and symptoms. This involves an improved ability to look for evidence relevant to competing accounts of their experiences and events. They learn problem-solving skills in which they generate specific and detailed plans and weigh up and consider the advantages and disadvantages of these plans. In the end they become open to alternative explanations, and more critical of their own inferences; they learn to be aware of their own primary appraisals and to examine a wide array of evidence as they revise these appraisals. Although Barber and DeRubeis concede that eventually a patient may learn to rely less on 'short-cut' heuristics, any change in schemas is more likely to occur following the changes in the way the patients deal with upsetting cognitions and problematic life situations. In other words 'compensation' comes first and cognitive processes or content change later.

While this model has been very helpful in describing a range of possible explanations for change in psychotherapy, I suggest that it is too ready to draw a distinction between the conscious 'compensatory' acquisition of problem-solving skills and the underlying cognitive processing which supports them. In other words the question implicit in the account given by Barber and DeRubeis (and to some extent implicit in Brewin's review), is 'Does cognitive therapy alter the fundamentals of information processing, or does it merely teach patients skills to cope with the information processing biases they have?' I hope to show that this is a false dichotomy and that it is, in practice, impossible to change one component without changing the others. What we need instead is a coherent functional account which describes in as much detail as our measures allow us, the subcomponents of cognitive processing and what changes in which components are likely to bring about changes in others. It does not matter that we do not know what initiates the change to bring about improvement. But we must be able as accurately as possible to specify these variables, so that when blockages in treatment occur, we may have some idea how to develop strategies to help the patient progress.

These models are not mutually exclusive. As I have already observed, Brewin's description of the information processing component could be said to give a more detailed account of the processing changes which are implicit in Teasdale's model, and occur later in the sequence envisaged by Barber and DeRubeis.

How does one judge what are the important aspects of these models? As I mentioned above, outcome studies appear to show that there is little to discriminate between different psychological treatments in the variables which each affects during therapy, and little to choose between psychological and drug treatments in their apparent mode of operation. It was these data that prompted Barber and DeRubeis to conclude that cognitive therapy could not be bringing about change by changing schemas, or by changing the relative activation of positive and negative schemas. If it had been so, would not dysfunctional attitudes be significantly lower after cognitive therapy than after antidepressant treatment?

CHANGING THE FOCUS

However, this line of reasoning does not adequately take account of the evidence on vulnerability for relapse that I reviewed in the previous chapter. This showed that one must distinguish between the 'resting state' of activation of a schema or dysfunctional attitude, and the 'arousability' of that schema or attitude. An example may help to illustrate this point. I recently had a leak in my car radiator which I suspected on the basis of the fact that the water level was rather low. But I did not know where the leak was, because, as far as I could see, no water was leaking out. However when I took the car to the garage they were able to find the leak by putting the system under pressure by pumping air into it. Under normal running conditions, one could not see the damage although one inferred that it was there. Under pressure, it became obvious where it was. I reviewed evidence in the previous chapter that if one assessed people when they were at least a little depressed, then those whose dysfunctional attitudes were then high or who were inclined to describe themselves in a negative way were more likely to become depressed again or to persist in the depression that they already had. Dysfunctional attitude scales, negative self-referent self-description, and cognitive-style tests, I suggest, represent the tendency to elaborate events in a negative way. But this tendency does not become manifest until a negative stimulus is present (e.g. a life event) or until there is an increase in transient state mood.

The data on dysfunctional attitudes and automatic thoughts from the outcome studies are consistent with the conclusion that change has been brought about in arousability – the ease with which such attitudes and thoughts are experienced in response to mood disturbance or negative events. At the end of treatment, the levels of attitudes do not differ between patients who have undergone different treatments. The difference lies in how arousable the dysfunctional attitudes remain in response to stress.

Note what has happened here. The focus of what needs to be explained has changed. We no longer need to explain how cognitive therapy brings about reduced frequency of automatic thoughts or reduced dysfunctional attitudes. All therapies which are effective do these things because these variables are state dependent. But (a) they are state dependent to different extents in different people; and (b) once recruited, they play a causal role in the maintenance of depression (Williams *et al.*, 1990). So the question has become: how does cognitive therapy reduce the reactivity of schemas and attitudes, etc.? How does it reduce the tendency for people to react to future negative events and downswings in mood by producing catastrophic thoughts?

I suggest that the answer lies in combining certain aspects of each of the three models outlined above. As Teasdale (1985) has suggested, cognitive therapy breaks the reciprocal link between mood and cognition. As Brewin (1989) has suggested, this takes place through some sort of re-categorization of events and moods. As Barber and DeRubeis (1989) have suggested, this itself involves an improved ability to look for evidence relevant to competing accounts of experiences and events.

Let me return to the example of the patient who found herself depressed on the way to the party. The critical question is this. Why did she, while she was depressed, believe her conclusion that she would not enjoy it, and that no-one wanted her around? To understand this, we need to understand the relationship between mood and cognition.

I want to suggest that mood and cognition are related in two ways in depression. First, mood and cognition spiral at times when there is no contrary information to interrupt the cycle or where the information that would normally interrupt it is accessed in a form which is too abstract or insufficiently detailed or imageable. Second, mood and cognition are related in that, in the absence of sufficiently concrete alternative criteria, mood is itself used as the criterion of truth of a self-statement (c.f. Schwarz and Clore, 1983). A proposition is taken to be true if it is consistent with the mood being felt at the time, however that mood has been caused.

Following cognitive therapy, a person may experience depressed mood, but they are more likely to have (a) learned to prevent it from activating negative thoughts and images; and (b) learned to ignore it as a source of information about the validity of current ideas (MacLeod, 1989). Common to both changes is the ability to retrieve alternative information in a form which will be useful – that is, specific, imageable and concrete. I predict that where this cannot be done, a person will respond more slowly to therapy, and will be more likely to relapse. In research at Cambridge and Newcastle-upon-Tyne we have investigated the role of autobiographical memory as the source of such information. I will describe these findings in detail below, focusing on the finding that depressed people find it difficult to retrieve specific information. (I offer these data on autobiographical memory as an example of the way in which knowledge of cognitive processes can inform clinical process issues. I do not claim that it exhausts the possibilities.) I and my colleagues have suggested that deficits in personal memories have three effects: it prevents the re-interpretation of old memories; it prevents the person seeing links between their mood, thoughts and behaviour; it prevents the production of effective alternative means of coping with current problems.

DEPRESSION AND THE SPECIFICITY OF AUTOBIOGRAPHICAL MEMORY

In our research, we have found that autobiographical memory in depressed people is not only biased, in the sense that they take longer to remember positive events that happened in their lives compared with negative events. In addition we have found that depressed people are more likely to be overgeneral in their memories (Williams and Scott, 1988; Moore et al., 1988). The basic phenomenon is established as follows. Patients are given words or phrases to cue their memories. These may be positive (e.g. happy, safe) or negative (e.g. angry, sorry). At the outset, it is explained that after each word, patients are to try and recall an event that the word reminds them of. It is emphasized that what is required is a specific event, something that happened at a particular place at a particular time. A few practice items are given until the patients understand what is required. Williams and Scott and Moore et al. found that depressed patients are more likely to respond to these cues not by giving specific events (e.g. going for a walk last Tuesday) but by giving generic statements which summarize events (e.g. going for walks).

This is a phenomenon similar to that which occurs in cognitive therapy for depression. From time to time, the therapist asks the patient a question about their past and the patient responds with a statement such as 'We always used to have such good times together' or 'I've always failed in everything I've done'. If the therapist tries to ask specific questions about the events on which such general statements are based, it sometimes takes the patient a long time to retrieve the specific events. This is true, not only for negative events (which people may not wish to talk about), but also in the case of positive events. In fact, when we looked at the memories of depressed people, we found that they have greater difficulty being specific about positive events in their life.

We have explained these phenomena in terms of those theories of memory which assume the existence of an intermediate stage in the encoding and retrieval of memories. When one tries to retrieve an event, one first generates a general description. This description is then used to search the memory 'database' for an appropriate candidate memory. For example, in response to the cue word 'happy', people generate an intermediate description based on the implicit question 'what sort of people, activities, places make me happy?' It appears that depressed patients get stuck at that intermediate stage, and cannot use the general descriptions that they generate at that stage to help them retrieve specific examples. What are the implications of this phenomenon for re-interpretation of old memories, for seeing thought-affect-behaviour connections, and for problem-solving?

The effect of overgeneral memory

The first significance of general encoding and retrieval of negative events is that it inhibits re-interpretation and re-schematization of the past. For example, if somebody has walked passed in the street and ignored the patient, then the patient may have encoded that as an example of 'people not bothering with me' or 'disliking me'. Only by retrieving details about what happened will other information be retrieved which might lead to a different conclusion and a different interpretation of that event. For example, the other person may have been a long way away, and therefore didn't see the patient; or they may have looked as if they were very preoccupied. Practising these skills will enable changes to take place in the way memories are represented. In particular, it is less likely that the description 'times when people have shown their dislike' will now fit the situation. The result will be that, although the person may well be upset when somebody next doesn't see them in the street, the mood is less likely to cause a series of negative elaborations which will end in a catastrophic thought such as 'nobody likes me anymore'. It is almost as if one has been able to put the mental equivalent of a fire-break in the forest which is the structure of memories in the person's mind. The fire may still burn, but it will not leap to the next part of the forest.

The second significance of general retrieval style shows up most clearly in the difficulty which patients often experience in using diaries. Since diaries (often completed at the end of each day) involve the retrieval of specific information, overgeneral retrieval style may inhibit this. Diaries are used to monitor events, feelings, and thoughts. In as much as a patient is unable to complete them, they will find it difficult to identify links between thoughts, feelings and behaviour. Since this ability to record aspects of daily life is fundamental to most structured psychotherapies, difficulty in encoding and retrieving specific events will retard progress in all such therapies.

Third, overgeneral retrieval has implications for problem-solving. In order to see this clearly, we need first to specify which aspects of problem-solving are likely to be affected. Problem-solving involves several steps (D'Zurilla and Goldfried, 1971; Goldfried and Goldfried, 1975). The first is the general orientation to a problem. People have to be able to recognize that a problem exists and to be able to articulate what the problem is as precisely as possible. The next stage is to generate as many alternative solutions as possible, and then to weigh up the advantages and disadvantages of implementing each one. The one that appears to be most likely to produce the best outcome is then selected, implemented, and its effects evaluated. There is little doubt that depressed patients find such problem-solving difficult. For example, they do not generate as many alternative solutions as non-depressed people do and what alternatives they do generate tend to be less effective (as rated by an independent judge) than those generated by non-depressed individuals (Marx *et al.*, in press).What is the connection between problem-solving and autobiographical memory?

Remember that the model of memory we use assumes that depressed people stop short of retrieving a specific memory and instead respond with an intermediate description. I suggest that problem-solving is inhibited because depressed people attempt to use these intermediate descriptions as a database to try and generate effective solutions. But this database is severely restricted because of the lack of specific information. For example, if a depressed person is feeling bad and they try to ask themselves 'what could I do to feel better?' then memory of past similar situations is clearly relevant. However, if the only memory they retrieve is the generic description (e.g. when I'm with my boyfriend) then that in itself will not contain enough specific information to cue different coping strategies for dealing with the current situation. By contrast, if a non-depressed person is feeling unhappy and tries to think to themselves 'what can I do to make myself better?', they are more likely to remember a specific event. Such a memory offers more cues for problem-solving. Although 'the boyfriend' may be part of this memory, there will be other details as well (e.g. 'a walk with my boyfriend last Friday when I met his friends and went to have a drink'). This specific event offers a far greater range of cues. As well as 'the boyfriend', there is also 'the walk', 'the meeting', 'the other friends', 'the pub' and 'last Friday', each of which may cue other potential coping strategies.

Evans *et al.* (in press) have recently tested these hypotheses directly in a suicidal population by measuring both the level of overgenerality in autobiographical memory, and the effectiveness of the solutions produced in response to the Means Ends Problem Solving Task (Platt and Spivack, 1975). They found that they were very highly correlated. People who had the most difficulty being specific in their memory produced the least effective solutions to the problems.

Is there any evidence that overgeneral retrieval retards progress in therapy? Wahler and Afton (1980) studied women who had relationship problems with their children, and found that these women, especially those with many additional stresses, had great problems in being specific in their descriptions of what their children were doing wrong. Wahler and Afton came to a conclusion similar to our own, that the mothers had difficulty in encoding and/or retrieving details of times when their children had been naughty. Importantly, as treatment progressed, the mothers were able to produce more and more detailed descriptions and those mothers whose relationship with their children had improved most by the end of treatment on various independent measures, were also those who had become more specific in their descriptions of the events. Second, some preliminary data from a recent study of prediction of recovery and relapse in depression has shown that overgenerality in the retrieval of positive memories (assessed at admission) predicts severity of depression seven months later (Brittlebank *et al.*, in preparation). In this study neither severity of depression nor dysfunctional attitudes assessed on admission predicted severity over this interval. Third, DeRubeis and Feeley (1990) found that more reduction in depression symptoms early in therapy occurred when the therapist used more 'concrete' strategies. All of these data are consistent with the suggestion that the way in which a person recalls events about themselves is very important in determining their mood and problem-solving abilities.

It is not surprising that a person's autobiographical memory should have such importance in determining the strength and persistence of emotional reactions. A person's memory provides all the information he or she has about themselves. The way that information has been encoded, and the different forms in which the information is retrieved is bound to play a critical role in determining a person's self-concept. In particular, I have suggested that the tendency to retrieve general rather than specific information about one's past may render a person vulnerable to uninterrupted spirals of mood and cognition, and vulnerable to mood being used as the sole criterion of the truth of current thoughts and ideas. Cognitive therapy, through its thought-catching, activity-scheduling and other procedures for reality-testing, provides specific information which will interrupt the mood-affect spiral and provide alternative criteria for reality, so that the hold that mood has on the person is weakened. It does so by facilitating the re-interpretation of past events, by allowing the person to appreciate links between thought, feeling and behaviour through the use of diaries, and by helping the person to generate more effective solutions to their problems.

COGNITIVE THERAPY AND THE MECHANISMS OF CHANGE

How does this way of thinking about change in psychotherapy relate to the three models I introduced at the outset? It builds upon that of Teasdale (1985) in specifying one way in which the break in reciprocal links between cognition and affect may occur. It is relevant to Brewin (1989), particularly his ideas on the re-categorization of memory, and shows how his theoretical ideas may be anchored in empirical data on autobiographical memory. It builds upon both Brewin and Teasdale's models by making explicit the role of mood as a criterion of validity and suggests the possibility that therapy works in part by providing alternative criteria, allowing mood to be distrusted as a guide to truth.

Third, the model I have suggested is relevant to that of Barber and DeRubeis (1989) (especially as regards problem-solving training as a compensatory strategy). However, I differ in emphasis from them, in that I do not believe that a compensatory strategy such as problem-solving training can be implemented without involving changes in information processing. I suggest that where such training is effective, it is because these strategies begin to enable the person to go beyond the general intermediate descriptions to the specifics of events in their encoding and retrieval of memory. Where positive events are involved, this has very clear implications for mood and for the generation of alternative coping strategies to deal with the current problem. Like the example of being able to recall the specific event of 'going for a walk' given above, there will be a richer database available to the person to help generate alternative coping strategies for current problems.

Let us look again now at the evidence that different types of therapy are indistinguishable in the way they bring about change. Note that studies find a lack of difference in *levels* of the variables measured. But does this mean that there are no differences? The problem has been that we have become content to look at the level of a variable rather than its reactivity in response to stress. As we saw at the end of the last chapter, vulnerability consists not in a particular level of dysfunctional attitude, but in how reactive a person is in their dysfunctional attitudes and in the global negative statements they make about themselves in response to mood. The argument is that one may only see vulnerability when people are under stress.

Consistent with this it is becoming clear that, independently of current level of depression, a previous history of depression exerts an influence on current cognition. A prior history of depression makes it more likely that current mood disturbance will be associated with increased negative self-reference (increased memory for negative self-referent adjectives; Hammen *et al.*, 1986; Teasdale and Dent, 1987). This is because a prior history of depression is more likely to have linked mood with a greater degree of elaboration on negative themes. People are more likely, if they have been depressed in the past, to encode and elaborate events using overgeneric concepts. It is also evident from the literature that a prior history of depression makes it more likely that a current high level of depression will be associated with more dysfunctional attitudes (Miranda and Persons, 1988). Each of these studies has found that if people have not previously been depressed, their current mood levels have less effect on cognition.

This is consistent with what is known in two other important areas of depression research: first, sex differences in depression; and second, prediction of relapse. It appears that the reason for the greater proportion of women than men who become depressed is not due to their being more likely to have a first episode (Amenson and Lewinsohn, 1981). The difference arises because, having had one episode of depression, women are much more likely than men to have a recurrence. Only further research will determine whether this is due to the difference between the sexes in the associations between mood and cognition which are set up during the initial depression (as Clark and Teasdale's 1985 results suggested), or whether the increased frequency of mood shift due to hormonal cycles in women tends to activate, and as it were, keep alive a prior depression. In any event, the influence of prior history of depression in helping to determine future tendencies for mood shifts to precipitate depression is clear from these data.

The evidence on prediction of relapse is similarly suggestive. Three studies (Eaves and Rush, 1984; Simons *et al.*, 1986; Evans *et al.*, submitted) have assessed dysfunctional attitudes when patients are discharged (at which point there is still some mild mood disturbance). In each case, level of dysfunctional attitudes contributed significantly to the prediction of relapse. The conclusion is that what we are measuring here is the capacity of small amounts of mood disturbance to precipitate large shifts in dysfunctional thinking. If dysfunctional attitudes are assessed at a time when a person is not depressed, they do not predict relapse (Segal *et al.*, in press).

CONCLUDING REMARKS

To summarize, cognitive therapy reduces vulnerability to further depression by preventing small amounts of mood disturbance from precipitating a large amount of cognitive change. In terms of the four meanings of 'cognitive', this will involve the prevention of large increases in negative thinking, in helplessness, in dysfunctional attitudes and mis-attributions, and in biased information processing that would normally occur (especially if the person has been depressed before).

Cognitive therapy provides compensation for the errors and biases which have become enslaved by depressive interpretation of events. In part this is done by giving patients methods by which they can manage their symptoms, and in part by making them aware of the way in which they are making errors in judgements under conditions of uncertainty. Cognitive therapy is not thereby restorative and could be called 'compensatory' in the sense that patients are becoming aware of things which non-depressed people are not aware of. On the other hand this does not mean that there is no influence on information processing. Information processing changes and compensatory processes are not mutually exclusive. Neither is it the case that compensation comes first and then, when it is practised, information processing changes later. Even at the outset, compensatory processing (involving problem-solving, thought-catching, and diary-keeping), involve changes to the way information is perceived, categorized, encoded, stored and retrieved. In particular I have pointed to a feature of autobiographical memory, the level of specificity or generality that people are able to achieve, as an indicator of the style in which people elaborate their memories. If they encode and retrieve memories in an overgeneric form, then it will lead to failures to generate effective problem-solving strategies. As people proceed to keep diaries of their thoughts, actions and feelings, they will come to encode events more specifically, thus releasing a block which has existed on their problem-solving abilities.

I suggest that these changes help to prevent mood from causing connections to be made which end up with catastrophic self-referent negative interpretations of events. After therapy, transient mood shifts will still occur, but these will have less influence on this elaborative process. This explains the difficulty in distinguishing between therapies on the basis of patients' level of dysfunctional attitudes at the end of therapy. This is because, when mood is reduced, the tendency to elaborate these self-referent concepts in a negative way will also reduce. The confusion has arisen a) because investigators have tended to look only at the level of a variable, rather than its reactivity in response to transient shifts in mood; and b) because they have tended to see attitudes as long-lasting permanent structures in a person's mind, rather than as predispositions to elaborate certain themes 'on line' under conditions of mood disturbance.

The hypothesis is testable. It predicts that patients who respond more slowly to therapy of any sort should be those who have most difficulty being specific across a range of their autobiographical memory. (We have seen that there is some preliminary evidence to support this suggestion.) Second, it predicts that if patients who had undergone antidepressant medication treatment were compared with patients who had undergone cognitive therapy at the end of treatment, then although they would not be able to be distinguished on the basis of their level of negative self-reference or in dysfunctional attitudes, they ought to be able to be distinguished when under stress (for example, following an interview in which they are recalling past negative experiences). Since such interviews are often given as part of the discharge procedure, such a study would not be difficult to arrange. Our model clearly predicts that this test should differentiate the groups. If cognitive-behavioural therapy has reduced vulnerability in this way, then these patients should show less transient increases in dysfunctional attitudes in response to mood, and less association between fluctuations in their mood and degree of belief in the validity of their negative thoughts.

We already know that levels of dysfunctional attitudes and negative self-referent descriptions can predict both relapse and persistence of depression. It is a small step, but an important one, to the hypothesis that the critical thing about cognitive therapy is (a) the breaking of the association between mood disturbance and elaboration of negative self-referent material; and (b) the weakening of mood as a criterion of the truth of negative thoughts, assumptions and fears. It is important progress to observe that where this occurs, there may be found no apparent difference in the levels of various measures of either mood or cognition at the end of different treatments. The important factor is how they shift in relation to each other, not what their 'resting state' is. Finally, it has been, and will continue to be important to search for critical cognitive processes (such as those aspects of autobiographical memory which we have identified), which help to explain how cognitive therapy acts to bring about such change.

NOTES

1   Note, however, that what specificity was found in the NIMH study suggested that cognitive therapy was, as predicted, specifically affecting a 'need for approval' factor on the DAS (Imber et al., 1990) and Whisman et al. (1991) have recently found similar specificity for cognitive therapy with depressed inpatients.

2   It is worth noting in passing that this conclusion is almost certainly wrong. Not only do depressed patients have genuine information processing problems with the registration of information and its later recall (Watts et al., 1987) they also have difficulties in retrieving autobiographical memories (see text) which is independent of the content of what is being recalled. This deficit in autobiographical memory acts as a vulnerability factor in the persistence of depression.

References

Abramowitz, S.I. (1969) 'Locus of control and self-reported depression among college students'. *Psychological Reports*, 25, 149–50.

Abramson, L.Y., Seligman, M.E.P. and Teasdale, J.D. (1978) 'Learned helplessness in humans: critique and reformulation'. *Journal of Abnormal Psychology*, 87, 49–74.

Alloy, C.B. and Abramson, L.Y. (1979) 'Judgements of contingency in depressed and nondepressed students: sadder but wiser?' *Journal of Experimental Psychology: General*, 108, 441–85.

Alloy, C.B., Abramson, L.Y., Metalsky, G.I. and Hartlage, S. (1988) 'The hopelessness theory of depression: attributional aspects'. *British Journal of Clinical Psychology*, 27, 5–21.

Altman, J.H. and Wittenborn, J.R. (1980) 'Depression-prone personality in women'. *Journal of Abnormal Psychology*, 89, 303–8.

Ambelas, A. (1979) 'Psychologically stressful events in the precipitation of manic episodes'. *British Journal of Psychiatry*, 135, 15–21.

Amenson, C.S. and Lewinsohn, P.M. (1981) 'An investigation into the observed sex differences in prevalence of unipolar depression'. *Journal of Abnormal Psychology*, 90, 1–13.

Antaki, C. and Brewin, C.R. (1982) *Attributions and Psychological Change*. Academic Press, New York.

Anton, J.L., Dunbar, J. and Friedman, L. (1976) 'Anticipation training in the treatment of depression' in J.D. Krumbolz and C.E. Thoresen (eds) *Counselling Methods*. Holt Rinehart and Winston, New York.

APA Task Force on Laboratory Tests in Psychiatry (1987) 'The Dexamethasone Suppression Test: an overview of its status in psychiatry'. *American Journal of Psychiatry*, 144, 1253–62.

Ayllon, Y. and Azrin, N.H. (1968) *The Token Economy: A Motivational System for Therapy and Rehabilitation*. Appleton Century Crofts, New York.

Barber, J.P. and DeRubeis, R.J. (1989) 'On second thoughts: where the action is in cognitive therapy for depression'. *Cognitive Therapy and Research*, 13, 441–57.

Barnett, P.A. and Gotlib, I.H. (1988) 'Psychosocial functioning and depression: distinguishing among antecedents, concomitants and consequences'. *Psychological Bulletin*, 104, 97–126.

Beck, A.T. (1963) 'Thinking and depression 1: idiosyncratic content and cognitive distortions'. *Archives of General Psychiatry*, 9, 324–33.

Beck, A.T. (1964) 'Thinking and depression 2: theory and therapy'. *Archives of General Psychiatry*, 10, 56–71.

Beck, A.T. (1967) *Depression: Clinical, Experimental and Theoretical Aspects*. Hoeber, New York (republished as *Depression: Causes and Treatment*, University of Pennsylvania Press, Philadelphia, 1972).

Beck, A.T. (1976) *Cognitive Therapy and the Emotional Disorders*. International Universities Press, New York.

Beck, A.T. (1988) *Love is Never Enough*. Penguin, Harmondsworth.

Beck, A.T., Ward, C.H., Mendelson, M., Mock, J.E. and Erbaugh, J.K. (1961) 'An inventory for measuring depression'. *Archives of General Psychiatry*, 4, 561–71.

Beck, A.T., Schuyler, D. and Herman, J. (1974) 'Development of suicidal intent scales' in A.T. Beck, H.L.P. Resnik and D.J. Lettieri (eds) *The Prediction of Suicide*. Charles Press, Bowie, Maryland.

Beck, A.T., Weissman, A.W., Lester, D. and Trexler, L. (1974) 'The assessment of pessimism: the Hopelessness Scale'. *Journal of Consulting Clinical Psychology*, 42, 861–5.

Beck, A.T., Rush, A.J., Shaw, B.F. and Emery, G. (1979) *Cognitive Therapy of Depression*. Guildford Press, New York.

Beck, A.T., Hollon, S.D., Young, J.E., Bedrosian, R.C. and Budenz, D. (1985) 'Treatment of depression with cognitive therapy and amitriptyline'. *Archives of General Psychiatry*, 42, 142–8.

Beck, A.T., Steer, R.A. and Garbin, M.G. (1988) 'Psychometric properties of the Beck Depression Inventory: 25 years of evaluation'. *Clinical Psychology Reviews*, 8, 77–100.

Bellack, A.S. and Schwartz, J.S. (1976) 'Assessment for self-control programs' in M. Hersen and A.S. Bellack (eds) *Behavioural Assessment: A practical handbook*. Pergamon, Oxford.

Bellack, A.S., Hersen, M. and Harmondsworth, J. (1981) 'Social skills training compared with pharmacotherapy and psychotherapy in the treatment of unipolar depression'. *American Journal of Psychiatry*, 138, 1562–7.

Bellack, A.S., Hersen, M. and Himmelhoch, J. (1983) 'A comparison of social skills training pharmacotherapy and psychotherapy for depression'. *Behaviour Research and Therapy*, 21, 101–7.

Bellew, M. (1990) *Information Processing Biases and Depression*. University of Keele, Unpublished PhD thesis.

Belsher, G. and Costello, C.G. (1988) 'Relapse after recovery from unipolar depression: a critical review'. *Psychological Bulletin*, 104, 84–96.

Benatov, R. (1981) *Evening Therapy: psychotherapy of short-term memory*, Paper presented at SPR European Conference on Psychotherapy Research, Trier FRG, Sept. 1981.

Bentall, R.P. and Kaney, S. (1989) 'Content specific information processing and persecutory delusions: an investigation using the emotional stroop test'. *British Journal of Medical Psychology*, 62, 355–64.

Billings, A.G. and Moos, R.H. (1985) 'Psychosocial processes of remission in unipolar depression: Comparing depressed patients with matched community controls'. *Journal of Consulting and Clinical Psychology*, 53, 314–25.

Blackburn, I.M. (1989) 'Cognitive therapy with severely depressed in-patients' in J. Scott, J.M.G. Williams and A.T. Beck (eds) *Cognitive Therapy in Clinical Practice: an illustrative casebook*. Routledge, London, New York.

Blackburn, I.M. and Smyth, P. (1985) 'A test of the cognitive vulnerability in individuals prone to depression'. *British Journal of Clinical Psychology*, 24, 61–2.

Blackburn, I.M., Bishop, S., Glen, I.M., Whalley, L.J. and Christie, J.E. (1981) 'The efficacy of cognitive therapy in depression: a treatment trial using cognitive therapy and pharmacotherapy, each alone and in combination'. *British Journal of Psychiatry*, 139, 181–9.

Blackburn, I.M., Eunson, K.M. and Bishop, S. (1986) 'A two year naturalistic follow-up of depressed patients treated with cognitive therapy, pharmacotherapy and a combination of both'. *Journal of Affective Disorders*, 10, 67–75.

Blackburn, I.M., Jones, S. and Lewin, R.J.P. (1986) 'Cognitive style in depression'. *British Journal of Clinical Psychology*, 25, 241–51.

Blaney, P.H. (1977) 'Contemporary theories of depression: critique and comparison'. *Journal of Abnormal Psychology*, 86, 203–23.

Blaney, P.H. (1981) 'The effectiveness of cognitive and behavioral therapies' in L.P. Rehm (ed.) *Behavior Therapy for Depression*. Academic Press, New York.

Bootzin, R. (1973) 'Stimulus control of insomnia'. Paper presented at annual meeting of APA Montreal, Sept. 1973.

Borkovec, T.D. and Boudewyns, P.A. (1976) 'Treatment of insomnia with stimulus control and progressive relaxation procedures' in J.D. Krumbolz and C.E. Thoresen (eds) *Counselling Methods*. Holt Rinehart and Winston, New York.

Bower, G. (1981) 'Mood and memory'. *American Psychologist*, 36, 129–48.

Bower, G.H., Monteiro, K.P. and Gilligan, S.G. (1978) 'Emotional mood as a context for learning and recall'. *Journal of Verbal Learning and Verbal Behaviour*, 17, 573–85.

Bowers, W.A. (1990) 'Treatment of depressed in-patients: cognitive therapy plus medication, relaxation plus medication, and medication alone'. *British Journal of Psychiatry*, 156, 73–8.

Brewer, D.W., Doughtie, E.B. and Lubin, B. (1980) 'Induction of mood and mood shift'. *Journal of Clinical Psychology*, 36, 215–26.

Brewin, C.R. (1985) 'Depression and causal attributions: what is their relation?' *Psychological Bulletin*, 98, 297–309.

Brewin, C.R. (1989) 'Cognitive change processes in psychotherapy'. *Psychological Review*, 96, 379–94.

Brittlebank, A., Scott, J., Ferrier, N. and Williams, J.M.G. (in preparation). 'Autobiographical memory predicts course of depression'.

Brown, G. and Harris, T. (1978) *Social Origins of Depression – a study of psychiatric disorder in women*. Tavistock, London.

Brown, G.W. (1989) 'Depression: a radical social perspective' in K. Herbst and E.S. Paykel (eds) *Depression: an integrative approach*. Heinemann Medical Press, London.

Brown, J.D. and Siegal, J.M. (1988) 'Attribution for negative life events and depression: the role of perceived control'. *Journal of Personality and Social Psychology*, 54, 316–22.

Burgess, E.P. (1969) 'The modification of depressive behaviours' in R.D. Rubin and C.M. Frank (eds) *Advances in Behaviour Therapy*. Academic Press, New York.

Burns, D.D. (1980) *Feeling Good: the new mood therapy*. Signet, New American Library, New York.

Burns, M.O. and Seligman, M.E.P. (1989) 'Explanatory style across the life-span: evidence of stability over 52 years'. *Journal of Personality and Social Psychology*, 56, 471–7.

Campbell, E.A. (1982) 'Vulnerability to depression and cognitive predisposition: psychosocial correlates of Brown and Harris's vulnerability factors'. Paper presented at BPS conference, York, April 1982.

Campbell, E.A., Cope, S.J. and Teasdale, J.D. (1983) 'Social factors and affective disorders: an investigation of Brown and Harris' model'. *British Journal of Psychiatry*, 143, 548–53.

Carney, N.W.P., Roth, M. and Garside, R.F. (1965) 'The diagnosis of depressive syndromes and prediction of ECT response'. *British Journal of Psychiatry*, 111, 659–74.

Carroll, B.J. (1982) 'The dexamethasone suppression test for melancholia'. *British Journal of Psychiatry*, 140, 292–304.

Carroll, B.J., Fielding, J.M. and Blashki, T.G. (1973) 'Depression rating scales: a critical review'. *Archives of General Psychiatry*, 28, 361–6.

Clark, D.M. (1983) 'On the induction of depressed mood in the laboratory: evaluation and comparison of the Velten and musical procedures'. *Advances in Behaviour Research and Therapy*, 5, 27–49.

Clark, D.M. and Teasdale, J.D. (1985) 'Constraints on the effects of mood on memory'. *Journal of Personality and Social Psychology*, 48, 1595–608.

Cleaver, S. (1981) 'Attributional modifications in the treatment of depression'. Unpublished MSc dissertation, University of Newcastle upon Tyne.

Cofer, D.H. and Wittenborn, J.R. (1980) 'Personality characteristics of formerly depressed women'. *Journal of Abnormal Psychology*, 89, 309–14.

Coleman, R.E. (1975) 'Manipulation of self-esteem as a determinant of mood of elated and depressed women'. *Journal of Abnormal Psychology*, 84, 693–700.

Cook, T.D. and Campbell, D.T. (1979) *The Design and Analysis of Quasi Experiments in Field Settings*. Rand McNally, Chicago.

Costello, C.G. (1972a) 'Depression: loss of reinforcement or loss of reinforcer effectiveness'. *Behaviour Therapy*, 3, 240–7.

Costello, C.G. (1972b) 'Reply to Lazarus'. *Behaviour Therapy*, 3, 251–3.

Costello, C.G. (1982) 'Social factors associated with depression: a retrospective community study'. *Psychological Medicine*, 12, 329–39.

Coyne, J.C. (1976) 'Depression and the response of others'. *Journal of Abnormal Psychology*, 85, 186–93.

Coyne, J.C., Metalsky, G.I. and Lavelle, T.L. (1980) 'Learned helplessness as experimenter induced failure and its alleviation with attentional redeployment'. *Journal of Abnormal Psychology*, 89, 350–7.

D'Zurilla, T.J. and Goldfried, M.R. (1971) 'Problem solving and behaviour modification'. *Journal of Abnormal Psychology*, 78, 107–26.

Davies, E. (1982) 'An investigation into the effect of internally and externally focussed tasks on depressed mood'. Unpublished MSc thesis, University of Newcastle-upon-Tyne.

Davis, H. (1979) 'Self-reference and the encoding of personal information in depression'. *Cognitive Therapy and Research*, 3, 97–110.

Davis, H. and Unruh, W.R. (1981) 'The development of the self-schema in adult depression'. *Journal of Abnormal Psychology*, 90, 125–33.

de Jong, R., Treiber, R. and Henrich, G. (1986) 'Effectiveness of two psychological treatments for in-patients with severe and chronic depression'. *Cognitive Therapy and Research*, 10, 645–63.

Dent, J. and Teasdale, J.D. (1988) 'Negative cognition and the persistence of depression'. *Journal of Abnormal Psychology*, 97, 29–34.

Depue, R.A. and Monroe, S.M. (1978) 'Learned helplessness in the perspective of the depressive disorders: conceptual and definitional issues'. *Journal of Abnormal Psychology*, 87, 2–20.

Derry, P.A. and Kuiper, N.A. (1981) 'Schematic processing and self-reference in clinical depression'. *Journal of Abnormal Psychology*, 90, 286–97.

DeRubeis, R.J. and Feeley, M. (1990) 'Determinants of change in cognitive therapy for depression'. *Cognitive Therapy and Research*, 14, 469–82.

DeRubeis, R.J. and Hollon, S.D. (1981) 'Behavioural treatment of the affective disorders' in M. Michelson, M.L. Hersen and S.M. Turner (eds) *Future Perspectives in Behaviour Therapy*. Plenum Press, New York.

Dobson, K. (1989) 'A meta analysis of the efficacy of cognitive therapy for depression'. *Journal of Consulting and Clinical Psychology*, 57, 414–19.

Eastman, C. (1976) 'Behavioural formulations of depression'. *Psychological Review*, 83, 277–91.

Eaves, G. and Rush, A.J. (1984) 'Cognitive patterns in symptomatic and remitted unipolar major depression'. *Journal of Abnormal Psychology*, 93, 31–40.

Elkin, I., Shea, M.T., Watkins, J.T., Imber, S.D., Sotsky, S.M., Collins, J.F., Glass, D.R., Pilkonis, P.A., et al. (1989) 'NIMH treatment of depression collaborative research program: general effectiveness of treatments'. *Archives of General Psychiatry*, 46, 971–83.

Evans, M., Hollon, S.D., DeRubeis, R.J., Piasecki, J.M., Tuason, V.B. and Vye, C. (1985) 'Accounting for relapse in a treatment outcome study of depression'. Paper presented at the Annual Meeting of the Association for the Advancement of Behaviour Therapy, November 1985.

Evans, M., Hollon, S.D., DeRubeis, R.J., Piasecki, J.M., Grove, W.M., Garvey, M.J. and Tuason, V.B. (submitted) 'Differential relapse following cognitive therapy, pharmacotherapy, and combined cognitive-pharmacotherapy for depression'.

Evans, J., Williams, J.M.G., O'Loughlin, S. and Howells, K. (in press) 'Autobiographical memory and problem solving in parasuicide'. *Psychological Medicine*.

Eysenck, H.J. and Eysenck, S.B.G. (1975) *Manual of the Eysenck Personality Questionnaire*. Hodder and Stoughton, Sevenoaks.

Feighner, J.P., Robins, E., Guze, S.B., Woodruff, R.A., Winokur, G. and Minoz, R.

(1972) 'Diagnostic criteria for use in psychiatric research'. *Archives of General Psychiatry*, 26, 57–63.

Fennell, M.J.V. and Campbell, E.A. (1984) 'The cognitions questionnaire: specific thinking errors in depression'. *British Journal of Clinical Psychology*, 23, 81–92.

Fennell, M.J.V. and Teasdale, J.D. (1982) 'Cognitive therapy with chronic, drug-refractory depressed out-patients. A note of caution'. *Cognitive Therapy and Research*, 6, 455–59.

Fennell, M.J.V. and Teasdale, J.D. (1987) 'Cognitive therapy for depression: individual differences and the process of change'. *Cognitive Therapy and Research*, 11, 253–72.

Fennell, M.J.V., Teasdale, J.D., Jones, S. and Damle, A. (1987) 'Distraction in neurotic and endogenous depression: an investigation of negative thinking in major depressive disorders'. *Psychological Medicine*, 17, 441–52.

Ferster, C.B. (1966) 'Animal behaviour and mental illness'. *Psychological Record*, 16, 345–56.

Ferster, C.B. (1973) 'A functional analysis of depression'. *American Psychologist*, 28, 857–70.

Fischhoff, B. (1977) 'Perceived informativeness of facts'. *Journal of Experimental Psychology: Human Perception and Performance*, 3, 349–58.

Fogarty, S.J. and Hemsley, D.R. (1983) 'Depression and the accessibility of memories: a longitudinal study'. *British Journal of Psychiatry*, 142, 232–7.

Free, M.L. and Oei, T.P.S. (in press) 'Biological and psychological processes in the treatment and maintenance of depression'. *Clinical Psychology Reviews*, in press.

Friedman, A.S. (1975) 'Interaction of drug therapy with marital therapy in depressive patients'. *Archives of General Psychiatry*, 32, 619–37.

Frost, R.O, Graf, M. and Becker, J. (1979) 'Self-devaluation and depressed mood'. *Journal of Consulting and Clinical Psychology*, 47, 958–62.

Fuchs, C. and Rehm, L.P. (1977) 'A self-control behaviour therapy program for depression'. *Journal of Consulting and Clinical Psychology*, 45, 206–15.

Garber, J. and Hollon, S.D. (1980) 'Universal vs personal helplessness in depression; belief in uncontrollability or incompetence?' *Journal of Abnormal Psychology*, 89, 56–66.

Geer, J.H. and Katkin, E.S. (1966) 'Treatment of insomnia using a variant of systematic desensitisation – a case report'. *Journal of Abnormal Psychology*, 71, 161–4.

Glen, A.M., Johnson, A.L. and Shephard, M. (1984) 'Continuation therapy with lithium and amitriptyline in unipolar depressive illness: a randomised double-blind controlled trial'. *Psychological Medicine*, 14, 37–50.

Goldfried, M.R. (1980) 'Toward a delineation of therapeutic change principles'. *American Psychologist*, 35, 991–9.

Goldfried, M.R. and Goldfried, A.P. (1975) 'Cognitive change methods' in F.H. Kanfer and A.P. Goldstein (eds) *Helping People Change*. Academic Press, New York.

Golin, S., Jarrett, S., Stewart, M. and Drayton, W. (1980) 'Cognitive theory and the generality of pessimism among depressed persons'. *Journal of Abnormal Psychology*, 89, 101–4.

Golin, S., Sweeney, P.D. and Shaeffer, D.E. (1981) 'The causality of causal attribution in depression. A cross-lagged panel correlational analysis'. *Journal of Abnormal Psychology*, 90, 14–22.

Gong-Guy, E. and Hammen, C. (1980) 'Causal perceptions of stressful events in depressed and nondepressed outpatients'. *Journal of Abnormal Psychology*, 89, 662–9.

Goodwin, A.M. and Williams, J.M.G. (1982) 'Mood-induction research; its implications for clinical depression'. *Behaviour Research and Therapy*, 20, 373–82.

Gotlib, I.H. (1981) 'Self-reinforcement and recall: differential deficits in depressed and nondepressed psychiatric in-patients'. *Journal of Abnormal Psychology*, 90, 521–30.

Gray, J.A. (1987) *The Psychology of Fear and Stress* (2nd edn). Cambridge University Press, Cambridge.

Gray, J.A. (1990) 'Brain systems that mediate both emotion and cognition'. *Cognition and Emotion*, 4, 269–88.

Greene, S. (1981) Levels of measured hopelessness in the general population. *British Journal of Clinical Psychology*, 20, 11–14.

Hale, W.D. and Strickland, B.R. (1976) 'Induction of mood states and their effect on cognitive and social behaviours'. *Journal of Consulting and Clinical Psychology*, 44, 155.

Hamilton, E.W. and Abramson, L.Y. (1983) 'Cognitive patterns and major depressive disorder. A longitudinal study in a hospital setting'. *Journal of Abnormal Psychology*, 92, 173–84.

Hamilton, M. (1960) 'A rating scale for depression'. *Journal of Neurology and Neurosurgical Psychiatry*, 23, 56–61.

Hamilton, M. (1967) 'Development of a rating scale for primary depressive illness'. *British Journal of Social and Clinical Psychology*, 6, 278–96.

Hamilton, M. (1982) 'The effect of treatment on the melancholias'. *British Journal of Psychiatry*, 140, 223–30.

Hamilton, M. and Shapiro, C.M. (1990) 'Depression' in D.F. Peck and C.M. Shapiro (eds) *Measuring Human Problems: a practical guide*. John Wiley and Sons, Chichester.

Hammen, C.L. (1978) 'Depression, distortion and life stress in college students'. *Cognitive Therapy and Research*, 2, 189–92.

Hammen, C.L. and Glass, D.R. (1975) 'Depression activity and evaluation of reinforcement'. *Journal of Abnormal Psychology*, 84, 718–21.

Hammen, C.L. and Peters, S.D. (1978) 'Interpersonal consequences of depression: responses to men and women enacting a depressed role'. *Journal of Abnormal Psychology*, 87, 322–32.

Hammen, C.L., Marks, T., Mayall, A. and De Mayo, R. (1985) 'Depressive self-schemas, life stress and vulnerability to depression'. *Journal of Abnormal Psychology*, 94, 308–19.

Hammen, C.L., Dyke, D.G. and Micklovitch, D.J. (1986) 'Stability and severity parameters of depressive self-schema responding'. *Journal of Social and Clinical Psychology*, 4, 23–45.

Hargreaves, I.R. (1982) 'A test of the reformulated learned helplessness model of depression'. Unpublished MSc dissertation, University of Aberdeen.

Hargreaves, I.R. (1985) 'Attributional style and depression'. *British Journal of Clinical Psychology*, 24, 65–6.

Healy, D. and Williams, J.M.G. (1989) 'Moods, misattribution and mania: an interaction of biological and psychological factors in the precipitation of mania'. *Psychiatric Developments*, 1, 49–70.

Hersen, M., Eisler, R.M., Smith, B.S. and Agras, W.S. (1972) 'A token reinforcement ward for young psychiatric patients'. *American Journal of Psychiatry*, 129, 228–32.

Hersen, M., Eisler, R.M., Alford, G.S. and Agras, W.S. (1973) 'Effects of token economy on neurotic depression: an experimental analysis'. *Behaviour Therapy*, 4, 392–7.

Hersen, M., Bellack, A.S., Himmelhoch, J.M. and Thase, M.E. (1984) 'Effects of social skills training, and psychotherapy in unipolar depressed women'. *Behaviour Therapy*, 15, 21–40.

Hiroto, D.S. and Seligman, M.E.P. (1975) 'Generality of learned helplessness in man'. *Journal of Personality and Social Psychology*, 31, 311–27.

Hirschfeld, R.M.A., Klerman, G.L., Gough, H.G., Barrett, J., Korchin, S.J. and Chodoff, P. (1977) 'A measure of interpersonal dependency'. *Journal of Personality Assessment*, 41, 610–18.

Hirschfeld, R.M.A., Klerman, G.L., Andreason, N.C., Clayton, P.J. and Keller, M.B. (1986) 'Psycho-social predictors of chronicity in depressed patients'. *British Journal of Psychiatry*, 148, 648–54.

Hockanson, J.E., DeGood, D.E., Forrest, M.G. and Brittain, T.M. (1971) 'Availability of avoidance behaviours in modulating vascular stress responses'. *Journal of Research and Social Psychology*, 19, 60–8.

Hollon, S.D. (1981) 'Comparisons and combinations with alternative approaches' in L.P. Rehm (ed.) *Behavior Therapy for Depression*. Academic Press, New York.

Hollon, S.D., Bedrosian, R.C. and Beck, A.T. (1979) 'Combined cognitive-pharmacotherapy vs cognitive therapy in the treatment of depression'. Paper presented at the Annual Meeting of the Society for Psychotherapy Research, Oxford.

Hollon, S.D., Yuason, V.B., Weiner, M.J. *et al.* (1984) 'Combined cognitive and pharmacotherapy versus cognitive therapy alone and pharmacotherapy alone in a treatment of depressed out-patients: differential treatment outcome in the CTP project'. Unpublished Ms. University of Minnesota and St Paul Ramsey Medical Centre, Minneapolis.

Hollon, S.D., DeRubeis, R.J. and Evans, M.D. (1987) 'Cause or mediation of change in treatment for depression: discriminability between non-specificity and non-causability'. *Psychological Bulletin*, 102, 139–49.

Hooley, J.M. and Teasdale, J.D. (1988) 'Predictors of relapse in unipolar depressives: expressed emotion, marital distress and perceived criticism'. *Journal of Abnormal Psychology*, 98, 229–35.

Howes, M.J. and Hokanson, J.E. (1979) 'Conversational and social responses to depressive interpersonal behaviour'. *Journal of Abnormal Psychology*, 88, 625–34.

Hunsley, J. (1989) 'Vulnerability to depressive mood: an examination of the temporal consistency of the reformulated learned helplessness model'. *Cognitive Therapy and Research*, 13, 599–608.

Imber, S.D., Pilkonis, P.A., Sotsky, S.M., Elkin, I., Watkins, J.T., Collins, J.F., Shea, M.T., Laber, W.R. and Glass, D.R. (1990) 'Mode specific effects among three treatments for depression'. *Journal of Consulting and Clinical Psychology*, 58, 352–9.

Ingham, J.G., Kreitman, M.B., Miller, P., Sashidharan, S.P. and Surtees, P.G. (1986) 'Self-esteem vulnerability and psychiatric disorder in the community'. *British Journal of Psychiatry*, 148, 375–86.

Jack, R.L. and Williams, J.M.G. (1991) 'The role of attributions in self-poisoning'. *British Journal of Clinical Psychology*, 30, 25–35.

Jackson, B. (1972) 'Treatment of depression by self-reinforcement'. *Behaviour Therapy*, 3, 298–307.

Kanfer, F.H. (1970) 'Self-regulation: research, issues and speculations' in C. Neuringer and J.L. Michael (eds) *Behaviour Modification in Clinical Psychology*. Appleton Century Crofts, New York.

Kanfer, F.H. and Hagerman, S. (1981) 'The role of self-regulation' in L.P. Rehm (ed.) *Behavior Therapy for Depression*. Academic Press, New York.

Kavanagh, D.J. and Wilson, P.H. (in press) 'Prediction of outcome with a group version of cognitive therapy for depression'. *Behaviour and Research Therapy*.

Keller, M.B., Klerman, G.L., Lavori, P.W., Coryell, W. and Endicott, J. (1984) 'Long-term outcome of episodes of major depression: clinical and public health significance'. *Journal of the American Medical Association*, 252, 788–92.

Kendall, P.C. and Korgeski, G.P. (1979) 'Assessment and cognitive-behavioral interventions'. *Cognitive Therapy and Research*, 3, 1–21.

Kendall, P.C., Hollon, S.D., Beck, A.T., Hammen, C.L. and Ingram, R.E. (1987) 'Issues and recommendations regarding use of the Beck Depression Inventory'. *Cognitive Therapy and Research*, 11, 289–300.

Kendall, R.E. (1976) 'The classification of depression: a review of contemporary confusions'. *British Journal of Psychiatry*, 129, 15–28.

Kenny, D.A. (1975) 'Cross-lagged panel correlation: a test for spuriousness'. *Psychological Bulletin*, 82, 887–903.

Klerman, G.L., DiMaschio, A., Weissman, M. *et al.* (1974) 'Treatment of depression by drugs and psychotherapy'. *American Journal of Psychiatry*, 131, 186–91.

Klerman, G.L., Weissman, M.M., Rounsaville, B.J. and Chevron, E.S. (1984) *Interpersonal Psychotherapy of Depression*. Basic Books, New York.

Knesevich, J.W., Biggs, J.T., Clayton, P.J. and Ziegler, V.E. (1977) 'Validity of the Hamilton Rating Scale for Depression'. *British Journal of Psychiatry*, 131, 49–52.

Kornblith, S.J., Rehm, L.P., O'Hara, M.W. and Lamparski, D.M. (1983) 'The contribution of self-reinforcement training and behavioural assignments to the efficacy of self-control therapy for depression'. *Cognitive Therapy and Research*, 7, 499–528.

Kovacs, M., Rush, A.J., Beck, A.T. and Hollon, S. (1981) 'Depressed out-patients treated with cognitive therapy or pharmacotherapy: a one-year follow-up'. *Archives of General Psychiatry*, 38, 33–9.

Lang, P.J. (1971) 'The application of psychophysiological methods to the study of psychotherapy and behaviour modification' in A.E. Bergin and S.L. Garfield (eds) *Handbook of Psychotherapy and Behaviour Change: an empirical analysis*. J. Wiley, New York.

Lavori, P.W., Keller, M.B., Klerman, G.L. (1984) 'Relapse in affective disorders: a reanalysis of the literature using life table methods'. *Journal of Psychiatric Research*, 18, 13–25.

Lazarus, A.A. (1968) 'Learning theory and the treatment of depression'. *Behaviour Research and Therapy*, 6, 83–9.

Lewinsohn, P.M. (1975) 'Engagement in pleasant activities and depression level'. *Journal of Abnormal Psychology*, 84, 729–31.

Lewinsohn, P.M. (1976) 'Activity schedules in the treatment of depression' in J.D. Krumbolz and C.E. Thoresen (eds) *Counselling Methods*. Holt Rinehart and Winston, New York.

Lewinsohn, P.M. and Graf, M. (1973) 'Pleasant activities and depression'. *Journal of Consulting and Clinical Psychology*, 41, 261–8.

Lewinsohn, P.M. and Amenson, C. (1978) 'Some relationships between pleasant and unpleasant mood related events and depression'. Unpublished Ms., University of Oregon.

Lewinsohn, P.M. and Shaw, D.A. (1969) 'Feedback about interpersonal behaviour as an agent of behavior change'. *Psychotherapy and Psychosomatics*, 17, 82–8.

Lewinsohn, P.M., Weinstein, M.S. and Shaw, D.A. (1969) 'Depression: a clinical research approach' in R.D. Rubin and C.M. Franks (eds) *Advances in Behavior Therapy*. Academic Press, New York.

Lewinsohn, P.M., Weinstein, M.S. and Alper, T.A. (1970) 'A behavioral approach to the group treatment of depressed persons: a methodological contribution'. *Journal of Clinical Psychology*, 26, 525–32.

Lewinsohn, P.M., Mischel, W., Chaplin, W. and Barton, R. (1980) 'Social competence and depression: the role of illusory self-perceptions'. *Journal of Abnormal Psychology*, 89, 203–12.

Lewinsohn, P.M., Steinmetz, J.L., Larson, D.W. and Franklin, J. (1981) 'Depression related cognitions: antecedents or consequences?' *Journal of Abnormal Psychology*, 90, 213–19.

Liberman, R.P. (1981) 'A model for individualizing treatment' in L.P. Rehm (ed.) *Behavior Therapy for Depression*. Academic Press, New York.

Liberman, R.P. and Roberts, J. (1976) 'Contingency management of neurotic depression and marital disharmony' in H.J. Eysenck (ed.) *Case Studies in Behaviour Therapy*. Routledge & Kegan Paul, London.

Libet, J. and Lewinsohn, P.M. (1973) 'The concept of social skill with special reference to the behaviour of depressed persons'. *Journal of Consulting and Clinical Psychology*, 40, 301–12.

Lloyd, G.G. and Lishman, W.A. (1975) 'Effect of depression on the speed of recall of pleasant and unpleasant experiences'. *Psychological Medicine*, 5, 173–80.

Lobitz, W.C. and Post, R.D. (1979) 'Parameters of self-reinforcement and depression'. *Journal of Abnormal Psychology*, 88, 33–41.

Loftus, E.F. and Palmer, J.C. (1974) 'Reconstruction of automobile destruction: an example of the interaction between language and memory'. *Journal of Verbal Learning and Verbal Behaviour*, 16, 585–9.

Louks, J., Hayne, C. and Smith, J. (1989) 'Replicated factor structure of the Beck Depression Inventory'. *Journal of Nervous and Mental Diseases*, 177, 473–9.

Lubin, D. (1965) 'Adjective checklists for the measurement of depression'. *Archives of General Psychiatry*, 12, 57–62.

McLean, P.D. (1976) 'Therapeutic decision-making in the treatment of depression' in P.O. Davidson (ed.) *The Behavioral Management of Anxiety, Depression and Pain*. Brunner Mazel, New York.

McLean, P.D. and Hakstian, A.R. (1979) 'Clinical depression: comparative efficacy of outpatient treatments'. *Journal of Consulting and Clinical Psychology*, 47, 818–36.

McLean, P.D., Ogston, K. and Grauer, L. (1973) 'A behavioural approach to the treatment of depression'. *Journal of Behaviour Therapy and Experimental Psychiatry*, 4, 323–30.

MacLeod, A.K. (1989) 'Anxiety and judgement of future personal events'. Unpublished PhD thesis, University of Cambridge.

MacPhillamy, D.J. and Lewinsohn, P.M. (1971) 'Pleasant Events Schedule'. Mimeograph, University of Oregon.

Maier, S.F. and Seligman, M.E.P. (1976) 'Learned helplessness: theory and evidence'. *Journal of Experimental Psychology: General*, 105, 2–46.

Malan, D.H. (1979) *Individual Psychotherapy and the Science of Psychotherapy*. Butterworth, London.

Mann, S. and Cree, W. (1976) 'New non-stay psychiatric patients: a national survey of fifteen mental hospitals in England and Wales 1972/3'. *Psychological Medicine*, 6, 603–16.

Martin, M. (1985) 'Neuroticism as predisposition towards depression: a cognitive mechanism'. *Personality and Individual Differences*, 6, 353–65.

Marx, E., Williams, J.M.G. and Claridge, G.S. (in press) 'Problem solving in depression'. *Journal of Abnormal Psychology*.

Marzillier, J.S. (1980) 'Cognitive therapy and behavioural practice'. *Behaviour Research and Therapy*, 18, 249–58.

Matussek, P. and Luks, O. (1981) 'Themes of endogenous and non-endogenous depressions'. *Psychiatry Research*, 5, 235–42.

Meichenbaum, D. (1974) *Cognitive Behaviour Modification*. General Learning Press, Morristown, New Jersey.

Meichenbaum, D. (1977) *Cognitive Behaviour Modification: an integrative approach*. Plenum, New York.

Metalsky, G.I., Abramson, L.Y., Seligman, M.E.P., Semmel, A. and Peterson, C. (1982) 'Attributional styles and life events in the classroom: vulnerability and invulnerability to depressive mood reactions'. *Journal of Personality and Social Psychology*, 43, 612–17.

Metalsky, G.I., Halberstadt, L.J. and Abramson, L.Y. (1987) 'Vulnerability to depressive mood reactions: toward a more powerful test of the diathesis/stress and causal mediation components of the reformulated theory of depression'. *Journal of Personality and Social Psychology*, 52, 386–93.

Mikulincer, M. (1989) 'Cognitive interference and learned helplessness: the effects of off-task cognitions on performance following unsolvable problems'. *Journal of Personality and Social Psychology*, 57, 129–35.

Miller, I.V., Bishop, S.D. and Keitner, G.I. (1985) 'Cognitive behavioural therapy and pharmacotherapy with chronic drug-refractory depressed in-patients: a note of optimism'. *Behavioural Psychotherapy*, 13, 320–7.

Miller, I.V., Norman, W.H. and Keitner, G.I. (1989) 'Cognitive-behavioural treatment of depressed in-patients: six and twelve month follow up'. *American Journal of Psychiatry*, 146, 1274–9.

Miller, W. and Seligman, M.E.P. (1975) 'Depression in humans'. *Journal of Abnormal Psychology*, 84, 228–38.

Mindham, R.H.J., Howland, C. and Shepherd, M. (1973) 'An evaluation of continuation therapy with tricyclic antidepressants in depressive illness'. *Psychological Medicine*, 3, 5–17.

Miranda, J. and Persons, J.D. (1988) 'Dysfunctional attitudes are mood-state dependent'. *Journal of Abnormal Psychology*, 97, 76–9.

Moore, R.G., Watts, F.N. and Williams, J.M.G. (1988) 'The specificity of personal memories in depression'. *British Journal of Clinical Psychology*, 27, 275–6.

Murphy, G.E., Simons, A.D., Wetzel, R.D. and Lustman, P.J. (1984) 'Cognitive therapy and pharmacotherapy: singly and together in the treatment of depression'. *Archives of General Psychiatry*, 41, 33–41.

Nekanda-Trepka, C.J.S., Bishop, S. and Blackburn, I.M. (1983) 'Hopelessness and depression'. *British Journal of Clinical Psychology*, 22, 49–60.

Nelson, R.E. and Craighead, W.E. (1977) 'Selective recall of positive and negative feedback, self-control behaviors and depression'. *Journal of Abnormal Psychology*, 86, 379–88.

Nelson, J.C. and Mazure, C. (1985) 'Ruminative thinking: a distinctive sign of melancholia'. *Journal of Affective Disorders*, 9, 41–6.

Norman, W.H., Miller, I.W. and Keitner, G.I. (1987) 'Relationship between dysfunctional cognitions and depressive subtypes'. *Canadian Journal of Psychiatry*, 32, 78–85.

O'Hara, M.W., Rehm, L.P. and Campbell, S.B. (1982) 'Predicting depressive symptomatology: cognitive-behavioural models and post-partum depression'. *Journal of Abnormal Psychology*, 91, 457–61.

Overall, J.E. and Hollister, L.E. (1966) 'Nosology and depression and differential response to drugs'. *The Journal of the American Medical Association*, 195, 946–8.

Overmier, J.B.L. and Seligman, M.E.P. (1967) 'Effect of inescapable shock upon subsequent escape and avoidance learning'. *Journal of Comparative and Physiological Psychology*, 63, 28–33.

Padfield, M. (1976) 'The comparative effects of two counselling approaches on the intensity of depression among rural women of low socioeconomic status'. *Counselling Psychology*, 23, 209–14.

Parker, G. and Brown, L. (1979) 'Repertoires of response to potential precipitants of depression'. *Australian and New Zealand Journal of Psychiatry*, 13, 327–33.

Parry, G. and Brewin, C.R. (1988) 'Cognitive style and depression'. *British Journal of Clinical Psychology*, 27, 23–35.

Patterson, G.R. and Hops, H. (1972) 'Coercion, a game for two: intervention techniques for marital conflict' in R.E. Ulrick and P. Mountjoy (eds) *The Experimental Analysis of Social Behaviour*. Appleton Century Crofts, New York.

Paykel, E.S. (1971) 'Classification of depressed patients: a cluster analysis derived grouping'. *British Journal of Psychiatry*, 118, 275–88.

Paykel, E.S. (1989) 'The background: extent and nature of the disorder', in K. Herbst and E.S. Paykel (eds) *Depression: an integrative approach*. Heinemann Medical Press, London.

Peselow, E.D., Robins, C., Block, P., Barouche, F. and Fieve, R.R. (1990) 'Dysfunctional attitudes in depressed patients before and after clinical treatment and in normal control subjects'. *American Journal of Psychiatry*, 147, (4), 439–44.

Peterson, C., Luborsky, L. and Seligman, M.E.P. (1983) 'Attributions and depressive mood shifts: a case study using the symptom-context method'. *Journal of Abnormal Psychology*, 92, 96–103.

Peterson, C., Seligman, M.E.P. and Vaillant, G. (1988) 'Pessimistic explanatory style is a risk factor for physical illness: a 35-year longitudinal study'. *Journal of Personality and Social Psychology*, 55, 23–7.

Peterson, C. and Vilanova, P. (1988) 'An expanded attributional style questionnaire'. *Journal of Abnormal Psychology*, 97, 87–9.

Platt, J.J. and Spivack, G. (1975) 'Manual for the means-ends-problem-solving (MEPS): a measure of interpersonal problem solving skill'. Hahnemann Medical College and Hospital, Philadelphia.

Polivy, J. and Doyle, C. (1980) 'Laboratory induction of mood states through the reading of self-referent mood-statements: affective changes or demand characteristics'. *Journal of Abnormal Psychology*, 89, 286–90.

Premack, D. (1959) 'Towards empirical laws 1: Positive reinforcement'. *Psychological Review*, 66, 219–33.

Prien, R.F., Clet, C.G. and Caffey, E.M. (1974) 'Lithium prophylaxis in recurrent affective illness'. *American Journal of Psychiatry*, 131, 198–203.

Rachman, S. (1971) 'Obsessional ruminations'. *Behaviour Research and Therapy*, 9, 229–35.

Rachman, S. (1976) 'The passing of the two stage theory of fear and avoidance'. *Behaviour Research and Therapy*, 14, 125–31.

Raps, C.S., Peterson, C., Reinhard, K.E. and Seligman, M.E.P. (1982) 'Attributional style among depressed patients'. *Journal of Abnormal Psychology*, 91, 102–8.

Reda, M.A., Carpiniello, B., Secchiaroli, L. and Blanco, S. (1985) 'Thinking, depression and antidepressants: modified and unmodified beliefs during treatment with amitriptyline'. *Cognitive Therapy and Research*, 9, 135–43.

Rehm, L.P. (1977) 'A self-control model of depression'. *Behaviour Therapy*, 8, 787–804.

Rehm, L.P. (1981) (ed.) *Behaviour Therapy for Depression*. Academic Press, New York.

Rehm, L.P. and Kornblith, S.J. (1979) 'Behavior therapy for depression: a review of recent developments' in M. Hersen and P.M. Eisler (eds) *Progress in Behavior Modification* (Vol. 7). Academic Press, New York.

Rehm, L.P., Fuchs, C.Z., Roth, D.M., Kornblith, S.J. and Romano, J.M. (1979) 'A comparison of self-control and assertion skills treatment of depression'. *Behaviour Therapy*, 10, 429–42.

Rehm, L.P., Kaslow, N.J. and Rabin, A. (1987) 'Cognitive and behavioural targets in a self-control therapy program for depression'. *Journal of Consulting and Clinical Psychology*, 55, 60–7.

Rippere, V. (1977) 'Commonsense beliefs about depression and antidepressive behaviour: a study of social consensus'. *Behaviour Research and Therapy*, 15, 465–73.

Rippere, V. and Adams, N. (1982) 'Clinical ecology and why clinical psychology needs it'. *Bulletin of the British Psychological Society*, 35, 151–2.

Robins, C.J. (in press) 'Congruence of personality and life events in depression'. *Journal of Abnormal Psychology*.

Robins, C.J. and Block, P. (1988) 'Personal vulnerability, life events, and depressive symptoms: a test of a specific interactional model'. *Journal of Personality and Social Psychology*, 54, 847–52.

Robins, C.J. and Block, P. (1991 submitted) 'Causal attributions for hypothetical situations, for stressful life events, and event frequency as predictors of depression: a test of the attributional diathesis stress model'.

Robins, C.J., Block, P. and Peselow, E.D. (1990) 'Endogenous and non-endogenous depressions: relation to life events, dysfunctional attitudes and event perceptions'. *British Journal of Clinical Psychology*, 29, 201–7.

Robinson, L.A., Berman, J.S. and Neimeyer, R.A. (1990) 'Psychotherapy for the treatment of depression: a comprehensive review of controlled outcome research'. *Psychological Bulletin* 108, 30–49.

Rosenbaum, M. (1980) 'A schedule for assessing self control behaviors: preliminary findings'. *Behaviour Therapy*, 11, 109–21.

Rosenberg, M. (1965) *Society and the Adolescent Self-image*. Princeton University Press, New Jersey.

Rothwell, N. and Williams, J.M.G. (1983) 'Attributions and life events'. *British Journal of Clinical Psychology*, 22, 139–40.

Rotter, J.B. (1966) 'Generalized expectancies for internal-external locus of control of reinforcement'. *Psychological Monograph*, 80, No. 1.

Rotzer, F.T., Koch, H. and Pflug, B. (1981) 'A cognitive-behavioral treatment program for depressed out-patients' in W.R. Minsel and W. Herff (eds) *Research on Psychotherapeutic Approaches*, Peter Lang, Frankfurt.

Rotzer-Zimmer, F.T., Axmann, D., Koch, H., Giedke, H., Pflug, B. and Heimann, H. (1985) 'One year follow-up of cognitive behaviour therapy for depressed patients: a comparison of cognitive behavioural therapy alone, in combination with pharmacotherapy and pharmacotherapy alone'. Paper presented at the 15th Annual

Meeting of the European Association for Behaviour Therapy, August-September 1985, München.

Rozensky, R.H., Rehm, L.P., Pry, G. and Roth, D. (1977) 'Depression and self-reinforcement behaviour in hospitalized patients'. *Journal of Behaviour Therapy and Experimental Psychiatry*, 8, 35–8.

Rush, A.J. (1983) 'A phase two study of cognitive therapy of depression' in J.B. Williams and R.L. Spitzer (eds) *Psychotherapy Research: Where are we and where should we go?* The Guildford Press, New York.

Rush, A.J., Weissenburger, J. and Eaves, G. (1986) 'Do thinking patterns predict depressive symptoms?' *Cognitive Therapy and Research*, 10, 225–36.

Sammons, R.A. (1974) 'Systematic resensitization in the treatment of depression'. Paper presented at the meeting of AABT, Chicago.

Sanchez, V.C. and Lewinsohn, P.M. (1980) 'Assertive behaviour and depression'. *Journal of Consulting and Clinical Psychology*, 48, 119–20.

Sanchez, V.C., Lewinsohn, P.M. and Larson, D.W. (1980) 'Assertion training: effectiveness in the treatment of depression'. *Journal of Clinical Psychology*, 36, 526–29.

Schwarz, N. and Clore, G.L. (1983) 'Mood, misattribution and judgements of well being: information and directive function of affective states'. *Journal of Personality and Social Psychology*, 45, 513–23.

Scott, J. (1988a) 'Chronic depression'. *British Journal of Psychiatry*, 153, 287–97.

Scott, J. (1988b) 'Cognitive therapy with depressed in-patients' in W. Dryden and P. Trower (eds) *Developments in Cognitive Therapy*. Sage, London.

Scott, J. (submitted) 'Chronic depression: can cognitive therapy succeed when other treatments fail?'

Scott, J., Barker, W. and Eccleston, D. (1988) 'The Newcastle chronic depression study: patient characteristics and factors associated with chronicity'. *British Journal of Psychiatry*, 152, 28–33.

Segal, Z.V. (1988) 'Appraisal of the self-schema construct in cognitive models of depression'. *Psychological Bulletin*, 103, 147–62.

Segal, Z.V., Shaw, B.F. and Vella, D.D. (1989) 'Life stress and depression: a test of the congruency hypothesis for life event content and depressive subtype'. *Canadian Journal of Behavioural Therapy*, 21, 389–400.

Segal, Z.V., Shaw, B.F., Vella, D.D. and Katz, R. (in press) 'Cognitive and life stress predictors of relapse in remitted unipolar depressed patients: a test of the congruency hypothesis'. *Journal of Abnormal Psychology*.

Seligman, M.E.P. (1974) 'Depression and learned helplessness' in R.J. Friedman and M.M. Katz (eds) *The Psychology of Depression: Contemporary Theory and Research*. J. Wiley, New York.

Seligman, M.E.P. (1975) *Helplessness: On Depression, Development and Death*. W.H. Freeman, San Francisco.

Seligman, M.E.P. (1978) 'Comment and integration'. *Journal of Abnormal Psychology*, 87, 165–79.

Seligman, M.E.P. (1981) 'A learned helplessness point of view' in L.P. Rehm (ed.) *Behavior Therapy for Depression*. Academic Press, New York.

Seligman, M.E.P. and Maier, S.F. (1967) Failure to escape traumatic shock. *Journal of Experimental Psychology*, 74, 1–9.

Seligman, M.E.P., Abramson, L.Y., Semmel, A. and Von Baeyer, C. (1979) 'Depressive attributional style'. *Journal of Abnormal Psychology*, 88, 242–7.

Seligman, M.E.P., Kanen, L.P. and Nolen-Hoeksoma, S. (1988) 'Explanatory style across the life-span: achievement and health' in R.M. Lehzer, E.M. Hetherington and M. Perlmutter (eds), *Child Development in Life-Span Perspective*. Erlbaum, Hillsdale, N.J.

Shaw, B.F. (1980) *Predictors of Successful Outcome in Cognitive Therapy: a Pilot Study*. Paper presented at the World Congress of Behaviour Therapy, Jerusalem, 1980.

Shea, M.T., Pilkonis, P.A., Beckham, E., Collins, J.F., Elkin, I., Sotsky, S.M. and Docherty, J.P. (1990) 'Personality disorders and treatment outcome in the NIMH

Treatment of Depression Collaborative Research Program'. *American Journal of Psychiatry*, 147, 711–18.

Shea, M.T., Elkin, I., Imber, S.D., Sotski, S.M., Watkins, J.T., Collins, J.F., Pilkonis, P.A., Laber, W.R., Krupnick, J., Dolan, R.T. and Parloff, M.B. (submitted) 'Course of depressive symptoms over follow-up: findings from the NIMH treatment of depression collaborative research programme'.

Silverman, J.S., Silverman, J.A. and Eardley, D.A. (1984) 'Do maladaptive attitudes cause depression?' *Archives of General Psychiatry*, 41, 28–30.

Simons, A.D., Garfield, S.L. and Murphy, G.E. (1984) 'The process of change in cognitive therapy and pharmacotherapy for depression'. *Archives of General Psychiatry*, 41, 45–51.

Simons, A.D., Lustman, P.J., Wetzel, R.D. and Murphy, G.E. (1985) 'Predicting response to cognitive therapy of depression: the role of learned resourcefulness'. *Cognitive Therapy and Research*, 9, 79–89.

Simons, A.D., Murphy, G.E., Levine, J.L. and Wetzel, R.D. (1986) 'Cognitive therapy and pharmacotherapy for depression'. *Archives of General Psychiatry*, 43, 43–50.

Snaith, R.P., Constantopoulos, A.A., Jardine, M.Y. and McGuffin, P. (1978) 'A clinical scale for the self-assessment of irritability'. *British Journal of Psychiatry*, 132, 164–71.

Spitzer, R.L., Endicott, J. and Robins, E. (1978) 'Research Diagnostic Criteria (RDC) for a selected group of functional disorders', 3rd edn. N.Y. State Psychiatric Institute, Biometrics Research.

Steinmetz, J.L., Lewinsohn, P.M. and Antolnuccio, D.O. (1983) 'Prediction of individual outcome in a group intervention for depression'. *Journal of Consulting and Clinical Psychology*, 51, 331–7.

Stuart, R.J. (1967) 'Casework treatment of depression viewed as an interpersonal disturbance'. *Social Work*, 12, 27–36.

Sutherland, G., Newman, B. and Rachman, S. (1982) 'Experimental investigations of the relations between mood and intrusive unwanted cognitions'. *British Journal of Medical Psychology*, 55, 127–38.

Taylor, F.G. and Marshall, W.L. (1977) 'Experimental analysis of a cognitive or behavioral therapy for depression'. *Cognitive Therapy and Research*, 1, 59–72.

Teasdale, J.D. and Fogarty, S.J. (1979) 'Differential effects of induced mood on retrieval of pleasant and unpleasant events from episodic memory'. *Journal of Abnormal Psychology*, 88, 248–57.

Teasdale, J.D. (1983) 'Negative thinking in depression: cause, effect, or reciprocal relationship?' *Advances in Behaviour Research and Therapy*, 5, 3–25.

Teasdale, J.D. (1985) 'Psychological treatment of depression: how do they work?' *Behaviour Research and Therapy*, 23, 157–65.

Teasdale, J.D. (1988) 'Cognitive vulnerability to persistent depression'. *Cognition and Emotion*, 2, 247–74.

Teasdale, J.D. and Dent, J. (1987) 'Cognitive vulnerability to depression: an investigation of two hypotheses'. *British Journal of Clinical Psychology*, 26, 113–26.

Teasdale, J.D. and Fennell, M.J.V. (1982) 'Immediate effects on depression of cognitive therapy interventions'. *Cognitive Therapy and Research*, 6, 343–51.

Teasdale, J.D. and Rezin, V. (1978) 'The effects of reducing frequency of negative thoughts on the mood of depressed patients – tests of a cognitive model of depression'. *British Journal of Social and Clinical Psychology*, 17, 65–74.

Teasdale, J.D., Fennell, M.J.V., Hibbert, G.A. and Amies, P.L. (1984) 'Cognitive therapy for major depressive disorder in primary care'. *British Journal of Psychiatry*, 144, 400–6.

Tversky, A. and Kahneman, D. (1974) 'Judgement under uncertainty: heuristics and biases'. *Science*, 185, 1124–31.

Vaughn, C.H. and Leff, J.P. (1976) 'The influence of family and social factors on the course of psychiatric illness. A comparison of schizophrenic and depressed neurotic patients'. *British Journal of Psychiatry*, 129, 125–37.

Velten, E. (1968) 'A laboratory task for the induction of mood states'. *Behaviour Research and Therapy*, 6, 473–82.

Wahler, R.J. and Afton, A.D. (1980) 'Attentional processes in insular and non-insular mothers: some differences in their summary reports about child problem behaviours'. *Child Behaviour Therapy*, 2, 25–41.

Watkins, J.T. and Rush, A.J. (1978) 'Measurement of cognitions, beliefs and thought patterns in depressed persons'. Presentation at Symposium 19, Twelfth Annual AABT, Chicago.

Watts, F.N., MacLeod, A.K. and Morris, L. (1988) 'A remedial strategy for memory and concentration problems in depressed patients'. *Cognitive Therapy and Research*, 12, 185–93.

Watts, F.N., Morris, L. and MacLeod, A.K. (1987) 'Recognition memory in depression'. *Journal of Abnormal Psychology*, 96, 273–5.

Weiner, B. (1986) 'An attributionally based theory of motivation and emotion: focus, range and issues' in R.M. Sorrentino and E.T. Higgins (eds) *Handbook of Motivation and Cognition – Foundations of Social Behaviour*. Wiley, Chichester and New York.

Weiner, B. and Heckhausen, H. (1972) 'Cognitive theory and motivation' in P.C. Dodwell (ed.) *New Horizons in Psychology*. Penguin, Harmondsworth.

Weissman, A.N. (1979) 'The Dysfunctional Attitudes Scale'. Doctoral thesis, University of Pennsylvania.

Weissman, A.N. and Beck, A.T. (1978) 'Development and validation of the Dysfunctional Attitude Scale'. Paper presented at the Annual Meeting of the Association for the Advancement of Behaviour Therapy, Chicago, 1978.

Weissman, M.M. (1979) 'The psychological treatment of depression. Evidence for the efficacy of psychotherapy alone in comparison with and in combination with pharmacotherapy'. *Archives of General Psychiatry*, 36, 1261–9.

Weissman, M.M., Prusoff, B.A., DiMascio, A., Neu, C., Goklaney, M. and Klerman, G.L. (1979) 'The efficacy of drugs and psychotherapy in the treatment of acute depressive episodes'. *American Journal of Psychiatry*, 136, 555–8.

Weissman, M.M. and Klerman, G. (1977) 'Sex differences and the epidemiology of depression'. *Archives of General Psychiatry*, 34, 98–111.

Weissman, M.M., Prusoff, B.A. and Klerman, G.L. (1978) 'Personality and predictors of long-term outcome of depression'. *American Journal of Psychiatry*, 135, 797–9.

Whisman, M.A., Miller, I.W., Norman, W.H. and Keitner, G.I. (1991) 'Cognitive therapy with depressed in-patients: specific effects on dysfunctional cognitions'. *Journal of Consulting and Clinical Psychology*, 59, 282–8.

Whitehead, A. (1979) 'Psychological treatment of depression: a review'. *Behaviour Research and Therapy*, 17, 495–509.

Wilkinson, I.M. and Blackburn, I.M. (1981) 'Cognitive style in depressed and recovered depressed patients'. *British Journal of Clinical Psychology*, 20, 283–92.

Williams, J.G., Barlow, D.H. and Agras, W.S. (1972) 'Behavioral measurement of severe depression'. *Archives of General Psychiatry*, 27, 330–3.

Williams, J.M.G. (1980) 'Generalisation in the effects of a mood induction procedure'. *Behaviour Research and Therapy*, 18, 565–72.

Williams, J.M.G. (1981) 'The use of satiation-distancing in the treatment of a chronically anxious patient'. *British Journal of Clinical Psychology*, 20, 297–8.

Williams, J.M.G. (1982) 'E x V: a model of how attributions affect educational attainment' in C. Antaki and C.R. Brewin (eds) *Attributions and Psychological Change*. Academic Press, New York.

Williams, J.M.G. (1984a) *The Psychological Treatment of Depression* (1st edn). Croom Helm, Beckenham; Free Press, New York.

Williams, J.M.G. (1984b) 'Cognitive-behaviour therapy for depression: problems and perspectives'. *British Journal of Psychiatry*, 145, 254–62.

Williams, J.M.G. (1985) 'The attributional formulation of depression as a diathesis stress model: Metalsky *et al.* reconsidered'. *Journal of Personality and Social Psychology*, 48, 1572–5.

Williams, J.M.G. (1989) 'Cognitive treatment for depression' in K. Herbst and E.S. Paykel (eds) *Depression: an integrative approach*. Heinemann Medical Books, London.

Williams, J.M.G. and Brewin, C.R. (1984) 'Cognitive predictors of reactions to a minor life event: the British driving test'. *British Journal of Social Psychology*, 23, 41–9.

Williams, J.M.G. and Broadbent, K. (1986a) 'Autobiographical memory in suicide attempters'. *Journal of Abnormal Psychology*, 95, 144–9.

Williams, J.M.G. and Broadbent, K. (1986b) 'Distraction by emotional stimuli: use of a stroop task with suicide attempters'. *British Journal of Clinical Psychology*, 25, 101–10.

Williams, J.M.G. and Dritschel, B. (1988) 'Emotional disturbance and the specificity of autobiographical memory'. *Cognition and Emotion*, 2, 221–34.

Williams, J.M.G. and Nulty, D.D. (1986) 'Construct accessibility and the emotional stroop task: transient mood or stable structure?' *Personality and Individual Differences*, 7, 485–91.

Williams, J.M.G. and Scott, J. (1988) 'Autobiographical memory in depression'. *Psychological Medicine*, 18, 689–95.

Williams, J.M.G. and Teasdale, J.D. (1982) 'Facilitation and helplessness: the interaction of perceived difficulty and importance of a task'. *Behaviour and Research Therapy*, 20, 161–71.

Williams, J.M.G., Watts, F.N., MacLeod, C. and Mathews, A. (1988) *Cognitive Psychology and Emotional Disorders*. John Wiley, Chichester.

Williams, J.M.G., Healy, D., Teasdale, J.D., White, W. and Paykel, E.S. (1990) 'Dysfunctional attitudes and vulnerability to persistent depression'. *Psychological Medicine*, 20, 375–81.

Wilson, P.H., Goldin, J.C. and Charbonneau-Powis, M. (1983) 'Comparative efficacy of behavioral and cognitive treatments of depression'. *Cognitive Therapy and Research*, 7, 111–24.

Wing, J.K., Cooper, J.E. and Sartorius, N. (1974) 'The description and classification of psychiatric symptoms: an instructional manual for the PSE and Catego programme'. Cambridge University Press.

Wolpe, J. (1972) 'Neurotic depression: experimental analog, clinical syndromes and treatment'. *American Journal of Psychotherapy*, 25, 362–8.

Wortman, C.B., Adesman, P., Herman, E. and Greenberg, R. (1976) 'Self-disclosure: an attributional perspective'. *Journal of Personality and Social Psychology*, 33, 184–91.

Young, J. (1989) 'Schema focussed cognitive therapy for difficult patients and characterological disorders'. Workshop presented at World Congress of Cognitive Therapy, Oxford 1989.

Young, M.A., Sheftner, W.A., Klerman, G.L., Andreason, N.C. and Hirschfeld, R.M. (1986) 'The endogenous subtype of depression: a study of its internal construct validity'. *British Journal of Psychiatry*, 148, 257–67.

Youngren, M.A. and Lewinsohn, P.M. (1980) 'The functional relation between depression and problematic interpersonal behaviour'. *Journal of Abnormal Psychology*, 89, 333–41.

Zeiss, A.M., Lewinsohn, P.M. and Munoz, R.F. (1979) 'Nonspecific improvement effects in depression using interpersonal skills training, pleasant activity schedules, or cognitive training'. *Journal of Consulting and Clinical Psychology*, 47, 427–39.

Ziegler, V.E., Co, B.T., Taylor, D.R., Clayton, P.J. and Biggs, J.T. (1976) 'Amitriptyline plasma levels and therapeutic response'. *Clinical Pharmacology and Therapeutics*, 19, 795–801.

Name index

Subject index